The Official®
Identification
and
Price Guide
to
ARTS
and
CRAFTS

The Official® Identification and Price Guide to

ARTS and CRAFTS

The Early Modernist Movement in American Decorative Arts: 1894–1923

BRUCE JOHNSON

With Introductions by
Thomas K. Maher
David Rago
Robert C. Rust and Kitty Turgeon

First Edition

House of Collectibles
New York, New York

Important Notice. All of the information, including valuations, in this book has been compiled from the most reliable sources, and every effort has been made to eliminate errors and questionable data. Nevertheless, the possibility of error, in a work of such immense scope, always exists. The publisher will not be held responsible for losses which may occur in the purchase, sale, or other transaction of items because of information contained herein. Readers who feel they have discovered errors are invited to *write* and inform us, so they may be corrected in subsequent editions. Those seeking further information on the topics covered in this book are advised to refer to the complete line of *Official Price Guides* published by the House of Collectibles.

Front Cover (left to right): Gustav Stickley #332 Morris chair (leather upholstery by Kim & Mike's Upholstery, Durham, NC); embroidered table scarves, unsigned; Gustav Stickley #649 table; 6″ Hampshire vase with matte green glaze; hammered copper bowl by Joseph Heinrichs; 12″ Fulper vase with crystalline glaze and 5″ Rookwood floral vellum (courtesy of Jay Dubiel, VA.); 22″ oak and slag glass table lamp, unsigned.

Published by: The House of Collectibles
                201 East 50th Street
                New York, New York 10022

Distributed by Ballantine Books, a division of Random House, Inc., New York and simultaneously in Canada by Random House of Canada Limited, Toronto.

Manufactured in the United States of America

ISBN: 0-876-37447-X

10 9 8 7 6 5 4 3 2 1

To my wife Lydia

For her support, her encouragement, and her friendship.
And for reminding me that our only regrets
have been those pieces we didn't buy.

For Carol —

Many thanks for your support to my A+C conference

Brad J— Feb 89

TABLE OF CONTENTS

Part Two: Art Pottery

EVALUATING ART POTTERY
by David Rago

Part Three: Metalware, Lighting, and Accessories

ACKNOWLEDGMENTS

REGARDLESS OF WHOSE NAME appears on the cover, no book of this type could ever have been written by one person. The completion of this book marks my twelfth year as an Arts and Crafts collector and writer, but I could never have reached this point were it not for the scores of other collectors along the way who have demonstrated their unselfish willingness to share their knowledge and experience. Perhaps the only way we can each repay the debt we owe to those who taught us is to teach others what we have learned. For the many individuals who have worked on this project, this book has come to be "the book we wish we had ten years ago." For some of them, there may be little new information between these covers, but they still offered what they knew in order that new Arts and Crafts collectors might have the benefit of their experience.

At the top of the list of those who have contributed to this book come the four individuals who have written introductory essays for the three major divisions. Thomas K. Maher, David Rago, Robert Rust, and Kitty Turgeon have each drawn on their experiences with the furniture, pottery, and metalware of the Arts and Crafts movement in order to enlarge the body of written information on the antiques of this era. Without their personal insight, this book would have fallen short of its goal.

Along with them, I wish to thank my two research assistants, Kacie Carroll in Los Angeles and Andrew Schiermeier in St. Louis. Ms. Carroll's interviews with important Arts and Crafts collectors and Mr. Schiermeier's research into shopmarks of the various craftsmen and women of the movement have each added a valuable dimension to this project.

The most challenging aspect in the writing of this book was the price guide. While information on prices was gleemed from various auctions, shows, shops, dealers, and collectors across the country, I wish to single out Dennis DeVona of Cranston,

RI, for his valuable assistance on the prices for Gustav Stickley and Roycroft furniture, Marilee Meyer of Skinner's in Boston and Bolton, MA, for her insight into furniture prices as well, David Rago of Trenton, NJ, for help on pottery values, and Thomas Maher for his advice and encouragement from the very beginning of this project.

In addition, a number of other individuals made important contributions to this book, either through their previous research or personal interviews. Among those whom I wish to thank are: Frederick Brandt, Emyl Jenkins, Bill Porter, D. J. Puffert, Randell Makinson, Dr. Eugene Hecht, Jay Dubiel, John Toomey, George Viall, Richard Rasnick, Cindy and Tommy Edwards, James and Janeen Marrin, Don Marek, Peter Smorto, Robert Melita, Bruce Bland, Jeffrey Hill, Mike Adams, Rosalie Berberian, Linda Brady, Boice Lydell, Harvey Kaplan, Michael FitzSimmons, Richard Caggiano, Ray Groll, Stephen Gray, Robert Edwards, Nancy McClelland, and N. I. "Sandy" Bienenstock, founder and curator of the Bernice Bienenstock Furniture Library in High Point, NC, and Carl Vuncannon, librarian.

Without a publisher, a book is destined to remain simply a manuscript. I would like to thank my literary agent, Susan Urstadt, for discovering both the best publisher and the best editor for my manuscript. Without an enthusiastic editor, even the best book may never find its way into the hands of readers. I have been fortunate to work under the direction of Dorothy Harris, editor-in-chief of House of Collectibles, who, like all of us, at one time was not even sure what the Arts and Crafts movement was, yet who immediately recognized its importance and convinced the staff at Ballantine Books that this was not "macramé and tole painting." They, in turn, have responded with a sincere show of support, which has produced a book far better than I had ever dreamed of. In particular, I wish to thank Barbara Goldstein and the House of Collectibles staff for all their assistance with the manuscript.

While I am certain it must have been a photographer and not a writer who said "a picture is worth a thousand words," I will be the first to insist that this book could never have fulfilled its purpose without the photographs that many people have provided from their files. While I have tried to credit each individual beneath each photograph, I would also like to thank the following people for doing more for this book's illustrations than a simple photo credit can ever indicate: David Rago and his staff in Trenton, NJ; Marilee Meyer and the staff at Skinner's in Bolton, MA; Nancy McClelland and the Art Nouveau and Arts and Crafts Department at Christie's in New York; D. J. Puffert and his assistants in Sausalito, CA; Don Treadway and Jerri Nelson Durham in Cincinnati; and Robert Edwards of the *Artsman.*

In closing, I would also like to express my gratitude to several writers whose works are included in the bibliography at the end of this book. Three writers, in particular, and their books deserve special mention: David Cathers, who wrote *Furniture of the American Arts and Crafts Movement,* the first in-depth study of the furniture of Gustav Stickley; Paul Evans, revered author of *Art Pottery of the United States,* the most extensive history of the art pottery of this era; and Wendy Kaplan and the many contributors to *The Art that is Life,* the far-ranging text which accompanied the 1987–1988 traveling Arts and Crafts exhibition.

These authors and those credited in the bibliography have given all subsequent Arts and Crafts writers a solid foundation of research upon which to build. Our debt to them is one which we may never be able to completely repay.

Finally, I would like to thank my wife, Lydia Jeffries, for her continual support of this and my many other projects. Her patience, her understanding, and her insight have all had a great effect on the final outcome of this book. When she chose the field of medicine, the publishing world lost the opportunity to benefit from another great editor. Fortunately, I did not.

A NOTE ON PRICES

SEVERAL YEARS AGO, when interest in the Arts and Crafts movement was just beginning to attract national attention, a freelance writer took a handful of record-setting New York auction house results and published them as a "price guide" to Arts and Crafts antiques. Prices at that particular auction reflected a buying frenzy that occurred after interest in the Arts and Crafts movement had rekindled, but before scholars had an opportunity to give us a better idea of just how much Arts and Crafts furniture was out there. Subsequently, many of those sales results were not surpassed for several years, yet Arts and Crafts collectors had the writer's article thrust in their faces every time they found any piece of signed Stickley—Gustav, Charles, or Albert—in a dealer's shop.

Unless they are placed in their proper perspective, price guides can be as dangerous as a loaded gun. Every author emphasizes that they are intended to be "guides" and not absolute minimums or maximums. They provide each reader with a starting point from which an example may or may not be informally appraised. From the beginning, certain rules do apply and must be understood:

Rule No. 1. Similar is not the same as identical. Unless the example at hand is a) made by the same individual, b) has the same form, and c) has the same dimensions, it cannot be considered identical in value to one listed in this book.

Rule No. 2. Unless noted differently, prices quoted in this book are for examples a) with their original finish, glaze, or patina, b) with no distracting repairs, chips or damage, and c) with their original upholstery. If the example at hand differs in any way from these criteria, then an appropriate downward adjustment must be made in its value.

Rule No. 3. New York prices only apply to New York pieces. The prices quoted in this book are intended as a national average, but in areas where the demand for Arts and Crafts antiques is low, values will have to be adjusted downward. In a similar but opposite manner, prices paid at New York auction houses may be higher than those suggested in this book, but that is only a reflection of what one bidder was willing to pay on one particular day at one particular auction—not what the piece is worth on the open market.

This price guide is intended to be a tool, but just as no tool is designed to meet every need, it may not be able to accurately evaluate every piece encountered. When in doubt, seek the advice of a qualified appraisor or experienced collector.

The
Arts and Crafts
Movement
in America

An Introduction

WHILE THE ARTS AND CRAFTS movement, a brief, but far-reaching revolution in the field of decorative arts, has often been reduced to its more plebian catchword "Mission oak," it began as an international movement in the latter part of the nineteenth century. It culminated between 1900 and 1910 in the development of a style of decorative arts that included furniture, pottery, metalware, linens, and lighting fixtures which, while distinctively American in style, combined crucial elements from several different countries. From England came the philosophy, in the writings of Thomas Carlyle, John Ruskin, and William Morris, who established the principles upon which the movement was built. From America came the entrepreneurs and industrialists, such as Gustav Stickley, Charles Limbert, and Elbert Hubbard, who embodied those principles in a new style of decorative arts made affordable to the middle class through carefully controlled mass production. And from Europe came the designers, Josef Hoffmann, Charles Mackintosh, and C. F. A. Voysey, whose influence brought grace and sophistication to the furniture, metalware, and decorative arts which have emerged as the best of the Arts and Crafts movement. Each individual had many goals, but all shared one desire: to raise the level of the craftsman to that of the artist, hence the name Arts and Crafts.

Carlyle, Ruskin, and Morris were among the first prominent Englishmen to recognize the dangers posed to the working class by the highly touted Industrial Revolution. Before James Watt harnessed steam and opened the doors to the factory system, the world was primarily an agricultural society, dependent on individual craftsmen for their furniture, silver, decorative arts, and accessories. By the middle of the nineteenth century, however, sleepy English villages were spouting blackened smokestacks, as the production of textiles and steel pulled farmers out of their fields and into the coal mines and factories. While capitalists boasted of the economic efficiency of the factory system and the improvements it would bring to the English lifestyle, sensitive observers found a voice in novelist Charles Dickens, whose characters demonstrated the plight of the working class, from young girls and their mothers toiling fourteen-hour days in the textile mills to their brothers, husbands, and fathers chipping out coal in wet, treacherous tunnels.

While social reformers fought to improve both the working conditions and housing for the lower class, Morris and his followers attacked the factory system from another direction. Dismayed by the crumbling quality of goods being mass-produced in England's factories, Morris and other reformers, such as A. H. Mackmurdo and Charles Robert Ashebee, attempted to establish guilds and cooperatives in which craftsmen and women could work under ideal conditions, selling their crafts to the English public. They believed that by raising the status of the craftsman, they would also increase the quality of the objects being produced. And by approaching each object, regardless of how utilitarian it might be, as a work of art, they hoped to also bring beauty, serenity, and happiness to the homes in which they would be used. "We should at all events take as our maxim 'the less, the better,' " Morris declared, "Have nothing in your houses that you do not know to be useful, or believe to be beautiful."[1]

Morris and Company was firmly established by 1875 in the production of hand-crafted furniture, wallpapers, rugs, draperies, fabrics, pottery, and books. What soon became evident, however, was the fact that the time and materials required by quality craftsmanship inflated the price of each article. Rather than reaching the homes of the lower and middle classes, Morris and Company discovered that the only people who could afford their products were members of the wealthy society. While the quality of their materials remained high, their impact was

1. Design Council, *William Morris & Kelmscott* (London: The Design Council, 1981), p. 85.

lessened by the limited availability and restrictive prices of their products.

The message broadcast by Carlyle, Ruskin, and Morris soon crossed the Atlantic, where Americans were wallowing, in the words of Gustav Stickley, in "badly-constructed, over-ornate, meaningless furniture that was turned out in such quantities by the factories ... that its presence in the homes of the people was an influence that led directly away from the sound qualities which make an honest man and a good citizen."[2] Stickley, himself, had been on both sides of the issue. During the 1880s, he and his brothers produced and marketed several lines of period reproductions imitating the styles of Chippendale, Sheraton, Hitchcock, and whomever else was popular at the time. Discontent with his role as a furniture salesman, Stickley left the family business and, for more than a decade, experimented with various styles of furniture in search of one which would embody the ideals of William Morris in a form that was honest, simple, and attractive. His debt to Morris was later revealed in the first issue of his monthly magazine, *The Craftsman* (1901–1916), which was dedicated to the English philosopher.

It is difficult to fully appreciate the radical departure of the new furniture style which characterized the Arts and Crafts movement in America without first visualizing that which had been previously popular. While America's factory system did not demoralize a class of people to the extent that it did in England, the mass-production of inexpensive goods did manifest itself in a number of garrish, often bizarre furniture abberations. Manufacturers invented elaborate machines to carve ornate scrollwork, turn bulbous table legs, slice paper-thin veneers, mold ornaments from plaster and pulpwood, cut recessed and raised panels, stamp out thin hardware, press designs in chair backs, and turn dozens of identical spindles simultaneously. Mass-produced, machine-spawned, inexpensive furniture reached its ignominious glory in the 1890s and early 1900s with what is now referred to as the Era of Golden Oak. Unfortunately, not all that glittered was golden oak, as

2. Gustav Stickley, *Stickley Craftsman Furniture Catalogs* (New York, Dover Publications, 1979), p. 3.

This advertisement appearing in the trade journal *Furniture World* from 1889 until 1900 reveals that Gustave Stickley (he later dropped the "e") began as a producer of the same style of furniture he later criticized. It is interesting to note that Stickley refers to this adjustable back chair as a Morris chair, but in his tenure as a designer and manufacturer of Arts and Crafts furniture, he preferred the term "reclining chair."

manufacturers freely substituted ash, hickory, and even pine and poplar under the disguise of an oak stain and a shellac finish.

Gustav Stickley was not alone in the search for an honest furniture style that would appeal to a large part of the populus. While Stickley was still making period reproductions, a young Chicago architect named Frank Lloyd Wright had already designed an oak dining room set in the style that would later be called Arts and Crafts. Wright, however, was first and foremost an architect, who insisted on designing the interior furnishings for each of his clients' homes; he appeared uninterested in manufacturing a line of Arts and Crafts furniture. Nevertheless, several other individuals were, and by 1900 the McHugh Company, the Michigan Chair Company, and the Roycrofters were each producing and selling a line of sturdy, simple, plain oak furniture. It remained for Gustav Stickley, though, to improve their early, almost crude forms, to promote the ideals of the Arts and Crafts movement through his magazine, and to develop an efficient, yet worker-conscious factory system that would produce moderately priced "simple, strong comfortable furniture."[3] Stickley was the first American industrialist to manufacture Arts and Crafts furniture that appeared to have been entirely built by hand, yet which depended on electrically powered woodworking machines to saw, plane, and sand the oak lumber. Workers then assembled, pegged, stained, and finished each piece by hand, thereby promulgating the principles of the Arts and Crafts movement while using modern technology to reduce production costs.

Stickley and the dozens of other furniture manufacturing firms that soon introduced their own lines of Arts and Crafts furniture or, as it was often called, "Mission oak" (tracing its heritage back to the California missions and their simple, sparse furniture), most often used white oak in their shops. Whereas the famous, early nineteenth-century furniture designers had often worked in mahogany, and the Victorian manufacturers who followed selected walnut for some of their best work, oak was the first choice of the Arts and Crafts designers. In addition to being both plentiful and less expensive than either Honduras mahogany or American black walnut, the dynamic flaking in quarter-sawn oak provided the furniture with the only decoration designers such as Stickley and Wright felt the furniture required. Quarter-sawn oak, however, was more expensive than plain sawn oak and remains as one of the distinguishing features between mediocre Mission oak and quality Arts and Crafts furniture.

Designers of the Arts and Crafts style were not limited to furniture. Just as quarter-sawn oak and pegged joints were associated with Arts and Crafts furniture, hand-beaten copper and brass, with a dark chemically induced patina, became characteristic of the metalware of the era. Once again, manufacturers

3. Gustav Stickley, *Stickley Craftsman Furniture Catalogs* (New York, Dover Publications, 1979), p. 3.

attempted to achieve the look of medieval handcraftsmanship while utilizing, as much as possible, the technology available to reduce production costs. Lighting fixtures, whether of oak or copper, incorporated mica shades or amber slag glass for a mellow glow similar to that of the satin furniture finishes. Art pottery firms gradually saw the demand for their high glaze vases dwindle as the public turned to matte glazes to complement the low gloss finishes on their furniture. While firms such as Rookwood, Weller, and Roseville remained popular with their hand-painted vellum glazes, other firms such as Teco, Grueby, Marblehead, and Hampshire produced simple, vertical forms featuring subtle, naturalistic decorations under matte glazes which became—and have remained—associated with the movement.

While the English provided the basis for the philosophy of the Arts and Crafts movement and the Americans popularized it, it remained for designers such as Arthur Mackmurdo, Baillie Scott, and C. F. A. Voysey in England, Charles Mackintosh in Scotland, and Josef Hoffmann in Austria to provide models that led designers such as Gustav Stickley, Charles Limbert, Harvey Ellis, and Dard Hunter beyond the early massive forms and into a realm of design that brought lightness, grace, and sophistication to what otherwise might still be known as the "chunky charm" of Mission oak furniture.[4] Subtle touches, such as arched toeboards and stretchers; thin overhanging tops; cut-out designs; tall chair backs; and long, delicate corbels, have proven that they can turn a formidable piece of furniture into a graceful, modern design.

The Arts and Crafts movement ended all too soon. By 1915, the world's attention was focused on troubles brewing in eastern Europe and America's approaching involvement in a struggle for power between the ancient nobility of two, small European countries. The world war that erupted made hand-hammered hardware, hand-painted vases, and quarter-sawn oak seem insignificant by comparison. By the time the war had ended in 1918, so had interest in the Arts and Crafts movement.

4. Thomas M. Voss. *The Bargain Hunter's Guide to Used Furniture* (New York: Delta, 1980), p. 82.

Charles Rennie Mackintosh's many contributions to the Art Nouveau and Arts and Crafts movements include the use of thin, curved, vertical slats, the arched seat apron, and decorative glass inserts demonstrated in this chair produced around 1904. The designs of Harvey Ellis foreshadow Mackintosh's influence on subsequent Craftsman furniture. *(Photo courtesy of the Virginia Museum of Fine Arts, the Sydney and Frances Lewis Collection)*

Returning soldiers brought back stories of a new style in Paris, soon to be called Art Deco; the surge of nationalism brought on by the war resurrected interest in Colonial reproductions, and the two new interests left no room for the Arts and Crafts movement. While Art Deco furniture failed to capture the emotions of most Americans, it provided another step toward the emergence of a style now referred to as Modernism. Originally called Swedish or Danish Modern, the furniture featured clean, crisp lines devoid of ornamentation, often in an oiled teak or walnut. Eventually the style dropped its Scandinavian association and expanded to include a variety of materials, from wood to chrome, glass, and plastic, but in retrospect, it becomes clear that what we today call Modern decorative arts had its first beginnings ninety years earlier with the introduction of the American Arts and Crafts movement.

PART 1

Arts and Crafts Furniture

Evaluating Arts and Crafts Furniture

□

Thomas K. Maher

Thomas and Marianne Maher have collected Arts and Crafts furniture and accessories since 1979. Mr. Maher has researched and lectured on the furniture and metalwork of the period for the Detroit Institute of Arts and was guest curator at the 1986 Pewabic Pottery exhibit, "The Arts and Crafts Movement in Michigan: 1886–1906." The Mahers reside in an Arts and Crafts home in Detroit and are board members of Preservation Detroit.

THE ARTS AND CRAFTS period had many individuals who claimed to be the first to produce Mission oak furniture. Their claims are interesting in the historical context, but in terms of the true test of how well their designs have weathered time, one individual stands clearly at the head of Arts and Crafts furniture development. Gustav Stickley manufactured the finest-proportioned Arts and Crafts furniture with the highest degree of factory-produced construction and finish details of any of the Arts and Crafts furniture manufacturers. While he may not be credited as the first producer of Arts and Crafts furniture, he has earned his place in design theory and history as the first major industrial designer in twentieth-century America. The popularization and marketing of Arts and Crafts furniture, lighting, textiles, metalwork, and accessories in a total house concept through *The Craftsman* magazine, which he published, ranks him with other major industrial designers who followed.

The democratization process of bringing artistically designed, well-constructed, factory-produced furniture to middle-class America was achieved by Gustav Stickley. The ideals of the Arts and Crafts movement came into the homes of many who previously had to be content with poorly made mass-produced furniture with little thought given to the design and the relationship of the furniture to its environment. Other manufacturers quickly picked up on this idea and produced furniture in all ranges of quality and budget for the mass market, with varying degrees of success.

This has created for the modern collector the problem of distinguishing between the most desirable and the less desirable of the furniture, which dozens of firms, from Gustav Stickley to the Barber Brothers Chair Company, produced between 1894 and 1923. The analysis of any example of Arts and Crafts furniture requires weighing several factors before drawing a conclusion. The elements outlined here are not all-inclusive, for any factor may be dismissed if you simply decide you like a piece and can afford it. However, a serious appreciation of an important example of furniture will usually include the following considerations.

Signatures

Is it signed?

That is usually the first question from a collector or dealer about a piece of furniture. The importance of whether or not a piece is signed varies with the experience of a collector. The fact that a piece of furniture is signed is no assurance that it is worth purchasing. If an example of Limbert furniture is signed with the branded mark but has been substantially altered and refinished, it may not be worth serious consideration. However, if the same piece is in pristine condition but does not bear a signature, although all measurements and other factors indicate it is by Limbert, then it should be acquired with all haste.

Every new collector places exaggerated importance on finding a signed piece. A signature helps identify the manufacturer and often will increase the value of a piece, but other factors carry much more significance in the evaluation of an example of Arts and Crafts furniture. Most important in acquiring the skill to determine the maker of a piece is careful study of reprints of manufacturers' catalogs and recent sale catalogs from the major auction houses. Many of the earliest examples of Arts and Crafts furniture were not signed and must be judged by their form and condition. Collectors should be aware that there are many bargains in the marketplace due to the investor mentality of some collectors who will buy only signed pieces. As a result, many times the identical form in better condition, but unsigned, will sell at a lower price.

Several of the major furniture manufacturers used large retail outlets in various cities to distribute their furniture. Montgomery Ward advertised Gustav Stickley's earliest production in a 1902 catalog, identifying it as having been acquired from a "major Eastwood, N.Y. manufacturer." The Marshall Field Company in Chicago, the Cobb-Eastman Company in Boston, and the A. A. Gray Company in Detroit all distributed Mission oak furniture, with their retailer label often obscuring the original maker's mark. Collectors should not be confused when they see this on a piece of furniture they may wish to acquire.

Original Finish

One of the first factors to consider is the finish: is it original? Many antique dealers and new collectors will dismiss this consideration as irrelevant in the selection of a piece of furniture, but experienced Arts and Crafts collectors insist that the finish is one of the most critical points.

The importance of original finish is not something promoted by a group of snobbish collectors attempting to create an elite category of furniture or to inflate the price of an original example. A serious collector of any artifact of the decorative arts appreciates an example that is most closely related to the concept and condition when the artisan or designer created it. The color of the finish and the patina that only age can give a piece of furniture contrasts sharply with a refinished example that has lost a great deal of its character.

Those who are not purists about original finish can certainly be won over to the cause by the current state of the price structure for Arts and Crafts furniture. Some early collectors refinished all of the furniture they acquired. Antiques dealers restored pieces that did not need it, to provide what they considered to be the appropriate color and gloss for selling furniture. Today serious collectors have come to appreciate an original finish, and original examples will bring 100 percent or more over the same piece in a refinished state.

When is an original finish still original? This is an extremely sensitive area among collectors, and there are three major schools of thought. The first view can be called the "strict interpretation" view: Any man-made alteration by chemicals or abrasion or any other form of restorative enhancement changes an original finish to a restored finish. Removing dirt and grime with mild cleansers is permissible, and a coat of paste wax may be used to bring back some of the gloss. The key is that any conservation must be possible to reverse. Applications of sprayed lacquer, tung oil, linseed oil, and the like do not fall into the category of acceptable treatments to preserve and enhance finishes.

The second view of an original finish is one that can be called a "functional approach." This view recognizes the fact that most collectors live in a home and not a museum and that some methods of conservation and restoration may be necessary to restore a piece for use in a room, while still retaining as much of the original patina as possible. Mild cleaning to remove dirt and grime is again permissible, and rough chipping and abrasions may be lightly colored with tinted waxes or aniline stains matching the color of the piece. Paint splatters may be lightly scraped off, and in many cases minor touch-ups may be done with dye on worn spots on the feet and legs of a piece.

The third view is one described as "anything goes." Collectors and dealers have used varnish and tung oil, sprayed colored lacquer, and so on to enhance pieces with some remnant of original finish, and they have still called it original. If you are buying an example strictly for its form, then finish may be a secondary consideration, and the restoration treatment used on a piece may not be a major concern. If, however, you are paying a premium for an original finish, then beware of examples described as "original color with a new finish," "skinned," or any number of vague phrases. It is far safer to buy a form in as-found condition, which allows you to determine the degree of restoration needed. Examples of Arts and Crafts furniture that have been oiled or had sprayed-lacquer finishes applied will plague the movement for years to come. These items almost fall into the same category as those that have been completely stripped and restored.

It is naive to assume that all Arts and Crafts furniture without its original patina is not worth collecting, or that a piece of furniture in use for over seventy years would survive without any distress. An examination of any piece of furniture should assume that certain areas of wear will occur, such as the tops of tables, arms of chairs, and front rails of settles. However, a second look needs to be taken at such wear; it is evidence of the age and use of the piece, rather than a sign that such a piece needs extensive restoration before using it in your home.

A beginning collector should also be aware that some common forms of Arts and Crafts furniture command a much higher premium in their original state. Dining chairs are frequently found distressed, with wear to the lower stretchers and chips and dents to the front posts. An ordinary dining chair in its original finish, with original upholstery and tacks if applicable, will command two to three times the price of the same chair stripped of its finish and without upholstery or tacks. Collectors are frequently puzzled by the apparent inconsistency of prices at auction; these factors play a considerable role in the determination of value.

One of the most difficult aspects of collecting for most beginning collectors is developing an ability to determine for oneself if a piece of furniture has its original finish. Many Arts and Crafts manufacturers produced pieces over a number of years in finishes that ranged from deep black to pale gold. The best opportunity to see a variety of furniture in its original state is at an Arts and Crafts auction, where careful examination and comparison of pieces in original and refinished condition can teach a collector more in a few hours than could be learned over a two- or three-year period.

Construction

The significance of the construction of an example of Arts and Crafts furniture relates directly to the philosophy of decoration espoused by the Arts and Crafts furniture designers. Gustav Stickley and other Arts and Crafts designers rebelled against the addition of decorative elements that did not relate directly to the overall design and function of the example. Claw feet, machine-applied carving, and other embellishments served no purpose in the function or construction of the chair or table; they were considered confusing and cluttered when several pieces of this furniture were combined in a room setting.

The only decorative elements that were considered important in Arts and Crafts furniture were those relating to the construction of the furniture. Tenons projecting through the posts of tables and chairs, tenon- and key-locking joints, and exposed-dowel-pin construction demonstrated the craftsmanship and served as a natural form of decoration that simply expressed the integrity of the object.

Any example of Arts and Crafts furniture can be judged by the genuine use of these elements of construction. The furniture of the major manufacturers frequently incorporated these elements in their furniture. Manufacturers of poor-quality furniture screwed or bolted it together or used quarter-sawn oak veneers to disguise maple, ash, and other less expensive woods. Some manufacturers copied these structural elements by applying them to their furniture. Charles Stickley and other imitators of Arts and Crafts–style designs often nailed on tenon and key joints or inserted false tenons to give the appearance of quality construction. All furniture needs to be examined carefully to determine if the exposed tenons are genuine or attached with small nails or glue.

Repairs

While Arts and Crafts furniture survives in much better condition than many other forms because of the strength and durability of the wood and the construction techniques, repairs made to Arts and Crafts furniture can dramatically affect the desirability and value of any example.

Any repair incorporating significant alterations, such as the replacement of a leg or tabletop, extensive reveneering, or replacement of the back of a piece may reduce the total value to less than 75 percent of its original value without the repairs. Repairs and replacement parts will not render a piece valueless, but collectors and antiques dealers must realize that a

This Gustav Stickley slant-arm Morris chair (No. 369, back cushion removed, 40″ × 33″ × 37″) demonstrates the decorative role that construction techniques such as exposed tenons, pegged joints, and supporting corbels can play when properly incorporated into an Arts and Crafts design. *(Photo courtesy of Robert W. Skinner, Boston)*

repaired piece cannot be appraised at the same level as a similar piece in better condition. There are collectors at all price ranges who will purchase an example based on its form, but it is unrealistic to expect a heavily restored example to bring the same price that a perfect one brings at auction. Many collectors enjoy pieces in rough condition that they can restore for home use at a fraction of the normal price, but they should always make full inquiries before purchase regarding the nature of any repairs made to the piece. An owner is under no obligation to disclose these repairs without inquiry, and you may later find that the example you have acquired is quite different from what it appeared to be when first found.

The nature of the problems a piece may have will indicate to a collector the feasibility of acquiring that piece and attempting restoration. Some thoughts to consider:

1. Is the piece painted or refinished? This can necessitate the restoration of the appropriate finish.

2. Was the piece sanded at any point in its restoration? This may result in a much more extensive restoration than originally planned. Several of the major Arts and Crafts furniture manufacturers fumed the oak before application of the final finish. Sanding destroys the effect of the fuming process on the grain. Refuming with ammonia is possible, but it is expensive and may lead to a decision not to purchase.

3. Has the hardware been polished or replaced? The hardware used on Arts and Crafts furniture was given a patina to match the dull sheen of the finish on the wood. If it has been polished, age will slowly darken and patinate the metal; to restore the piece appropriately it should be professionally repatinated by a metalworker. This adds to the cost and difficulty of the restoration. If the hardware has been replaced, this may be a serious problem. Unless you have access to authentic pulls from another piece of Arts and Crafts furniture, it can be very expensive to have replacement pulls made, and the use of anything other than the original or an accurate reproduction destroys the original appearance and intent of the maker. Unless the piece is extremely reasonable, I would suggest passing it by for a better example.

4. If the piece originally had a leather top, is it missing or replaced? This is important in direct relationship to the original appearance of the piece and its value in today's market. Several library tables, desks, and occasionally taborets by various makers originally had leather hides covering their tops. These were dyed to match the finish of the wood and affixed with brass or iron nails with a dark patina. The effect of a missing or replaced top on a piece is debatable among collectors. Some feel that although an original leather top brings a substantial premium, a replaced one should not dramatically alter the value of the piece. Others, including myself, feel that a

piece with a missing or replaced leather top can never accurately duplicate the original.

In evaluating an example a collector or dealer should realize that the piece with the original top in good condition is much more desirable than one without, and the price you pay for it should reflect this.

Frequency of Appearance and Demand

Two factors, frequency of appearance and demand, are closely linked when making a determination as to whether or not to acquire a particular piece of furniture. Certain examples of Arts and Crafts furniture are commonly found in the marketplace, and their prices reflect this fact. Library tables and rocking chairs appear frequently and are at the lowest end of desirability when evaluation is strictly on form. Dining room furniture also comes up for sale frequently, sideboards and chairs being the most frequent in appearance. China closets and the nicer forms of dining room tables are seen much less often and usually command premium prices, especially tables in original condition and with leaves. Bookcases appear with some consistency, but demand for them always outstrips their supply, and they disappear as fast as they appear.

Living room furniture and bedroom furniture are much more difficult to find. Even-arm settles and Morris chairs are two examples of Arts and Crafts furniture that are in high demand by collectors, especially those furnishing only one or two rooms, not an entire household. Large bench settles (those with high backs and low arms) are in very little demand due to their level of discomfort and space considerations in the modern home. Bedroom furniture is at the rarest end of the scale in Arts and Crafts furniture, but the demand is somewhat less than in other areas because many collectors either work on acquiring bedroom furniture last, due to cost and rarity, or in many cases do not even attempt to furnish an entire home in the Arts and Crafts style, leaving the bedroom off the list. The rarest of all forms of Arts and Crafts furniture is probably the double bed. Most period journals, reflecting the mores of the period, picture twin beds in the master bedroom suite. Consequently, new collectors should not be surprised at finding single beds at a five-to-one ratio over double beds.

Demand enters the overall pricing scheme in a manner different from frequency of appearance. The cut-out designs of Charles Limbert, the inlaid and spindle designs of Gustav Stickley, and the tall-back chairs and Prairie school designs of L. & J. G. Stickley are all examples of furniture that meets the approval of the majority of collectors and frequently brings high prices regardless of how frequently they appear on the scene.

Design

Analysis of the furniture of any major decorative arts period usually will focus on condition and rarity factors in the evaluation process. One important factor that also must be discussed is the emphasis placed on specific designs of the major manufacturers of the period. The characteristic of Arts and Crafts furniture design that each collector should evaluate when deciding on what examples to acquire should be the visual elements of proportion and utility, with thought to which designs are truly innovative in comparison to the work available at the time from other designers.

Several design classics of the period, by various makers, stand out from other production when closely examined. Gustav Stickley produced furniture that, by its proportions, comfort, finish, and adherence to Arts and Crafts principles of decorative elements expressed through construction details, includes some of the purest examples of the movement. The even-arm settle is one of the true classics of the Arts and Crafts period. Gustav Stickley's design No. 208—the low height emphasizing the length, the proportion of the slats and their equal placement on the sides and rear of the piece, and the depth of

Even with its cushion temporarily removed, Gustav Stickley's No. 208 box settle (29″ × 76″ × 32″) displays the crucial balance between dimension and design. Notice how the slats are proportionally spaced to provide enough contrasting light for the dark oak without resulting in detracting gaps. *(Photo courtesy of Don Treadway, Cincinnati)*

the seat—is one of the finest forms of this period. While other manufacturers produced these settles with varying numbers of slats and combinations of detail, many are too high in proportion to their length, or the spacing of the slats may not have been well planned. The key is choosing one that is comfortable and proportioned in its concept.

Examples such as this illustrate the variety and excellence of the innovative designs of Arts and Crafts makers. The boldness and excitement created by these designs has not dimmed since their introduction and should be considered when choosing a piece for your collection, for they represent some of the forms that are most in demand, most difficult to find, and most highly valued.

Conclusion

Regardless of whether you are beginning to assemble a collection of Arts and Crafts furniture or just want to purchase a piece for your home, a checklist you may find helpful would include the following points:

1. What condition is the piece in? Are there factors such as a new finish, missing hardware, leather top replacement, or serious wood damage that may make restoration more expensive than the piece is worth?

2. Is it a difficult form to find? An even-arm settle, whether Gustav Stickley or generic, is much more difficult to find than a rocking chair or library table. If it is a relatively common form and there are factors that cast doubt on its condition, then you may decide not to purchase it.

3. Is it well made? A piece with heavy veneering and exposed-screw construction is not the equal of a piece by any one of over a dozen manufacturers who used solid-wood construction with quarter-sawn tops and, at the very least, internally doweled construction.

4. Is it a great design? Certain examples by the major manufacturers are considered by many to be design classics that will never go out of style and are the most desirable forms by that designer. Previously mentioned examples of these will consistently generate high prices and competition among buyers.

5. Is the piece signed? If the furniture you are examining meets the preceding four criteria, the fact that it is signed only enhances the value of the piece.

6. Is there a provenance? This factor is only now beginning to be appreciated by Arts and Crafts collectors. Older collectors in other fields know well the cachet attached to an article belonging to a celebrated early collector in a field or one from an important estate originally furnished by a major furniture maker. This, like the signature, only adds bonus points to the piece.

A perfect ten in Arts and Crafts furniture occurs when a rare form, in original finish, signed, considered a great design, with attention paid to the selection of the wood, and with a

Gustav Stickley's massive Eastwood chair measures thirty-six inches in height and width yet is considered extremely rare and valuable to collectors. This example was discovered in a garage in Maine in 1987 with its original rope cushion support intact. *(Photo courtesy of Robert W. Skinner, Boston)*

provenance, appears on the marketplace. An example of this occurred at the Robert Skinner auction gallery on October 24, 1987. An Eastwood chair, the largest chair produced by Gustav Stickley, appeared at auction. The first of its kind to appear at auction in ten years, this chair was incredibly rare, in original condition, signed, and with a known provenance from an inn furnished by Gustav Stickley. The final price of $30,800 reflects the importance of all of these factors coming together on a great example of furniture. A similar chair, stripped, unsigned, and without provenance, could bring 20 to 30 percent less when sold in the future.

These points, along with others in this introduction, are not to be considered the beginning and end of all discussion and evaluation but should serve as a basic guide to your evaluation of various factors that may affect the ultimate wisdom of your acquisition. A knowledge of Arts and Crafts furniture makers, developed in the following sections by Bruce Johnson, and the selection of your own evaluation criteria, best suiting your finances and interests, will soon lead to the enjoyment of acquiring examples for your collection and the satisfaction of living in an Arts and Crafts–furnished environment.

BYRDCLIFFE
ARTS & CRAFTS COLONY

Shopmark:
Branded mark with the word *BYRDCLIFFE* and the year 1904
around a lily and enclosed an an octagon

Principal Contributions:
Furniture, pottery, textiles, and metalware

Founder:
Ralph Radcliffe-Whitehead
Born: 1854   Died: 1929
Founded: 1902   Closed: ca. 1910

Workshops and Salesrooms:
Byrdcliffe Arts & Crafts Colony
Woodstock, New York
1902–ca. 1910

"Now I think not of such large beginnings, but of quietly finding out something which I shall be capable of doing as an individual, trusting that when I am master of that, I shall not fail to gather one or two around me."

—*Ralph Radcliffe-Whitehead*
ca. 1892[1]

While men such as Gustav Stickley, Charles Limbert, and Elbert Hubbard chose to work within the factory system,

---

1. Ralph Radcliffe-Whitehead, *Grass of the Desert* (London: Chiswick Press, 1892), p. 61.

attempting to raise the status of the craftsman through an improved working environment, a few highly motivated and financially secure individuals elected to attempt to establish small utopian communities for craftsmen during the Arts and Crafts movement. In retrospect, all seemed doomed to failure from the start, but Ralph Radcliffe-Whitehead's Byrdcliffe Colony had a particularly bright flowering before it too withered and died.

An Englishman by birth, Whitehead inherited his family's textile manufacturing fortune at the age of thirty-two; and after several years of leisurely travel, study with John Ruskin, and romantic dreams of establishing an artisan colony "on a Ruskinian mountainside with a stream, some pine trees, and a view of the ocean in the distance,"[2] he purchased thirteen hundred acres of land outside Woodstock, New York, in 1902. He christened it Byrdcliffe, combining portions of his name and that of his second wife, Jane Byrd Whitehead.

As author Coy Ludwig has observed, "Byrdcliffe was to be a place where the fusion of ideas and the teaching and production of crafts could take place among compatible, intelligent friends in an inspiring rural setting."[3] Whitehead poured thousands of dollars into Byrdcliffe, constructing more than thirty buildings, including houses, a dining hall, artist studios, a dormitory for students, and a furniture workshop equipped with the most modern machinery. He and his associates, Hervey White and Bolton Coit Brown, planned to ship their furniture by rail to retail outlets in New York City, but their output, while unique and well built, was extremely small, fewer than fifty pieces by one estimate.[4]

It appears that what little furniture was made at Byrdcliffe was constructed between 1903 and 1905, although the branded shopmarks on the furniture always bear the date 1904. The only style of shopmark discovered consists of an octagon surrounding

2. Robert Edwards, *The Byrdcliffe Arts & Crafts Colony* (Wilmington, DE: Delaware Art Museum, 1984), p. 6.

3. Coy L. Ludwig, *The Arts & Crafts Movement in New York State: 1890's–1920's* (Hamilton, NY: Gallery Association of NY State, Inc., 1983), p. 45.

4. Wendy Kaplan, *The Art That Is Life* (Boston: Museum of Fine Arts, 1987), p. 229.

a stylized lily, the word *Byrdcliffe*, and the date 1904. The principal furniture designers were Zulma Steele and Edna Walker,
both Pratt graduates, who favored hand-carved floral themes,
often highlighted with naturalistic colors, including greens and
reds. The pores of the oak and poplar furniture were generally
left unfilled and the wood unfinished so as not to detract from
the beauty of the natural pattern of the grain.

As Byrdcliffe scholar Robert Edwards has noted, "Even
though Whitehead had intended to make the colony pay for itself, he gave little thought to the portability of the furniture
produced. Many of the cabinets were over six feet tall, and the
oak used in their construction ensured a weight so great as to
prevent easy transportation to the nearby Kingston freight de-
pot. As a result, more than half of the pieces known were relegated to shadowy corners of the corridors at 'White Pines,'
where they remained for eighty years."[5] By 1905 Whitehead
had become disenchanted with his dreams of Arts and Crafts–
style furniture production at Byrdcliffe and closed the wood-
shops, turning his attention to pottery and weaving.

The few pieces of Byrdcliffe furniture that did leave the
mountainside colony in 1904 encountered many of the same marketing problems as did the products of Morris and Company in
the 1880s. The handcraftsmanship involved in carving the panels and staining the wood inflated the price beyond that of its
competition—and the budgets of all but a few potential buyers.
"Though some Byrdcliffe furniture lacks refinement in proportion, and all is simple," interprets Robert Edwards, "it remains
an instructive manifestation of the Arts and Crafts idea that
beauty found by the craftsmen in their daily lives was more
important than the finished product."[6]

While the colony never achieved self-sustainment, Whitehead's fortune kept it open for several years after the close of
the cabinet shops. The artists, designers, teachers, and students
eventually departed, leaving Whitehead with the skeletal

5. Robert Edwards, *The Byrdcliffe Arts & Crafts Colony* (Wilmington,
DE: Delaware Art Museum, 1984), p. 10.
6. Ibid., p. 11.

The Byrdcliffe designers often preferred to use poplar, whose subtle grain would not compete with the carving and naturalistic staining of their furniture. This hanging cabinet (18″ × 40″ × 8″) was designed by Zulma Steele and stained green. *(Photo by Rick Echelmeyer, courtesy of* The Artsman)

remains of a glorified country estate. He died in 1929, one year after his oldest son was lost at sea. His wife Jane continued to live at Byrdcliffe, selling off portions of the estate to support her and their other son, who lived there in quiet seclusion from the time his mother died in 1952 until he too passed away at Byrdcliffe in 1976.

Although Whitehead's experiment failed to meet his expectations, "the Byrdcliffe experiment attracted many talented people to the area, beginning a tradition that to this day makes Woodstock an important center for artists."[7]

Selected Prices

The rarity of Byrdcliffe furniture, plus the individual nature of each piece, makes establishing a price guide both impractical and quite possibly misleading, for the value of any example will be influenced by factors beyond the scope of this study. Therefore, in lieu of price ranges, recent auction reports have been listed, including their presale estimates. However, it must be understood that auction estimates and final bids are often

7. Coy L. Ludwig, *The Arts & Crafts Movement in New York State: 1890's–1920's* (Hamilton, NY: Gallery Association of NY State, Inc., 1983), p. 45.

influenced by factors that cannot always be anticipated, fully explained, or duplicated. Auction prices quoted reflect the final bid plus the 10 percent buyer's premium.

Bench, double-back: oak, with four carved back panels above twin upholstered slip seats, 60″ wide, Phillips 4/87 (est. $1000–$1500) *$930*.

Blanket chest: poplar, stained dark green, each post with carved lilies, stained naturalistic colors, wrought-iron hardware, 29″ × 50″ × 22″, Phillips 6/87 (est. $3000–$5000) *$8800*.

Dining suite: oak, rectangular table with four carved legs joined by H-stretcher, 29″ × 66″ × 35″; four dining chairs with carved back panels and upholstered slip seat, Phillips 4/87 (est. $3000–$5000) failed to clear reserve.

Hanging cabinet: poplar, stained light green, small door on left with carved red iris, one shelf, closed back, branded inside door, 18″ × 39″ × 8″, Phillips 6/87 (est. $2000–$3000) *$3740*.

HARVEY ELLIS

Shopmark:
(illustrations only) Initials "H.E." over the last two digits of the year, all enclosed in a circle
(furniture) See Gustav Stickley

Principal Contributions:
Inlay furniture designs, architectural drawings
Born: 1852   Died: January 2, 1904

Studios and Workshops:
Harvey and Charles S. Ellis
Rochester, New York
1879–1885
1895–1903

Various firms, including:
LeRoy Buffington, St. Paul, Minnesota
J. Walter Stevens, St. Paul, Minnesota
George R. Mann, St. Louis
1885–1895

Gustav Stickley's Craftsman Shops
Syracuse, New York
1903–1904

"Care has also been taken properly to adjust the movable furnishings to the size of the room: as apparent space may be rapidly diminished by the introduction of pieces too large and too massive."

—*Harvey Ellis*
The Craftsman
October 1903[1]

While to their contemporaries it may have seemed an unlikely match, the brief collaboration between the frail, itinerant architect Harvey Ellis and the robust, headstrong Gustav Stickley left an indelible impression on the Arts and Crafts movement. When they met at Stickley's Syracuse exhibition in March 1903, Ellis was but a few months from his death, a victim of chronic alcoholism. Stickley's empire was just beginning to take shape: both his new furniture designs and *The Craftsman* magazine

1. Harvey Ellis, "A Simple Dining Room," *Craftsman Magazine* (October 1903), p. 92.

were gaining popularity steadily—and once again he was ready to expand, this time into the field of residential architecture.

Stickley, however, had no formal training as an architect. His attempts at designing bungalows that he felt were appropriate for his massive Arts and Crafts furniture inevitably reflected his own personal bias toward interior design rather than critical aspects of the exterior structure. Finding an available architect who shared his enthusiasm for the Arts and Crafts ideals and who could provide plans and articles for *The Craftsman* could well have been difficult in 1903; Stickley undoubtedly felt fortunate that Ellis, even with his nomadic reputation, would leave his brothers' established practice to join him in Syracuse. As the Rochester *Times* reported at the end of May 1903, "Mr. Harvey Ellis, one of the most successful architects and one of the best-known and most talented of Rochester's artists has accepted a position with Mr. Gustav Stickley of Syracuse, who will hereafter control Mr. Ellis' designs and work."[2]

What the newspaper did not report, however, was that the talents and career of Harvey Ellis had been victimized by his bouts with alcohol addiction. An appointment to West Point at the age of eighteen lasted only six months before he was dismissed. After a trip to Europe he served a brief apprenticeship in Albany before opening an architectural office with his brothers, Charles and Frank, in Rochester in 1879. He was still in his twenties when it first became apparent that his genius for design and his talent as an artist were to be diluted by his addiction to alcohol. After a disagreement with Charles in 1885, Harvey left the firm and chose to become a journeyman architect, traveling around the country, occasionally working for architectural firms in need of an experienced draftsman, apparently unconcerned about whose name and whose reputation were built on his work. It was left to later scholars to determine from visual analysis which buildings Harvey Ellis had designed while serving under various New York and Midwestern architects. LeRoy Buffington in St. Paul, Minnesota, for whom Ellis did extensive work, recalled that he "gave Harvey,

2. *Times* (Rochester, NY, May 29, 1903).

at the end of every day, amounts varying from a quarter to several dollars; and whatever the sum, in the morning it was gone."[3] Ellis, though intensely private, could joke at his own expense. "You must remember," he replied to a friend who once complimented him on how well he looked, "that I've been preserved in alcohol for twenty years."[4]

In 1895 Ellis returned to Rochester once again to work with his brothers. This time he was sober and apparently stayed away from alcohol until "a few months before his melancholy death, weakened by disease, he sought its aid to give him strength for his daily task."[5] His interest and energies were soon drawn away from their architectural practice and into the emerging Arts and Crafts movement; in 1897 he played a crucial role in the founding of the Rochester Arts and Crafts Society, the first of its kind in New York. His efforts were rewarded by its members, who elected him their first president. As a friend reminisced a few years after his death, Ellis loved "to talk about anything under the sun except himself to anyone who would listen . . . he was easily and without effort the center of a charmed attention."[6] The Society's first show reflected Ellis's infatuation with Japanese art. "His love for things Japanese (at a time when most of us had never seen a Japanese print)," a friend later wrote, "influenced all of his later work, and particularly his color."[7]

When Gustav Stickley announced that he was sponsoring an Arts and Crafts exhibition in Syracuse in the spring of 1903, Harvey Ellis took personal responsibility for arranging for the exhibition to travel to Rochester for a subsequent showing in

3. Claude Bragdon, "Harvey Ellis: A Portrait Sketch," *Architectural Review* (December 1908), p. 20.

4. Ibid., p. 21.

5. Ibid., p. 19.

6. Ibid., p. 20.

7. Hugh Garden, "Harvey Ellis, Designer and Draughtsman," *Architectural Review* (December 1908), p. 38.

April. The two worked closely together on the exhibition and decided that Ellis, though it was reported that he was drinking heavily again at the time, should come to work for Stickley in Syracuse around the first of June. According to Stickley's daughter, "Gustav took care of Harvey, but he also recognized Ellis' design genius . . . [and] above anyone else at the United Crafts, Harvey understood Gustav's ideas about furniture."[8]

Given the fact that Stickley had no formal training as an architect and that Ellis had never ventured into serious furniture design, it would appear that Ellis was hired to design Craftsman houses for Stickley's magazine. As he delved into his projects with renewed enthusiasm, the design of interiors, walls, and furniture seemed a natural extension of his work as an architect. The July issue featured an Ellis article, "A Craftsman House Design," with the trademark Ellis emphasis on color and his hope that "the owner is fortunate enough to possess, or can obtain two or three Japanese prints of a good period and by approved masters, such as Hokusai, Hiroshige, Toyokuni or Utarmaro."[9] The furniture pictured is definitely of Gustav Stickley design, but the first glimpse of Harvey Ellis's furniture designs appears later in the same issue in "A Child's Bedroom." Here can be found the arched toeboards inspired by Charles Rennie Mackintosh, the first sign of any inlay or bowed sides, the Voysey-like thin, overhanging tops, and a lighter, more sophisticated look than Stickley had been designing. As the year progressed, Ellis's architectural and furniture drawings continued to evolve issue by issue until, in the January 1904 publication, several pages of photographs of Harvey Ellis–designed furniture appeared. If Ellis had the opportunity to see this important issue, it was on his deathbed, for he had been hospitalized in December and died shortly afterward, on January 2. It fell to Gustav to write the article accompanying this new line of Craftsman furniture and to explain how the presence of inlay

8. Barry Sanders, "Harvey Ellis: Architect, Painter, Furniture Designer," *Art & Antiques* (January-February 1981), p. 64.

9. Harvey Ellis, "A Craftsman House Design," *Craftsman Magazine* (July 1903), p. 275.

Harvey Ellis brought sophistication to the early designs of Gustav Stickley. While the inlay was never put into production, the crucial elements in the design of this desk (44″ × 30″ × 13″)—the overhanging top, arched sides, and delicate proportions—remained for another decade. *(Photo courtesy of Christie's, New York)*

fit within his declaration to "do away with needless ornamentation."

"It is used ... to relieve and make interesting what otherwise would have been a too large area of plain, flat surface," Stickley wrote, but as if not totally convinced, he continued, "It, in every case, emphasizes the structural lines; accenting in most instances the vertical elements, and so giving a certain slenderness of effect to a whole which were otherwise too solid and heavy."[10] While his reasoning may have been weak, Stickley was correct in his realization that the designs of Harvey Ellis brought a needed sense of lightness and reduced emphasis on the structural elements—exposed and keyed tenons, trumpet-flared stretchers and massive legs—that had characterized Stickley's powerful pre-1903 designs.

10. Gustav Stickley, "Structure and Ornament," *Craftsman Magazine* (January 1904), pp. 395–396.

The inlaid furniture that Harvey Ellis designed for Gustav Stickley bears no special signature different from that used by Stickley on all of his Arts and Crafts furniture produced in 1903 and 1904. Many of those piece produced in 1903 bear the red decal featuring the name Stickley encompassed in a red box. Also in 1903 and on into 1904, a variation of the red decal was used in which the entire logo is contained within a box. While no special mark was used to indicate which pieces were designed by Ellis, the characteristics of his work—from the inlay to the bowed sides to the sweeping arches—are more identifiable than any decal could be. In those rare instances in which a watercolor or painting of Harvey Ellis's surfaces, his own mark—the initials *H* and *E* above the last two digits of the year, all encompassed in a circle—may be found. Some paintings and his architectural drawings, if signed, will bear his name clearly printed or written in longhand, often followed by the month and the year.

Regardless of how Stickley felt about the philosophical justification for the presence of inlay in his Arts and Crafts furniture, economic considerations prevented the line from ever being put into production. Only a few exhibition and floor samples with inlays of pewter and exotic woods were produced in oak, and their rarity has made them the most valuable of all of the work produced by either Gustav Stickley or Harvey Ellis. On October 24, 1987, an inlaid-oak secretary designed in collaboration by Harvey Ellis and Gustav Stickley was offered for sale at Robert W. Skinner's, Inc., outside Boston. The final price, including the buyer's premium, was $102,300, a new record for Stickley furniture. Ironically, the desk had sold virtually unrecognized a few months earlier at a Virginia estate sale for only $700.

In instances such as this, the inlaid furniture has overshadowed the more important contribution Harvey Ellis made both to Gustav Stickley's development and to the entire Arts and Crafts furniture movement. Ellis softened the impact made by the massive furniture of Stickley and his imitators by eliminating keyed tenons; replacing severe, straight aprons with sweeping curves, heavy chamfered backs with laminated panels, and

Although manufactured several years after his death in 1904, this Ellis-designed server (39″ × 40″ × 18″) reveals the impact he had on Stickley's subsequent production. The bowed sides, arched apron, and invisible tenons eliminate the ponderousness often associated with Mission oak furniture. *(Photo courtesy of D. J. Puffert, Sausalito)*

straight sides with gentle bows; reducing both the number of pegged joints and the emphasis on heavy, hand-hammered hardware; and installing thin, overhanging tops and narrow chair stretchers. In short, Ellis brought style and sophistication to the basic Arts and Crafts furniture designs that Gustav Stickley had introduced and that his competitors continued to imitate. Although the inlay was discontinued shortly after his death, Harvey Ellis's more important contributions remained evident in Gustav Stickley's designs to the end of the Arts and Crafts movement. Stickley continued to produce Ellis-designed furniture (minus the inlay) until the close of his factory in 1916; these pieces still command premiums from current collectors. Around 1912 Stickley also released a few bedroom pieces made of curly maple and featuring Harvey Ellis inlay, but they have thus far failed to inspire the interest demonstrated in the earlier inlaid-oak furniture.

In the February 1904 issue of *The Craftsman* there appears a brief obituary, presumably written by Stickley. In it he declares that "Mr. Ellis was a man of unusual gifts; possessing an accurate and exquisite sense of color, a great facility in design and a sound judgment of effect. . . . Altogether, he is to be regretted as one who possessed the sacred fire of genius."[11]

Selected Prices

Although actual figures have never been discovered, it has been reported that the inlaid furniture designed by Harvey Ellis was never put into full production at the Craftsman Workshops. As might be expected, inlaid chairs appear most frequently, although still only rarely. In most other instances, the number of examples of each form ranges from two to less than a dozen. For that reason, plus the volatile nature of the current market, it is impossible to establish reliable price ranges. Therefore, in lieu of such, recent auction reports have been listed for both Ellis-designed inlaid furniture and non-inlaid furniture, including their presale estimates. However, it must be understood that auction estimates and final bids are often influenced by factors that cannot always be anticipated, fully explained, or duplicated. Auction prices quoted reflect the final bid plus the buyer's 10 percent premium.

Armchair: inlaid central central slat in back, flanked by pair of narrow slats, open arms, arched seat aprons, shoe feet, drop-in leather seat, red decal, 47″ high, Christie's 6/86 (est. $8000–$12,000) *$12,100* and *$13,200.*

Armchair: three inlaid back slats beneath a double crest rail, open arms, drop-in seat with arched seat aprons, red decal, 43″ high, Christie's 6/86 (est. $2500–$3500) *$8250.*

Bookcase: #700, single-door with three sections of leaded panes at the top over three vertical panes, overhanging top, arched toeboard, exposed tenons, 58″ × 36″ × 14″, Christie's 6/87 (est. $7000–$9000) *$11,000.*

11. Gustav Stickley (untitled), *Craftsman Magazine* (February 1904), p. 520.

China cabinet: #803, single door beneath overhanging top, bowed sides, chamfered board back, arched toeboard, early red decal, 60″ × 36″ × 15″, Christie's 12/87 (est. $4000–$6000) *$5500*.

Desk, drop-front: rectangular fall front with three inlaid panels, flanked by two narrow doors above three drawers and open shelf, arched toeboard, overhanging top, fitted interior, early red decal, 46″ × 42″ × 12″, Christie's 12/83 $42,000; Skinner's 10/87 (est. $40,000–$60,000) *$102,300*.

Desk, drop-front: #706, rectangular fall front with three inlaid panels, open shelf below, overhanging top, arched toeboard, fitted interior, red decal, 44″ × 30″ × 13″, Christie's 6/87 (est. $10,000–$15,000) *$30,800*; Skinner's 10/87 (est. $18,000–$22,000) *$22,000*.

Music cabinet: pair of inlaid cupboard door panels below an overhanging top, four vertical compartments below, arched toeboard, early red decal, 50″ × 24″ × 15″, Christie's 6/86 (est. $7000–$10,000) *$8800*.

Piano: upright form with inlaid panels flanking central music rest, additional inlaid banding, 62″ × 55″ × 29″, Christie's 6/86 (est. $15,000–$20,000) *$13,200*.

Rocking chair: curly maple, three inlaid vertical back slats, no arms, arched seat aprons, drop-in leather seat, red decal, ca. 1912, 34″ × 17″ × 26″, *$3300–$3500*.

Rocking chair: high back with three inlaid vertical slats, two horizontal top bars, open arms, arched aprons, early red decal under arm, 39″ × 24″ × 28″, *$6000–$7000*.

Screen: three panels, each with inlay in top section, cloth panels, arched crest, red decal, 67″ × 20″, Skinner's 10/87 (est. $15,000–$20,000) *$19,800*.

GEORGE GRANT ELMSLIE

Shopmark:
Does not appear on furniture

Principal Contributions:
Architectural and furniture designs
Born: 1871   Died: 1952

Studios and Workshops:
Louis Sullivan
Chicago
1890–1909

Purcell, Feick and Elmslie
Minneapolis and Chicago
1910–1913

Purcell and Elmslie
Minneapolis and Chicago
1914–1922

"After the motif is established the development of it is an orderly procession from start to finish, it is all intensely organic, proceeding from main motif to minor motifs, interblending, interrelating and to the last terminal, all of a piece."

—*Purcell and Elmslie*
January 1913[1]

Of all of the future Prairie school architects who trained under the great master Louis Sullivan in his Chicago offices—Frank

1. Marian Page, *Furniture Designed by Architects* (New York: Whitney Library of Design, 1980), p. 115.

Lloyd Wright, William Gray Purcell, Parker Berry, and William Steele—none remained with him as long or was as greatly influenced by his designs as was George Grant Elmslie.

Elmslie had emigrated from Scotland at the age of thirteen and four years later was sharing a drafting table with the twenty-one-year-old Frank Lloyd Wright in the offices of Joseph Silsbee. George Washington Maher was also working for Silsbee but departed in 1888 to establish his own practice; Elmslie and Wright both left to take drafting positions with the firm of Adler and Sullivan in 1890. Wright and Sullivan parted company after a quarrel over Wright's moonlighting residential practice in 1893, but Elmslie was to remain for nearly twenty years, until Sullivan's alcohol-induced behavior drove him away as it had Sullivan's partner, Dankmar Adler, in 1895.

In 1910 Elmslie joined a pair of younger architects, William Gray Purcell (1880–1965) and George Feick (1881–1945), whom he had known and worked with on occasion during his last years with Sullivan. Purcell had worked briefly for Sullivan in 1903 but left Chicago to travel and gain additional experience. He and George Feick had formed a partnership in Minneapolis in 1907, but six years later Feick chose to pursue other interests, at which time the name of the firm changed to Purcell and Elmslie. The popularity of their partnership is evidenced by the fact that in ten years, from 1910 through 1920, Purcell and Elmslie executed more than seventy commissions, many of which included designing the interior furnishings.[2] Much of their work was residential and was built in the Minneapolis region; like most Prairie school architects, Purcell and Elmslie "involved themselves in the total design of their buildings from furniture to landscape."[3]

Even though Purcell maintained the firm's office in Minneapolis while Elmslie supervised a branch in Chicago, the two had strong ideological bonds. That coupled with what has been described as Elmslie's "extraordinary modesty" when it came to taking credit for his work, often has made it difficult for

2. Wendy Kaplan, *The Art That Is Life* (Boston: Museum of Fine Arts, 1987), p. 204.
3. Marian Page, *Furniture Designed by Architects* (New York: Whitney Library of Design, 1980), p. 114.

scholars to distinguish between the individual designs of the two architects. Researchers have determined that Elmslie, while still working for Sullivan, played an influential role in some of Purcell's pre-1910 designs. It was during that same time period, 1907–1909, that three of Sullivan's most impressive commissions were completed: the Babson House (Riverside, Illinois, 1907), the National Farmers' Bank (Owatonna, Minnesota, 1908) and the Bradley House (Madison, Wisconsin, 1909). By this time Elmslie had risen to become Sullivan's chief draftsman and designer and as such would have been "responsible for detailing and supervising the famous architect's last important commissions."[4]

Other scholars have been more outspoken regarding the extent to which these three commissions reflect Elmslie's creative involvement, claiming that Elmslie "should be credited with most of the design, ornamentation and furniture"[5] for these important projects, most notably "the Bradley House furnishings including the ornamental glass windows, lamps, tables and chairs."[6] In a letter written to the owner of the Owatonna Bank shortly after he and Sullivan severed their working relationship, Elmslie declared that Sullivan "did none of the work you see on your building, none whatsoever."[7] As an interesting note, the furniture designed by Elmslie for both the Babson House and the Owatonna Bank was supplemented at the time with additional desks and chairs from the Craftsman Shops of Gustav Stickley.

Although Elmslie was a multifaceted interior designer, working in stained glass, draperies, linens, clocks, and metalware, it is his furniture for which he is best remembered today. For the Bradley House (1909) he designed a tall-back chair with a

4. Sharon Darling *Chicago Furniture: 1833–1983* (Chicago: Chicago Historical Society, 1984), p. 253.

5. Marian Page, *Furniture Designed by Architects* (New York: Whitney Library of Design, 1980), p. 112.

6. Ibid., pp. 112–114.

7. Wendy Kaplan, *The Art That Is Life* (Boston: Museum of Fine Arts, 1987), p. 208.

"central V-shaped splat pierced with an intricate motif of inter-
laced floral and geometric forms. He liked the effect so much
that he created variations of these chairs for several of his clients as well as for his own house."[8] His continued insistence on
decorative ornament in the backs of this series of dining chairs
ran counter to what many other Prairie school and Arts and
Crafts designers were doing, most notably Wright and Stickley,
but it served to unify the overall plan for the residence, as the
pattern in the chair was repeated in the leaded glass windows,
the rugs, and even the linens used on the table.

Regardless of his feelings for Sullivan at this time, it also
seems obvious that Elmslie's intricate floral and geometric designs are reflective of the lasting impression left by his former
employer and teacher, who years earlier had begun combining
"luxurious foliage with striking geometric patterns"[9] in his ornament. Elements of Wright's influence can be seen in the slight
outward curve of the rear feet and the central back slat extending nearly to the floor, as well as elements of the general Arts
and Crafts furniture movement: quarter-sawn oak, drop-in
leather seats, rectilinear design, and wide stretchers.

As Marian Page has observed, "There is no doubt that Elmslie was a highly gifted ornamentalist and the individuality and
appeal of much of Purcell and Elmslie furniture is based on
ornament. In fact, ornament is one of the essential elements
contributing to the overall harmony of their interiors."[10]

Selected Prices

The rarity of Elmslie furniture, plus the individual nature of
each piece, makes establishing a price guide both impractical
and quite possibly misleading, for the value of any example will

8. Sharon Darling, *Chicago Furniture: 1833–1983* (Chicago: Chicago Historical Society, 1984), p. 254.

9. Wendy Kaplan, *The Art That Is Life* (Boston: Museum of Fine Arts,
1987), p. 194.

10. Marian Page, *Furniture Designed by Architects* (New York: Whitney Library of Design, 1980), p. 115.

A number of these chairs (36″ × 24″ × 26″) were designed by Purcell, Feick, and Elmslie for the waiting room in the Merchants Bank of Winona, Minnesota (1911–1912). The projecting seat and spindle sides are indicative of the impact Frank Lloyd Wright and the Prairie school of architecture had on the firm's designs. *(Photo courtesy of Christie's, New York)*

be influenced by factors beyond the scope of this study. Therefore, in lieu of price ranges, recent auction reports have been listed, including their presale estimates. However, it must be understood that auction estimates and final bids are often influenced by factors that cannot always be anticipated, fully explained, or duplicated. Auction prices quoted reflect the final bid plus the buyer's 10 percent premium.

Armchair: three even sides with numerous square spindles, upholstered seat, and separate back cushion, on four ball feet, by Purcell, Feick, and Elmslie; Merchants Bank of Winona, MN (1912) 36″ × 24″ × 26″, Christie's 6/85 (est. $9000–$13,000) *$9350.*

Window: Babson House (1907), leaded glass, featuring circular, square, and rectangular patterns, 44″ × 16″, Christie's 6/86 (est. $4000–$6000) *$4950.*

GREENE AND GREENE

Shopmark:
Branded script SUMNER GREENE/HIS TRUE MARK

Principal Contributions:
Architectural, furniture, and lighting designs

Founders:
Charles Sumner Greene
Born: 1868   Died: 1957
Henry Mather Greene
Born: 1870   Died: 1954

Studios and Workshops:
Greene and Greene, Architects
Pasadena, California
1893–1922

Henry Greene
Pasadena, California
1922–1930

Charles Greene
Carmel, California
1916–1934

"Here things were really alive—and the "Arts and Crafts" that
all the others were screaming and hustling about are here actually being produced by a young architect, this quiet, dreamy,

nervous, tenacious little man, fighting single-handed until recently against tremendous odds."

—C. R. Ashbee, architect
1909[1]

"Business, I admit must run upon business lines, but this is not business, this art of helping to make living pleasurable and beautiful beyond the merely useful."

—Charles Greene
1928[2]

The brothers Charles and Henry Greene grew up in St. Louis and attended Washington University's Manual Training High School, where each student was required "to study woodworking and metalwork with emphasis on understanding the inherent nature of wood and metal as well as the use of tools and machinery, along with a regular liberal arts curricula."[3] Both went on to study architecture and joined influential Boston firms, but in 1893 they traveled together to Pasadena, California, to visit their parents and stayed to open their own architectural office.

It was not until 1900, however, and the emergence of the Arts and Crafts movement in America that Charles Greene began designing furniture. When the first issues of *The Craftsman* magazine appeared in October 1901, both brothers were so impressed with Gustav Stickley's new line of furniture that they ordered their next client's furniture directly from the magazine's first two issues. The bungalow concept championed by Stickley, with an emphasis on unity of architectural design and interior furnishings, appealed to the brothers. Charles's first commercial furniture designs in 1903 are reflective of those of Gustav Stickley both in design and in his selection of oak as his

---

1. Marian Page, *Furniture Designed by Architects* (New York: Whitney Library of Design, 1980), p. 121.
2. Randell L. Makinson, *Greene & Greene: Furniture and Related Designs* (Salt Lake City, UT: Peregrine Smith Books, 1979), p. 131.
3. Marian Page, *Furniture Designed by Architects* (New York: Whitney Library of Design, 1980), p. 121.

primary working material; but, as Randell Makinson has pointed out in his definitive work on the brothers, "influenced as he was by Stickley's work, he added his own personal touch in the subtle variations."[4]

Unlike many turn-of-the-century furniture manufacturers who were content to copy the designs of Stickley, Charles Greene used the Arts and Crafts concepts exemplified by Stickley in both his magazine and his furniture as a foundation for his more imaginative and creative work. As Makinson so aptly states:

> What wrenched Charles from his earlier precedents and established a recognizable Greene and Greene style was his effort to blend subtly curved forms into an otherwise linear composition and, by combining an honest use of joinery giving interest and variation, arriving at a less harsh overall effect. He accomplished this with such finesse that there was no need for applied decoration. . . . The departure from the total use of the straight line removed the harsh architectural character often associated with furniture designed by architects and, instead, created pieces with a scale and appearance more humanly pleasing.[5]

The execution of the imaginative plans flowing from the drafting table of Charles Greene (though subject to Henry's more disciplined and practical review) fell to two other highly skilled brothers. Peter and John Hall, Swedish immigrants as young boys, were self-taught woodworkers who had settled in Pasadena and who, beginning in 1906, transformed Charles's and Henry's drawings into finished furniture. It was also about this time that Greene and Greene began using mahogany rather than oak as their principal wood; square ebony pegs began replacing oak dowels, and graceful Oriental designs began playing a major role in their renditions.

Demand for their services increased significantly the number of employees in both the Greene and Greene drafting rooms and the workshops of Peter and John Hall, as well as the delay in the completion of their projects. "Do you wish me to make a

---

4. Randell L. Makinson, *Greene & Greene: Furniture and Related Designs* (Salt Lake City, UT: Peregrine Smith Books, 1979), p. 20.
5. Ibid., p. 27.

The pierced slats and stepped apron reflect the Oriental influence on the furniture of Greene and Greene. Notice the square, raised ebony pegs and the inlaid design on the crest rail. Like most of their important work, this chair (39″ × 19″) was made of Honduras mahogany. It was part of the furnishings for the Pratt House (1909) in Ojai, California. *(Photo courtesy of Christie's, New York)*

will telling who is to have the house if it is finished?" a client once inquired.[6] While Henry managed the office and supervised on-site construction, Charles would often be found in the Hall woodshop, working alongside the other craftsmen and devising new forms of joinery to give him additional freedom in design. His structural trademark—the raised, square ebony peg—actually disguised screws purposely placed in oversize holes to permit the boards to expand and contract without either splitting

6. Randell L. Makinson, *Greene & Greene: Furniture and Related Designs* (Salt Lake City, UT: Peregrine Smith Books, 1979), p. 62.

or warping. Additional decorative pegs were occasionally added to complete the design.

The full development and exercise of the creative talents Charles possessed—in designing furniture, lighting, stained glass, wood carving, ironwork, even carpets, linens, and small accessories—was dependent on wealthy, imaginative, and patient clients. Between the years 1907 and 1909, five such clients commissioned Greene and Greene to design their homes and furnishings: the Robert Blacker house (1907), the David Gamble house (1908), the Freeman Ford house (1908), Pasadena, CA; the William Thorsen house (1909), Berkeley, CA; and the Charles Pratt house (1909), Ojai, CA.

The range of creativity and level of craftsmanship demonstrated in the furnishings of these homes is simply astonishing and certainly without equal. In the skillful hands of Peter and John Hall the designs of Charles Greene passed beyond furniture forms into sculptured art. The finest Honduras mahogany, rosewood, walnut, and teak were often inlaid with subtle fruitwoods, contrasting ebony, fine silver, or semiprecious stones. Makinson's research into the Halls' finishing methods revealed that "soft stains were rubbed repeatedly with boiled linseed oil and Japan dryer until the friction produced the heat necessary for the final finish."[7]

Both the number and the size of the commissions declined after completion of the famous Greene and Greene "ultimate bungalows." Fewer clients seemed prepared to offer Charles Greene the unlimited budget he required, and the general sway away from natural woods in the Arts and Crafts style to darker period reproductions eliminated all but a few sizable commissions. Charles was drawn to the community of artists living around Carmel, California, and moved his family there in 1916, effectively ending the working partnership he and Henry had established in 1893 and which they officially dissolved in 1922. Both continued to work on smaller commissions the remainder of their productive years, retiring shortly after 1930.

Like the early furniture of Frank Lloyd Wright and George Grant Elmslie, Greene and Greene furniture was designed for

7. Randell L. Makinson, *Greene & Greene: Furniture and Related Designs* (Salt Lake City, UT: Peregrine Smith Books, 1979), pp. 113–114.

specific clients and never intended to be marketed by retail merchants, thus the need to "sign" each piece was never a pressing concern. In 1912, however, Charles registered a branded trademark which, at that time, he stated had been in use since 1910 (it does appear on furniture from the 1909 Pratt House). After receiving trademark status, Charles went back to at least one of the other homes they had built prior to 1909 and branded numerous pieces of his furniture. In the sample he provided the patent office, the words "His True Mark" appear along with the signature "Sumner Greene" (Charles had apparently decided no longer to be called by his first name). Although it was used inconsistently and on furniture spanning only a few years, the brand is readily apparent, often appearing in two or three places on the underside of his furniture.

As with all Arts and Crafts furniture, however, a brand or decal can be reproduced and for that reason should not be used as the primary means of identifying any purported piece of Greene and Greene furniture. At least two pieces of furniture that, to the trained eye, were obviously not designed by Greene and Greene have surfaced bearing a counterfeit Sumner Greene brand.

Of the five "ultimate bungalows" designed between 1907 and 1909, in only one, the Gamble House, are the furnishings and fixtures still intact and the house open to public viewing. During the 1940s and 1950s the furniture in the Blacker, Ford, and Thorsen Houses was sold or dispersed and still surfaces occasionally; in the case of the Thorsen House, more than forty pieces of Greene and Greene furniture went to one heir, and it is hoped they may someday be placed on permanent public display. In 1985 trustees of the Pratt House suddenly consigned nearly a dozen pieces of Greene and Greene furniture to Christie's auction house in New York, where one inlaid fall-front desk immediately soared to a record-setting $242,000.

Greene and Greene furniture is considered to be among the most important and scarcest of the Arts and Crafts movement, and it certainly displays the most unique and complex construction techniques. While their shopmark may again be duplicated, thus far no counterfeiter has been willing to make the commitment necessary to duplicate accurately both the designs of Charles and Henry Greene and the workmanship of John and Peter Hall.

Selected Prices

The rarity of Greene and Greene furniture, plus the individual nature of each piece, makes establishing a price guide both impractical and quite possibly misleading, for the value of any example will be influenced by factors beyond the scope of this study. Therefore, in lieu of price ranges, recent auction reports have been listed, including their presale estimates. However, it must be understood that auction estimates and final bids are often influenced by factors that cannot always be anticipated, fully explained, or duplicated. Auction prices quoted reflect the final bid plus the 10 percent buyer's premium.

Armchair: Blacker House (1909), mahogany, single vertical back splat inlaid with silver, pewter, and exotic woods, crest rail with ebony pegs and spline, open arms, drop-in trapezoidal seat, unsigned, 42″ × 25″ × 18″, Christie's 12/85 (est. $28,000–$36,000) *$41,800.*

Armchair: Pratt House (1909), mahogany, crest rail with pierced hand-hold flanked by inlaid tree, leather-upholstered back, and drop-in seat, open arms, pierced stretchers, branded, 35″ × 23″, Christie's 6/85 (est. $18,000–$24,000) *$20,900.*

Blanket chest: Pratt House (1909), oak and pine, double-section hinged top, wooden handles at either end, raised pegs at corners, unsigned, 18″ × 65″ × 21″, Christie's 6/85 (est. $3000–$5000) *$3300* and *$4180* and *$3520.*

Chair, side: Pratt House (1909), mahogany, five horizontal back slats, each pierced with wavy design, crest rail inlaid in tree design, drop-in seat, ebony pegs, branded, 39″ × 19″, Christie's 6/85 (est. $10,000–$15,000) *$16,500.*

Desk, drop-front: Pratt House (1909), mahogany, overhanging top over lid with inlaid fruitwoods to represent a gnarled fruit-laden tree, over two half drawers with handles inlaid with silver and ebony, both sides with inlaid trees, branded three places, 48″ × 47″ × 22″, Christie's 6/85 (est. $100,000–$150,000) *$242,000.*

Rocking chair: Pratt House (1909), mahogany, seven horizontal back slats, each pierced with wavy design, open arms, crest rail inlaid with tree, drop-in leather seat, branded, 40″ × 23″, Christie's 6/85 (est. $12,000–$18,000) *$9900* and *$15,400*.

Stool: Culbertson House (1911), upholstered seat supported by four legs inlaid with ivory and ebony, branded, 19″ × 25″ × 20″, Christie's 6/85 (est. $2500–$3500) *$2640*.

Table, living room: Pratt House (1909), mahogany, octagonal overhanging top, the edge splined with ebony, double-sided drawer, handle inlaid with silver and ebony, lower shelf, stretchers with pierced design, branded three times, 29″ × 54″ × 36″, Christie's 6/85 (est. $25,000–$35,000) *$44,000*.

LIFETIME FURNITURE
(Grand Rapids Bookcase & Chair Company)

Shopmark:
Decal, paper label, or brand, LIFETIME/ FURNITURE in rectangle, occasionally over GRAND RAPIDS BOOKCASE & CHAIR CO./ HASTINGS, MICH.

Principal Contributions:
General line of Mission oak furniture

Founder:
A. A. Barber

Founded: 1911   Closed: undetermined

Workshops and Salesrooms:
Grand Rapids Bookcase Company
Hastings, Michigan
1896–1911

Barber Brothers Chair Company
Grand Rapids, Michigan
ca. 1900–1911

Grand Rapids Bookcase & Chair Co.
Hastings, Michigan
1911–undetermined

"During the Medieval period Master Craftsmen when joining together parts that were subject to a severe strain, knew no other way than by the use of the mortise and tenon joint, locking it together with cross pins. The Manufacturers of Lifetime furniture know of no other way as good."

—*Lifetime Catalog*
ca. 1911[1]

In 1911 two neighboring Grand Rapids furniture companies, the Grand Rapids Bookcase Company and the Barber Brothers Chair Company, merged to form a new company—the Grand Rapids Bookcase and Chair Company.

The firm was headed by A. A. Barber, an enterprising salesman who previously had worked as a sales representative for several Grand Rapids furniture companies in addition to his own. The new company remained in Hastings, just outside Grand Rapids, in a modern factory boasting several innovative production features. Barber, however, continued to lease showroom space for their products in the Blodgett Building in Grand Rapids, which Charles Limbert had first conceived as a central retail outlet for area manufacturers.

Both parent companies had been producing a line of Arts and Crafts furniture since 1903, and their Mission oak line under

1. *Lifetime Furniture Catalog* (New York: Turn of the Century Editions, 1981), p. ii.

their new company name was called Lifetime Furniture. In their first catalog, reprinted in 1981 by Turn of the Century Editions, the author of the introduction borrowed a well-known phrase from William Morris, the founder of the Arts and Crafts movement, when he declared that the Lifetime designers have "incorporated only that which is useful and beautiful."[2]

Morris, who throughout his life had steadfastly protested the role of the machine in furniture production, may have rolled over in his grave, however, when the author continued: "A thorough and systematic organization has been perfected and division of labor has been carefully systematized. Every modern machine and appliance that can be utilized to increase production and efficiency has been installed."[3]

Barber, the firm's president, called their new Mission oak line "Cloister Furniture," in an apparent attempt to associate their furniture with the high level of handcraftsmanship associated with medieval England. He even went so far as to picture at the front of their catalog a thoughtful monk, diligently watering a lush bed of flowers, implying, perhaps, that their furniture was somehow inspired or even constructed by dedicated monks in a secluded abbey.

The Cloister line of Lifetime furniture included several designs originally popularized by Gustav or L. & J. G. Stickley, including, to mention a few of the more obvious, a trestle library table, a drawer-over-door cellarette, a drink stand, a magazine rack, and a bow-arm Morris chair; but many of their larger case pieces featured distinctive design elements, such as exposed tenons on the fronts rather than the sides of bookcases, rocking chairs, and china cabinets. They often incorporated a sweeping-arch toeboard across the fronts of bookcases and other case pieces, giving them a look not unlike that associated with the Stickleys. However, whereas Gustav and L. & J. G. Stickley used small individual panes of glass in each door (as many as twelve per door), Lifetime bookcases and china cabinets are

2. *Lifetime Furniture Catalog* (New York: Turn of the Century Editions, 1981), p. ii.
3. Ibid.

Arts and Crafts collectors are beginning to appreciate the quality workmanship displayed in much of the Lifetime furniture. This typical sideboard (No. 5272, 55″ × 60″ × 23″) incorporates authentic exposed tenons; heavy, hammered hardware; and a practical, if not inspiring, design. *(Photo courtesy of Robert W. Skinner, Boston)*

more apt to be found with one large pane of glass set behind a gridwork of mullions, giving the appearance of several individual panes with but a fraction of the effort or cost.

In the preface to their 1911 catalog the firm guarantees that "in Lifetime construction the front and back rails of all settees, chairs and rockers are tenoned on the ends, each tenon passing into a mortise in the post in its respective position. Holes are then bored through the post passing through the tenon. . . . Straight grained oak pins are then covered with glue and driven snugly into the holes. The posts are fastened into the arms in a like manner, in fact every joint that receives the least strain is fitted with this mortise and tenon pinned construction."[4]

Generally speaking, the quality of construction of most Lifetime furniture is admirable; Grand Rapids authority Don Marek states that "at its best, their Arts and Crafts furniture rivaled

4. *Lifetime Furniture Catalog* (New York: Turn of the Century Editions, 1981), p. ii.

the quality of the largest makers."[5] Unfortunately, the majority of their best designs, original or imitations, lack the grace and delicate balance of proportion required to make the leap from functional furniture to furniture that is also artistic and that, as Morris had recommended in 1880, "you know to be useful or believe to be beautiful."

One of the distinctive design elements often found on Lifetime furniture is an extremely wide and large corbel placed at the point where the arm of a chair or settle joins the rear post. The corbel serves no important structural purpose but exists to soften visually the impact of the sharp ninety-degree angle created by the two boards. The company produced a large number of settles and armchairs, the majority of which are characterized by sturdy, nearly massive posts and boards. In addition, a large number of Lifetime drop-front desks have also surfaced, many of which are uninspiring in design; a few, however—most notably those with rectangular sides, exposed tenons on the front posts, and arched aprons—command a great deal of respect.

A. A. Barber, though not a great designer, certainly was a smart businessman. Even when the Arts and Crafts movement was at the height of its popularity, the Grand Rapids Bookcase and Chair Company still issued "two catalogs yearly, one illustrating our line of Cloister Styles in Lifetime Furniture, and another that will illustrate our large and comprehensive line of Mahogany and Oak Dining Room Furniture in Period and Modern Styles."[6] Here was a captain who was determined not to go down with the Arts and Crafts ship.

The Lifetime shopmark, according to their catalog, "can always be found either in the form of a colored transfer or burned into the wood with an electric branding iron,"[7] although paper

5. Don Marek, *Arts and Crafts Furniture Design: The Grand Rapids Contribution* (Grand Rapids, MI: Grand Rapids Art Museum, 1987), p. 56.

6. *Lifetime Furniture Catalog* (New York: Turn of the Century Editions, 1981), p. 109.

7. Ibid.

labels have also been discovered.[8] In any instance, the shop-marks are relatively easy to locate and identify, appearing even on the insides of the backs of bookcases and china cabinets. Earlier Barber Brothers Chair Company shopmarks appeared as paper labels, and the Grand Rapids Bookcase and Chair Company occasionally used a metal tag to identify their furniture.

Lifetime hardware is often hand-hammered copper, similiar to that found on L. & J. G. Stickley bookcases and china cabinets, yet not as heavy or as impressive as that of Gustav Stickley. Other pieces bear hardware similar to that used by several Grand Rapids firms and that appear to have been purchased from the Grand Rapids Brass Company.[9]

While it is already evident that the largest percentage of Lifetime furniture will never attract the following or earn the respect accorded that of Gustav Stickley, L. & J. G. Stickley, the Roycrofters, Charles Limbert, or the best of the Stickley Brothers, it does stand at the top—in terms of both quantity and quality—of the other Mission oak manufacturers. For that reason, the sharp collector will continue to inspect each piece of Lifetime furniture carefully, for on occasion a piece will emerge combining the necessary elements of proportion, design, quality materials, and sound construction that make it a proud addition to any collection.

Selected Prices

Model numbers correspond with those in the *Lifetime Furniture Catalog* (New York: Turn of the Century Editions, 1981).

Armchair: #624½, three vertical slats in the back above two horizontal slats, open arms, drop-in spring seat, 37″ × 20″, *$125–$150.*

8. Don Marek, *Arts and Crafts Furniture Design: The Grand Rapids Contribution* (Grand Rapids, MI: Grand Rapids Art Museum, 1987), p. 66.
9. Ibid., p. 63.

Armchair: #689½, two vertical slats in the back, three under each arm, exposed tenons on tops of arms, corbels, drop-in spring seat, 36″ × 20″, *$175–$200*.

Bookcase: #7604, triple door with six panes each, gallery top, keyed tenons on sides, raised straight toeboard, metal hardware, 44″ × 55″ × 12″, *$1250–$1500*.

Bookcase: #7625, double door with one large pane each, exposed tenons on front, eight adjustable shelves, 56″ × 42″ × 12″, *$700–$800*.

Chair, side: #113, three vertical slats in back, drop-in leather seat, 36″ × 16″ × 16″, $65–$75, set of four, *$325–$375*.

China cabinet: #6478, double door with one large pane each, overhanging top, three adjustable shelves, interior mirror above top shelf, 59″ × 44″ × 13″, *$800–$900*.

Desk: #8567, gallery top over drop front and long drawer, wide board sides, lower shelf, arched toeboard and sides, 45″ × 28″ × 16″, *$300–$350*.

Desk: #8570, drop front, rectangular sides with exposed tenon stretchers top and bottom, two drawers beneath drop front, fitted interior, hammered hardware, paneled sides, decal, 43″ × 42″, *$675–$775*.

Dresser: #4007, two half drawers above two long, splashboard on overhanging top, metal hardware, slight arch to sides, straight toeboard, no mirror, 38″ × 48″ × 22″, *$500–$600*.

Footstool: #403, tray top with loose cushion, narrow stretchers, 15″ × 16″ × 15″, *$125–$150*.

Morris chair: #569, five slats under each flat arm, posts tenoned through arms front and back, seat apron tenoned through posts, adjustable wooden rod, four corbels under arms, 42″ × 23″, *$1000–$1250*.

Morris chair: #584, open flat arms, exposed tenons in tops of arms, drop-in spring seat and loose back cushion, corbels, adjustable wooden rod, 41″ × 21″, *$600–$700.*

Rocking chair: #623, three horizontal slats in back, open arms, no corbels or exposed tenons, drop-in spring seat, 39″ × 20″, *$100–$125.*

Rocking chair: #689, two wide vertical slats in back, three under each arm, exposed tenon on top of each arm, corbels, drop-in spring seat, 36″ × 20″, *$175–$200.*

Server: #5160, overhanging top with open plate rail, one long drawer with metal hardware, open lower shelf resting on side stretchers, 38″ × 39″ × 18″, *$500–$600.*

Settle: #614¾, even-arm, with ten vertical slats in back, three under each arm, exposed tenons on front posts, drop-in spring cushion seat, 36″ × 73″ × 24″, *$1750–$2000.*

Settle: #688¾, drop-arm with wide slats under arms and headrail, exposed tenons, spring cushion seat, 34″ × 72″ × 28″, *$1250–$1500.*

Sideboard: #5272, overhanging top supporting mirrored panel and shelf, three short drawers over one long drawer over two cabinet doors, hammered hardware, exposed tenons on front posts, 55″ × 60″ × 23″, *$700–$800.*

Table, dining: #1069, circular overhanging top with apron atop octagonal pedestal with four radiating feet, five leaves, 30″ × 54″, *$800–$900.*

Table, lamp: #930, circular top over small circular shelf atop straight cross stretchers, exposed tenons, 30″ × 24″ diameter, *$325–$375.*

Table, lamp: #917, circular overhanging top over apron, supported by four flared legs with arched cross-stretchers, exposed tenons, 27″ × 18″ × 18″, *$500–$600.*

Table, library: #8557, overhanging top above single drawer with hinged interior writing surface, metal pulls, open lower shelf, no exposed tenons, 30″ × 36″ × 24″, *$200–$225.*

Taboret: #257, square overhanging top with cut corners, lower shelf supported by arched stretchers, 18″ × 16″ × 16″, *$300–$350.*

CHARLES LIMBERT

Shopmark:
Paper label or brand of craftsman working at a bench, with the words LIMBERTS ARTS CRAFTS FURNITURE/ MADE IN GRAND RAPIDS/ MICHIGAN
(After 1906) Addition of the words TRADE MARK and replacement of MICHIGAN with AND HOLLAND

Principal Contributions:
General line of Arts and Crafts furniture

Founder:
Charles P. Limbert
Born: 1854   Died: 1923
Founded: 1894   Closed: 1944

Workshops and Salesrooms:
C. P. Limbert & Co.
Grand Rapids, Michigan
1894–1944

Holland, Michigan
1906–1944

"In this age of affected ornamentation, it is the unique piece of
furniture with its striking, pleasing outlines and rigid simplicity,
and harmonious colorings, that is made for comfort and service,
that marks the tastefully furnished home."

—*Charles Limbert*
1905[1]

Charles Limbert, like many other prominent Arts and Crafts
furniture manufacturers, first learned his trade by designing,
producing, and selling the period reproductions that were popular in the two decades immediately after the 1876 Centennial
celebration. At the age of thirty-five he left a secure future with
the large Chicago furniture firm of John A. Colby and Company
and moved to Grand Rapids, Michigan, rapidly becoming known
as the furniture capital of the world. There he and former co-
worker Philip Klingman formed the Limbert and Klingman
Chair Company and in 1890 began manufacturing a line of period reproduction chairs.

The firm was dissolved in 1892, and Limbert returned to a
career in sales, representing a number of furniture manufacturers in his rented Grand Rapids showroom. Two years later,
however, in 1894, Charles Limbert returned to furniture production with the announcement of the formation of C. P. Limbert and Company. The first few years may have been rough
ones for the forty-year-old entrepreneur, for from 1896 until at
least 1905 he continued to serve as a major sales representative
for the Indiana-based Old Hickory Furniture Company.

When the popularity of Arts and Crafts furniture began to
blossom in the early years of the new century, Limbert began
producing his own line of "Dutch Arts and Crafts" furniture.

1. Charles Limbert, *Limberts Arts and Crafts Furniture Catalog*, ca.
1905, introduction.

Much of his early furniture was experimental in nature, at times incorporating elements of both the waning Art Nouveau style and the severe rectilinear form characterizing the emerging Arts and Crafts movement. His continued interest in outdoor furniture and the Old Hickory Company undoubtedly influenced his 1902 line of ash "summer furniture" with its trademark exposed-carriage-bolt construction. Though not highly regarded by collectors today, Limbert's summer furniture, described as "well made, attractive, strong and comfortable [that looks] especially well in natural ash, light green and Weathered finish,"[2] remained in production for more than a decade.

The years 1902 to 1910 saw major advancements in Limbert's line of interior oak furniture. His Arts and Crafts furniture of that period reveals a man unafraid of experimentation, as it often incorporates elements of Art Nouveau, English medieval, Japanese, Glasgow School, and Austrian Secession styles. As Grand Rapids author Don Marek summarizes, Limbert's "early pieces are a little heavier and almost crude, with more elements from folk traditions and more experimentation (many of the more unusual pieces are from 1902–1904). The 1904–1910 period is characterized by increasing sophistication and the prominence of Glasgow School, Viennese and Prairie School influences."[3]

To illustrate, by 1905 Limbert had begun to phase out his use of Art Nouveau–influenced stained glass in the doors of his case pieces, had introduced a line of inlaid furniture, and had switched his emphasis to cutouts reflective of Charles Rennie Mackintosh of the Glasgow School and Josef Hoffmann in Vienna. The popular success of the Limbert production was reflected not only in his freedom to experiment with various forms but in the physical expansion of his factory. Until 1906 Limbert furniture was both manufactured and displayed in Grand Rapids. That year, however, in an effort to locate "an environment more

2. *The Arts & Crafts Furniture of Charles P. Limbert,* introduction by Robert Edwards (Watkins Glen, NY: The American Life Foundation, 1982), p. 21.

3. Don Marek, *Arts and Crafts Furniture Design: The Grand Rapids Contribution, 1895–1915* (Grand Rapids, MI: Grand Rapids Art Museum, 1987), p. 49.

This massive Limbert drop-front secretary is representative of much of his early work. The cutouts, the arched opening, and the flared form are all reflective of the influence of the Scottish and European designers on the Michigan furniture manufacturer. *(Photo courtesy of David Rago, Trenton)*

conducive to artistic effort and a higher quality of craftsmanship,"[4] Limbert established a new factory in the small rural town of Holland, Michigan. The plant continued to expand after its 1906 opening, prompting the local newspaper in 1912 to characterize "the Limbert company as one of the most progressive in the country. The business is on a sound financial footing and Holland foresees nothing but success for the enterprise."[5]

What Charles Limbert began to foresee, though, was a swing in public tastes away from Mission oak. Hordes of imitators had flooded the market with furniture that Limbert described as early as 1909 as being "poorly-constructed, ill-proportioned and

4. Deborah DeVall Dorsey Norberg, "Charles P. Limbert: Maker of Michigan 'Arts and Crafts' Furniture," *The Herald* (Henry Ford Museum, Dearborn, MI, 5: October 1976), p. 28.

5. Ibid., p. 30.

uncraftsmanlike."[6] Unlike Gustav Stickley and many other Arts and Crafts manufacturers, Limbert was prepared for 1915, the pivotal year in the turn of events. His new line of oak Arts and Crafts furniture was lightened, both in color and in structure, and upholstered fabrics began to replace the dark look of leather. As if to assure his customers that this lighter look was not to be mistaken for a reduction in quality, Limbert reintroduced in 1915 a line of inlaid Arts and Crafts furniture. The "Ebon-Oak" furniture featured thin lines and small squares of ebony inlay, occasionally accented with copper. The following year Limbert introduced his first period reproductions in nearly two decades and by 1918 had phased out the sixteen-year-old line of Limbert's Arts and Crafts Furniture.

Even though his health was beginning to fail, Limbert oversaw his factory's transition from Mission oak furniture to a variety of period reproductions. While on a winter trip to Hawaii in 1921 he became ill and never fully recovered. In late 1922 the lifelong bachelor reluctantly retired, and he died the following July at the age of sixty-eight. The company he founded in 1894, though, remained in business for twenty-one more years, until 1944, its fiftieth anniversary.

Limbert appears to have been among the first of the Arts and Crafts manufacturers to use a permanent branded shopmark in place of the traditional but fragile paper label or decal. His pre-1906 furniture bears a paper label, which can be identified by the location reference only to Grand Rapids. Sometime after 1906 and the opening of his Holland factory, the paper label was changed and a branded mark added, both of which include the words "Grand Rapids and Holland." In a few instances, small copper tags similar to those used by Stickley Brothers have been discovered on Limbert armchairs.

Unlike the Stickleys in New York, Limbert refrained from affixing his shopmark to the stretchers of chairs and tables. Armchairs and settles will invariably have a branded mark on the underside of the arm; tables will have either a brand or a paper label attached to the underside of the top. Case pieces

6. Limbert, Charles P., "The Arts and Crafts Furniture," *Furniture* (October 1909), p. 31.

with drawers will most often have a shopmark on the inside of a drawer; those without drawers, such as bookcases and china closets, will most often have either a brand or a paper label on the back. In nearly every case, the brand of paper label will be approximately two inches wide by three inches high and easily recognizable, for all feature a craftsman poised next to a workbench as he planes the edge of a board.

In those instances when either the paper label has been destroyed by a careless refinisher or a piece had left the factory without a brand, Limbert furniture can usually be distinguished from that of his competitors. With the exception of his summer furniture, Limbert Arts and Crafts furniture exhibits the quality of material and degree of craftsmanship associated with that of either Gustav or L. & J. G. Stickley. His hardware, unfortunately, appears to have been purchased from the Grand Rapids Brass Company and is neither as substantial nor as artistic as that of Gustav or L. & J. G. Stickley. Like the Stickleys, Limbert often used graceful, curved brackets beneath chair arms and overhanging tops and gently arched aprons and toeboards on tables and case pieces to lessen the severity of the rectilinear form. His tops are occasionally splined for greater stability between glue joints, and keyed tenons and pinned joints are often found; but the most unique feature characteristic to some of the most highly desirable Limbert furniture is the cutout.

Will Bradley's series of household interiors drawn for *Ladies Home Journal* from 1901–1902 introduced the American public to a number of English and European Arts and Crafts elements that were to become characteristic of much of their forthcoming furniture: exposed tenons, strap hinges, pinned joints, and extensive use of cutouts. Limbert's adaptation of various square, rectangular, and spade-, arrow- and heart-shaped cutouts can be traced back to the furniture of Mackintosh, Baillie-Scott, and Voysey, plus Bradley's popular line of illustrated interiors. The combination of quality craftsmanship and materials, plus this unique design aspect, can enable a collector to identify many examples of Limbert furniture without a shopmark.

Limbert furniture appears in a variety of wood tones, from a dark ebony to a much lighter reddish-brown color. It appears

As Limbert's style evolved, massive forms gave way to practical considerations, but this oval table (No. 146, 30″ × 45″ × 30″) with canted sides and trapezoidal cutouts remains distinctively Limbert and extremely popular. *(Photo courtesy of Robert W. Skinner, Boston)*

that all of his oak Arts and Crafts furniture was fumed with ammonia, although as in most Arts and Crafts furniture factories, hand staining was also utilized to achieve an even color. Their most popular finish, according to one catalog, was

> . . . autumn leaf brown . . . produced by placing White Oak, which contains tannic acid, in air tight boxes, and bringing it in contact with strong ammonia fumes for a number of days, until the fumes have thoroughly penetrated through the pores of the wood, and come in contact with the tannic acid, when a chemical change takes effect and discolors the wood through and through. After the furniture made of this wood is finished by our special process and waxed, a finish has been produced which is at once clear, translucent and smooth. This color never wears off or shows white on the edges or corners, as the wood is thoroughly impregnated with the ammonia fumes.[7]

His finishes have proved to be as durable as that of Gustav or L. & J. G. Stickley.

7. *Limberts Holland Dutch Arts and Crafts Furniture* (New York: Turn of the Century Editions, 1981), pp. 15–16.

As Deborah Norberg observed early in the current Arts and Crafts revival, "Though by no means profoundly innovative, the Limbert production was nonetheless more original than the majority of straight line furniture and was designed and handcrafted in an effort to provide quality goods to satisfy its middle-class patronage."[8] While collectors of early Limbert furniture might disagree with her assessment of Limbert's creativity in designs, it is true that he offered a line of less expensive Arts and Crafts–style furniture, including plank-seat chairs, open arm settles, and uninspiring tables. Until it became evident that the swing away from the Arts and Crafts style was inevitable, however, he continued to produce another line of high-quality, artistic furniture, including buffets and china cabinets with overhanging tops supported by long, graceful corbels, oval tables with cut-out bases, and a number of pleasing taborets.

Thus, while Charles Limbert never attempted to match the rhetoric of either Gustav Stickley or Elbert Hubbard, nor did he stoop to the depths of their unscrupulous imitators, his furniture struck a middle chord by demonstrating that it could please both the Arts and Crafts enthusiast and the casual observer who admires the style without needing the Stickley shopmark.

Selected Prices

Armchair: #933, three vertical slats in back, open arms, corbels, wide stretchers, drop-in spring seat, 43″ × 27″ × 28″, $150–$175.

Armchair: #1643, four vertical slats in back, three under each arm, arched front apron, exposed tenon on each arm, long corbels, drop-in spring seat, 38″ × 30″ × 26″, $225–$275.

Bookcase: #357, single door with two vertical panes, overhanging top supported by four long corbels, splashboard,

8. Deborah DeVall Dorsey Norberg, "Charles P. Limbert: Maker of Michigan 'Arts and Crafts' Furniture," *The Herald* (Henry Ford Museum, Dearborn, MI, 5: October 1976), p. 33.

While considered by some collectors to be slightly awkward in proportion, triple-door bookcases (No. 359, 67″ × 57″ × 14″) surface less frequently than the Limbert single- and double-door versions. The flared form, arched toeboard, and corbel-supported overhanging top have been carried over from his earlier designs, sacrificing power in the transition but gaining practicality. *(Photo courtesy of Robert W. Skinner, Boston)*

flaring base with arched toeboard, adjustable shelves, 57″ × 30″ × 14″, *$1250–$1500.*

Bookcase: #358, double doors, each with two vertical panes, overhanging tops supported by four long corbels, splashboard, flaring base with arched toeboard, adjustable shelves, 57″ × 48″ × 14″, *$1500–$1750.*

Bookcase: #359, triple doors, each with two vertical panes, overhanging top supported by four long corbels, splashboard, flaring base with arched toeboard, adjustable shelves, 57″ × 66″ × 14″, *$1750–$2000.*

Chair, side: #951, five vertical slats in back beneath curved crest rail, double side and front stretchers, scooped plank seat, 37″ × 17″ × 20″, *$65–$75;* set of four, *$325–$375.*

Chair, side: #851, same as #951, but with wraparound leather seat, 37″ × 18″ × 21″, *$85–$95;* set of four, *$425–$475.*

Chest of drawers: #486¼, four half-drawers over four long drawers, all with metal hardware, through tenons at top and bottom of front and back posts, 60″ × 40″ × 22″, *$1500–$1750.*

China cabinet: #448, overhanging top with plate rack, double doors, each with three small panes over one large pane, adjustable shelves, arched toeboard, 62″ × 46″ × 17″, *$1250–$1500.*

Desk: #1151, recessed flat top over two half-drawers, each over a smaller drawer flanking knee compartment, lower open shelf, exposed tenons, brass knobs, 30″ × 42″ × 28″, *$325–$375.*

Desk: #732, drop front over two short drawers over three long, each with brass knobs, arched toeboard and sides, gallery top, 42″ × 43″ × 19″, *$500–$600.*

Dresser: #479½, three short drawers over two long drawers, all with metal hardware, arched apron, recessed top, attached mirror, exposed tenons, 80″ × 49″ × 23″, *$900–$1100.*

Footstool: #201, "cricket," side panels with teardrops and heart cutout supporting leather-top surface, 12″ × 20″ × 12″, *$200–$225.*

Magazine stand: #300, four open shelves between canted sides, oval cutout on each lower side, buttons disguising screws, 37″ × 20″ × 14″, *$400–$450.*

Magazine stand: #301, gallery top over two shelves over arched toeboard, single slat in each side, 29″ × 16″ × 11″, *$325–$375.*

Morris chair: #521, flat arms over single wide slat with three square cutouts, stretchers flush with floor, long corbels under arms, drop-in spring seat, loose back cushion, 43″ × 34″ × 43″, *$2250–$2750*.

Pedestal: #269, square top supported by square post and four full-length tapering corbels, 36″ × 13″ × 13″, *$650–$750*.

Rocking chair: #932, three vertical slats in back, open arms with long corbels, drop-in spring seat, 35″ × 27″ × 27″, *$150–$175*.

Rocking chair: #1656, five vertical slats in tall back, curved crest rail, three slats under each arm, exposed tenons on arms, drop-in spring seat, 43″ × 28″ × 29″, *$350–$400*.

Server: #456, overhanging top with closed plate rail, two short drawers over one long, each with brass knobs, open lower shelf, 41″ × 42″ × 18″, *$700–$800*.

Settle: drop-arm, ebony inlay on front posts, two caned back sections, front posts tenoned through arms, supported by corbels, eight slats in back, arched apron, drop-in spring seat, 38″ × 47″ × 25″, *$1100–$1350*.

Settle: #570, drop-arm with wide crest rail over nine wide slats, five slats under each arm, exposed tenons, drop-in spring seat, 29″ × 76″ × 32″, *$1500–$1750*.

Settle: #618, drop-arm with 11 slats in back, open arms supported by long corbels, stretchers near floor, drop-in spring seat, 40″ × 76″ × 29″, *$850–$950*.

Sideboard: early design with four doors with Art Nouveau–inspired stained glass, three lower drawers, four keyed tenons per side, chamfered board back, 53″ × 64″ × 23″, *$2500–$3000*.

Sideboard: #1380, mirrored back panel with top shelf, two half-drawers over one long drawer over two cabinet doors, arched apron, 51″ × 45″ × 19″, *$600–$700*.

Table, dining: #1480, circular top supported by center pedestal and four pairs of slanted legs, each pair joined by arched stretchers, exposed tenons, four leaves, 30″ × 54″, $2250–$2750.

Table, dining: #419, circular overhanging top supported by five legs, no stretchers, corbel on outside of each leg, four leaves, 30″ × 54″, $1750–$2000.

Table, lamp: #110, circular top, cross-stretcher base on tapering legs, 29″ × 24″, $300–$350.

Table, lamp: #214, square recessed top with arched aprons, two with small caned sections, single vertical slat beneath caned aprons, lower shelf, 30″ × 11″ × 11″, $425–$475.

Table, library: #1140, overhanging top, single drawer with square wooden pulls, corbels on each leg, lower shelf, exposed tenons, 29″ × 42″ × 30″, $500–$600.

Table, library: #146, oval overhanging top above four legs with cross-panel shelf and square cutouts, 30″ × 45″ × 30″, $950–$1200.

Table, octagon: #120, overhanging top over four splayed legs, each with spade-shaped cutout, flat cross-stretchers tenoned through each leg and secured with pair of wedges, paper label beneath top, 30″ × 45″ × 45″, $1750–$2000.

Taboret: #251, square overhanging top with cut corners, supported by four corbels, solid sides, each with a trapezoidal cutout, 24″ × 17″ × 17″, $1500–$1750.

GEORGE WASHINGTON MAHER

Shopmarks:
None appearing on furniture

Principal Contributions:
Architectural and furniture designs
Born: 1864   Died: 1926

Workshops and Studios:
George W. Maher
Chicago
1888–1926

"There must be evolved certain leading forms that will influence the detail of the design; these forms crystallize during the progress of the planning and become the motifs that bind the design together."

—*George Washington Maher*
1907[1]

George Washington Maher was one of the leading proponents in the Prairie school of design that expanded the architect's role beyond the planning of the exterior structure to include the design of the interior furnishings as well: furniture, rugs, lighting fixtures, and decorative accessories. Led by Frank Lloyd Wright, the Prairie school architects found a willing clientele in the affluent Chicago suburbs between 1900 and 1915 and created one of the first truly American styles of architecture.

Ironically, three of the most important Prairie school designers—Frank Lloyd Wright, George Grant Elmslie, and George Washington Maher—all served simultaneous apprenticeships under Chicago architect Joseph Silsbee. Maher left in 1888, at the age of twenty-three, to form his own practice; Wright and Elmslie went on to work for Louis Sullivan before they too struck out on their own. While all of the Prairie school architects stressed unity of site, materials, and design—internal and external—Maher soon developed his unique "motif rhythm" theory.

1. Wendy Kaplan, *The Art That Is Life* (Boston: Museum of Fine Arts, 1987), p. 396.

In each commission he sought "to receive the dominant inspiration from the patron, taking into strict account his needs, his temperament, and environment, influenced by local color and atmosphere in surrounding flora and nature. With these vital impressions at hand, the design naturally crystallizes and motifs appear which being consistently utilized will make each object, whether it be of construction, furniture or decoration, related."[2]

Maher's motif generally consisted of a plant form in conjunction with a repeating geometric shape. Among those with which he worked between 1901 and 1906 were a thistle and an octagon, a hollyhock and a simple band, a poppy and a straight line, and a tulip and an arch. Both his early houses and the furniture he designed for them were massive and solidly built; as one reporter noted, "everything seemed to have been designed to withstand an earthquake."[3]

In 1904, however, Maher traveled to St. Louis for the Louisiana Purchase Exposition, where he had the opportunity to study closely the German and Austrian furniture exhibits that proved popular with both the critics and the general public.[4] What he saw there, combined with the emerging influence of Frank Lloyd Wright over the entire Prairie school, was to affect all of his future work. "Maher veered away from the overwhelming monumentality and elaborate carving of earlier work and began to design with a lighter hand, emphasizing architectural details and favoring geometric patterns rather than excessive floral decoration."[5] Maher's subsequent work also began to reflect the designs of Englishman C. F. A. Voysey, for as Edward S. Cooke, Jr., has observed, "many of Maher's residential structures for the period of 1905 to 1915 combine Voysey-influenced domestic forms with a midwestern horizontality."[6]

2. Marian Page, *Furniture Designed by Architects* (New York: Whitney Library of Design, 1980), pp. 109–110.

3. Sharon Darling, *Chicago Furniture: 1833–1983* (Chicago: Chicago Historical Society, 1984), p. 252.

4. See Gustav Stickley, "The German Exhibit at the Louisiana Purchase Exposition," *The Craftsman* (June 1904), pp. 488–506.

5. Wendy Kaplan, *The Art That Is Life* (Boston: Museum of Fine Arts, 1987), p. 396.

6. Ibid.

Like nearly all of the Prairie school architects, Maher's furniture is closely tied to each house he designed. His early work reflects a Victorian influence, with elaborate carvings and sinuous lines, while his later furniture designs reveal that the carving was dropped and severe geometric forms adopted. Voysey's influence and that of the Austrian Secessionist style can be found in many of Maher's later Prairie designs that combine a rectilinear framework with segmented arches and a wide base that seems rooted to the ground. Richard Guy Wilson, in an essay entitled "Arts and Crafts Architecture," describes Maher as one of the "Prairie school independents . . . whose interpretation of the midwest displays the same geometry and reliance on nature for detail [as Frank Lloyd Wright] but in a very personal way."[7]

Maher's early furniture was more elaborate than that which he designed after 1904, revealing the growing influence Wright, the German and Austrian designers, and the emerging Prairie school of architecture had on him. His motif-rhythm theory was more evident in the design of the furniture than in the structure of the home, as in the John Farson House (1897), wherein the chairs featured an elaborately carved lion's head under each arm as well as on the upper rear posts. After 1904 his furniture designs began to focus more on geometric patterns and less on ornate carvings and floral decorations, culminating, many believe, in his finest Prairie school design: Rockledge.

Rockledge was designed for a Minnesota businessman who wanted a summer home overlooking the Mississippi River. Maher drew on both the natural colors found at the site and the segmental arch as the key elements for his motif rhythm. The furniture he designed for Rockledge incorporated both: the wood was tinted a greenish-brown and featured segmented arches above the back splat and each of the wide side slats. The flaring legs, segmented arches, and overall design reveal more of an Austrian influence than the Oriental that is so often found in Wright's work. The 1987–1988 "Art That Is Life" exhibition gave thousands of people the opportunity to view examples of

7. Wendy Kaplan, *The Art That Is Life* (Boston: Museum of Fine Arts, 1987), p. 123.

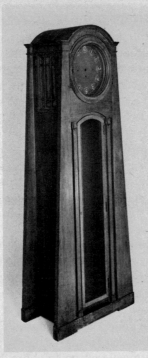

This oak tall-case clock (80″ × 31″ × 15″) was designed by Maher for the E. L. King House (1912), Rockledge, overlooking the Mississippi River in Minnesota. The arched bonnet, trapezoidal case, and green stain all corresponded with Maher's theme for the entire commission. *(Photo by Rick Echelmeyer, courtesy of* The Artsman)

the wide range of talents of George Washington Maher, as an armchair, a tall-case clock, a table lamp, a pair of andirons, and a rug—all of which he designed for Rockledge—were included in the traveling display and discussed at length in the exhibition catalog.

Selected Prices

The rarity of the furniture designed by George Maher, plus the individual nature of each piece, makes establishing a price guide both impractical and quite possibly misleading, for the value of any example will be influenced by factors beyond the scope of this study. Therefore, in lieu of price ranges, recent auction reports have been listed, including their presale estimates. However, it must be understood that auction estimates and final bids are often influenced by factors that cannot always be anticipated, fully explained, or duplicated. Auction prices reflect the final bid plus the 10 percent buyer's premium.

Armchair: Rockledge (1912), arched crest rail over single curved upholstered center splat, arms with arched apron above a vertical panel, drop-in seat, light green stain, 46″ × 25″ × 22″, Phillips 6/87 (est. $6000–$8000) *$7500* and *$10,000.*

Chest of drawers: Rockledge (1912), poplar, painted ivory, four short drawers over four long, with bronze pulls, trapezoidal backsplash and sides, 72″ × 42″ × 22″, Phillips 6/87 (est. $4000–$6000) *$2600.*

Clock, shelf: Rockledge (1912), poplar, painted ivory, trapezoidal case with arched hood, molded base on block feet, 11″ × 8″ × 5″, Phillips 6/87 (est. $1500–$2500) *$900.*

Clock, tall case: Rockledge (1912), arched bonnet above circular glass door, trapezoidal case, glass door revealing brass weights and pendulum, light green stain, 80″ × 31″ × 15″, Phillips 6/87 (est. $6000–$8000) *$27,000.*

Dresser: Rockledge (1912), poplar, painted ivory, two short drawers over two long, with bronze pulls, swivel mirror, trapezoidal sides, 67″ × 58″ × 24″, Phillips 6/87 (est. $3000–$5000) *$2100.*

Floor lamp: Rockledge (1910), a bronze shaft set on a bronze square platform with arched sides, a stained glass shade featuring tiger lilies, 62″ high, Christie's 12/86 (est. $5000–$7000) failed to clear reserve.

Floor lamp: Hiram Stewart House (1906), a hexagonal shade with striated glass, the shaft narrowing as it rises from the square base, 78″ × 26″ × 26″, Christie's 12/86 (est. $4000-$6000) *$3200*.

Library table: Hiram Stewart House (1906), mahogany with massive square legs ending in molded feet, overhanging top with wide apron, lower shelf, 30″ × 66″ × 36″, Christie's 12/86 (est. $4000-$6000) *$2600*.

Rocking chair: Rockledge (1912), poplar, painted ivory, arched crest rail above caned back and caned seat, flared legs, 35″ high, Phillips 6/87 (est. $2000-$3000) failed to meet reserve.

Table lamp: Rockledge (1912), the overhanging top featuring a segmented arch, each end with stained glass panel depicting a tiger lily, 16″ × 22″ × 12″, Phillips 6/87 (est. $10,000-$15,000) *$23,000*.

Vanity table: Rockledge (1912) poplar, painted, mirror panel with arched frame above hidden central drawer, flanked by two small drawers, 69″ × 45″ × 22″, Phillips 6/87 (est. $4000-$6000) failed to meet reserve.

JOSEPH P. McHUGH & CO.

Shopmark:
Paper label, decal, or brass tag with JOSEPH P. MCHUGH/ MISSION FURNITURE

Principal Contributions:
Limited line of early Mission oak furniture

Founder:
Joseph P. McHugh
Born: 1854   Died: 1916

Workshops and Salesrooms:
The Popular Shop
New York
ca. 1884–1916

"In the early part of 1894, an interior decorator of San Francisco
sent me a simple rush-seated chair similiar to some used by a
local architect to take the place of pews in a church of that city;
certain details of the form and construction attracted me, and I
set about making a variety of pieces which suggested the motive
of the single model."

—Joseph McHugh
1900[1]

While neither the name nor the furniture of Joseph P. McHugh
is widely known today, this New York City retailer has the
dubious distinction of being the first person to coin the phrase
"mission furniture."

In 1894 the thirty-year-old Joseph P. McHugh moved what
was to be known as The Popular Shop to the corner of Fifth
Avenue and West Forty-Second Street in Manhattan. He had
grown up and been trained in his family's dry-goods store and
learned early in his career the difference good publicity can make
to a business. Through his efforts The Popular Shop proved as
popular as its name, as McHugh made regular trips to England
and Europe, bringing back upholstery fabrics, wallpapers, pottery, William Morris chintzes, and Liberty and Company metalware and furniture for his Fifth Avenue clientele.

Shortly before his introduction to the "simple rush-seated
chair" that was to make him famous, albeit briefly, McHugh had
experimented with manufacturing his own line of wicker furniture. But when his friend A. Page Brown, a San Francisco designer, shipped him one of the chairs for a church interior he
and two other architects, A. C. Schweinfurth and Bernard

1. David Cathers, *Furniture of the American Arts and Crafts Movement* (New York: New American Library, 1981), p. 15.

This well-known McHugh chair (36″ × 17″ × 18″) may have
been the first commercially produced example of Mission oak furniture in the United States. Although the Michigan Chair Company sold a similar version, the McHugh chair differs in its raised
front-stretcher arrangement. Unlike later Mission oak furniture,
the joints were not pegged. *(Photo by Rick Echelmeyer, courtesy
of* The Artsman)

Maybeck, had designed,[2] Joseph McHugh saw the opportunity to
create and market a totally new line of furniture.

"The name McHugh mission furniture, which I used to distinguish the style, seemed appropriate, in view of the purpose
for which the single chair had been used, and the part of the
country from which it had been sent to me," McHugh explained
a few years later.[3] McHugh displayed the first samples of his
"McHugh mission furniture" in his Manhattan showrooms,
where it proved popular. The impending success of an extensive
line of Mission furniture led McHugh to hire a major designer,
Walter J. H. Dudley, in 1896. Dudley, a trained architect and

2. Wendy Kaplan, *The Art That Is Life* (Boston: Museum of Fine Arts,
1987), p. 124.
3. *American Cabinetmaker and Upholsterer* (July 14, 1900).

an accomplished artist, was instructed "to develop a line of furniture based on the simple, structural chairs in the Swedenborgian Church in San Francisco."[4]

It was that same year, 1896, that Elbert Hubbard in East Aurora, New York, had local carpenters building plain, simple furniture for his expanding operation, but Hubbard wasn't as quick as McHugh to realize the potential popularity of the emerging style. By 1899, though, Hubbard had begun to advertise his line of Roycroft furniture "made after the William Morris fashion."[5] Gustav Stickley was developing his own line of furniture at that time, but much of it was still in a transitional stage between Art Nouveau and Arts and Crafts. By 1900, however, both Stickley and Hubbard were ready to compete with McHugh for the developing Mission oak market.

While Stickley and Hubbard both soon had their own publications in which they advertised and promoted their products, McHugh was adept at reminding the public that he had been the first to introduce Mission furniture. The May 1900 issue of *Ladies Home Journal* featured the designs of McHugh and Dudley and helped make him one of the most successful and widely publicized furniture manufacturers of the times. McHugh and Company's early designs met with critical as well as popular approval. His furniture exhibit at the 1901 Pan-American Exposition in Buffalo was only a short distance away from the booth shared by Stickley's United Crafts and the Grueby Faience Company of Boston, affording visitors their first opportunity to view a large assemblage of Mission oak furniture. While it is widely known that the exposition gave Stickley vital public exposure, Joseph P. McHugh and Company walked away with that and more—a silver medal for their Mission-style furniture.

As has been pointed out, "McHugh's furniture was praised in 1901 as epitomizing an effort to capture the simplicity and

4. Coy L. Ludwig, *The Arts & Crafts Movement in New York State: 1890's–1920's* (Hamilton, NY: Gallery Association of NY State, Inc., 1983), p. 61.

5. David Cathers, *Furniture of the American Arts and Crafts Movement* (New York: New American Library, 1981), p. 88.

harmony preached by William Morris and his followers."[6] But whereas the furniture designs of Gustav Stickley, the Roycrofters, and later those of Charles Limbert and L. &. J. G. Stickley continued to improve, to evolve into more sophisticated forms, McHugh was unable to maintain both a consistency and the necessary high standards of workmanship to compete with the others—then or now. As David Cathers observed, "while being first may have been important to McHugh, the fact is that his mission designs were inept and their execution substandard."[7]

McHugh utilized a variety of different types of shopmarks—a brand, an oval paper label, and a brass tag—but each bore basically the same words: "Joseph P. McHugh/ Mission Furniture." The so-called McHugh chair, though not the only style made by the company, is indicative of their early designs. The massive legs and posts are unpegged, and the feet end in a mild variation of the Mackmurdo foot, also used both by Stickley Brothers and the Roycrofters. The seat of the McHugh chair may be either rush or leather. The Michigan Chair Company offered a similar chair in their 1898 catalog; but whereas the McHugh chair features a front stretcher slightly higher than the other three, the Michigan Chair Company version reveals all four stretchers at the same level.

McHugh lived long enough to see Gustav Stickley's empire crumble, to read of Elbert Hubbard's untimely death, and perhaps to sense that when the definitive history of the Arts and Crafts movement in America is finally written, Joseph P. McHugh will have become an important footnote.

Selected Prices

Other than the well-known and widely distributed McHugh chair, relatively few signed examples of McHugh furniture have surfaced. Those few have inspired only a lukewarm response,

6. Wendy Kaplan, *The Art That Is Life* (Boston: Museum of Fine Arts, 1987), p. 185.
7. David Cathers, *Furniture of the American Arts and Crafts Movement* (New York: New American Library, 1981), p. 15.

appealing for the most part to Arts and Crafts collectors interested more in the historical role than the intrinsic design. Until additional examples are identified and tested on the market, a comprehensive price guide will remain elusive.

Chair, side: the McHugh chair, two horizontal slats across the back between two massive posts, square legs ending in tapering, flared feet, rush seat, 36″ × 17″ × 18″, *$275–$325.*

Table, card: flip top above a single drawer, supported by four square, tapering posts with straight cross-stretchers, 28″ × 30″ × 30″, *$425–$475.*

GEORGE MANN NIEDECKEN

Shopmark:
None appearing on his furniture

Principal Contributions:
Interior architectural and furniture designs
Born: 1878   Died: 1945

Studios and Workshops:
Frank Lloyd Wright
Oak Park, Illinois
ca. 1904

Niedecken-Walbridge Co.
Milwaukee, Wisconsin
1907–ca. 1940

"Nine tenths of the men following the profession of interior decoration in America are in the business merely from a commercial
standpoint, and in no sense of the word are they artists. The
client consulting men of this type cannot expect to get anything
more than a stereotyped reproduction of things carried out in a
time and place when social conditions were wholly different from
our present day mode of living."

—*George Niedecken*
1913[1]

For many years it was incorrectly assumed that George Niedecken was simply the cabinetmaker who had built much of the
furniture that Frank Lloyd Wright had designed between 1902
and 1911. To his credit, George Niedecken undoubtedly was familiar with the skills required to be a cabinetmaker, for he oversaw the manufacture of much of the furniture he and other
architects, including Wright, had designed; but his contribution
to both the Arts and Crafts movement and the Prairie school of
architecture go far beyond that of a woodworker.

After studying at the Wisconsin Art Institute and the Art
Institute in Chicago, a young George Niedecken spent several
months traveling in Europe and England, where he studied the
work of important Arts and Crafts designers, including William
Morris, as well as Art Nouveau artists in Paris and Arts and
Crafts architects in Vienna, many of whom were to influence his
later designs. He returned to Milwaukee in July 1902 and re-
sumed painting, displaying his work in exhibitions he helped to
organize.

Soon thereafter Niedecken met Frank Lloyd Wright, "who
cultivated a working relationship with Niedecken that spanned
fifteen years and a dozen commissions."[2] In 1904 Niedecken was

1. George Niedecken, "Relationship of Decorator, Architect and Client," *The Western Architect* (May 1913).
2. Rosalie Goldstein, ed, *The Domestic Scene (1897–1927): George M.
Niedecken, Interior Architect* (Milwaukee, WI: Milwaukee Art Museum,
1981), p. 11.

Though not indicative of his best work, this oak rolltop desk (43″ × 50″ × 34″) reflects Niedecken's attempt to design an Arts and Crafts rolltop desk for the Irving House (1910), which Frank Lloyd Wright had begun before leaving for Europe in 1909. None of the Arts and Crafts designers, including Wright and Stickley, seemed able to design a successful rolltop desk. *(Photo courtesy of Phillips, New York)*

hired by Wright to design and paint the sumac dining room frieze in the Susan Dana House in Springfield, Illinois. The two developed a working friendship that almost led, according to John Walbridge, Niedecken's brother-in-law and eventual business partner, to a formal partnership.[3]

The work Niedecken did for Wright and other Chicago area architects led to the establishment of a business partnership between Niedecken and Walbridge in 1907. The partners offered a variety of services, from upholstery and refinishing of existing furniture to custom-designed furniture, fabrics, draperies, rugs, and lighting fixtures. They continued to collaborate with Wright on many of his interiors, at times transforming his

3. Rosalie Goldstein, ed., *The Domestic Scene (1897–1927): George M. Niedecken, Interior Architect* (Milwaukee, WI: Milwaukee Art Museum, 1981), p. 11.

rough sketches into finished drawings ready to be taken to a cabinetmaker and at other times designing the furniture itself.

In 1907, when both his reputation and his business were blossoming, Wright hired the firm of Niedecken-Walbridge to assist with the furnishings for the Frederick C. Robie and the Avery W. Coonley houses in Chicago. At this point the partnership had not yet established its own woodworking shop, so the finished furniture plans were turned over to the F. H. Bresler firm for execution under George Niedecken's close supervision. By 1910, though, Niedecken and Walbridge were no longer subcontracting furniture construction to local cabinet shops but had set up their own factory. They completed the furniture for the Robey House and also began making furniture for William Purcell, George Elmslie, William Drummond, and other Midwestern architects. One of the most famous pieces that the Niedecken-Walbridge furniture shop built was the tall-case clock with mahogany and brass inlay designed by George Elmslie in 1912 for the Babson House in Riverside, Illinois. The hands and gold face for the clock were provided by none other than Robert R. Jarvie of Chicago.

Wright left Chicago in 1909, but he and Niedecken later worked together on the design of the furniture for the Allen House in Wichita, Kansas (1917–1918) and the Bogk House in Milwaukee (1917–1918), all of which was produced by the Niedecken-Walbridge furniture factory. The furniture reveals a Niedecken touch that was not typically Wright: decorative inlay.

Whereas Wright chose to stress the plane geometry of his early furniture by adding linear wood strips, Niedecken's own contemporary style often relied on inlay to achieve the same effect. It is significant that Niedecken's own furniture shop, set up in 1910, was headed by Dutch immigrant Herman Tenbroeke, who specialized in veneered cabinetwork. . . . Niedecken apparently derived geometric inlay not from the oriental sources that inspired Wright but from the innovative architects associated with the Arts and Crafts Movement in Vienna.[4]

4. Rosalie Goldstein, ed., *The Domestic Scene (1897–1927): George M. Niedecken, Interior Architect* (Milwaukee, WI: Milwaukee Art Museum, 1981), p. 47.

As Edward S. Cooke, Jr., has noted, Niedecken, both through the work he did for Wright and other Prairie school architects and through the plans he designed for his own individual clients, "was one of the first to give definition to a new profession: that of the interior architect."[5] Niedecken's work reveals an ability to work in a variety of styles and woods, depending on the needs and desires of his client, but his personal Prairie school designs reveal the influence both Wright and the Austrian school of design had on him. Like Wright, Niedecken embraced the machine in the design and execution of his furniture plans, utilizing its ability to quickly cut precision dovetails, doweled joints, and splined miters, but as Chicago-based author Sharon Darling has pointed out, "At first view Prairie style furniture gave the illusion of simplicity; in fact it was quite complex. While its relatively straight lines allowed the use of modern woodworking machinery, a great deal of additional handwork was also required."[6]

The furniture produced by Niedecken-Walbridge was well constructed, utilizing both mortise-and-tenon and doweled joints, dovetailed drawers, mitered corners, tongue-and-groove joinery, and internal splines. Both the insides of drawers and the backs of case pieces were finished as if they were going to be on display. Unlike Wright, Niedecken was as concerned with the comfort of his furniture as he was with how it fit within the overall plan. Whereas Wright would later joke about his inability to design comfortable chairs, Niedecken's redesign of Wright's chairs for the Bogk House "involved shortening and contouring the backs to bring them more in line with human anatomy."[7]

Like most of the Prairie school architects and interior designers, Niedecken's work is identified not through shopmarks

5. Wendy Kaplan, *The Art That Is Life* (Boston: Museum of Fine Arts, 1987), p. 237.

6. Sharon Darling, *Chicago Furniture: Art, Craft & Industry 1833–1983* (Chicago: Chicago Historical Society, 1984), p. 265.

7. Rosalie Goldstein, ed., *The Domestic Scene (1897–1927: George M. Niedecken, Interior Architect* (Milwaukee, WI: Milwaukee Art Museum, 1981), p. 65.

but by studying documents and photographs of the rooms in which it appeared. Unlike the furniture of any of the Stickleys or other furniture manufacturers, the clients' tastes generally took precedence over that of the architect's in the design of their furniture. While Wright proved to be the exception to this and many other rules, George Niedecken's work reflects the variety of styles inherent in the number of architects and private clients he served. One observer has surmised that, in part at least, "Niedecken's willingness to temper his creativity to conform with an architect's comprehensive plan stemmed from contact with Wright's dominant personality and exceptional conceptual powers."[8] Niedecken proved that he not only could work in a wide range of styles, from Art Nouveau to Prairie to Georgian Revival, but that he could master them as well. "Whether called upon to decorate a colonial mansion or a historical Prairie residence, Niedecken faced the same challenge of interrelating facade, woodwork, fabrics, cabinetry and seating furniture."[9]

Selected Prices

The rarity of the furniture designed by George Niedecken, plus the individual nature of each piece, makes establishing a price guide both impractical and quite possibly misleading, for the value of any example will be influenced by factors beyond the scope of this study. Therefore, in lieu of price ranges, recent auction reports have been listed, including their presale estimates. However, it must be understood that auction estimates and final bids are often influenced by factors that cannot always be anticipated, fully explained, or duplicated. Auction

8. Rosalie Goldstein, ed., *The Domestic Scene (1897-1927): George M. Niedecken, Interior Architect* (Milwaukee, WI: Milwaukee Art Museum, 1981), p. 69.
9. Ibid., p. 70.

prices reflect the final bid plus the 10 percent buyer's premium.

Chair, side: Irving House (1910), oak, square back with inset cushion mounted between canted uprights, above a trapezoidal seat with inset cushion, Phillips 4/87 (est. $7000–$9000) failed to clear reserve.

Chair, side: Irving House (1910), oak, tall, rectangular slab back with inset cushion canted between two square uprights, above a trapezoidal seat with inset cushion, Phillips 4/87 (est. $8000–$12,000 for pair) failed to clear reserve.

Desk, rolltop: Irving House (1910), oak, with fitted interior, seven drawers, with C-curve roll, 43″ × 50″ × 34″, Phillips 4/87 (est. $10,000–$25,000) failed to clear reserve.

Rug, wool: Wilcox House (ca. 1923), ivory pattern on beige ground, 81″ × 61″, Phillips 4/87 (est. $1200–$1800) *$1210*.

Table, lamp: Irving House (1910), oak, square top with wood band detailing, supported by an angular planar pedestal raised on stepped square base, Phillips 4/87 (est. $5000–$7000) *$3300*.

Taboret: Irving House (1910), oak, molded square top above a molded frieze, the square legs joined by a medial shelf, 16″ × 14″ × 14″, Phillips 4/87 (est. $6000–$8000) *$4620*.

CHARLES ROHLFS

The unique pierced designs and Art Nouveau flavor of Rohlfs's work are exhibited in this oak library table (29″ × 43″ × 34″). The Rohlfs shopmark is visible inside the door, which opens to reveal a storage compartment. *(Photo courtesy of the Virginia Museum, Richmond, Sydney and Frances Lewis Collection)*

Shopmark:
Incised or branded, the letter *R* within the outline of a saw, occasionally with the year underneath

Principal Contributions:
Uniquely designed oak interior furnishings and accessories
Born: 1853   Died: 1936
Founded: ca. 1890   Closed: ca. 1925

Studios and Workshop:
Charles Rohlfs Workshop
Buffalo, New York
ca. 1890–ca. 1925

"In other words my feeling was to treat my wood well, caress it perhaps, and that desire led to the idea that I must embellish it to evidence my profound regard for a beautiful thing in nature. This embellishment consisted of line, proportion and carving."

—Charles Rohlfs
1925[1]

A few miles away from the village of East Aurora, New York, where Elbert Hubbard and his colony of artisans were busily producing a line of severely plain and straight-lined Mission oak furniture, Charles Rohlfs and seven or eight German craftsmen were meticulously designing, carving, and producing a limited number of privately commissioned pieces. And while both the Roycrofters and Charles Rohlfs worked in close proximity to one another, both utilizing quarter-sawn white oak and designing furniture with exposed structural details, in many cases the similarities end there.

Charles Rohlfs was born in New York City and as a youth learned the trades of both barrel maker and a cast-iron stove designer. While in his mid-twenties he left the factory environment to take to the stage, where he quickly established a reputation as a fine Shakespearean actor. Soon thereafter he fell in love with Katherine Green, a popular writer of detective novels and daughter of a prominent socialite—who refused to accept Rohlfs as a son-in-law so long as he remained an actor.[2]

Within a few years Rohlfs had decided to forgo a career in the theater, and in 1884 he married Katherine Green. As Rohlfs recalled years later, he and Katherine had hoped to furnish their home in Buffalo with antiques, but since they could not yet afford them, he drew on his basic woodworking skills and began designing and constructing furniture in a makeshift attic

1. Charles Rohlfs, "My Adventure in Woodcarving," *Arts Journal* (September 1925).
2. Coy L. Ludwig, *The Arts and Crafts Movement in New York State: 1890's–1920's* (Hamilton, NY: Gallery Association of New York State, 1983), p. 87.

workshop. Even his earliest projects reveal that Charles Rohlfs had a rare talent for design that enabled him successfully to blend elements of the flowing Art Nouveau style with the linear look and structural expressiveness characteristic of Arts and Crafts-style furniture. His love for his work, his admiration and devotion to both his subject and his material, and his dedication to his craft are revealed in one statement: "If I make a chair, I am a chair."[3]

Unhappy with his job in a Buffalo foundry, Rohlfs pursued his woodworking hobby, transforming it, as he turned forty, into a new career. By 1898 he had moved his shop out of the attic of his home and into a commercial building, but "instead of mass-producing a 'line' of furniture, Rohlfs believed in maintaining the high quality of art in his work by limiting production to pieces, suites, and ensembles that were unique."[4] Rohlfs and his furniture gained international acclaim at the 1901 Pan-American Exposition in Buffalo, where a new line of oak furniture by an Eastwood, New York, furniture maker by the name of Gustav Stickley was also being introduced. Subsequent expositions in St. Louis, Canada, and Europe brought honors and commissions from around the world, from Buckingham Palace to the home of Marshall Field, as well as inclusion in London's Royal Society of Arts; yet Rohlfs steadfastly refused to enlarge his small staff of craftsmen and woodcarvers.

Like most Arts and Crafts designers, Rohlfs worked primarily in oak, often pegging joints and utilizing keyed tenons. Unlike any of the same major designers and manufacturers, however, Rohlfs's furniture is often decorated with elaborate carvings, motivated in traditional Art Nouveau style by natural plant forms. According to his son, Rohlfs was once inspired by the smoke curling up from the bowl of his pipe, and he preserved that image in the carvings on the sides of a chest of

3. Michael James, "The Philosophy of Charles Rohlfs: An Introduction," *Arts & Crafts Quarterly* (April 1987), p. 15.

4. Coy L. Ludwig, *The Arts and Crafts Movement in New York State: 1890's–1920's* (Hamilton, NY: Gallery Association of New York State, 1983), p. 87.

drawers he designed for their home.[5] Like Charles Greene on
the West Coast, Rohlfs worked in the Arts and Crafts style, but
his creative talents were never bound by convention. While most
Arts and Crafts designers shunned the added decorative effect
of carving, Rohlfs approached it as an art form, often letting the
grain of the wood determine the direction his carving took. "If
you have the feeling for this work," he later explained, "the
carving will look after itself."[6]

Much of Rohlfs's early furniture was either darkly stained or
fumed oak, as was the reigning fashion. Unlike the Roycrofters
or any of the Stickleys, though, Rohlfs appeared to be con-
stantly testing current fashion, incorporating curved cutouts and
flowing lines into his designs at a time when rectilinear forms
without elaborate oramentation were prevalent within the
movement. While most of the major Arts and Crafts furniture
manufacturers used flush pegs to strengthen critical joints,
Rohlfs drew attention to his pegs by letting them protrude
above the wood. In addition, Rohlfs used raised pegs for their
decorative effect, as he also did brass tacks and wood buttons.
The buttons, however, often disguised screws used in place of
dowels or tenons—a practice other important firms generally
avoided and that has been attributed to Rohlfs's lack of extensive training in joinery.[7]

When Rohlfs's work, like that of all of the Arts and Crafts
designers, fell out of style between the late 1920s and the early
1970s, it was scattered across the country as households to which
it originally had been commissioned were disposed of and heirs
sold off the contents. Robert Judson Clark and the organizers
of the 1972 landmark exhibition "The Arts and Crafts Movement in America: 1876–1916" were the first to call attention
to Rohlfs's role as an important Arts and Crafts furniture

5. Judson Clark, *The Arts and Crafts Movement in America, 1876–1916*
(Princeton, NJ: Princeton University Press, 1972), pp. 28–29.

6. Eve Warner, "Charles Rohlfs: In Step with a Different Drummer,"
The New York–Pennsylvania Collector (November 1986), p. 6.

7. Wendy Kaplan, *The Art That Is Life: The Arts and Crafts Movement
in America, 1875–1920* (Boston: Museum of Fine Arts, 1987), pp. 98–
99.

designer;[8] respect and demand for his work has increased tremendously since then. As would be expected, important examples from Rohlfs's workshop surface only on rare occasions and are almost always recognized immediately because of their distinctive style. The combination of quality Art Nouveau carving and curved lines within an obviously well-constructed, often startling Arts and Crafts form is difficult for even an inexperienced collector to overlook.

While large case pieces, generally made on commission, are considered extremely rare, smaller forms intended to be sold to the public—from stamp boxes and candlesticks to chairs and rockers—continue to surface. The collector who cannot justify spending $28,000 for a rare Rohlfs chair or even $3000 for an oak sewing cabinet could still have purchased a signed Rohlfs picture frame for less than $100 or a 1901 stamp box for less than $500 at the major auction houses in 1987.

Much of the Rohlfs furniture that was not intended for use in his own home was signed with a shopmark as unique as his furniture. The letter *R*, carved or burned into the wood, was encompassed by the rectangular outline of a wood saw. In many instances the year in which the piece was made will also be incised into the wood next to his shopmark, leading people unfamiliar with Rohlfs's work to refer occasionally to a piece as being "dated Roycroft furniture." Examples have been found in which the carved Rohlfs shopmark and date have been highlighted with either red or white paint, making them even easier to distinguish.

Although some people have difficulty understanding how the fanciful and often elaborate designs of Charles Rohlfs can be included with the severely plain and unadorned work of Arts and Crafts spokesmen such as Gustav Stickley, Elbert Hubbard, and Frank Lloyd Wright, his independent and creative spirit, his demand for quality craftsmanship, and his respect for the nature of his materials represent the very spirit of the Arts and Crafts movement.

8. Judson Clark, *The Arts and Crafts Movement in America, 1876–1916* (Princeton, NJ: Princeton University Press, 1972), pp. 28–31.

As Coy Ludwig concluded, "Rohlfs furniture is the work of a self-assured individualist. His high ideals were nurtured by the courage of his conviction to pursue them, and his work genuinely deserves the name by which it is commonly called: art furniture."[9]

Selected Prices

Since Charles Rohlfs and his assistants worked primarily on private commissions, their furniture is considered both rare and extremely valuable. For that reason, recent auction results have been substituted for price ranges that, in light of the current Rohlfs market, could prove misleading. Rohlfs also designed smaller accessories for his assistants to complete, such as candlesticks and stamp boxes, which surface on a regular basis and for which price ranges are included.

Candleholder: mahogany, with a triangular column resting on a triangular base, a copper bobeche on the column, incised shopmark and 1902 painted red, 4½″ × 11″, *$250–$300*.

Candleholder: oak, with a triangular column resting on a triangular base, a copper bobeche set on the column, incised shopmark and 1902 painted red, 4½″ × 11″, *$300–$350*.

Candlestick: a triangular form with overhanging top drilled and fitted for candle, behind which is a triangular copper reflector, triangular shaft with cutouts on triangular base, incised shopmark and 1901, 25″ high, Christie's 6/87 (est. $2000–$3000) *$3520*.

Chafing set: an earthenware chafing dish sitting on a copper scrolled platform on a triangular oak base, incised

9. Coy L. Ludwig, *The Arts and Crafts Movement in New York State: 1890's–1920's* (Hamilton, NY: Gallery Association of New York State, 1983), p. 88.

shopmark, 20″ high, Christie's 12/86 (est. $1200–$1500) *$3850.*

Chair, swivel: wide back panel with pierced cutouts, carved rear posts and arm supports, incised shopmark and 1902, 46″ high, Christie's 12/87 (est. $2000–$3000) *$2860.*

Chair, side: octagonal rear posts joined by four horizontal slats, seat apron arched with cutouts, raised pegs, loose cushion seat, incised shopmark and 1901 painted red on rear apron, 47″ high, Christie's 6/87 (est. $7000–$9000) *$28,600.*

Chair, side: single wide slat in back with pierced ovals and incised carving, seat apron cut out and carved, curved cross-stretcher base, incised shopmark, 38″ × 18″, Skinner's 4/87 (est. $3000–$5000) *$9075.*

Chest: overhanging hinged top with carving, copper hardware, curved aprons, raised pegs, incised shopmark and 1906, 24″ × 48″ × 24″, Christie's 12/87 (est. $9000–$13,000) *$8800.*

Frame, picture: rectangular form, incised shopmark on back, 16″ × 26″, *$100–$125.*

Sewing cabinet: overhanging top over single paneled door with cut-out apron, two keyed tenons on either side, fitted interior with sliding trays, incised shopmark and 1907 on door, 25″ × 17″ × 17″, Christie's 6/87 (est. $2500–$4000) *$3080.*

Stamp box: hinged top opening to reveal four square compartments, curved sides, incised shopmark and 1901 colored red, 2″ × 6″, *$325–375.*

Taboret: octagon overhanging top over an eight-sided base with hinged door to storage compartment, each side with cutouts and raised pegs, incised shopmark inside door, 29″ × 32″ × 32″, Christie's 12/85 (est. $10,000–$14,000) *$9900.*

THE ROSE VALLEY ASSOCIATION

Shopmark:
Branded mark, ROSE VALLEY SHOPS, and a rose and the
letter *V* enclosed by a buckled belt

Principal Contributions:
Furniture, pottery, and *The Artsman* magazine

Founder:
William L. Price
Born: 1861　　　　Died: 1916
Founded: 1901　　　Closed: ca. 1909

Furniture Workshops:
The Rose Valley Shops
Rose Valley, Pennsylvania
1901–1906

"the art that is life. . . ."

—*William L. Price*
1903[1]

Among the experimental utopian crafts communities that were
inspired by John Ruskin and William Morris was the Rose Valley Association outside Philadelphia. Architect Will Price
founded the colony in 1901 after having secured financial backing from prominent Philadelphia philantropists, including the
influential Edward Bok, founder of the *Ladies Home Journal*
and an early supporter of the Arts and crafts movement. Price

1. This phrase was adopted by William L. Price for the subtitle of his
periodical *The Artsman,* which was published from 1903 to 1907.

established the Rose Valley Shops amid the ruins of a bankrupt textile factory, a move that proved to be as prophetic as it was symbolic.

Though idealistic, Price was not devoid of practical considerations, "situating his experiment within commuting distance of Philadelphia, where he maintained his architectural practice and where most of the original Valley residents worked."[2] The corporation papers for the Rose Valley Shops indicated Price's intention to "manufacture structures, articles, materials and products involving artistic handcraft."[3] It was clear from the beginning that one of the principal endeavors at Rose Hill was going to be the production of handcrafted furniture. Price installed several workbenches and a minimum number of woodworking machines, for it appears that most of the relatively small number of examples that were produced at Rose Valley were made primarily by hand. Price employed an average of four to six craftsmen, generally European woodcarvers, who, in turn, attempted to train some of the residents, since Price believed that "Americans had already lost their craft skills to machinery."[4]

The furniture designs that Price provided for the Rose Valley woodworkers featured extensive hand carving, often in a Gothic or Renaissance style. Keyed tenons were often incorporated, enabling many of the pieces to be disassembled for shipping. As Robert Edwards observed, "In some instances, three-dimensional figures formed the fully functional mortise pins of the tables and chairs that were the mainstay of Rose Valley production. Comparatively few case pieces were made and all of the known examples of the five hundred pieces estimated to have been made are of quartered oak finished with dark Cabot's stain."[5]

2. Wendy Kaplan, *The Art That Is Life* (Boston: Museum of Fine Arts, 1987), p. 223.
3. Ibid., p. 314.
4. Ibid., p. 225.
5. Ibid., p. 229.

Although not a commercial success, the artistic quality of Rose Valley furniture was undeniable. The figural keyed tenons could be removed to allow the table to be disassembled for shipping, but internal problems proved to be insurmountable at the Arts and Crafts retreat. *(Photo by Rick Echelmeyer, courtesy of* The Artsman)

Problems soon surfaced at Rose Valley as Price, his associates, and his woodworkers "wrestled with the compromise reality forces upon the ideal. Woodworkers had no creative control over the products' designs nor were they accepted as peers by the residents of the community (where most workers did not reside)."[6] They were excluded from the other activities at Rose Valley, including the plays, publication of *The Artsman* (1903–1907), and cultural events that highlighted life in the utopian community.

Price arranged for an exhibit of Rose Valley crafts and furniture at the prestigious 1904 Louisiana Purchase Exposition in St. Louis, which, along with ads and features in magazines such as Bok's *Ladies Home Journal*, helped increase demand for their work, which they also sold through a retail outlet in Philadelphia. Nevertheless, as Edwards reveals, "workers were

6. Wendy Kaplan, *The Art That Is Life* (Boston: Museum of Fine Arts, 1987), p. 229.

content neither with pity nor with the damp stone mill in which they worked. After five years, the woodworking shop closed amid complaints about poor working conditions."[7]

The few examples of Rose Valley furniture that surface can be recognized both by their high quality of workmanship and the Rose Valley shopmark: a branded rose and the letter *V* encompassed by a buckled belt and the inscription "Rose Valley Shops." Although their designs may not be considered strictly Arts and Crafts, the inspiration, motivation, and handcraftsmanship that were behind each example were clearly derivative of the principles of both John Ruskin and William Morris.

Selected Prices

The rarity of the furniture designed and produced at Rose Valley, plus the individual nature of each piece, makes establishing a price guide both impractical and quite possibly misleading, for the value of any example will be influenced by factors beyond the scope of this study. Therefore, in lieu of price ranges, recent auction reports have been listed, including their presale estimates. However, it must be understood that auction estimates and final bids are often influenced by factors that cannot always be anticipated, fully explained, or duplicated. Auction prices reflect the final bid plus the 10 percent buyer's premium.

Chair, side: carved and pierced back panel with leather stretched between the two carved uprights, leather seat with brass tacks, 39″ × 15″ × 15″, Phillips 6/87 (est. $2500–$3500) *$2200*.

Table, library: rectangular top constructed of four boards joined with butterfly joints, sides with Gothic carving, through tenons and carved keys holding lower shelf, Phillips 6/87 (est. $20,000–$25,000) failed to clear reserve.

7. Wendy Kaplan, *The Art That Is Life* (Boston: Museum of Fine Arts, 1987), p. 229.

THE ROYCROFT SHOPS

One of the most popular examples of Roycroft furniture today is this six-foot-tall bookstand with the carved orb-and-cross shop-mark. Collectors need to realize, however, that an identical, high-quality reproduction is currently being marketed. The modern example is signed with the craftsman's mark on the underside of the bottom shelf. *(Photo courtesy of David Rago, Trenton)*

Shopmark:
Carved letter *R* within a circle topped by a cross; carved wood *ROYCROFT* in Gothic lettering

Principal Contributions:
Oak furniture, metalware, and books

Founder:
Elbert Hubbard

Born: 1856   Died: 1915
Founded: 1895   Closed: 1938

Workshops and Salesrooms:
The Roycroft Shops
East Aurora, New York
1895–1938

"We would ask you not to class our products as "Mission," or so-called "Mission Furniture." Ours is purely Roycroft—made by us according to our own ideas. We have eliminated all unnecessary elaboration, but have kept in view the principles of artistic quality, sound mechanical construction and good workmanship."

—Elbert Hubbard
1906[1]

"Elbert Hubbard has gone on his last Little Journey . . . ," a sentimental prologue to the Roycroft Shops' 1919 catalog laments. Hubbard's untimely death aboard the *Lusitania* in 1915 ended the stormy and controversial career of an enterprising soap salesman turned publisher, who, according to one of his respected peers "started more people to thinking in the last fifteen years than any man who has been talking or writing, or both, in this country."[2]

Hubbard's story is one many people are familiar with, for more information has survived regarding his life than that of all but a few other figures in the Arts and Crafts movement. Among his many talents, two served him best: a natural knack for promotion and a charisma that attracted talented individuals and

1. *Roycroft Furniture Catalog* (New York: Turn of the Century Editions, 1981), p. 3.
2. Freeman Champney, *Art & Glory: The Story of Elbert Hubbard* (Kent, OH: Kent State University Press, 1983), p. 199.

artists to his fold. In 1892, in the midst of a successful career
with the John Larkin soap company, Elbert Hubbard, married
and the father of three boys, sold his stock in the firm for
$75,000[3] and left to pursue his other interests. During the next
two years he enrolled briefly in Harvard, wrote an unsuccessful
novel, and traveled extensively. In 1894 he hiked across England, met William Morris, and returned home to await the births
in September of two daughters—one by his wife, the other by
his mistress.

Elbert Hubbard soon embarked on a Morris-inspired publishing career that blossomed under his prolific pen and promotional
campaigns. By 1895 he had established his press in East Aurora
and named it after two brothers, Thomas and Samuel Roycroft,
printers who had lived in London in the seventeenth century.
His new shopmark, an orb-and-cross, had been used by a four-
teenth-century monk, Cassiodorus; he and other monks had inscribed it at the end of each book they meticulously hand-copied
to signify that each work was "the best they knew how."[4] Hubbard combined the two—the letter *R* from the Roycroft brothers and the orb-and-cross from the monks—to create the
Roycroft shopmark that was to become a prominent element in
all of their work.

As his regular publications, *Little Journeys* and *The Philis-
tine*, grew in popularity, so did his need for additional staff and
space. Local carpenters were hired in 1896 to construct and furnish a book bindery and soon thereafter a leather shop, a larger
print shop, and eventually the Roycroft Inn. The simple,
straight-lined furniture the carpenters produced for the buildings quickly became popular with visitors to the Roycroft campus, and Hubbard, never one to let opportunity slip away, was
offering it for sale by 1897.[5] An early advertisement stated
that "no stock of furniture is carried—the pieces are made as

3. Mary Roelofs Stott, *Rebel with Reverence: Elbert Hubbard* (Watkins
Glen, NY: American Life Foundation, 1984), p. 20.

4. Nancy Hubbard Brady, ed., *The Book of the Roycrofters* (East Aurora, NY: House of Hubbard, 1977), p. 4.

5. David Cathers, *Furniture of the American Arts and Crafts Movement* (New York: New American Library, 1981), p. 87.

ordered, and about two months will be required to fill your order. Every piece is signed by the man who made it."[6]

Hubbard's first love was always the printed word, and it does not appear that he played a major role in the design or production of Roycroft furniture. As with many of his projects, Hubbard attracted talented craftsmen to his East Aurora workshops, including Santiago Cadzow, Albert Danner, Victor Toothaker, and Herbert Buffum, all of whom contributed in various ways to Roycroft design and production. As David Cathers observed, Hubbard may have occasionally injected his opinions, but "the enormous variety in designs found in Roycroft furniture indicates that no one designer ever dominated its appearance."[7] That fact is unfortunate, for Roycroft designs often fail to equal the high quality of materials and level of workmanship evidenced in all of their work. Uncompromisingly severe, Roycroft furniture often lacks the warmth and almost personal nature other firms achieved through a careful use of tapering corbels, sweeping arches, and lighter finishes. Their massiveness and sheer weight are enough to convince even those unfamiliar with cabinetry that these are quality pieces; but the bullish, masculine character of most Roycroft furniture, along with its relative rarity, has prevented it from becoming as widely collected as that of Gustav Stickley.

The Roycrofters encouraged visitors to the Inn and readers of their catalogs to commission special orders, as evidenced both in the number of pieces of furniture that surface with a particular person's name carved into them, and in a line from their catalog: "We do not confine ourselves to the designs shown herein, but, will, if you wish, make special pieces to your order, embodying your own ideas."[8]

What Hubbard no doubt did have a hand in was the promotional descriptions of their furniture: "Roycroft furniture resembles that made by the old monks, in its simple beauty, its

6. Nancy Hubbard Brady, *Roycroft Handmade Furniture* (East Aurora, NY: House of Hubbard, 1973), p. 57.

7. David Cathers, *Furniture of the American Arts and Crafts Movement* (New York: New American Library, 1981), p. 91.

8. Nancy Hubbard Brady, *Roycroft Handmade Furniture* (East Aurora, NY: House of Hubbard, 1973), p. i.

strength and its excellent workmanship. We use no nails—but are generous in the use of pegs, pins, mortises and tenons. Our furniture is made of the solid wood—no veneer. We use only the best grade of quarter-sawed oak and African or Santo Domingo mahogany. The oak is finished in our own weathered finish, a combination of stain, filler and wax polish, that produces a satisfying and permanent effect."[9] While Roycroft furniture is distinguished by its exceedingly high quality of materials and workmanship, their finishes have not proved to be as durable as those of Gustav Stickley or Charles Limbert. For that reason many pieces have been refinished, but collectors have demonstrated that they are willing to pay a premium for those pieces that have retained their original finish.

Roycroft furniture is by far some of the heaviest and the most massive produced in this era. Whereas even Gustav Stickley, late in his career, began to attempt to reduce both the weight and the cost of his furniture using veneers, plywood panels, thinner woods, and more advanced production techniques, the Roycrofters continued to use thicker woods, bulbous feet, keyed tenons, and coppered glass doors in a shop where it was claimed, though not substantiated, that "each piece was made by one man and each man could make any piece."[10] Hubbard's solution to the cost problem was simple: whereas a flat-arm Gustav Stickley Morris chair (No. 332) cost $33.00 in 1910, a similiar Roycroft model (No. 045) was priced in 1912 at $55.00— a difference representing more than two weeks' pay for an average worker.

Even though the Roycroft craftsmen may have made Arts and Crafts furniture longer than anyone else—from 1897 until nearly 1925—their level of production lagged far behind that of other well-known manufacturers. Large case pieces are considered extremely rare and, when in excellent, original condition, very valuable. Large bookcases, flat-topped desks, buffets, and china cabinets are among the hardest to find; dining chairs,

9. Nancy Hubbard Brady, *Roycroft Handmade Furniture* (East Aurora, NY: House of Hubbard, 1973), p. 1.
10. Ibid.

In 1913, the Roycrofters manufactured approximately 300 dining chairs for the Grove Park Inn outside Asheville, North Carolina. Originally, the chairs looked like the chairs pictured on the right, but around 1917, arms were added for the convenience of the diners. The chairs are marked with both the Roycroft orb-and-cross and the letters *G.P.I.*

library tables, and rocking chairs are among the most common. One form that appears quite often is a small bookstand, often referred to as a "Little Journeys table." It was designed after 1915 to hold the fourteen-volume complete works of Elbert Hubbard's *Little Journeys* series. The table is distinguished by four keyed tenons on each side and is marked with a small metal tag bearing the orb-and-cross. Once considered unimportant by most Roycroft collectors, these small, convenient tables have become more popular than the Elbert Hubbard books they were intended to promote.

Each piece of furniture that left the Roycroft shops was a literal advertisement for Hubbard's enterprises. The Roycroft shopmark or, on special commissions, the entire word in Gothic script was boldly enblazoned across the front of each piece in letters large enough to be read from across the room, a barely silent reminder from Elbert Hubbard himself that this is not just a piece of furniture; this is ROYCROFT furniture.

As fate would have it, the most common example of Roycroft furniture, the "Little Journeys bookstand" (26″ × 26″ × 14″), is the least representative of their work. This three-tiered stand is held together with four screws and eight wedges, making it easy to mail from the Roycroft gift shop but unstable once it arrives. It is the only Roycroft furniture signed with a brass tag. *(Photo courtesy of Christie's, New York)*

Selected Prices

Model numbers correspond with those in the catalog reprints *Roycroft Furniture* (New York: Turn of the Century Editions, 1981) and *Roycroft Handmade Furniture* (East Aurora, NY: House of Hubbard, 1973). Unless otherwise indicated, all examples are made from oak, and both the finish and the leather upholstery are in excellent, original condition.

Note: Pieces signed with the word *ROYCROFT* carved in the wood are considered more desirable by many Roycroft collectors and up to 15 percent more valuable.

Armchair: #106, five vertical slats across back, open arms, tacked leather seat, tapered feet, 40″ × 22″ × 20″, *$300–$350.*

Armchair: #28, two horizontal slats in back, open arms butting front posts, tacked leather seat, 38″ × 25″ × 22″, *$700–$800.*

Bench, "Ali Baba": #46, halved oak log, flat side finished, underside bark, with four splayed legs, cross-stretcher keyed through side stretchers, 20″ × 42″ × 11″, *$2250–$2750.*

Bench, piano: rectangular overhanging top over beveled legs and lower shelf tenoned through side stretchers, 36″ × 16″, *$1500–$1750.*

Bookcase: #84, single door over single drawer, copper hardware, straight toeboard, arched sides, adjustable shelves, 67″ × 32″ × 14″, *$3750–$4500.*

Bookcase: #82, double doors, each with 12 panes of glass, two drawers, copper pulls, overhanging top with arched splashboard and letter rack, two keyed tenons at bottom of each side, 62″ × 52″ × 14″, *$4500–$5000.*

Bookrack: #0116, two fixed ends joined by flat board, orb incised in side, 6″ × 15″, *$250–$300.*

Bookstand: "Little Journeys," rectangular overhanging top, two open shelves with exposed keyed tenons and shoe foot base, 26″ × 26″ × 14″, *$375–$475.*

Box, "Goody": mahogany lidded box with iron hardware, 9″ × 25″ × 12″, *$275–$325.*

Cellaret: #1, overhanging top over two half-drawers over two doors with strap hinges, copper hardware, two keyed tenons on each flared side, 32″ × 40″ × 18″, *$3000–$3500.*

Chair, child's: #37, four vertical slats across back, tacked leather seat, Mackmurdo feet, 29″ × 14″ × 13″, *$325–$375.*

Chair, side: #27, two horizontal slats in back, drop-in leather seat, 37″ × 17″ × 18″, *$225–$275.*

Chair, side: #30, single wide vertical slat in back, tacked leather seat, bulbous feet, stacked stretchers, 44″ × 17″ × 17″, *$350–$400.*

Chair, side: incised "GPI" (Grove Park Inn) on crest rail, single vertical slat in back, tacked leather seat, open half-arms, stacked stretchers, 41″ × 25″ × 18″, *$375–$425.*

Chest of drawers: #113, two half-drawers over four long, splashboard, paneled sides, copper hardware, 60″ × 42″ × 24″, *$2750–$3250.*

China cabinet/server: #8, overhanging top with plate rail, one long drawer over two leaded glass doors, copper hardware, tapered feet, paneled sides, 45″ × 42″ × 20″, *$2250–$2750.*

Desk, drop-front: #91, strap hinges on the front, oval metal pulls on long drawer, tapering legs with bulbous feet, fitted interior, 46″ × 36″ × 18″, *$2200–$2450.*

Dresser: #108, two half-drawers over two long drawers, all with copper hardware, attached mirror, 34″ × 43″ × 25″, *$1500–$2000.*

Magazine pedestal: #80, square overhanging top over flared sides, each with four keyed tenons, five fixed shelves, arched sides, 63″ × 18″ × 18″, *$4000–$5000.*

Morris chair: #45, large paddle arms over four vertical slats, adjustable bar, drop-in cushion, Mackmurdo feet, 41″ × 37″ × 40″, *$2250–$2500.*

Rocking chair: #39A, five vertical slats across back, no arms, drop-in seat, 35″ × 19″ × 18″, *$200–$225.*

Rocking chair: #39, single curved slat in back, open arms, tacked leather seat, 38″ × 21″ × 19″, *$250–$300.*

Rocking chair: #51, four slats under each arm, loose cushion back and seat, 39″ × 25″ × 22″, *$400–$500.*

Server: #10, overhanging top with plate rail, long drawer with copper hardware, open shelf below, tapered feet, 36″ × 44″ × 22″, *$1500–$1750*.

Server: #11, half-round table, overhanging top supported by three legs, 36″ × 48″ × 24″, *$1000–$1250*.

Table, dining: #112, overhanging top over wide apron, supported by four square legs ending on X cross-stretchers, 30″ × 54″, *$1250–$1500*.

Table, lamp: #102, circular top, no apron, supported by four tapering legs ending in bulbous feet, lower circular shelf rests atop straight cross-stretchers, 23″ × 23″, *$600–$700*.

Table, lamp: #73½, circular top and apron supported by four curving legs, 30″ × 30″, *$700–$800*.

Table, library: overhanging rectangular top supported by four legs joined by crossing stretcher arrangement, 30″ × 42″ × 30″, *$600–$700*.

Table, library: #18, overhanging rectangular top over one long drawer with copper hardware, five vertical slats on each side, lower shelf through-tenoned and keyed twice at each end, bulbous feet, 30″ × 48″ × 30″, *$1750–$2000*.

Table, library: #72, overhanging top, lower shelf with keyed tenons, 28″ × 30″ × 22″, *$850–$950*.

Table, library: #74, circular top with apron, four tapering legs with straight cross-stretchers, bulbous feet, incised orb in leg, 30″ × 36″, *$750–$850*.

Taboret: #50, overhanging top over four flared sides, each with circular cutout extending to floor, narrow stretchers, 21″ × 16″ × 16″, *$1400–$1650*.

THE SHOP OF THE CRAFTERS

Shopmark:
Paper label SHOP OF THE CRAFTERS/ AT CINCINNATI/
OSCAR ONKEN CO. SOLE OWNERS around drawing of
lantern

Principal Contributions:
Inlaid oak furniture

Founder:
Oscar Onken
Born: 1858   Died: 1948
Founded: 1904   Closed: 1920

Workshops and Salesrooms:
The Shop of the Crafters
Cincinnati, Ohio
1904–1920

"The Crafter movement seeks to obliterate overdecoration, pur-
poseless, meaningless designs and to install, instead, a purity of
style, which will express at once, beauty, durability and usefulness. Working in harmony with this idea Professor Paul Horti

has introduced a touch of inlay work of colored woods or metal, that enlivens the strong simple lines of Mission furniture."

—*Catalog introduction*
ca. 1906[1]

Although the Pan-American Exposition held in Buffalo, New York, in 1901 marked the first official introduction of American Arts and Crafts furniture through the exhibits of Gustav Stickley and Joseph McHugh, it was the 1904 Louisiana Purchase Exposition held in St. Louis that gave people from across the entire country the opportunity to inspect Arts and Crafts–style furniture, glassware, and metalware from firms and individuals such as Charles Rohlfs, Louis C. Tiffany, Arthur Stone, and the Rose Valley Shops, plus pottery designed by Artus Van Briggle, Grueby, Teco, Newcomb, and Rookwood. The St. Louis exposition drew national attention, including coverage in a young periodical, *The Craftsman*. Among the thousands of viewers of the various displays were two young architects, Frank Lloyd Wright and Charles Sumner Green—and a businessman from Cincinnati, Ohio, by the name of Oscar Onken.

In 1904 Oscar Onken was a successful retailer who had started a picture frame business more than twenty years earlier and expanded it into the manufacture of moldings and the sale of mirrors, etchings, and artwork. He had secured a prestigious downtown Cincinnati location to serve as his retail outlet, and a manufacturing plant he established on the outskirts supplied much of his merchandise. In 1903 he incorporated the Oscar Onken Company in preparation for a major expansion of his enterprise.

Onken's journey to the exposition in St. Louis was to have a dramatic impact on the next fifteen years of his life. As scholar Kenneth Trapp has observed, Onken was enamored of the "contemporary designs of furniture and interiors from Germany and the Austro-Hungarian Empire that were first introduced to a large American audience at the Louisiana Purchase

---

1. Stephen Gray, ed., *Shop of the Crafters Catalog* (ca. 1906). Introduction by Kenneth Trapp (New York: Turn of the Century Editions, 1983), p. 4.

Exposition."[2] Unlike most casual visitors, however, Onken was not content simply to return to Cincinnati with illusive visions. Before leaving St. Louis he introduced himself to the acclaimed Budapest designer Paul Horti (1865–1907), who was an exhibitor at the exposition and who had already received numerous awards and recognition of his avant-garde furniture designs. The two quickly reached an agreement by which Horti, who had formerly worked for Charles Limbert in Grand Rapids, Michigan, was to begin designing furniture for the Oscar Onken Company.

By the fall of that same year ads were appearing in the *Saturday Evening Post* for Oscar Onken's new venture: The Shop of the Crafters, "Makers of Arts and Crafts Furniture, Hall Clocks, Shaving Stands, Cellarettes, Smokers' Cabinets and Mission Chairs."[3] Subsequently, ads also began appearing in other popular magazines, such as *Scribners*, *Harpers*, and *Literary Digest*. By 1906 Onken was prepared to issue his first catalog, featuring an extensive line of Arts and Crafts furniture for every room in the home.

The Shop of the Crafters at Cincinnati, as it was often referred to, featured "Furniture of Austrian Design" with a distinctive and unique flair. Horti often incorporated inlaid "marquetry panels of colored imported Austrian woods,"[4] which Onken described as being "out of the usual and not to be duplicated."[5] Unlike many of the firms that entered the Arts and Crafts market after it had been popularized by pioneers like Gustav Stickley and Elbert Hubbard, the Shop of the Crafters

2. Stephen Gray, ed., *Shop of the Crafters Catalog* (ca. 1906). Introduction by Kenneth Trapp (New York: Turn of the Century Editions, 1983), p. 69.

3. Ibid., p. 3.

4. Ibid., p. 6.

5. Ibid., p. 68.

This trio of Shop of the Crafters furniture reveals the impact European furniture designers had on this Cincinnati firm. The marquetry panels in the sideboard doors (58″ × 54″ × 25″) and backs of the chairs (47″ × 27″) are as much a Crafter trademark as their applied paper label. *(Photo courtesy of Robert W. Skinner, Boston)*

was not content to duplicate Craftsman furniture designs. While their striking European flavor may have seemed a bit unorthodox for a severe American interpretation of the Arts and Crafts ideal, their designs were a refreshing change from the flood of Stickley imitators that were entering the market at the same time.

Onken brought to his new line of furniture two distinct skills: In addition to being an experienced businessman with sound promotional ideas, he also experimented with and developed a number of furniture finishes, including, as his catalog recommends, his "dull waxed finishes, such as Weathered, Fumed, Flemish, Austrian or Early English shades."[6] His

6. Stephen Gray, ed., *Shop of the Crafters Catalog* (ca. 1906). Introduction by Kenneth Trapp (New York: Turn of the Century Editions, 1983), p. 4.

advertisements and promotional material made reference to his work force, "comprised of a number of skilled Germans who represent the best handiwork of our day,"[7] reminiscent of Charles Limbert's proud references to his skilled staff of Dutch craftsmen and Albert Stickley's Russian coppersmiths.

In addition to stressing the quality handcraftsmanship of his German workers, Onken also appealed to the American desire to remain fashionable by European standards. As Trapp explains, Onken's advertisements implied that "by using Mission furniture purchased of course from the Shop of the Crafters, Americans could create rooms consonant with European high style to demonstrate that they were au courant in matters of international design."[8]

Trapp goes on: "The furniture that Onken manufactured, such as shaving stands, cellarettes, smokers cabinets, and pieces for the library, traditionally the refuge of men, appealed directly to a male clientele. Moreover, the use of oak and leather and large metal fittings, the emphasis on muted earthen-colored stains and the massive forms of some of the furniture give it a distinct masculine character that accorded with the cultural norms of the turn of the century."[9]

The furniture produced by the Shop of the Crafters exhibits a variety of Arts and Crafts features. Most often it was produced in oak, although some mahogany, "dull or polished," was offered. In addition to Horti's unique inlay, pieces often displayed keyed tenons (though on occasion they were false tenons), Limbert-style cutouts, Art Nouveau–inspired stained and leaded glass, and variations of Mackmurdo-style feet not unlike those already in use by the Roycrofters and Stickley Brothers.

7. Stephen Gray, ed., *Shop of the Crafters Catalog* (ca. 1906). Introduction by Kenneth Trapp (New York: Turn of the Century Editions, 1983), p. 68.

8. Ibid., p. 69.

9. Ibid.

Their advertisements described the hardware as being "old copper trimmings ... old brass drawer pulls" and leather tops "heavily studded with old brass nails."[10] The Shop of the Crafters furniture also often featured strap hinges and beveled square brass knobs. Interestingly enough, elements of the Victoria era also appear occasionally, including claw feet, fancy drawer pulls, and applied trim.

The Shop of the Crafters shopmark apparently remained consistent throughout the sixteen years the firm produced Arts and Crafts furniture. A gold paper label with black lettering reading "Shop of the Crafters" appears above a simple lantern, below which are found the words "at Cincinnati/ Oscar Onken Co. Sole Owners."

Although Arts and Crafts furniture production had ceased by 1920, the Oscar Onken Company remained in business until 1931. Onken passed away in 1948, at the age of ninety, and was remembered in his obituaries not as the founder of the Shop of the Crafters but as "a prominent businessman and philanthropist, active in some of Cincinnati's most distinguished clubs and organizations."[11] The Shop of the Crafters furniture remained in the shadows for several decades, even after the recent revival of interest in the Arts and Crafts movement. Had it not been for the 1983 facsimile of their 1906 catalog and the research done by scholars such as Kenneth Trapp, the Shop of the Crafters might have been denied the recognition that it so well deserves. Fortunately, it received additional attention when an inlaid china cabinet, attributed to Paul Horti, was selected for "The Art That Is Life" exhibition that premiered in Boston in 1987,[12] sustaining Oscar Onken's belief that "handmade things are slow in the making, and they are made by hand that style

10. Stephen Gray, ed., *Shop of the Crafters Catalog* (ca. 1906). Introduction by Kenneth Trapp (New York: Turn of the Century Editions, 1983), pp. 8, 16.

11. Ibid., p. 3.

12. Wendy Kaplan, *The Art That Is Life* (Boston: Museum of Fine Arts, 1987), pp. 21, 248.

and distinction may be preserved, and that they may look as well fifty years hence as when first made."[13]

Selected Prices

A comprehensive price guide for the Shop of the Crafters furniture will be dependent on the identification of additional examples. While interest in the Shop of the Crafters furniture is growing, it remains to be seen how the market will respond to the additional pieces that are expected to surface as the furniture from this firm receives additional exposure. Until that time collectors are advised to consider carefully both the condition and the attractiveness of the design of any Shop of the Crafters furniture.

Armchair: #321, solid back with four vertical cutouts, inlaid panel in center, open arms, flared legs, attached leather seat, *$600–$700.*

Bookcase: #360, single door with Art Nouveau–inspired leaded and stained glass, gallery top, copper hardware, molded base 60″ × 29″ × 12″, *$1250–$1500.*

Cellarette: #264, overhanging top with copper tray, single solid door with strap hinges, solid sides with lower cutouts, shoe feet, interior with revolving bottle rack, paper label, 35″ × 22″ × 16″, *$600–$700.*

Chair, side: #320, solid back with four vertical cutouts, inlaid panel in center, flared legs, attached leather seat, 43″ × 18″, *$200–$225;* set of four, *$900–$1000.*

China cabinet: #326, single wide door flanked by four narrow doors, lower two with vertical inlaid panels, overhanging top, molded block base, 63″ × 42″ × 16″, *$1250–$1500.*

Clock: Van Dyke model with six leaded-glass panels, exposed tenon construction, brass numerals and hands, 74″ × 20″ × 13″, *$500–$600.*

13. Stephen Gray, ed., *Shop of the Crafters Catalog* (ca. 1906). Introduction by Kenneth Trapp (New York: Turn of the Century Editions, 1983), p. 68.

Desk: #279, shaped crest over drop front and leaded glass side doors, surface support over single drawer with dowel pulls, lower shelf, 46″ × 42″ × 18″, *$350–$400.*

Floor lamp: #153, Art Nouveau–inspired stained-glass shade with four panels, supported by four arms, flared base with three open shelves and oval cutouts, paper label, 72″ × 24″ × 24″, *$1250–$1500.*

Mirror, hall: #222½, center mirror flanked by inlaid peacock feathers, crest rail with small cutouts, five hat hooks, 26″ × 40″, *$500–$600.*

Morris chair: #13, one wide slat under each arm, massive front legs, adjustable rod, two loose cushions, *$900–$1000.*

Morris chair: #333, flat arms supported by sides with multiple vertical cutouts, front legs inlaid, front apron arched, cushion seat and back, *prices yet to be determined.*

Rocking chair: #32, inlaid slat in back flanked by two plain slats, three slats under each arm, massive front posts tenoned through tops of arms, long corbels with false through tenons on each front post, loose cushion seat, *$350–$400.*

Settee: #34, back divided into two matching sections, each with middle inlaid slat flanked by four plain slats, three slats under each arm, massive front posts tenoned through tops of arms, long corbels with false through tenons on each front post, two loose cushions, *prices yet to be determined.*

Sideboard, inlaid: #323, arched mirror and gallery surface, long drawer over two inlaid cabinet doors centering three half-drawers and open shelf, molded base, 58″ × 54″ × 25″, *$750–$850.*

Table, library: #116, overhanging top supported by sides with large rectangular cutouts, lower shelf, 30″ × 48″ × 30″, *$350–$400.*

STICKLEY BROTHERS, INC.

Shopmark:
(Early) Oval paper label MADE BY STICKLEY BROS. CO./
GRAND RAPIDS, MICH.

(Later) Brass tag or decal QUAINT FURNITURE/
STICKLEY BROS. CO./ GRAND RAPIDS, MICH.;
branded QUAINT with stylized letters *S* and *B*

Principal Contributions:
General line of Arts and Crafts furniture, plus
metalware and lighting

Founders:
Albert Stickley
Born: 1862   Died: 1928

John George Stickley
Born: 1871   Died: 1921
Founded: 1891   Closed: ca. 1940

Workshops and Salesrooms:
The Stickley Brothers Company
Binghamton, New York
1884–1890

Stickley Brothers, Inc.
Grand Rapids, Michigan
1891–ca. 1940

"A chair ought to be well built and its structural qualities should be exemplified in two ways: first, the greatest possible amount of structural strength and dignity should be obtained with the smallest amount of wood; next, the wood must be handled expertly as wood, and not made to simulate properties of any other material."

—*Albert Stickley*
1909[1]

Had the five Stickley brothers—Gustav, Albert, Charles, Leopold, and John—been able to control their strong, independent spirits and to combine their individual talents—Gustav's eye for design, Leopold's management skills, Charles's production talents, Albert's marketing techniques, and John's sales ability—they could well have built a furniture empire that would have survived long after Arts and Crafts furniture fell out of favor. Instead, they eventually formed their own competing furniture companies that flourished while the Arts and Crafts movement

1. Albert Stickley, "The Merits of Arts and Crafts," *Furniture, A Magazine of Education for the Home* (April 1909), p. 30.

was in full bloom but that quickly withered as furniture styles changed after 1915.[2]

The Stickley brothers did not have an easy childhood. Their father left home when Gustav, the eldest, was not yet sixteen and John, the youngest, was but three, leaving their mother to raise and support eleven children. In 1874 she moved her family from their home in rural Wisconsin to Brandt, Pennsylvania, where Gustav, Albert, and Charles went to work in their uncle's small chair factory. In 1884 the three older brothers formed what was to be known as the Stickley Brothers Company, which sold and later manufactured popular reproduction period chairs. Their business grew rapidly, and by early 1888 it appears that all five brothers were working together in the Stickley Brothers firm. That same year, however, Gustav left to pursue other projects, coaxing Leopold to join him the following year; but Albert, Charles, and John kept the family business going in Binghamton, New York.

In 1891 another division occurred. Charles and Schuyler Brandt, their uncle and financial backer, took over the operation in Binghamton, which was soon to be renamed the Stickley and Brandt Chair Company, while Albert and John moved to Grand Rapids, Michigan, taking with them the name Stickley Brothers Company. The two brothers worked together in Grand Rapids until 1900, when John moved back to New York to establish yet another Stickley furniture factory in partnership with brother Leopold, who had previously been working as a foreman in Gustav's Eastwood, New York, factory, overseeing the production of a new line of Arts and Crafts furniture.

By 1901, then, the picture was nearly in focus: Gustav was designing and manufacturing Arts and Crafts furniture in his Eastwood shops; Charles was a partner and general manager of Stickley and Brandt in Binghamton; Leopold and John George were making plans to form the L. & J. G. Stickley Company in Fayetteville, New York; and Albert had maintained the name Stickley Brothers Company in Grand Rapids. Within five years,

2. The technical exception was Leopold Stickley, but his later line of Colonial reproductions marketed under the Cherry Valley trademark did not surpass the recognition or production of his earlier Arts and Crafts designs.

THE STICKLEY BROTHERS

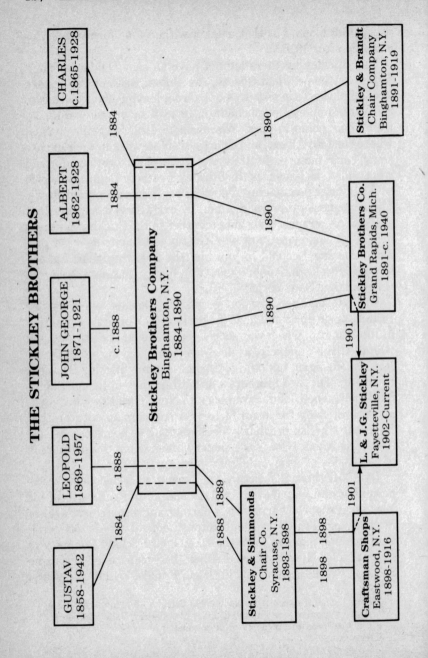

all four firms would be nationally recognized manufacturers of Arts and Crafts furniture—and rivals with one another in a highly competitive market.

While Gustav quickly became the most widely publicized of the five Stickley brothers, Albert worked very diligently in his older brother's long shadow. He was among the first American furniture manufacturers to reverse the centuries-old tradition of importing furniture from England. From 1897 until 1902 he shipped unfinished furniture from his Michigan base of operations to his London factory, where it was assembled and finished by seventy-five workers before being sold to the English public.

Marketing was not the only area in which Albert Stickley was not afraid to experiment. In the early years of the new century, before Harvey Ellis had an opportunity to introduce his inlaid designs to Gustav Stickley in 1903, Timothy A. Conti was executing exquisite inlay for Albert Stickley, often in forms directly influenced by both Japanese art and the innovative English and Scottish schools of design. As early as 1901 Albert was also producing high-quality furniture featuring circular, heart-shaped, and abstract cutouts, a clear reflection of his admiration for the work of the British designers C. R. Mackintosh and Charles Voysey.

Albert's adoption of the British term for the Arts and Crafts style of furniture—"Quaint"—as part of his trademark is another indication of the impact the British designers had on the Stickley Brothers firm. Just as Gustav believed the furniture of this period would someday be referred to as Craftsman furniture, D. Robertson Smith, a major designer for Albert Stickley, predicted in 1902 that "this new school of furniture and decoration . . . will most likely be called 'Quaint,' for that is what it has been called in the country to which we are indebted for it, namely, Scotland."[3]

It is apparent from the Stickley Brothers furniture that has surfaced in recent years that Albert was far more than just another furniture designer attempting to capitalize on the

3. Don Marek, *Arts and Crafts Furniture Design: The Grand Rapids Contribution* (Grand Rapids, MI: Grand Rapids Art Museum, 1987), p. 52.

popularity of Mission oak. He hired and utilized some of the best furniture designers of the day, including Smith, who remained with the firm from 1902 until 1915, and Arthur Teal, who had studied in Scotland before joining Albert in 1904. At the same time that his designers were creating costly inlaid, carved, and cut-out furniture, however, Albert Stickley's workers were also producing lines of less ornate, less expensive furniture, much of which was purchased for use in meeting halls, offices, and other businesses, "as well," according to his advertisements, "as for the club, the cafe [and] the hotel."[4]

In the introduction to his 1908 catalog, Albert Stickley declares that "Quaint Furniture in Arts and Crafts has made ideals possible which might otherwise have been impossible—has brought within the means of those with even the most modest of incomes the possibility of artistic homes."[5] Even so, at a time when a typical factory worker was being paid an average of $10 per week, a standard Stickley Brothers ladder-back side chair was selling for $8, and a five-legged, round oak dining room table for $38. Gustav Stickley, in his 1910 catalog, advertised a similiar chair for $6.50 and a table for $47. In contrast, Sears, Roebuck & Company was then selling pressed-back dining room chairs with leather seats for $3 and a five-legged dining room table for only $12.

Stickley Brothers furniture was produced primarily in oak, though a number of pieces were turned out in mahogany after 1907. "Quality is always sought," the 1908 catalog states, "even in the most trivial details. All drawer ends are solid black walnut. The joints are all the old fashioned tongue-and-groove kind."[6] Many pieces have a unique concave lower leg, apparently a modification of the Arthur Mackmurdo foot design, which the Roycrofters also often duplicated. Despite Albert's romantic description of his copper workers—whose "experience is augmented by the teachings of their fathers and their fathers'

4. *Quaint Furniture Catalog* (New York: Turn of the Century Editions, 1981), p. 5.

5. Ibid., p. 4.

6. Ibid., p. 5.

fathers, all copper workers for generations"[7]—rarely will Stickley Brothers hardware equal the weight and quality of that found on Craftsman furniture. Comparisons with hardware advertised at the same time by the Grand Rapids Brass Company leads to the conclusion that, like several other Arts and Crafts firms, Stickley Brothers purchased hardware in large quantities from speciality metal shops.[8]

Like his brothers, Albert Stickley adopted the practice of affixing a shopmark to much of his furniture. Of the brand, paper label, gold decal, and metal tag shopmarks Stickley Brothers used, only the early oval paper label does not carry the trade name "Quaint." The decal, paper label, and metal tag make bold and clear reference to the factory location in Grand Rapids, proof that Albert Stickley did not intend customers to confuse his shopmark or his furniture with that of any of his brothers in New York.

What has happened on more than one occasion, however, is that a damaged Stickley Brothers paper label has mysteriously lost those portions containing the words "Brothers" and "Grand Rapids, Mich." The result can be a paper label simply reading "Stickley"—and price tag that would be more appropriate on a piece of Gustav Stickley furniture. Fortunately, if a collector becomes familiar with the shopmarks of both Gustav and Albert Stickley, such incidents will not prove confusing. Many times the outline of the oval label or unique brass tag will still be evident in the wood even though the shopmark itself may be missing.

While Albert Stickley was a successful Mission oak manufacturer, the majority of the Stickley Brothers' most pleasing designs are those that appear to be copies or slight modifications of his older brother's Craftsman furniture. After 1904 Stickley Brothers furniture designs failed to progress with any consistency, and as the 1908 catalog demonstrates, when Albert's craftsmen ventured off into their own designs, such as their

7. *Quaint Furniture Catalog* (New York: Turn of the Century Editions, 1981), p. 5.
8. Don Marek, *Arts and Crafts Furniture Design: The Grand Rapids Contribution* (Grand Rapids, MI: Grand Rapids Art Museum, 1987), p. 63.

This Stickley Brothers sideboard (54″ × 48″ × 22″) illustrates the problems their designers often had in achieving the delicate balance between proportion and practicality. Although well constructed, the light hardware, oversize mirror, and unbalanced drawer and door arrangement detract from the strength and harmony of the piece. *(Photo courtesy of D. J. Puffert, Sausalito)*

buffets and china cupboards, Quaint furniture often suffered from either a degree of misproportion, a disturbing lack of harmony, or mediocre workmanship.

The large volume of utilitarian furniture bearing the Stickley Brothers shopmark has adversely affected the firm's current reputation and status as designers and manufacturers of quality Arts and Crafts furniture. The fact that Albert was able to survive the swing away from Mission oak furniture after 1915 is a tribute to his business ability, but the ready availability of the transitional furniture (characterized by spiral-turned legs) his firm produced between 1918 and his death in 1928 has tarnished his reputation as an Arts and Crafts manufacturer.

Astute collectors, however, have recognized that much of the early Stickley Brothers furniture is destined to increase in both demand and value. Early inlaid and cut-out designs have already begun selling above their presale estimates at major Arts and Crafts auctions. As additional research is conducted, such as that presented in 1987 by Don Marek in his book *Arts and Crafts Furniture Designs: The Grand Rapids Contribution 1895–1915*, much of the early, high-quality furniture produced by Albert Stickley will undoubtedly step out of the shadow cast by his older brother.

Selected Prices

Model numbers, when applicable, correspond with those in the catalog reprint *Quaint Furniture* (New York: Turn of the Century Editions, 1981).

Armchair: #873, three vertical slats in back, open arms, drop-in seat, 37″ × 19″ × 19″, *$100–$125*.

Armchair: #389½, three slats under each arm, loose cushion back and seat, arms notched around front posts, 38″ × 19″ × 21″, *$175–$200*.

Bookcase: double doors with one large pane each, overhanging top with flared supports, hammered copper pulls, canted feet, 58″ × 42″ × 12″, *$750–$850*.

Bookcase: #4690, double doors, each with two small panes above one large, recessed top, exposed tenons on front posts, straight toeboard, metal pulls, 56″ × 36″ × 13″, *$700–$800*.

Bookcase, revolving: four corner posts extending through top, four-sided center section pivoting on cross-stretchers, 32″ × 25″ × 25″, *$650–$750*.

Chair, side: #412½, three vertical slats in back, wraparound leather seat, concave feet, 37″ × 19″ × 16″, *$75–$85*; set of four, *$375–$425*.

China cabinet: #8745, arched crest rail with plate rack, overhanging top, double doors with single large pane each, adjustable shelves, metal hardware, 61″ × 32″ × 14″, *$750–$850*.

Clock, tall: four corner posts joined by stretchers, sides and back consisting of thin slats, open face with brass numerals, brass pendulum and weights, 79″ × 20″ × 15″, *$400–$500.*

Costumer: double posts supported by four flared feet, copper hooks on posts and joining stretchers, 70″ × 16″ × 20″, *$425–$475.*

Desk: #6500, drop front with decorative strap hinges, gallery top, two short drawers over two long, lower open shelf flanked by two pairs of cutouts in sides, exposed tenons in sides, metal pulls, 48″ × 36″ × 14″, *$650–$750.*

Footstool: #674-5265, upholstered insert, narrow stretchers, rectangular framework, 12″ × 18″ × 12″, *$150–$175.*

Footstool: leather-covered, with seven spindles on each narrow end, 12″ × 20″ × 16″, *$1000–$1250.*

Magazine stand: three spindles on either side with four open shelves, each with backsplash, 39″ × 26″ × 13″, *$475–$550.*

Morris chair: #343, three vertical slats under each arm, supported by four corbels, front posts tenoned through tops of arms, two loose cushions, adjustable back, 38″ × 21″ × 22″, *$650–$750.*

Morris chair: #780½, open arms, front posts tenoned through tops of arms, no corbels, stretcher around seat, drop-in spring cushion seat, adjustable back, 36″ × 21″ × 20″, *$300–$350.*

Rocking chair: #790, three short vertical slats in back over lower back upholstered section, drop-in seat, open arms, front posts tenoned through tops of arms, 36″ × 19″ × 20″, *$175–$200.*

Rocking chair: #910, four short vertical slats in back over two horizontal slats, open arms, no corbels, drop-in spring seat, 35″ × 20″ × 20″, *$100–$125.*

Rocking chair: four vertical slats across back, three beneath each arm, front posts tenoned through arms, floor-length corbels, drop-in spring seat, 37″ × 28″ × 30″, *$250–$300.*

Settle: #905-3865, even-arm, with narrow vertical slats cut out with repeating arches, slightly canted sides, cushion seat on slats, 36″ × 84″ × 29″, *$1250–$1500.*

Sideboard: #8610, open plate rail with five short slats on overhanging top, two upper drawers over open shelf over two lower drawers, metal hardware, 46″ × 54″ × 21″, *$450–$500.*

Sideboard: overhanging top supporting paneled plate rail, two split drawers over two half-drawers centered by two cabinet doors, arched corbels on legs, 46″ × 60″ × 22″, *$600–$700.*

Trumpet stretchers, pegged joints, and exposed tenons can be found on a Stickley Brothers leather-top table (30″ × 36″), just as they can on a Gustave Stickley lamp table; but whereas Gustav used a more expensive, circular apron, this Stickley Brothers table employs a simple, straight one. *(Photo courtesy of D. J. Puffert, Sausalito)*

Stand, drink: #2615, circular overhanging copper top over four flared legs, arched aprons, 28″ × 18″, *$700–$800.*

Table, dining: #2640, overhanging top supported by five square legs, wide apron, three leaves, 30″ × 54″, *$700–$900.*

Table, lamp: #2504, circular overhanging top supported by four legs, lower square shelf resting on cross-stretchers, exposed tenons, 30″ × 26″ diameter, *$300–$350.*

Table, lamp: circular top notched around four legs, lower square shelf, concave feet, 30″ × 20″ diameter, *$225–$250.*

Table, library: #2606, overhanging top over single long drawer with metal hardware, two vertical slats at either end, lower shelf, 30″ × 24″ × 36″, *$250–$300.*

Taboret: #314½, circular overhanging top supported by three flared legs joined by triangular lower shelf, exposed tenons, 18″ × 15″ diameter, *$175–$200.*

CHARLES STICKLEY and STICKLEY AND BRANDT

Shopmark:
(Early) Rectangular decal with STICKLEY & BRANDT CHAIR COMPANY/ signature, CHARLES STICKLEY/ GENL.MGR
(Later) Impressed signature CHARLES STICKLEY

Principal Contributions:
Chairs, rockers, and dining room furniture

Founders:
Charles Stickley

Born: ca. 1865   Died: ca. 1928

Schuyler C. Brandt

Born: unknown   Died: ca. 1913

Founded: 1891   Closed: 1919

Workshops and Salesrooms:
The Stickley Brothers
Binghamton, New York
1884–1891

Stickley and Brandt Chair Company, Inc.
Binghamton, New York
1891–1919

"You can visit the prominent Furniture stores in the large cities, and you will hear on every hand that "Stickley's Furniture" has a reputation for quality. Good furniture is a permanent investment and one of the requisites of comfortable living—not a luxury, but a necessity."

—*Stickley-Brandt Furniture Company catalog*
1908[1]

Little is known about Charles Stickley, the forgotten brother of the Stickley furniture manufacturing family. His career has been pieced together primarily through fragmented references found among the records of his more publicized brothers, such as in a 1906 *Furniture Journal* magazine article, which reported that

1. *Stickley-Brandt Furniture Company* catalog #A-11 (dated 1908).

around 1874 "three of the boys were old enough to work and the chair factory [of their uncle, Schuyler C. Brandt] needed hands. It was a far cry from Stillwater [Minnesota] to Binghamton, but the trip was made, and Gustav, Charles and Albert Stickley were put to work in the factory. . . . In the course of events Gustav became the general foreman of the factory; Charles became skilled in the weaving of rush fibre seats, then much used in chair making, while Albert showed skill in decorating old Boston rockers, which were among the products of the factory."[2]

In 1884 the three older Stickley brothers, with the financial backing of their benevolent uncle, Schuyler Brandt, established a new furniture business, selling a variety of styles of chairs to both the wholesale and the retail trade from a storefront in Binghamton, New York. Two years later, again with the help of Schuyler Brandt, the Stickley Brothers Company expanded, adding the machinery necessary to produce their own line of simple Colonial chairs. When the elder Gustav left in 1888 to pursue other interests, Charles and Albert remained in Binghamton and continued to run the Stickley Brothers Company.

In 1890, when Albert and John George Stickley decided to move to Grand Rapids, Michigan, to establish a new Stickley Brothers Company, Charles chose to remain in Binghamton, where, in December of 1891, the Stickley and Brandt Chair Company was incorporated. Charles, though only twenty-six, was named the new general manager. His uncle, Schuyler Brandt, was listed as president in the firm's incorporation papers, but judging from the fact that business directories during the time the Stickley and Brandt Chair Company was in business cite Brandt's home address as Oak Park, Illinois, it would appear that Charles Stickley was solely responsible for the daily operation of the company.

Despite the defection and eventual competition of the other brothers, Stickley and Brandt continued to grow. In 1900,

---

2. David Cathers, *Furniture of the American Arts and Crafts Movement* (New York: New American Library, 1981), pp. 258–260.

according to Binghamton public records, they purchased a larger and better-equipped facility and soon had "one of the best factories in the city with a large force of men."[3] In 1905 Charles was listed as the factory superintendent and manager. It appears that at that time the Stickley and Brandt Chair Company was still selling period reproduction furniture, for the record goes on to state that they were "turning out an excellent line of chairs and fancy furniture which is sold in large quantities in all parts of the country."[4]

If they were not manufacturing Mission oak–style furniture in 1905, they were soon after. It is difficult to interpret what was meant by "large quantities" of furniture, but when the number of surviving examples of signed Stickley and Brandt furniture is compared with that of Gustav, L. & J. G., or Albert Stickley, it would appear that Stickley and Brandt produced a limited line of Mission oak furniture. As both their 1904 and 1908 catalogs reveal,[5] the Stickley and Brandt Chair Company was also a large mail-order distributor, with over seventy-two different types of chairs (most manufactured by other firms) to choose from: fancy golden oak, Queen Anne, Art Nouveau, even wicker, but no Mission oak. In addition, Stickley and Brandt offered fancy parlor and bedroom suites and served as sales representatives for both Macy sectional bookcases and the Hoosier Kitchen Cabinet Company.

Like his brothers, Charles Stickley instructed his workers to affix a shopmark to the Mission oak furniture they produced. At least two forms have surfaced: a yellow rectangular decal trimmed in red and bearing the words "Stickley & Brandt Chair Company" above the signature of Charles Stickley and his title "GENL.MGR." The Stickley and Brandt decals have been found on Mission oak arm chairs and rocking chairs with heavy structural features: wide slats, exposed wide tenons, double-pegged joints, wide arms, and massive ($2'' \times 4''$) front legs. The decal

3. Broome County Public Library (Binghamton, NY).
4. Ibid.
5. Henry Francis Du Pont Winterthur Museum (Wilmington, DE).

While the arms appear to have been placed too high in proportion to the height of the back, this stout Stickley & Brandt rocker (34″ × 29″ × 26″) is actually quite comfortable. The front posts are solid quarter-sawn two-by-fours with authentic exposed tenons. *(Private collection)*

has most often been found on the rear seat apron of these particular chairs.

In what would appear by design to be later, lighter chairs, in which there were no pegs or exposed tenons and no unusually massive boards, the decal was replaced by an incised script signature of Charles Stickley. In nearly every instance the signature was stamped into the center of the rear apron of the chair. The exact date at which the Stickley and Brandt Chair Company decal was replaced by the Charles Stickley signature is unknown, but it may have been around 1913, shortly after Schuyler Brandt's death.

Although he obviously changed the shopmark at some time during the reign of Arts and Crafts furniture, Charles Stickley either could not or chose not to change the name of the original corporation, for Binghamton court records indicate that the firm of Stickley and Brandt Chair Company, Inc., declared bankruptcy in 1919—nearly four years after Gustav Stickley's Craftsman empire had crumbled.

It is interesting to speculate why, in 1918, when Leopold, John George, Albert, and a reluctant Gustav formed the Stickley Associated Cabinetmakers, Inc., Charles either declined their invitation or was not asked to join the new firm. In any event, by 1928 John George, Albert, and Charles had all passed away, Gustav was living with his daughter in quiet retirement, and only Leopold remained active in the furniture business, overseeing the production of Colonial reproductions until his death in 1957.

In his 1981 work, *Furniture of the American Arts and Crafts Movement*, David Cathers states that "Charles Stickley in Binghamton, New York produced a mission line called 'Moderncraft' with many direct copies of Gustav's work. Albert Stickley in Grand Rapids also made mission furniture under the brand name 'Quaint.' Both Moderncraft and Quaint are characterized by shabby workmanship and inept design."[6] As additional examples of both the work of Charles Stickley and that of Albert Stickley have surfaced, however, it has become evident that Cathers's blanket dismissal is no longer valid.[7]

It cannot be denied that Charles Stickley, along with numerous other manufacturers, openly duplicated many popular Craftsman designs, but not all of the workmanship exhibited on his furniture deserves to be characterized as "shabby." While verifiable examples of the work of Stickley and Brandt are relatively scarce compared to works by any of the other Stickleys, examples of their early chairs, rockers, and settles reveal the use of quarter-sawn oak, pegged joints, massive front legs, leather upholstery, and exposed tenons. Although in these examples their designs may suffer in comparison with those of Gustav Stickley's, no apology need be made for their workmanship.

6. David Cathers, *Furniture of the American Arts and Crafts Movement* (New York: New American Library, 1981), p. 16.

7. See Don Marek, *Arts and Crafts Furniture Design: The Grand Rapids Contribution, 1895–1915* (Grand Rapids, MI: Grand Rapids Art Museum, 1987).

In other examples, one particular china cupboard closely resembling Gustav Stickley's model No. 803 exhibits materials and workmanship equal to that displayed in the Craftsman Shops' original version. In another example, a set of four ladder-back side chairs stamped with Charles Stickley's signature and clearly modeled after a standard Craftsman design (No. 370) featured quarter-sawn oak, authentic leather upholstery, a durable original finish, and sturdy construction—despite the fact that none of the joints were pegged, a detail in Gustav Stickley furniture at least that is not considered detrimental to the value.

Although Charles Stickley occasionally produced quality Mission oak furniture, a large part of his work suffered from a lack of consistency. Too often, it seems, when the workmanship excelled, the design faltered; when the design excelled, the workmanship faltered. For that reason, each piece of Charles Stickley or Stickley and Brandt furniture must be closely examined and evaluated on the basis of the design, the materials, and the workmanship. When all three are in harmony, the result may well be a fine example of Arts and Crafts furniture.

Selected Prices

Although the Stickley and Brandt Chair Company remained in business longer than Gustav Stickley did, fewer examples of their Mission oak furniture have surfaced than of any of the other Stickley brothers. Arts and Crafts furniture production was not their primary concern but represented only a small portion of their large wholesale chair distribution. As was stated earlier, Stickley and Brandt and Charles Stickley Mission oak furniture varies considerably in the quality of materials, design, and workmanship; thus, the collector should use only the few representative prices included in this study as a basis from which to begin a careful appraisal.

Armchair: three wide vertical slats across the back, open arms, massive front posts with exposed tenons from the seat apron, drop-in spring seat, 34″ × 29″ × 22″, *$225–$250*.

Armchair: four vertical slats in back, open arms, plank seat, impressed signature on rear seat apron, 36″ × 26″ × 21″, *$125–$150*.

Bookcase: double door, each with eight panes formed by gridwork of mullions over large sheets of glass, gallery top, straight toeboard, 56″ × 48″ × 12″, *$700–$800*.

Chair, side: three horizontal slats across the back, wide stretchers, wraparound leather seat, 36″ × 17″ × 16″, *$85–$95;* set of four, *$400–450*.

China cabinet: (similar to Craftsman #803) overhanging top, single door with large pane of glass, arched toeboard, Gustav Stickley hardware, 60″ × 36″ × 15″, *$1750–$2000*.

Desk, drop-front: slant front opening to reveal fitted interior, narrow splashboard across top, two short drawers over one long, open base, 39″ × 30″ × 14″, *$300–$350*.

Rocking chair: three vertical slats across the back, open arms, massive front posts with exposed tenons from the seat apron, drop-in spring seat, 34″ × 29″ × 26″, *$250–$300*.

Sideboard: overhanging top supporting tall, paneled plate rail, three drawers centered by two cabinet doors over long lower drawer, Gustav Stickley hardware, 53″ × 56″ × 22″, *$1100–$1350*.

GUSTAV STICKLEY and the CRAFTSMAN WORKSHOPS

A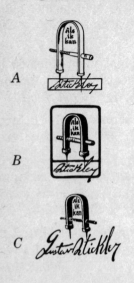

B

C

 D

Shopmarks:

(1902–1903) Red decal: joiner's compass around words *ALS IK
KAN* with *STICKLEY* in script in a rectangle below it
(1903–1904) Same as before but with entire decal
enclosed in a rectangle (see Shopmark *A, B* above)

(1904–1912) Red decal: joiner's compass around words *ALS IK
KAN* with *GUSTAV STICKLEY* in script below it
(no rectangle) (see Shopmark *C* above)

(1912–1916) Branded mark: joiner's compass around words *ALS
IK KAN* with *STICKLEY* in script below it (no rectangle)

(1905–1907) Large paper label: joiner's compass, *GUSTAV
STICKLEY* in script, and *EASTWOOD, N.Y.*

(1907–1912) Large paper label: joiner's compass, *GUSTAV
STICKLEY* in script, large word *CRAFTSMAN*, and address
of New York City salesrooms

(1912–1916) Large paper label: joiner's compass, *STICKLEY* in
script, large word *CRAFTSMAN*, but no reference to New
York City salesrooms (see Shopmark *D*)

Principal Contributions:
Oak furniture, metalware, lighting fixtures

Founder:
Gustav Stickley

Born: 1858   Died: 1942

Founded: 1898   Closed: 1916

Workshops and Salesrooms:
The Stickley Brothers
Binghamton, New York
1884–1888

Stickley & Simmonds
Syracuse, New York
1893–1898

The United Crafts   Craftsman Workshops
Eastwood, New York   Eastwood, New York
1898–1904   New York
                         1905–1916

"In the beginning there was no thought of creating a new style,
only a recognition of the fact that we should have in our homes
something better suited to our needs and more expressive of our
character as a people than imitations of the traditional styles,
and a conviction that the best way to get something better was
to go directly back to plain principles of construction and apply
them to the making of simple, strong, comfortable furniture."

—Gustav Stickley
1909[1]

Unlike the vast majority of American furniture manufacturers
working in the popular Mission oak style, Gustav Stickley was
a vocal proponent of the tenets of the Arts and Crafts movement. Regardless of whether or not it began as a conscious de-

1. Gustav Stickley, *Craftsman Homes* (New York: Dover Publications,
1979), p. 158.

cision, from 1900 until his bankruptcy in 1915, "he designed a new kind of American furniture, promulgated the Arts and Crafts philosophy to an educated and influential segment of the public and created a domestic architecture in which both his furniture and his philosophy were at home."[2]

Gustav Stickley was a stubborn and steadfast man with a creative and fiercely independent spirit. He demonstrated from the beginning of his career that he was unafraid to walk away from financial security in search of his beliefs and a form in which he could express them. Once discovered, he held to them doggedly, even in the face of financial ruin; yet he was also able to recognize that the early Arts and Crafts movement founders, Englishmen John Ruskin and William Morris, "have striven for a definite and intentional expression of art that was largely for art's sake and had little to do with satisfying the plain needs of the people."[3]

Though initially trained by his father in Wisconsin to be a stonemason, Stickley began his career as a furniture maker at the age of sixteen in his uncle's modest chair factory in Brandt, Pennsylvania. Lured by the prospect of self-employment, Gustav encouraged two of his brothers, Albert and Charles, to start with him in 1884 the Stickley Brothers Company in nearby Binghamton, New York. Four years later, about the time that their success as manufacturers and retailers of period reproduction furniture would have been assured, Gustav broke away to experiment in a variety of projects and careers but returned to period furniture production in 1893 in yet another partnership.

Five years later that partnership also dissolved, and after a year's sojourn in England and Europe, Gustav Stickley returned to establish what would eventually be known as the Craftsman Workshops in Eastwood, New York. His travels abroad had taken him into the homes and studios of many of the leading designers of the Arts and Crafts movement, and he returned to the United States determined to establish his personal interpretation of the medieval guild system. His idealized

2. Mary Ann Smith, *Gustav Stickley: The Craftsman* (Syracuse, NY: Syracuse University Press, 1983), p. xvi.
3. Gustav Stickley, *Craftsman Homes* (New York: Dover Publications, 1979), p. 154.

Characteristic of many of his early designs, this Stickley book-case (56″ × 45″ × 11″) features keyed tenons, mitered mullions, filed (not hammered) hardware, and a chamfered-board back. By 1904 each of these had been replaced by less expensive tech-niques. *(Photo courtesy of D. J. Puffert, Sausalito)*

vision of United Crafts eventually evolved into the Craftsman Workshops, a more conventional factory system, but Gustav nevertheless strove to design and produce "furniture which would be simple, durable, comfortable and fitted for the place it was to occupy and the work it had to do."[4]

Gustav Stickley's first public exhibition of his Arts and Crafts furniture took place in 1900 at the semiannual Grand Rapids furniture show and led to a brief arrangement in which he pro-vided, without public recognition, furniture for the Tobey Fur-niture Company, a Chicago furniture manufacturer and retailer. Examples of this early Stickley furniture can only be identified either by comparison with that pictured in the Tobey ads[5] or by a Tobey paper label, since Gustav had not yet begun affixing his own shopmark to his work. (See Tobey Furniture Company.)

The line of furniture that he soon thereafter began selling under his own shopmark displayed heavy structural features, such as keyed tenons and chamfered boards, as well as pegged joints, forged or hammered hardware, wide chair stretchers,

4. *Stickley Craftsman Furniture Catalogs* (New York: Dover Publica-tions, 1979). p. 3.
5. David Cathers, *Furniture of the American Arts and Crafts Move-ment* (New York: New American Library, 1981), p. 37.

and flaked quarter-sawn oak. In 1903, however, Stickley hired the itinerant architect Harvey Ellis, whose subsequent furniture designs "brought a new sense of lightness and color to the Craftsman Workshops."[6] Although Ellis died tragically nine months later, his influence can be traced through Stickley designs for the next twelve years. (See Harvey Ellis.)

As a result of his experience with Ellis, an ever-changing public taste, and his own design evolution, Stickley's later furniture had less emphasis on structural details. Exposed tenons diminished in size and number; keyed tenons were almost eliminated; legs and chair stretchers were reduced in size; and plywood panels replaced chamfered board backs. For a few years, beginning in 1905, spindles replaced slats in a number of chairs and settles, though hand-hammered hardware, pegged joints, leather upholstery, and quarter-sawn oak remained standard on nearly all Craftsman furniture.

In the years just prior to his bankruptcy in 1915, many of Stickley's designs suffered from too much reduction in structural expression: curved aprons were replaced by stagnant straight boards, strap hinges were dropped altogether, chair stretchers shrank, and keyed and even exposed tenons became scarce. Although it has been argued that his furniture thus became pure in form, much of it pales in comparison with his earlier "simple, strong and comfortable furniture."[7]

Perhaps the most famous of all Arts and Crafts shopmarks, the Gustav Stickley joiner's compass appeared in one form or another on nearly all of his furniture produced between 1902 and 1916. Within each compass appear the Flemish words "Als ik kan," loosely translated "As best I can." Prior to 1904, only his last name appeared on the red decal; but when youngest brothers, Leopold and John George, continued to expand their Arts and Crafts line of furniture only a few miles away, Gustav added his first name to the Craftsman shopmark, where it remained until 1912, the same year L. & J. G. Stickley suddenly

6. David Cathers, *Furniture of the American Arts and Crafts Movement* (New York: New American Library, 1981), p. 47.

7. *Stickley Craftsman Furniture Catalogs* (New York: Dover Publications, 1979), p. 3.

This Harvey Ellis–influenced bookcase (No. 703, 57″ × 48″ × 14″) can be identified by the deeply arched toeboard, overhanging top, paneled back, minimum pegging, and reduced emphasis on hammered hardware and exposed tenons. When compared with Stickley's earlier bookcases, the lighter, more sophisticated look becomes obvious. *(Photo courtesy of David Rago, Trenton)*

changed their red shopmark to one totally different from that of Gustav's (see L. & J. G. Stickley). Although Gustav must have felt that their new shopmark would erase any confusion on the part of the public, when he dropped his first name from his shopmark, he also switched from using decals to a permanent brand.

Stickley's shopmark appears repeatedly in certain locations on his furniture. Side chairs, footstools, and settles often reveal one on either the inside or the outside of the rear stretcher. Rocking chairs, armchairs, and adjustable Morris chairs may have a decal underneath either arm or on a rear stretcher. Library tables and desks may have either a red decal inside the drawer or a brand on the outside of the drawer. Case pieces, such as bookcases and chin cupboards, will often have a red decal centered near the top of the back and may be accompanied by a large rectangular paper label. Labels also appear on the bottoms of upholstered seats and tables after 1904, but many of them, like many of the red decals, were later destroyed by upholsterers and refinishers.

Undoubtedly, the most highly valued Gustav Stickley furniture is that from the experimental line of inlaid furniture designed by Harvey Ellis between June and December 1903. The inlay proved to be too expensive to put into production and may have come too close to compromising Gustav's desire "to do away with all needless ornamentation."[8] In 1905 the Craftsman Workshops began producing a line of patented spindle furniture that Stickley had designed. The new line included Morris chairs, footstools, a library table with spindles at either end, a settle, and several varieties of chairs, most of which were produced until 1909, but fine examples are considered relatively scarce. Auction prices for Stickley slant-arm Morris chairs with spindles, for instance, took a major jump in 1987 from a previous year's average of $5,000 to $7,000 each to a record-breaking $17,000 for one outstanding example at David Rago's May 31 Arts and Crafts auction in New York City.[9]

Other highly desirable characteristics sought in Craftsman furniture include arched aprons, stretchers, and toeboards; wide, overhanging tops; strap hinges across buffet doors; settles and chairs with sides the same height as the back; bookcases and china cupboards with gently bowed sides; and desks and tables with original leather tops. Library tables, rocking chairs, and dining chairs are the most commonly found examples of Craftsman furniture; bedroom furniture—especially tall chests of drawers and full-size beds—are among the most difficult to locate.

One of the lingering unanswered questions regarding Craftsman furniture involves plant production. Whereas Morris and Ruskin advocated handcraftsmanship, their American counterparts—most notably Gustav Stickley, Frank Lloyd Wright, and Elbert Hubbard—recognized that woodworking machines not only could eliminate much of the drudgery associated with

8. Gustav Stickley, *Craftsman Homes* (New York: Dover Publications, 1979), p. 158.
9. David Rago, *Arts and Crafts Auction Catalog* (May 31, 1987, Lot 205), p. 24.

The combination of rare spindles, a highly desirable slant-arm Morris chair form (42″ × 33″ × 37″) in its original finish, and a competitive New York auction is bound to set new records. Repaired and refinished examples of this same form, however, have not fared nearly as well. *(Photo courtesy of David Rago, Trenton)*

cabinetmaking but could also reduce the time, materials, and cost involved in furniture production, thus making their furniture available to people of moderate incomes. Publicly, Stickley and Hubbard emphasized the handcraftsmanship that went into each piece of furniture they produced, preferring not to draw attention to the number of electric planers, tenoners, shapers, and mortisers in their factories.[10] In contrast, L. & J. G. Stickley claimed that their furniture was "built in a scientific manner, [and] does not attempt to follow the traditions of a bygone day."[11]

Regardless of the impression left by either his magazine articles or his catalog introductions, the fact remains that for the

10. Wendy Kaplan, ed., *The Art That Is Life: The Arts and Crafts Movement in America, 1875–1920* (Boston: Museum of Fine Arts, 1987), p. 230.

11. *Stickley Craftsman Furniture Catalogs* (New York: Dover Publications, 1979), p. 131.

Original leather tops are not difficult to recognize, and authentic Craftsman leather tops are most often encircled by a tacked leather band. This hexagonal table (30″ × 48″ × 48″) also features exposed tenons, "button" pegs, and arched cross-stretchers. *(Photo courtesy of D. J. Puffert, Sausalito)*

largest part of sixteen years Gustav Stickley employed approximately two hundred craftsmen working six days each week in a well-equipped furniture factory.[12] Calculating precisely how many Morris chairs, simple footstools, or double-door bookcases would have been made in that span requires additional information yet unavailable; but when other factors are taken into consideration—such as Stickley's continued factory expansion; the gradual elimination of time-consuming inlay, spindles, keyed tenons, chamfered backs, and arched toeboards; the impressive number of major retail stores across the country that sold Craftsman furniture; the number of different designs offered each year in his catalogs; and the fact that at a time when the average factory worker made less than $500 per year, Gustav Stickley drew more than that amount each month[13]—it becomes

12. Wendy Kaplan, ed., *The Art That Is Life: The Arts and Crafts Movement in America, 1875–1920* (Boston: Museum of Fine Arts, 1987), p. 235.

13. Ibid., p. 236.

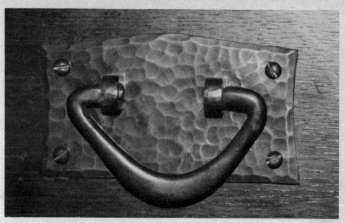

Gustav Stickley drawer pulls in copper, brass, or iron can generally be identified by their hammered surface and unique shape. No other firm is known to have gone to the expense of duplicating this form.

evident that the Craftsman Workshops were both efficient and prolific. With a few notable exceptions, today's perceived scarcity may still be due to the fact that much of Stickley's furniture remains unrecognized, continuing to serve the practical roles for which it was intended in homes where parents or grandparents purchased it either new or used little more than seventy years ago. Too substantial to throw out, too well made to wear out, it may have been relegated to the basement, back porch, or storage room and in some cases painted or refinished. But chances are the majority of what was originally produced, whatever that number, is still in existence.

And as Gustav Stickley predicted in 1910, "in fifty or a hundred years [it] will be worth many times its first cost, for the time is coming when good oak furniture will be as valuable on account of its permanent worth and also of its scarcity."[14]

14. *Stickley Craftsman Furniture Catalogs* (New York: Dover Publications, 1979), p. 9.

Selected Prices

Model numbers correspond with those appearing in the *Stickley Furniture Catalogs* (New York: Dover Publications, 1979) and the *Collected Works of Gustav Stickley* (New York: Turn of the Century Editions, 1981). Unless otherwise indicated, all examples are made from oak, and both the finish and the leather upholstery are in excellent original condition.

Armchair: #310½, three horizontal slats in back, wide front stretcher, wraparound leather seat, open arms, 36″ × 20″ × 19″, *$225–$250.*

Armchair: #312½, five wide vertical slats across back under V-back headrail, wraparound leather seat, open arms, front posts tenoned through tops of arms, 37″ × 20″ × 19″, *$350–$400.*

Armchair: #318, five wide vertical slats across back, open arms, front posts tenoned through tops of arms, drop-in spring seat, 38″ × 21″ × 19″, *$300–$350.*

Armchair: #324, five vertical slats under each arm, front posts tenoned through arms, fixed back with four horizontal slats and loose cushion, drop-in spring seat, 41″ × 22″ × 25″, *$650–$700.*

Armchair, office: #361, swivel seat with wraparound leather, leather back, open arms, 35″ × 22″ × 19″, *$825–$950.*

Bookcase: #715, single door with 16 panes, gallery top, four exposed tenons per side, straight toeboard, arched sides, 56″ × 36″ × 13″, *$1750–$2000.*

Bookcase: #716, double doors with eight panes each, gallery top, four exposed tenons per side, straight toeboard, arched sides, 56″ × 42″ × 13″, *$2250–$2500.*

The No. 715–719 series of bookcases remains one of the most popular of the period. Notice that the mullions of this model (No. 718, 56″ × 54″ × 13″) are butted rather than mitered, and the earlier keyed tenons have been reduced to slight protrusions. The recessed toeboard fills the awkward gap left in Stickley's earlier bookcase forms. *(Photo courtesy of D. J. Puffert, Sausalito)*

Bookcase: #717, double doors with 12 panes each, gallery top, four exposed tenons per side, straight toeboard, arched sides, 56″ × 48″ × 13″, *$2500–$2750.*

Bookcase: #718, double doors with 12 panes each, gallery top, four exposed tenons per side, straight toeboard, arched sides, 56″ × 54″ × 13″, *$2750–$3250.*

Bookcase: #719, double doors, with 12 panes each, gallery top, four exposed tenons per side, straight toeboard, arched sides, 56″ × 60″ × 13″, *$3250–$3750.*

Chair, side: #306½, three horizontal slats across back, wide stretchers front and rear, wraparound leather seat, 36″ × 16″ × 16″, *$125–$150;* set of four, *$750–$900.*

The outstanding characteristic of No. 353 is the arched seat apron first introduced on the Harvey Ellis–designed inlaid chair. Stickley dropped the inlay and the double-crest rail but continued to incorporate the delicate arch into this series. It was also available with a drop-in leather seat. *(Photo courtesy of Robert W. Skinner, Boston)*

Chair, side: #308, wide H-shaped slat in back, drop-in seats, 39″ × 17″ × 15″, *$150–$175;* set of four, *$900–$1000.*

Chair, side: #353, three vertical slats in back, wraparound leather seats, arched seat aprons, wide stretchers front and rear, 39″ × 16″ × 16″, *$200–$225;* set of four, *$1250–$1500.*

Chest of drawers: #909, two half-drawers over three long, with wooden knobs, overhanging top with splashboard, on legs, 42″ × 36″ × 20″, *$900–$1100.*

Chest of drawers: #913, six half-drawers over three long, with wooden knobs, overhanging top with back splashboard, bowed sides, arched apron, Harvey Ellis design, 51″ × 36″ × 20″, *$4500–$6000.*

China cabinet: #820, single door with 12 panes, over-hanging top with splashboard, straight apron, 63″ × 36″ × 15″, *$1750–$2000*.

China cabinet: #815, double doors with eight panes each, gallery top, exposed tenons on sides, arched toeboard and sides, 65″ × 42″ × 15″, *$3000–$3500*.

Costumer: #53, double posts on shoe feet, through tenons on both tapered posts, three hammered hooks on each side, 72″ × 13″ × 22″, *$900–$1100*.

Desk, "Chalet": #505, drop front beneath gallery top, with closed lower shelf, shoe feet, keyed tenons on either side, 46″ × 23″ × 16″, *$800–$900*.

Desk: #720, overhanging top with upper section composed of slots and two small drawers, two regular drawers with metal hardware, 38″ × 38″ × 23″, *$700–$800*.

Desk: #732, veneered drop front, gallery top, two half-drawers over two long, arched sides, exposed tenons, 42″ × 32″ × 14″, *$1000–$1250*.

Dresser: #911, two half-drawers over two long, arched toe-board, bowed sides, attached mirror, overhanging top, 67″ × 48″ × 22″, *$2250–$2500*.

Footstool: #300, wraparound leather seat, four stretchers, 15″ × 20″ × 16″, *$900–$1100*.

Footstool: #302, wraparound leather seat on four short flared feet, 5″ high, 12″ × 12″, *$250–$300*.

Liquor cabinet: #86, lift top revealing copper-lined inte-rior, single drawer over door opening to interior with ro-tating bottle rack, 42″ × 24″ × 17″, *$2200–$2500*.

Magazine stand: #72, overhanging top, three open shelves, arched sides, Harvey Ellis design, 42″ × 21″ × 13″, *$1100–$1350*.

Harvey Ellis has also been credited with the design of this magazine stand (No. 72, 42″ × 22″ × 13″). The arched sides complement the subtle curve in the top support, while the thin, overhanging top caps a pleasing balance between the vertical sides and the horizontal shelves. *(Photo courtesy of Christie's, New York)*

Magazine stand: #500, overhanging top, relief carving of tree on either side, four open shelves with leather strips, unsigned, 43″ × 12″ × 12″, *$650–$750.*

Morris chair: #332, flat arms over five vertical slats, exposed tenons on each leg and arm, drop-in seat, loose cushion back, 40″ × 23″ × 27″, *$2500–$2850.*

Morris chair: #336, open bow arms supported by short corbels, arched seat aprons, three horizontal rails around seat cushion, drop-in spring seat, loose cushion back, 40″ × 30″ × 36″, *$3500–$4000.*

Morris chair: #346, open flat arms, legs tenoned through tops of arms, two corbels under each arm, drop-in spring seat, loose cushion back, 41″ × 21″ × 23″, *$800–$950.*

Morris chair: #369, slant arms with five slats under each, exposed tenons on each leg and arm, four long tapering corbels, drop-in spring seat, loose cushion back, 40″ × 23″ × 27″, *$4500–$5000.*

Rocking chair: #305½, three horizontal slats in back, no arms, wraparound leather seat, wide stretchers front and rear, 31″ × 16″ × 16″, *$90–$115.*

Rocking chair: #309½, three horizontal slats in back, open arms, wraparound leather seat, wide stretchers front and rear, 32″ × 20″ × 19″, *$250–$300.*

Rocking chair: #311½, five vertical slats under V-back headrail, wraparound leather seat, exposed tenons on arms, 34″ × 25″ × 28″, *$375–$425.*

Rocking chair: #323, five vertical slats under each arm, drop-in spring seat, loose cushion back, exposed tenons on arms, 40″ × 22″ × 25″, *$400–$450.*

Rocking chair, child's: #345, three horizontal slats in back, open arms, wraparound leather seat, 26″ × 18″ × 12″, *$375–$425.*

Server: #818, two or three drawers with metal pulls, overhanging top with splashboard, lower open shelf, 39″ × 48″ × 20″, *$1400–$1600.*

Settle, hall: #205, even-arm, five slats across back, one wide slat under each arm, exposed tenons on each post, drop-in spring seat, 30″ × 56″ × 22″, *$2250–$2750.*

Settle: #208, even-arm, eight slats across back, three under each arm, exposed tenons on each post, drop-in spring seat, 29″ × 76″ × 32″, *$6000–$7000.*

Settle, bench: #212, 12 slats across back, open arms, exposed tenons on tops of arms, wide front stretcher, wraparound leather seat, 36″ × 48″ × 21″, *$1000–$1250.*

Stickley's most successful dining table design is No. 634, available in either 54-inch or 60-inch diameters. While the trumpet stretchers and exposed tenons solve both practical and decorative problems, the dramatic overhanging top, uncommon on large circular tables, sets this table apart from most others. *(Photo courtesy of D. J. Puffert, Sausalito)*

Sideboard: #814, overhanging top above three short drawers flanked by two doors with strap hinges, over long bottom drawer, open plate rail, metal hardware, straight toeboard, 49″ × 66″ × 24″, *$1850–$2100.*

Sideboard: #816, overhanging top above long drawer above three short drawers flanked by two doors, open plate rail, straight toeboard, 48″ × 48″ × 18″, *$1000–$1250.*

Sideboard: #819, overhanging top supporting attached mirror, with three short drawers over one long, 50″ × 52″ × 20″, *$850–$950.*

Table, dining: #632, circular top supported by five square legs without stretchers, apron, six leaves, 30″ × 54″, *$2000–$2250.*

Table, dining: #634, circular top supported by five square legs joined with stretchers, exposed tenons on outside legs, apron, six leaves, 30″ × 54″, *$3750–$4250*.

Table, dining: #638, drop-leaf style with cut corners on leaves, two swing-out legs, exposed tenons, 29″ × 40″ × 42″ (open), *$1500–$1750*.

Table, dining: #656, circular top supported by center pedestal, four flared feet, apron, six leaves, 30″ × 54″, *$2250–$2500*.

Table, lamp: #604, circular top over four legs joined by two arched cross-stretchers, no apron, 26″ × 20″, *$500–$600*.

Table, lamp: #607, circular top over four legs joined by arched cross-stretchers, lower circular shelf, apron, 29″ × 24″, *$750–$850*.

Table, lamp: #611, square top with cut corners, four legs joined by cross-stretchers supporting lower square shelf, no apron, 29″ × 24″ × 24″, *$500–$600*.

Table, library: #615, rectangular overhanging top, two drawers with metal pulls, two corbels on each leg, exposed tenons on legs and side stretchers, open lower shelf, 30″ × 48″ × 30″, *$700–$800;* with original leather top, *$1250–$1500*.

Table, library: #653, overhanging top above single drawer with metal pull, open lower shelf, 29″ × 48″ × 30″, *$750–$850*.

Table, trestle: #637, rectangular overhanging top over double side legs, lower shelf, two exposed and keyed tenons on each side, 29″ × 48″ × 30″, *$900–$1000;* with original leather top, *$1500–$1750*.

Trestle tables were popular in Arts and Crafts households, and nearly every major furniture firm manufactured its own version. Most are amazingly similar and, once the shopmark has been removed, must be identified by comparing the decorative shape of the feet with those pictured in their original catalogs. *(Photo courtesy of D. J. Puffert, Sausalito)*

Taboret: #601, circular overhanging top supported by four legs joined by arched cross-stretchers, 16″ × 14″, $300–$350.

Taboret: #602, same as #601, 18″ × 16″, $350–$400.

Taboret: #603, same as #601, 20″ × 18″, $400–$450.

Umbrella stand: #54, four tapering posts with stretchers top and bottom, copper drip pan, 29″ × 12″ × 12″, $400–$450.

L. & J. G. STICKLEY
FURNITURE COMPANY

A

B

C

D

Shopmarks:
(1902–1906) Rectangular decal, THE ONONDAGA SHOPS/
L.&J.G. STICKLEY/ FAYETTEVILLE, N.Y.
(1902–1906) Oval paper label with large *S* and
THE ONONDAGA SHOPS (see Shopmark *A* on p. 159)
(1906–1912) Red decal of handscrew with L.&J.G. STICKLEY
on jaws (see Shopmark *B* on p. 159)
(1912–1918) Red and yellow rectangular decal around THE
WORK OF L.&J.G. STICKLEY (see Shopmark *C* on p. 159)
(1912–1918) Branded mark, THE WORK OF
L.&J.G. STICKLEY
(1918) Red and yellow circular decal with joiner's compass and
handscrew encircled by STICKLEY HANDCRAFT
CRAFTSMAN/ SYRACUSE & FAYETTEVILLE, N.Y. (see
Shopmark *D* above)

Principal Contribution:
Extensive line of Arts and Crafts furniture

Founders:
Leopold Stickley
Born: 1869   Died: 1957

John George Stickley
Born: 1871   Died: 1921
Founded: 1902   Closed: current

Workshops and Salesrooms:
The Onondaga Shops
Fayetteville, New York
1902–1904

L. & J. G. Stickley, Inc.
Fayetteville, New York
1904–current

"Fumed by ammonia in air-tight compartments and stained in tones that show beautiful undertints, the furniture is next given, through sanding and waxing, a smooth bloom-like texture, so that the arm or back of your chair is delightful to the touch. . . ."

"Where hinges and pulls are needed, as upon chests of drawers and bookcases, these metal fixtures are of copper hand-wrought in simple designs. The copper is hammered to obtain texture and is dulled and modulated in color by various processes until the soft tones of old metal are secured."

—*Catalog introduction*
1912[1]

Unlike their older brother Gustav and their popular competitor Elbert Hubbard, Leopold and John George Stickley were solely occupied with the business of making furniture. They were neither Arts and Crafts philosophers, editors, nor writers. Leopold was a sharp businessman who managed the firm's factory in Fayetteville, New York, only a few miles away from Gustav Stickley's Eastwood plant where he had trained; John George was considered one of the best furniture salesmen of his day. In later years he oversaw their main sales office in New York City until his early death at age 50 in 1921.

The two youngest Stickley brothers joined forces in 1901, Leopold having worked as plant supervisor in Gustav's new furniture factory for two years and John having spent nine years in partnership with brother Albert in the Stickley Brothers Company in Grand Rapids, Michigan. In 1902 they began producing a line of Arts and Crafts furniture under the trademark

1. *Stickley Craftsman Furniture Catalogs*, introduction by David Cathers (New York: Dover Publications, 1979), p. 130.

of the Onondaga Shops, named after the New York county in which Fayetteville is located. Their immediate success is reflected in the rapid expansion of both their facility and their furniture line; in 1904 they incorporated and continued to enlarge their factory, constructing both a metal shop and leather shop soon thereafter. Early the following year they exhibited for the first time at the semiannual Grand Rapids trade show. Shortly afterward it was reported in one of the important furniture trade journals that "the only trouble they are experiencing is an inability to fill orders."[2]

A few miles away Gustav Stickley must have been painfully aware of his younger brothers' success, for in 1904 he redesigned the Craftsman shopmark, including his first name to help distinguish between the two companies. The confusion must have continued, however, fueled not only by the two firms' close proximity to one another and their similar names but by the adoption, in 1906, by Leopold and John George of a red shopmark similar to that of their brother's. Gustav must have felt that the L. & J. G. Stickley "Handcraft" decal was an infringement on his red joiner's compass trademark and may even have threatened legal action to stop them from using it. In 1912, for whatever reason, L. & J. G. Stickley dropped their red Handcraft decal and replaced it with a yellow decal and a branded mark, both of which clearly read "THE WORK OF L.&J.G. STICKLEY."

The L. & J. G. Stickley firm issued five catalogs between 1905 and 1922, the year before they phased out their Arts and Crafts line. All five catalogs reveal the debt the majority of their furniture designs owe to those of Gustav Stickley, especially early in their careers, which is not surprising in light of the fact that Leopold had trained under Gustav during the time that Gustav developed and introduced his first line of Arts and Crafts furniture. During those two years he would have assimilated the philosophy, the design, and the construction techniques that propelled Craftsman furniture to the top of the Arts and Crafts furniture world. Family members recalled that Leopold sketched some of the early Onondaga Shops designs himself,

2. David Cathers, *Furniture of the American Arts and Crafts Movement* (New York: New American Library, 1981), p. 72.

While this L. & J. G. Stickley box settle (No. 216, 36″ × 70″ × 30″) is one of the best of its types, it provides a lesson in design when compared with the Craftsman No. 208 pictured in Thomas Maher's introduction. A seemingly minor adjustment in the overall dimensions and a wider spacing of the slats creates a major difference in appearance. The net result is that the back of this settle seems a little too high for the seat. *(Photo courtesy of D. J. Puffert, Sausalito)*

which were then transformed into working plans by the firm's experienced designers. Peter Hansen, one of their best-known designers in later years, had also once worked for Gustav.[3]

In some instances the L. & J. G. Stickley firm made only subtle changes (the length of the corbel, the sweep of an arch, the arrangement of drawers, etc.) in what had obviously originated as a Craftsman design. A comparison of the L. & J. G. Stickley server No. 741 with the slightly earlier Gustav Stickley No. 818, both of which are pictured and discussed in detail by David Cathers in *Furniture of the American Arts and Crafts Movement*,[4] illustrates the extent to which Gustav Stickley often influenced the designs of L. & J. G. Stickley. The large

3. Wendy Kaplan, *The Art That Is Life: The Arts and Crafts Movement in America, 1875–1920* (Boston: Museum of Fine Arts, 1987), p. 168.

4. David Cathers, *Furniture of the American Arts and Crafts Movement* (New York: New American Library, 1981), pp. 196–197.

This double-door bookcase (No. 746, 58″ × 44″ × 16″) was obviously inspired by the Harvey Ellis bookcase pictured earlier. Minor changes in the dimensions, the number of leaded glass windows, and the more moderate arch in the toeboard do not detract from this example but only further illustrate Ellis's genius for design. To their credit, no other firm came closer than L. & J. G. Stickley to duplicating his work. *(Photo courtesy of Robert W. Skinner, Boston)*

number of L. & J. G. Stickley pieces bearing more than just a coincidental resemblance to those from the Craftsman shops have, unfortunately, overshadowed many of their own designs and improvements on those of Gustav's.

Unlike most of Gustav Stickley's imitators, however, Leopold and John George did not resort to sloppy workmanship or inferior materials. The majority of their furniture was made from Kentucky quarter-sawn white oak and was pegged at crucial joints. In a few instances they experimented with false exposed tenons but appear to have concluded that it required nearly as much time to imitate an exposed tenon as it did to make one. Although their hardware may not have been as impressive as Gustav's, it certainly was better than that of every other major Arts and Crafts firm.

Leopold and John George were proud of their "scientific manner" of furniture construction, using "all the resources of modern invention."[5] In their 1910 catalog the brothers implied that they had been the first to adapt the spring seat from the fledgling automotive industry to Arts and Crafts chairs, rockers, and settles[6]—an innovation Gustav, in turn, incorporated into his large chairs around 1909. Whereas Gustav often veneered two sides of the legs of his Morris chairs and dining room tables, Leopold developed an interlocking design wherein "four pieces of solid oak, with a tiny core, [are] all so tightly welded together that no cracking is possible."[7] The firm also utilized thin splines in assembling the tops of tables, dressers, and buffets, stating in their catalog introduction that "no splitting is possible." Regardless of the validity of their claims, both the interlocking post system and the use of splines between boards may help distinguish between what might otherwise be two very similar designs from the shops of either Gustav or L. & J. G. Stickley.

The craftsmen in both shops, however, were permitted to make minor changes as deemed necessary, as is reflected in variations between the dimensions listed in the catalogs and those found on some of the pieces. In addition, a great deal more experimentation went on in these shops than in modern furniture factories. For instance, while the interlocking leg system is commonly associated with L. & J. G. Stickley, it has also been found on some signed Gustav Stickley library tables.

L. & J. G. Stickley furniture is generally well marked, but their early paper label and their later decals can both easily be destroyed by a careless refinishing. In these instances identification is dependent on comparisons of designs and dimensions illustrated in their original catalogs, many of which have been reproduced and widely distributed. Even without a catalog, an astute collector will recognize the unique L. & J. G. Stickley hand-hammered copper hardware found on many of their case pieces built after 1906. Another design characteristic that was often repeated was the long, tapering corbel, located under the

5. *Stickley Craftsman Furniture Catalogs* (New York: Dover Publications, 1979), p. 131.

6. Ibid.

7. Ibid.

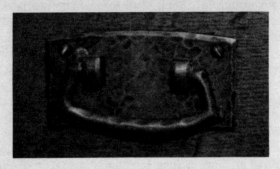

As far as has been determined, L. & J. G. Stickley did not produce their own hardware, which may account for the lack of evolution in its design. The hammered copper pulls are similar to those of Gustav Stickley yet are not as large nor as substantial. Nevertheless, they are of higher quality than those of any other Arts and Crafts firm and can be used to help identify an unmarked piece.

arms of rocking chairs, settles, and armchairs, that ends with a unique flare.

In 1918, perhaps in an attempt to restore Gustav's tarnished image in the Arts and Crafts furniture industry, Leopold and John George bought controlling interest in Gustav's bankrupt factory and formed, along with Gustav and Albert (who was and remained in Grand Rapids), Stickley Associated Cabinetmakers. The reunion was short-lived; before the year had ended, so had the relationship. Gustav left to live with his daughter, and Leopold and John George began the gradual transformation from the production of Arts and Crafts furniture to "Cherry Valley" Colonial reproductions. Their last Arts and Crafts furniture was produced in 1923; since then the factory has continued to manufacture quality reproductions of classic Early American designs bearing the Stickley name branded in the wood.

Selected Prices

Model numbers correspond with those in the *Stickley Craftsman Catalogs* (New York: Dover Publications, 1979) and *The Mission Furniture of L. & J. G. Stickley* (New York: Turn of the Century Editions, 1983). Unless otherwise indicated, all examples are made from oak, and both the finish and the leather upholstery are in excellent original condition.

Armchair: #818, four horizontal slats across the back, open arms, wide front stretcher, corbels, drop-in spring seat, 39″ × 23″, *$225–$250*.

Armchair: #836, four vertical slats in tall back, open arms, drop-in spring cushion seat, flat arms with exposed leg tenons, 44″ × 23″, *$350–$400*.

Armchair: #450, six vertical slats across the back, five under each arm, front posts tenoned through tops of arms, corbels, drop-in spring seat, 40″ × 24″, *$475–$525*.

Bookcase: #641, single door with sixteen panes of glass, four keyed tenons on each side, gallery top, 55″ × 30″ × 12″, *$1500–$1750*.

Bookcase: #644, open front, gallery top over four shelves, keyed tenons on sides, arched sides, 55″ × 36″ × 12″, *$1250–$1500*.

Bookcase: #645, double doors, with twelve panes of glass each, four keyed tenons on each side, metal pulls, chamfered board back, 56″ × 49″ × 14″, *$2000–$2250*.

Chair, side: #350, three horizontal slats in back, wraparound leather seat, wide stretcher front and rear, 35″ × 17″, *$100–$125*; set of four, *$600–$750*.

Chair, side: #820, four vertical slats across back beneath scooped crest rail, drop-in spring cushion seat, wide stretchers front and rear, 36″ × 20″, *$125–$150*; set of four, *$750–$900*.

China cabinet: #761, overhanging top over single door with one large sheet of glass, arched sides and toeboard, copper pull, 60″ × 36″ × 16″, *$1750–$2000*.

Like most of the major furniture companies, L. & J. G. Stickley produced a line of bookcases of various sizes, but they were the only firm to continue using authentic keyed tenons to the end of Arts and Crafts production. Without them, this open bookcase (No. 644, 55″ × 36″ × 12″) would lose the greater part of its power, its presence, and its value. *(Photo courtesy of Robert W. Skinner, Boston)*

China cabinet: #746, double doors with 12 small leaded glass panels in the top of each, large single pane below, overhanging top, arched toeboard, adjustable shelves, 58″ × 44″ × 16″, *$2750–$3250.*

Desk, drop-front: #613, overhanging top above slanted lid and single long drawer, fitted interior, lower shelf, arched sides, 40″ × 32″, *$375–$450.*

Desk, flat-top: #502, overhanging top over single drawer and book shelf at either end, 30″ × 48″ × 28″, *$375–$425.*

Desk, flat-top: #610, overhanging top supporting compartment of slots across back, two short drawers over knee compartment, wooden knobs, 38″ × 40″ × 22″, *$500–$600.*

Dresser: #99, overhanging top with splashboard, two short drawers over three long, arched sides and toeboard, wooden knobs, 38″ × 40″ × 22″, *$850–$950*.

Footstool: #391, leather-wrapped seat with two narrow stretchers at ends and one wide stretcher along each side, 18″ × 19″ × 16″, *$350–$450*.

Footstool: loose cushion set in rectangular frame with concave sides, stretcher base, 15″ × 20″ × 16″, *$175–$200*.

Magazine stand: #46, with four shelves, open back, three slats on either side beneath arched crest rail, arched toeboards, 42″ × 19″ × 12″, *$875–$975*.

Morris chair: #830, open flat-arm style, adjustable bar, front legs tenoned through arms, drop-in spring seat, loose cushion back, 41″ × 25″, *$450–$550*.

Morris chair: #471, flat arms with six slats under each, front posts tenoned through tops of arms, four long corbels, adjustable bar, drop-in spring seat, cushion back, 41″ × 26″, *$1000–$1250*.

Morris chair: #498, slant arms with five slats under each arm, exposed tenons on front legs and tops of arms, adjustable rod, drop-in spring cushion seat, loose cushion back, 41″ × 28″, *$2250–$2750*.

Morris chair rocker: #831, open arms, front posts tenoned through tops of arms, long corbels on front posts, adjustable rod, 38″ × 25″, *$500–$600*.

Rocking chair: #823, four vertical slats across the back beneath scooped crest rail, open arms with exposed tenons on tops, wide front stretcher, drop-in spring seat, 36″ × 23″, *$250–$300*.

Rocking chair: #837, tall-back version with four vertical slats, open arms with exposed tenons on tops, corbels, drop-in spring seat, 44″ × 23″, *$450–$500*.

This three-drawer server/sideboard (No. 750, 49″ × 48″ × 22″) with an open plate rail and standard L. & J. G. Stickley hammered-copper hardware is functional but lacks charm. The lower shelf rests on the side stretchers rather than being tenoned into or through them, just as the plate rail rests on the top rather than extending up through it. *(Photo courtesy of Don Treadway, Cincinnati)*

Server: #741, splashboard and overhanging top over three drawers and lower open shelf, copper hardware, 38″ × 44″ × 18″, *$850–$950.*

Settle, bench: #263, seven slats across the back beneath a scooped crest rail, arms slanted slightly over two vertical slats, corbels, drop-in spring seat, 37″ × 72″ × 25″, *$1250–$1500.*

Settle: #215, even arms with five vertical back slats, two under each arm, slightly curved apron, drop-in spring cushion seat, 36″ × 54″ × 24″, *$1500–$1750.*

Settle: #281, even arms with 16 back slats and five side slats, drop-in spring cushion seat, 34″ × 76″ × 31″, *$2000–$2250.*

Sideboard: #707, overhanging top supporting closed plate rail, two half-drawers over two doors, slightly arched apron, copper hardware, 44″ × 48″ × 20″, *$500–600.*

Sideboard: #731, overhanging top supporting paneled plate rail, four short drawers centered by two cabinet doors with strap hinges over long drawer, arched toeboard, 49" × 72" × 25", *$1750–$2000*.

Table, dining: #720, overhanging circular top supported by five tapering legs, three leaves, 30" × 48", *$800–$900;* 54", *$1250–$1500;* 60", *$1750–$2000*.

Table, dining: #713, circular top supported by pedestal of four curved supports mounted on four wide feet, apron, 30" × 54", *$1500–$1750*.

Table, lamp: #576, square top with cut corners, no apron, lower square shelf on arched cross-stretchers, 29" × 24" × 24", *$375–$425*.

The L. & J. G. Stickley version of the trestle table (No. 593, 29" × 48" × 30") is one of the best of the era. Unlike Gustav's, the boards in their tops are splined together for greater stability. They also added a little embellishment in the curve of the feet on their table; the slight difference neither increases nor decreases its value but merely provides another means of identifying an unmarked example. *(Photo courtesy of D. J. Puffert, Sausalito)*

Table, lamp: #538, overhanging circular top with narrow skirt, straight cross-stretchers, 29″ × 30″, *$350–$400*.

Table, lamp: #577, circular top with lower circular shelf on cross-stretchers, 29″ × 30″, *$350–$400*.

Table, library: #543, circular top with narrow skirt, circular lower shelf on cross-stretchers, 29″ × 48″, *$500–$600*.

Table, trestle: #593, overhanging top supported by dual column sides, lower shelf with big key tenons, shaped feet, 29″ × 48″ × 30″, *$800–$900*.

Table, library: #521, overhanging top over long single drawer with metal pulls, two long tapering corbels on each leg, lower shelf with through-tenons, 29″ × 42″ × 28″, *$600–$700; with leather top, $900–$1000*.

Taboret: #558, four legs protruding through octagonal overhanging top, arched cross-members, 17″ × 15″ × 15″, *$400–$450*.

THE TOBEY FURNITURE COMPANY

Shopmarks:
(Pre-1900) Circular tag, TOBEY HAND-MADE FURNITURE/ ESTABLISHED 1856/ CHICAGO

(1900–1901: furniture designed by Gustav Stickley) Circular label, THE NEW FURNITURE/ THE TOBEY FURNITURE COMPANY/ CHICAGO
(After 1902) Metal tag, RUSSMORE/ THE TOBEY FURNITURE COMPANY/ TRADEMARK/ CHICAGO

Principal Contribution:
Early distributor and producer of Arts and Crafts furniture

Founders:
Charles Tobey
Born: 1831   Died: 1888

Frank Tobey
Born: 1833   Died: 1913
Founded: 1856   Closed: 1954

Workshops and Salesrooms:
Charles Tobey
Chicago
1856–1857

Charles Tobey & Brother
Chicago
1858–1869

Thayer and Tobey Furniture Company
Chicago
1870–1874

The Tobey Furniture Company
Chicago
1875–1954

"It is but a beginning—the first slight harvest in this new field of furniture. Now that it has met with success, nothing will hinder its development. New pieces—pieces hitherto impossible to find— are being made, and it will be our constant endeavor to produce a variety of furniture that will be thoroughly practical, not too good for daily use, moderate in price, in demand by people of culture and taste, and that will help to make life better and truer by its perfect sincerity."

—Tobey advertisement
1900[1]

Charles Tobey was an American success story. In 1855, at the age of twenty-one, he left his home in Massachusetts to make his fortune in the fastest-growing city in the country: Chicago. He soon opened a small furniture store, expanding it on the arrival of his brother Frank. The Panic of 1857 drove several companies to bankruptcy, but the two brothers weathered the economic storm, managing even to buy the inventories of several firms that went out of business—a move that proved profitable when Chicago's financial misfortunes were suddenly reversed by the Civil War. The firm soon expanded into furniture production, securing large contracts to fill Chicago's new hotels with hundreds of bedroom suites. Twelve years after he had arrived in Chicago, Charles Tobey owned his own store on bustling State Street, where he and Frank continued to prosper, furnishing homes across the city with a variety of styles of furniture, draperies, and wallpapers.

The company continued to expand both its facilities and its furniture line. In the 1880s they were simultaneously selling high-quality Victorian bedroom suites in native black walnut and imported mahogany, a line of Colonial reproductions, oak Eastlake parlor sets, and the newest rage: horn furniture—perhaps utilizing the sprawling Chicago stockyards as a convenient source. Charles Tobey died in 1888, but his younger brother Frank proved to be a capable and innovative president. That same year he and a Norwegian woodworker, Wilhelm Christiansen, founded the Tobey & Christiansen Cabinet Company, a custom furniture factory that quickly developed a reputation as one of the finest in the country. Under Christiansen's capable leadership, the firm produced high-quality furniture in a variety of woods and styles that attracted wealthy clients and many of

1. Chicago *Tribune* (October 7, 1900).

Chicago's growing number of important architects. "Furniture made in the cabinet shop, identified as Tobey Hand-Made Furniture by the use of metal tags after 1898, was distinguished by excellent craftsmanship and perfection of detail. Made from hardwoods like mahogany, maple, and oak, Tobey's pieces were finished on all sides, with as much attention lavished on the surfaces that stood against the wall as on the visible surface."[2]

It was at this same time that Frank Tobey also hired George F. Clingman, who first worked as a wholesale buyer and occasional designer but who eventually became the firm's manager. It was Clingman who later claimed to have sketched the first Mission-style furniture prior to 1900.[3] In July 1900, however, he traveled to Grand Rapids for the semiannual furniture trade show, where he saw Gustav Stickley's new line of furniture that incorporated elements of both the waning Art Nouveau and the emerging Arts and Crafts styles. Clingman immediately purchased Stickley's entire line and negotiated an exclusive arrangement wherein the Tobey Furniture Company would market Gustav Stickley's furniture.

As Clingman recalled years later, "I took a piece of paper out of my pocket, or in fact several pieces, and told him that if he was going to make a success of the furniture that he was making it would be necessary for him to make some more important pieces than he was making at that time. On this paper I drew out several large sofas with square posts with flat arms with loose pillow seats and backs; some broad arm rockers and chairs, several styles of tables and one or two screens, and from these Gustave Stickley made what he now claims to be the originator of, that is his so-called arts and crafts furniture . . . [but] instead of Gustave Stickley being the originator of this kind of furniture I claim the honor of being the first to introduce to the public generally this plain, simple kind of furniture."[4]

2. Sharon Darling, *Chicago Furniture: Art, Craft & Industry 1833–1983* (Chicago: Chicago Historical Society, 1984), pp. 235–236.
3. Don Marek, *Arts and Crafts Furniture Design: The Grand Rapids Contribution 1895–1915* (Grand Rapids, MI: Grand Rapids Art Museum, 1987), p. 35.
4. Ibid.

The concern over who was the first to introduce the Arts and Crafts–style furniture did not become an issue until several years later, when its success was assured. In July 1900 Gustav Stickley was content to permit the Tobey Furniture Company to advertise and sell his line of furniture without any reference to him or his shops in Eastwood, New York; at that point economic survival took precedence over shopmarks. The ads that appeared that fall in *House Beautiful* magazine and the Chicago *Tribune* bore a new Tobey paper label: "The New Furniture" encompassed by four branches. The name of Gustav Stickley never appeared in any of the advertisements.

Identifying the Stickley-designed pieces in the Tobey ads that appeared that fall has been made possible through the recent publication of Gustav Stickley's first catalog, which was originally printed just before the Grand Rapids exhibition in July 1900.[5] Clingman simply clipped Stickley's drawings out of his catalog, retained the same names and dimensions and added the prefix 3 to each model number. One of the most common of these early and rare pieces is the Chalet magazine cabinet, which featured a carved plant form on either side, reflecting the comment in the Tobey ad stating that "such ornament as it bears is incut carving . . . something from nature, a flower or a leaf, as its motive, and all the carving is in bold line."[6] Although the ad also declared that "each piece of 'new furniture' bears our special trademark here shown,"[7] most of the pieces that came from Stickley's Eastwood shops either never received the paper labels or did not retain them over the course of the next eighty-eight years. Identification is most often made using the illustrations and dimensions listed in Stickley's catalog.

Stickley soon grew disillusioned with the terms he and Clingman had agreed to and by that same December was no longer shipping furniture to the Tobey salesrooms on State Street. The ads for Tobey's New Furniture continued through 1901, however, leading author Sharon Darling to suggest that "it is possible that the original contract with the Tobey Company was

5. See Stephen Gray, *The Early Work of Gustav Stickley* (New York: Turn of the Century Editions, 1987).
6. Chicago *Tribune* (October 7, 1900).
7. Ibid.

Although this magazine stand was not manufactured by the To-bey company, it remains their best-known example. Gustav Stickley designed and manufactured this particular stand (43″ × 12″ × 12″) in 1901, but Tobey and several other firms were duplicating it by 1902. Almost all are unsigned, but the Stickley model generally excels in the quality of the carving on the sides. *(Photo courtesy of Don Treadway, Cincinnati)*

fulfilled by Leopold Stickley,"[8] who, incidently, had left Gus-tav's employment that same December to begin organizing his own furniture manufacturing company in nearby Fayetteville, New York, with his brother John George.

Back in Chicago, Clingman and Christiansen were busy ini-tiating a new line of Mission oak furniture for the Tobey Fur-niture Company. Introduced in 1902, the Russmore line featured several new designs, along with some that were obviously in-spired by Gustav Stickley. The major difference, though, was apparent to the trained observer: whereas Gustav Stickley pre-ferred the more expensive and more durable quarter-sawn white oak, the Russmore line was constructed of plain sawn oak "to meet the growing demand for a type of furniture of artistic

8. Sharon Darling, *Chicago Furniture: Art, Craft & Industry 1833–1983* (Chicago: Chicago Historical Society, 1984), p. 235.

simplicity in design, richness in finish, durability in construction, and of low price."[9] At first glance Russmore furniture can be confused with that of Gustav Stickley, especially if the brass plaque has been removed, but a closer examination will often reveal a lack of pegging of key joints, the use of thinner boards, less expensive construction techniques and, as mentioned, plain sawn oak lumber. While the Russmore line may have appealed to the growing numbers of young people who were clamoring for Mission oak furniture for their homes, Gustav Stickley was not left out of the Chicago scene. Not far from Tobey's State Street showrooms, Marshall Field and Company introduced their line of Mission oak–style furnishings in 1902 as well—with an entire showroom of Gustav Stickley's Craftsman furniture.

Although the Tobey Furniture Company had an auspicious beginning, introducing the early Arts and Crafts furniture of Gustav Stickley to a large audience, they, like several other Midwest furniture manufacturers and distributors—Sears, Roebuck & Company, the Hartman Furniture Company, S. Karpen & Brothers, and the Chicago Mission Furniture Company—were motivated not by the writings of William Morris or John Ruskin but by the potential for profit in a new fashion. More often than not, their motivation is reflected in the workmanship, design, and materials of the furniture they produced, leaving the collector to determine the level of quality achieved by each piece encountered. In the case of the Tobey Furniture Company, it is the search for those rare early pieces designed and executed by Gustav Stickley, not the Russmore line of inexpensive Mission oak furniture, that will ensure continued, though limited, recognition.

Selected Prices

Armchair: slant arm rising sharply from front posts to rear, posts tenoned through tops of arms, leather swing seat from front seat apron to crest rail, unsigned, 46″ × 26″ × 30″, $500–$600.

9. Sharon Darling, *Chicago Furniture: Art, Craft & Industry 1833–1983* (Chicago: Chicago Historical Society, 1984), p. 240.

China cabinet: double doors with eight false-mullion panes each, overhanging top, adjustable shelves, straight toe-board, Russmore brass tag on back, 60" × 42" × 15", *$700–$800.*

Magazine stand: designed and produced by Gustav Stickley, square overhanging top supported by six small corbels, splayed sides featuring incised plant form, arched at bottom, four fixed shelves, unsigned, 43" × 12" × 12", *$500–$600.*

Magazine stand: similiar to previous entry, but with inferior carving, plain sawn oak, and Russmore brass tag, 41" × 12" × 12", *$150–$175.*

Plant stand: #3137 or #137, flush top with high-gloss green Grueby tile set in, top notched around four corner posts, lower square shelf, unmarked, 24" × 14" × 14", *$1500–$1750.*

Trestle table: overhanging top supported by dual-column sides ending in shoe feet, lower shelf with two keyed tenons per side, unmarked, 29" × 48" × 35", *$700–$800.*

FRANK LLOYD WRIGHT

Shopmark:
None appearing on Arts and Crafts or Prairie style furniture
Red square on architectural drawings

Principal Contribution:
Architectural and furniture designs
Born: 1867   Died: 1959

Studio and Workshops:
Frank Lloyd Wright, Architect
Oak Park and Chicago, Illinois
1887–1910

Spring Green, Wisconsin
1911–1959

Scottsdale, Arizona
1933–1959

"This is the modern opportunity—to make of a building, together with its equipment, appurtenances and environment, an entity which shall constitute a complete work of art, and a work of art more valuable to society as a whole than has ever before existed."

—*Frank Lloyd Wright*
1908[1]

"I have done the best I could with this "living room chair" but, of course, you have to call for somebody to help you move it. All my life my legs have been banged up somewhere by the chairs I have designed."

—*Frank Lloyd Wright*
1954[2]

As one might expect from a career that spanned seven decades, the furniture, lighting fixtures, and stained-glass windows designed by Frank Lloyd Wright, like his buildings, fall into several different cagetories: Arts and Crafts, Prairie school, Art Deco, International, Usonian, and Modern. Unlike any of the other Arts and Crafts furniture designers, Wright not only survived the sudden swing in public tastes after World War I, he embraced it. The end of the Arts and Crafts and Prairie school movements coincided with the end of Wright's days of innocence and glory, but his endless stream of plans, projects, and

1. Frank Lloyd Wright, *In the Cause of Architecture* (1908).

2. Frank Lloyd Wright, *The Natural House* (1957), as quoted in Marian Page, *Furniture Designed by Architects* (New York: Whitney Library of Design, 1980), p. 106.

visions for the future carried him from one style to another, through personal tragedy, public rejection, and, finally, nearing the end of his seventy-two-year career, to recognition as America's greatest architect.

The stylistic development of the furniture of Frank Lloyd Wright parallels the buildings he designed, for Wright was the first Prairie school architect to insist that all of the furnishings of the home—woodwork, windows, lights, carpets, and furniture—are each a part of the more important whole and for that reason can only be designed by the architect. The Prairie school movement took root and flourished in turn-of-the-century Chicago, due in no small part to the influence of the young architect from Wisconsin. Wright's career had taken a major step forward when, in 1887, he was accepted into the prestigious architectural firm of Adler and Sullivan. Six years later, however, after a stormy argument with Louis Sullivan over Wright's moonlighting activities, Frank Lloyd Wright established his own firm in the Oak Park, Illinois, house and studio Sullivan had financed for him a few years earlier. From 1893 until 1915, when he moved to Tokyo to supervise the seven-year construction of the Imperial Hotel, Frank Lloyd Wright served as the spokesman and chief architect of the Prairie school movement.

"The decorative designs of the Prairie school architects were an outgrowth of the Arts and Crafts movement, ideologically and stylistically," observed David Hanks in a 1972 essay. "From the larger movement the Prairie architect derived an emphasis on unity of exterior and interior, the respect for natural materials, a desire for simplicity, the interest in Japanese art, and a geometric, rectilinear style."[3]

The furniture Wright designed for early Prairie school homes was, as one author has pointed out, "highly architectural and seemingly rooted to the floor as the houses are rooted to the earth."[4] Wright himself, years later, insisted that his furniture "should be seen as a minor part of the building itself even if

3. Robert Judson Clark, *The Arts and Crafts Movement in America 1876–1916* (Princeton, NJ: Princeton University Press, 1972), p. 59.

4. Marian Page, *Furniture Designed by Architects* (New York: Whitney Library of Design, 1980), p. 101.

detached or kept aside to be employed on occasion."[5] Perhaps
the realization that Wright designed furniture for his homes
and not for the general public will help explain why the volatile architect bristled at the suggestion that he was designing Mission oak furniture similar to that promoted by Gustav
Stickley in *The Craftsman* magazine and by his friend Elbert
Hubbard at the Roycroft shops. Wright was well aware of
the work of both Stickley and Hubbard, whom he visited on
occasion, and in his typical outspoken manner pronounced it
"plain as a barn door."[6]

To Wright's credit it should be pointed out that while Elbert
Hubbard was yet a struggling writer and Gustav Stickley was
still making reproduction Chippendale chairs on a farm in up-
state New York, Frank Lloyd Wright, at the tender age of
twenty-six, had already designed the now-famous set of Arts
and Crafts dining room furniture for his home in Oak Park
(1893–1895). By the time Gustav Stickley had placed his first
spindle furniture designs into production in 1905, Frank Lloyd
Wright had experimented with it ten years earlier, had incorporated it into two major commissions—the Francis Little House
(1902) and the George Barton House (1903)—and had moved on
to conquer other challenges.

To Wright, oak seemed the natural choice for both the woodwork and the furniture of his Prairie school designs. While he
may have disliked being associated with the more plebian Mission oak, Wright's furniture is clearly reflective of the Arts and
Crafts movement, as evidenced by its simple, crisp, rectilinear
design; his preference for natural or fumed oak under a varnish
or wax finish; his choice of authentic leather upholstery; and his
incorporation of narrow slats or square spindles. Where his custom-designed furniture differed with that associated with the
major Arts and Crafts furniture manufacturers was in his cal-
culated omission of pegged joints, hand-hammered hardware,
and exposed tenons, a detail that on more than one occasion has

5. Marian Page, *Furniture Designed by Architects* (New York: Whitney
Library of Design, 1980), p. 94.
6. Frank Lloyd Wright, *An Autobiography* (New York: Longmans
Green, 1932), p. 138.

The spindle furniture of Frank Lloyd Wright had been well publicized long before Gustav Stickley or any of the other Arts and Crafts furniture manufacturing concerns introduced their own versions. This tall-back chair was designed in 1906 and is representative of Wright's Prairie school side chairs. Unlike any of the major firms, Wright did not see the need to design pegs into his furniture. The original seat was leather. *(Photo courtesy of the Virginia Museum, Richmond, the Sydney and Frances Lewis Collection)*

confused collectors who have unexpectedly come upon a Frank Lloyd Wright–designed piece of furniture and have failed to recognize it.

Unlike Stickley, Limbert, or Hubbard, Wright was first and foremost an architect. Whereas the others employed cabinetmakers, Wright employed draftsmen. Rather than involve himself in furniture production, Wright sent his furniture plans to a number of different custom furniture shops in the Chicago and Milwaukee areas, which explains the subtle differences in woodworking techniques and the omission of Wright's shopmark from his Arts and Crafts furniture.[7]

7. David Hanks, *The Decorative Designs of Frank Lloyd Wright* (New York: E. P. Dutton, 1979), pp. 41–42.

Identifying furniture designed by Frank Lloyd Wright requires an eye trained more for research than for recognizing the remnants of a hidden shopmark. Although his early furniture does not bear any shopmark, original drawings, blueprints, photographs, contracts, and letters have been used to identify his furniture. Although even a novice stumbling upon an early Wright high-back spindle chair would realize, simply by its sheer architectural impact, that it is a piece of major importance, identifying a copper urn, a small end table, a stained-glass window, a floor lamp, a modest side chair, or a library table as having originated from the drafting room of Frank Lloyd Wright requires an acquired familiarity with his career, his philosophy, and his designs.

Fortunately for the Arts and Crafts collector, Wright's prolific career has been well documented. No serious work on twentieth-century architecture is complete without a major section on Wright and the Prairie school movement. Scores of newspaper and magazine articles trace both his stormy career and his sensational private life—a life that was marred by two exhausting divorces, bankruptcy, lawsuits, arrests, and the harrowing ax murders in 1914 of his mistress and her two small children in his Spring Green retreat. With the encouragement and assistance of his third wife, Wright undertook the writing of *An Autobiography*, first published in 1932 when Wright was sixty-three years old and when his most important contribution to modern architecture—the Guggenheim Museum in New York City—was still more than twenty-five years away.

Although the prices that fine examples of Frank Lloyd Wright Arts and Crafts furniture have brought in recent years are indicative of its relative rarity, the collector should not presume that he or she will never have the opportunity to inspect, let alone purchase, one of Wright's works. Between the years 1893 and 1909, when he left a lucrative practice and a growing family for a two-year sojourn in Europe with the wife of one of his clients, more than one hundred of Wright's commissions were completed.[8] In nearly every instance, Wright designed the

8. Robert C. Twombly, *Frank Lloyd Wright in Spring Green* (Madison, WI: State Historical Society of Wisconsin, 1980), p. 2.

furnishings for each project, his wealthy clients concurring with his persuasive insistence that they replace their previous furniture with pieces Wright had designed exclusively for their home.

Dining room chairs and tables, desks, library tables, and armchairs are the most commonly discovered examples of early Wright furniture, for whenever possible, Wright incorporated built-in furniture—buffets, window seats, hall benches, and lamp tables—into his homes, both as an integral aspect of his philosophy of organic architecture and, indirectly or directly, as a way to prevent his present clients and future owners from replacing them with furniture from other designers. In at least one instance, however, one of Wright's clients was granted permission by the architect—grudgingly, it is reported—to furnish the secondary rooms with the less expensive Arts and Crafts furniture of L. & J. G. Stickley. This instance led to the erroneous conclusion that the firm of L. & J. G. Stickley had been contracted by Wright in 1900 to execute his furniture designs for the Bradley house in Kankakee, IL.[9] Additional research has revealed, however, that Chicagoan John Ayers rather than the Stickleys deserves that credit.[10]

During the 1930s and 1940s, while Wright fought for national recognition and major commissions, both the Arts and Crafts and the Prairie school movements remained out of vogue. Many Wright houses, as they either passed to the next generation or were sold to new owners, were destroyed, remodeled, redecorated, or, as in the case of Wright's original Oak Park home and studio, transformed into multiple apartments. Now priceless examples of Frank Lloyd Wright furniture were literally hauled out onto lawns to be sold, given away, or even thrown away. Today they continue to surface, but it seems inevitable that within another decade all but a few lost examples will have found their way into museum exhibitions and important collections, such as the National Center for the Study of Frank Lloyd

9. Robert Judson Clark, *The Arts and Crafts Movement in America 1875-1916* (Princeton, NJ: Princeton University Press, 1972), p. 44.

10. David Hanks, *The Decorative Designs of Frank Lloyd Wright* (New York: E. P. Dutton, 1979), pp. 41-42.

Wright at the Domino's Pizza headquarters in Ann Arbor, Michigan, where pizza magnate Thomas S. Monagham continues to assemble what will inevitably become the most important collection of Frank Lloyd Wright furniture, drawings, papers, books, and related items.

Selected Prices

The rarity of Prairie school and Arts and Crafts–style furniture designed by Frank Lloyd Wright, plus the individual nature of each piece, makes establishing a price guide both impractical and quite possibly misleading, for the value of any example will be influenced by factors beyond the scope of this study. Therefore, in lieu of price ranges, recent auction reports have been listed, including their presale estimates. However, it must be understood that auction estimates and final bids are often influenced by factors that cannot always be anticipated, fully explained, or duplicated. Auction prices reflect the final bid plus the 10 percent buyer's premium.

Beds, twin: Evans Residence, Chicago (ca. 1909), solid headboard and foot, each topped by heavy rail, 47″ × 47″, Christie's 6/86 (est. $6000–$9000) *$6600*.

Chair, dining: Evans Residence, Chicago (ca. 1908), high back with six square spindles extending to floor, curved feet, drop in seat, 44″ high, Christie's 6/86 (est. $20,000–$25,000) *$35,200*.

Chair, dining: Imperial Hotel, Tokyo (ca. 1916–1922), upholstered seat and hexagonal back, three spindles extending from floor upward to support back, 40″ high, Christie's 6/85 *$13,200*; Christie's 12/86 (est. $12,000–$15,000) *$20,900*.

Chair, dining: Little House, Peoria, IL (ca. 1902), single wide back slat extending from crest rail to rear stretcher, drop-in seat, 40″ high, Christie's 6/87 (est. $7000–$9000) *$25,300*; Christie's 12/87 (est. $12,000–$18,000) *$11,000*.

Chair, hexagonal: Little House, Peoria, IL (ca. 1902), the five sides with square spindles extending from top rail to stretchers, drop-in seat, 23″ × 25″ × 27″, Christie's 6/87 (est. $25,000–$35,000) *$28,600*.

Chair, side: Willits House, Highland Park, IL (ca. 1901), 11 square spindles extending from broad crest rail to lower stretcher, drop-in seat, rear feet canted slightly, 56″ high, Christie's 12/86 (est. $60,000–$70,000) *$198,000*.

Chair, side: Coonley House, Riverside, IL (ca. 1908), single slab back extending above crest rail and extending to lower stretcher, drop-in seat, 40″ high, Christie's 12/87 (est. $6,000–$8,000) *$8250* and *$9900*.

Daybed: Little House, Peoria, IL (ca. 1902), both ends of equal height connected by broad sideboards with applied moldings, 25″ × 79″ × 40″, Christie's 12/87 (est. $10,000–$15,000) *$16,500* and *$19,800*.

Desk: Bradley House, Kankakee,IL (ca. 1900), overhanging top supported by eight legs, with six drawers on one side, two cabinet doors on the other, 27″ × 92″ × 34″, Christie's 12/87 (est. $50,000–$70,000) *$176,000*.

Library table: Coonley House, Riverside, IL (ca. 1908), overhanging top and lower shelf, between which is a projecting middle tier between four massive square legs, 29″ × 53″ × 20″, Christie's 12/87 (est. $18,000–$24,000) *$77,000*.

Library table: Coonley House, Riverside, IL (ca. 1908), overhanging top supported by two massive sides, joined with lower shelf, 28″ × 65″ × 39″, Christie's 12/87 (est. $15,000–$20,000) *$38,500*.

Morris chair: Little House, Peoria, IL (ca. 1902), wide single slat in back, which slides forward with seat, paneled sides, 40″ × 32″ × 27″, Christie's 6/87 (est.

As one would expect, Wright's rendition of a reclining chair (Martin House, 1902, 29″ × 29″ × 33″) differed significantly from those of other Arts and Crafts designers. The flared feet, capped rear posts, and paneled sides give this chair an architectural look, and its size made it difficult to move, which is precisely what Wright confessed to having intended on more than one occasion. *(Photo courtesy of Christie's, New York)*

$20,000–$30,000) *$60,500;* Christie's 12/87 (est. $30,000–$40,000) *$77,000.*

Server: Bradley House, Kankakee, IL (ca. 1900), with two tiers, the lower tier extending beyond the upper, which is supported by four square posts, with one drawer with ring pulls, 41″ × 36″ × 21″, Christie's 12/87 (est. $8000–$12,000) *$11,000.*

Table, dining and eight chairs: Barton House, Buffalo, NY (ca. 1903), table with overhanging top supported by four massive octagonal legs, spindles along two sides, 29″ × 60″ × 54″; chairs with ten square spindles extending from crest rail to lower stretcher, drop-in seats, 46″ high, Christie's 6/87 (est. $200,000–$300,000) *$594,000.*

Urn, copper: Dana House (ca. 1903) spherical form on four-part foot with raised design, 18″ high, Christie's 6/86 (est. $40,000–$60,000) *$82,500.*

Window, leaded: Bradley House (ca. 1900), 63″ × 14″, Christie's 6/86: *$3850*.

Window, leaded: Martin House (ca. 1904), 38″ × 19″, Christie's 12/87 (est. $14,000–$18,000) *$24,200*.

OTHER MISSION OAK FURNITURE MANUFACTURERS

"Do not confuse Limbert's Holland Dutch Arts and Crafts furniture with the many poorly constructed, ill-proportioned and uncraftsmanlike specimens of straight line furniture with which the market is flooded at the present time, and called all manner of names, such as "Crafts Style", "Mission", etc. etc. simply because it is devoid of ornamentation. This is not Arts and Crafts furniture. Take the two words, "Arts" and "Crafts," and think of them separately and try to define each. You will see that the expression really means that which is beautiful, truly artistic, and expressive of the highest ideals and purest conceptions of a talented mind combined with the cleverness, ingenuity and mechanical ability of a well trained craftsman."

—*Charles Limbert*[1]

As Thomas K. Maher explained in his introduction, once Gustav Stickley had demonstrated by 1902 that the American public was ready for a new style of furniture, dozens of factories soon thereafter began producing their own version of Mission oak furniture. While some of these companies were new, the majority had been producing period reproductions, fancy golden oak, or utility household furniture. For most the switch to Mission oak was simple; few of these companies went to the lengths of

1. Charles Limbert, *Limberts Holland Dutch Arts and Crafts Furniture Catalog* #112.

Stickley, Charles Limbert, or the Roycrofters to manufacture consistently high quality oak furniture.

Like Stickley, Limbert, and the Roycrofters, however, many of these companies adopted the practice of affixing a shopmark to their furniture. Unfortunately, since the quality varied tremendously even within the same firm, shopmarks do little but provide evidence as to which firm produced a particular piece; determining the quality of that same piece remains a separate task. Signed and unsigned pieces have since been commonly called "generic Mission oak," a term that is not entirely accurate since most of this furniture was at some time signed or identifiable. An unsigned piece should no more be deemed poor quality than a signed piece should be considered worthy of a premium simply because a paper label managed to survive for eighty years on the underside of a table. A label, decal, or brass tag can indicate only who made the piece, not how well it was made. In the final analysis, each piece must speak for itself.

Distinguishing between a well-constructed and a poorly constructed example of Mission oak furniture is relatively easy once the characteristics of low-quality Mission oak furniture are identified. In most cases, ample evidence will be found, including a number of the following:

- lack of pegged joints
- thin, lightweight hardware
- plain sawn lumber
- ash or hickory rather than quarter-sawn oak
- square chair stretchers
- flimsy drawer construction
- exposed screw heads or bolts
- no corbels under the arms
- false tenons
- awkward proportions
- imitation leather upholstery
- thin tops
- excessive use of veneers
- false mullions over a single sheet of glass
- gimmicks and novelties
- design characteristics from other furniture styles (Victorian paw feet, Queen Anne legs, barley-twist legs, scrollwork, etc.)

Advertisement from an August 1904 issue of *Furniture World*.
Note their slogan: "Originators of Bolted Mission Furniture."

While even the most respected furniture manufacturers of
the Arts and Crafts era may not have avoided each of these
characteristics on every piece of furniture, the inexpensive imitations will inevitably exhibit several. Some of the most valuable examples of Gustav Stickley furniture were not pegged
and his dining armchairs often did not have corbels under their
arms, but when all of the factors are considered on each piece
of furniture, it will become clear that the low-quality imitations suffer in comparison in not just one or two but in several
respects.

The list of companies included in this category will probably
never be complete, nor is any firm's inclusion indicative of the
quality of its furniture. The works of several companies, such
as Plail and Harden, are today sought by astute collectors
aware that the high quality of their furniture has thus far been
overlooked. As additional examples of such work surfaces—
while at the same time furniture by Stickley, Limbert, and
Roycroft grows more difficult to find—collectors will soon be
turning to the less publicized manufacturers of quality Mission
oak furniture.

BERKEY & GAY FURNITURE CO.
Grand Rapids, Michigan
  Active: 1873—ca. 1930
  General line of Mission oak furniture
  Shopmark: BERKEY & GAY FURNITURE CO in circle

BLACK RIVER BENDING CO.
Black River, New York
  Active: early 20th century
  General line of Mission oak furniture
  Shopmark: undetermined

BRIAR CLIFF
(see Craftsman's Shop of Ossining)

CADILLAC CABINET CO.
Detroit, Michigan
  Active: early 20th century
  General line of Mission oak furniture
  Shopmark: paper label

CATSKILL MISSION FURNITURE
Woodstock, New York
  Active: early 20th century
  Small Mission oak furniture
  Shopmark: CATSKILL MISSION FURNITURE/ WOODSTOCK, N.Y.

CHICAGO MISSION FURNITURE CO.
Chicago, Illinois
  Active: ca. 1904
  Mission oak chairs and tables
  Shopmark: paper label

COLUMBIA PARLOR FRAME COMPANY
Chicago, Illinois
  Active: early 20th century
  Line of Mission oak chairs, settles, and rockers
  Shopmark: undetermined

COME-PACKT FURNITURE COMPANY
Toledo, Ohio
  Active: early 20th century
  Mail order line of Mission oak furniture
  Shopmark: decal, COME-PACKT in rectangle

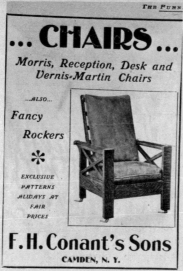

F. H. Conant's Sons were regular advertisers in *Furniture World* during the Arts and Crafts era, but their inventory was not restricted to Mission oak furniture. The cross-stretcher arrangement was repeated in several of their Mission oak forms.

F. A. CONANT'S SONS
Camden, New York
  Active: early 20th century
  General line of Mission oak furniture
  Shopmark: paper label

CONREY & BIRELY TABLE CO.
Shelbyville, Indiana
  Active: early 20th century
  General line of Mission oak furniture
  Shopmark: undetermined

CRAFTSMAN'S SHOP OF OSSINING
Ossining, New York
  Active: early 20th century
  General line of Mission oak furniture
  Shopmark: BRIAR CLIFF

H. T. CUSHMAN MFG. CO.
North Bennington, Vermont
  Active: early 20th century
  General line of Mission oak furniture
  Shopmark: undetermined

DELAWARE CHAIR CO.
Delaware, Ohio
  Active: early 20th century
  Mission oak chairs
  Shopmark: undetermined

M. C. DEXTER CHAIR CO.
Black River, New York
  Active: early 20th century
  General line of Mission oak furniture
  Shopmark: undetermined

J. S. FORD, JOHNSON & CO.
Chicago, Illinois
  Active: early 20th century
  Line of Mission oak chairs and library tables
  Shopmark: undetermined

FRANCISCAN SHOPS
Apulia, New York
  Active: early 20th century
  General line of Mission oak furniture
  Shopmark: paper label

L. G. FULLAM & SONS
Ludlow, Vermont
  Active: early 20th century
  General line of Mission oak furniture
  Shopmark: undetermined

GRAND LEDGE CHAIR COMPANY
Grand Ledge, Michigan
  Active: early 20th century
  General line of Mission oak furniture
  Shopmark: undetermined

GRAND RAPIDS BRASS & IRON BED CO.
Grand Rapids, Michigan
  Active: early 20th century
  Mission-style brass and iron beds
  Shopmark: undetermined

GRAND RAPIDS CHAIR COMPANY
Grand Rapids, Michigan
  Active: 1872–undetermined
  Extensive line of Mission oak furniture
  Shopmark: brass plaque

GRAND RAPIDS DESK COMPANY
Grand Rapids, Michigan
  Active: 1893–undetermined
  Limited line of Mission oak rolltop desks
  Shopmark: embossed brass escutcheon

GRAND RAPIDS FANCY FURNITURE CO.
Grand Rapids, Michigan
  Active: early 20th century
  General line of Mission oak furniture
  Shopmark: paper label

GRAND RAPIDS FURNITURE MFG. CO.
Grand Rapids, Michigan
  Active: early 20th century
  General line of Mission oak furniture, including unassembled mail
  order line
  Shopmark: undetermined

GRAND RAPIDS TABLE COMPANY
Grand Rapids, Michigan
  Active: early 20th century
  Mission oak tables
  Shopmark: undetermined

CHARLES A. GREENMAN CO.
Grand Rapids, Michigan
  Active: 1904–undetermined
  General line of Mission oak furniture
  Shopmark: undetermined

Camden, New York, was the site of several furniture companies, including the Harden Company, which manufactured a respected line of Mission oak furniture. The curved arms and double-crest rail illustrated in these two pieces are characteristic of their work. *(Photo courtesy of Robert W. Skinner, Boston)*

STANTON H. HACKETT
Philadelphia, Pennsylvania
  Active: early 20th century
  General line of Mission oak furniture
  Shopmark: undetermined

HARDEN FURNITURE COMPANY
Camden, New York
  Active: early 20th century
  General line of quality Mission oak furniture
  Shopmark: paper label

HARTMAN FURNITURE & CARPET CO.
Chicago, Illinois
  Active: early 20th century
  Mail-order line of Mission oak furniture
  Shopmark: undetermined

HUBBARD & ELDRIDGE CO.
Rochester, New York
  Active: early 20th century
  Mission oak chairs, rockers, footstools
  Shopmark: decal HUBBARD & ELDRIGE CO/ ROCHESTER NY

IMPERIAL FURNITURE COMPANY
Grand Rapids, Michigan
  Active: early 20th century

  General line of Mission oak furniture

  Shopmark: paper label

JAMESTOWN LOUNGE COMPANY
Jamestown, New York
  Active: early 20th century

  General line of Mission oak furniture

  Shopmark: undetermined

S. KARPEN & BROS.
Chicago, Illinois
  Solomon Karpen

  Active: 1880–1952

  Mission oak chairs, rockers, and parlor suites

  Shopmark: metal tag, KARPEN/ GUARANTEED/ UPHOLSTERED/ FURNITURE/ CHICAGO.

KIMBALL & CHAPPELL COMPANY
Chicago, Illinois
  Active: 1897–ca. 1920

  Mission-style brass and iron beds

  Shopmark: undetermined

LARKIN FURNITURE COMPANY
Buffalo, New York
  John D. Larkin (1845–1926)

  Active: 1901–1941

  General line of household furniture

  Shopmark: large paper label

LUCE FURNITURE CO.
Grand Rapids, Michigan
  Active: early 20th century

  General line of Mission oak furniture

  Shopmark: brass tag

MICHIGAN CHAIR COMPANY
Grand Rapids, Michigan
　Active: 1893–undetermined
　Complete line of Mission oak furniture
　Shopmark: circular paper label

MICHIGAN DESK COMPANY
Grand Rapids, Michigan
　Active: 1905–undetermined
　General line of Mission oak furniture
　Shopmark: undetermined

MILLER CABINET COMPANY
Rochester, New York
　Active: early 20th century
　General line of Mission oak furniture
　Shopmark: undetermined

MUELLER & SLACK
Grand Rapids, Michigan
　Active: early 20th century
　Upholstered Mission oak furniture
　Shopmark: undetermined

MUSKEGON FURNITURE CO.
Muskegon, Michigan
　Active: early 20th century
　General line of Mission oak furniture
　Shopmark: undetermined

NELSON-MATTER COMPANY
Grand Rapids, Michigan
　Active: 1885–1917
　"Modern English" Mission oak bedroom suites
　Shopmark: undetermined

OAK-WORTH SHOPS
Gouverneur, New York
　Active: early 20th century
　General line of Mission oak furniture
　Shopmark: OAKWORTH label

Few Mission oak firms went to the trouble and expense to produce a high-quality line of barrel-back furniture, but Plail & Company was an exception. The canted rear feet and other design elements may have been inspired by Frank Lloyd Wright. *(Photo courtesy of Robert W. Skinner, Boston)*

C. S. PAINE COMPANY
Grand Rapids, Michigan
Active: 1900–undetermined

Upholstered Mission oak chairs and settles

Shopmark: undetermined

PLAIL BROTHERS
Wayland, New York
Active: ca. 1910.

Quality Mission oak chairs and settles, often in a multiple-slat barrell-back design

Shopmark: oval paper label, PLAIL BROS. / WAYLAND, NY

PORTLAND FURNITURE COMPANY
Portland, Michigan
Active: early 20th century

Mission oak chairs

Shopmark: undetermined

PREMIER MANUFACTURING CO.
Grand Rapids, Michigan
Active: early 20th century

General line of Mission oak furniture

Shopmark: undetermined

JOHN D. RAAB CHAIR COMPANY
Grand Rapids, Michigan
  Active: early 20th century
  Mission oak chairs
  Shopmark: undetermined

RAMSEY-ALTON COMPANY
Portland, Michigan
  Active: early 20th century
  General line of Mission oak furniture
  Shopmark: "OAKCRAFT" brand

SHEYBOYGAN FURNITURE COMPANY
Sheyboygan, Wisconsin
  Active: ca. 1910
  Line of small Mission oak furniture: plant stands, wastebaskets, smoking stands, bookracks, etc.
  Shopmark: paper label

SKANDA FURNITURE CO.
Rockford, Illinois
  Active: early 20th century
  General line of Mission oak furniture
  Shopmark: undetermined

SKINNER AND STEENMAN
Grand Rapids, Michigan
  Active: early 20th century
  Line of Mission oak dining room suites
  Shopmark: undetermined

SWAN FURNITURE
Wadhams Mills, New York
  Active: early 20th century
  General line of Mission oak furniture
  Shopmark: MAYFLOWER label

SWEET AND BIGGS
Grand Rapids, Michigan
  Active: early 20th century
  Line of Mission oak chairs
  Shopmark: undetermined

SLIGH FURNITURE COMPANY
Grand Rapids, Michigan
Active: 1880–undetermined
Limited line of Mission oak furniture
Shopmark: brass tag

THOMPSON MANUFACTURING CO.
Holland, Michigan
Active: early 20th century
General line of smaller Mission oak furniture
Shopmark: paper label

TRAVERSE CITY CHAIR COMPANY
Traverse City, Michigan
Active: early 20th century
Line of Mission oak chairs
Shopmark: undetermined

MARTIN TROMP
Holland, Michigan
Active: early 20th century
Line of smaller Mission oak furniture
Shopmark: undetermined

UDELL WORKS
Indianapolis, Indiana
Active: early 20th century
General line of Mission oak furniture
Shopmark: red rectangular decal

C. A. WARNER & CO.
New York, New York
Active: early 20th century
Mission oak tall clocks
Shopmark: undetermined

WILKINSON & EASTWOOD
Binghamton, New York
Active: early 20th century
General line of Mission oak furniture
Shopmark: undetermined

While few of the thousands of Mission oak slat-sided clocks ever appear signed, the numerous ads placed in the trade publication *Furniture World* by C. A. Warner & Company could lead to the conclusion that many of them came from this New York factory.

WISCONSIN MANUFACTURING CO.
Jefferson, Wisconsin
 Active: early 20th century
 General line of Mission oak furniture
 Shopmark: undetermined

WOLVERINE MANUFACTURING CO.
Detroit, Michigan
 Active: early 20th century
 General line of Mission oak furniture
 Shopmark: large circular decal

PART 2
Art Pottery

Evaluating
Art Pottery

☐

David Rago

*David Rago has been involved in the Arts and Crafts field
since 1972. He has written extensively on a variety of topics within the Arts and Crafts spectrum, including a regular column for* The Antique Trader Weekly. *Since 1984
he has organized twice-yearly Arts and Crafts auctions,
which are currently held in New York City. Rago is the
founder and publisher of the* Arts & Crafts Quarterly *(P.O.
Box 3592, Station E, Trenton, New Jersey 08629), designed
for collectors, dealers, and scholars with an interest in the
furniture, pottery, and metalware of this period.*

WHAT YOU ARE ABOUT to read are the words of one attempting
the impossible. Establishing an evaluation scale for catalog furniture is difficult enough, where the variables between several
examples of any given form are usually restricted to date or
period, condition, and quality of finish. Presuming to do so for
art pottery is courting lunacy.

Nevertheless, some guidelines for specific potteries can be
established, based on prices realized at shows, in auction, and
privately. Please remember that the following information is
presented in an idealized format and is perhaps more valuable

if one uses the *ideas* implicit in these examples, rather than the examples themselves.

While there can be dozens of points to consider when determining the value of any given piece of pottery, we can simplify matters greatly if we concentrate on several key areas of concern:

1. *Maker or producer*. All things being equal, a vase by the Rookwood Pottery will always be worth two to three times more than an identical example by the Weller Pottery, for example. Similarly, Grueby Pottery will always be worth two to three times what a copy by the Hampshire Pottery will bring. What Rookwood and Grueby have in common is that both were the creators of a specific style of art pottery and both spawned their share of imitators who, generally, produced inferior work.

2. *Artistry*. Who decorated the pot? Rookwood's Kataro Shirayamadani was a man who understood ceramic decoration; he didn't decorate a vase but painted a vision; he didn't paint on the side of a pot but used the entire surface as a single canvas on which to give his ideas life. On a very bad day he could still paint his fellow artist Chlotilda Zannetta under the table, and his work will always be more valuable than hers.

   And what did the artist paint? By the very nature of the bloom, the fleshy voluptuousness of a poppy, with its sinewy tendril-like stems and broad-petaled flowers, will almost always be more visually appealing than a tighter, less interesting geranium. A rose by any other name would still smell as sweet and still bring twice the price of a spray of forsythia.

   As for style, at least at present, Victorian is out and Art Nouveau is in. Accordingly, our fleshy poppy rendered in a less fluid, more restrained Victorian palette and scheme will simply not command the same interest or price as a more vividly colored and visually stimulating Art Nouveau version.

3. *Form and size*. If you were a collector with limited shelf space, would you want ten low bowls occupying the same

area that twenty vases would use? And more, would you prefer the decoration on a pot being compressed into the restricted surface area of a low, wide bowl rather than seeing similar artistry rising up the surface of a vase form, dipping and winding its way around the hidden sides and offering new perspectives with each quarter turn?

A low bowl will never bring what a ten-inch vase is worth; nor will a ten-inch vase realize the same price as an eighteen-inch handled ewer, which is probably not as valuable as a twenty-four-inch floor vase. Form is crucial for both aesthetic and practical reasons. Size is and always has been an essential element of value.

While some have difficulty with this concept because bigger doesn't necessarily mean better, period artists understood that when working on a large piece, they were decorating an object that was to be priced at a much higher level and would receive much more attention in sales catalogs. You can believe with certainty that the bigger a pot, the more likely extra care was lavished on it; the more it cost at the time it was made, the more it is worth today.

4. *Condition.* That the condition of a piece affects price is obvious, but not all damage was created equally. Does a tight hairline hurt as much as a firing crack? How much does a chip affect the value of a Rookwood vase? How much does that same chip hurt a Grueby piece? What does a drill hole through the base of a Marblehead vase do to its price? To that of a Rookwood vase? You'll have to strap on the helmets for this part because this is where the ride really gets rough; the answers have more to do with the types of buyers certain potteries attract than with the damage or the potteries themselves.

Rookwood buyers, for example, are looking for the finest in representational art. A squash blossom painted on the side of a pot is to look like a squash blossom, with no frou-frou, stylization, or subterfuge. Anything that detracts from that exactness of appearance, that illusion of perfection, is a markdown. (Imagine an American diver at the Moscow Olympics performing in front of a panel of

Russian and East German judges.) And so that small chip at the top rim means the pot is now not perfect, nor is the visual magnificence unimpeded. Knock off about 50 percent for that minor flaw.

Grueby collectors are of a different breed. They are more emotionally inclined, buying for that particular interpretation of an organic naturalism expressed in true Arts and Crafts ceramic. They are hopeless romantics (which is considerably better than hopeful ones). That chip will not add to the value of a Grueby pot, but if the pot is particularly good, it won't hurt it much either. Take 10 percent off the top.

One could go on at length, criss-crossing the above variables into a scheme that could actually yield less clarity. Rather, for the purposes of presenting a cogent and useful package for the beginning ceramiphile, we will machete our way through the cornfield by working with some fixed variables:

1. *Form and size.* In all cases the example used will be the eight-inch vase form. Perhaps the average size of all art pottery, it is the neatest to grasp visually.

2. *Condition.* All examples should be considered perfect (i.e., free of chips, cracks, glaring manufacturing flaws, etc.). Comments will occasionally be made concerning the effect of damage on a particular piece.

3. *Style.* William Grueby basically worked in a single style, so when comparing different pieces of his pottery, that will not be an issue. Rookwood, however, produced work spanning many years and exhibiting many different decorative techniques. When style is a factor, it will be clearly defined as such. If it is not mentioned, assume it is not relevant.

4. *Quality of decoration and of the overall product.* As good a painter as Kataro Shirayamadani was, he was as susceptible to a beer binge as the next slip-decorator. Rather than weigh ourselves down with the nuances of an individual artist's highs and lows, let's assume that all examples used are above average in quality, though less than great. On a scale of one to ten, let's call our idealized examples

sevens. Occasionally, where fitting, comments will appear that will reflect on how lesser or better work would influence value.

5. *Subject matter*. While the decoration on the comparisons below will be concisely articulated, it is important for you to understand that we are going to work with readily accessible and extremely appropriate images. Rookwood pieces do occasionally surface decorated with mushrooms. However, because you are much more likely to find a vase with nasturtiums, we will be more likely to use the latter in our examples.

6. *Marks*. The purpose of this book is not to make experts of beginners but rather to assist beginners in their quest of establishing an expertise. As such, it is foolish to attempt to use this time to train a new eye so that it might learn to determine an unmarked Weller vase from an unmarked Roseville example. Let's assume that all pieces are either clearly marked in the proper manner or possess enough distinguishing characteristics that a proper mark is superfluous. Because it would take time and practice to understand exactly how a Van Briggle feathered, green, matte glaze differs from the one William Grueby used, believe that it is clearly discernible and that the examples used below are based on that assumption.

OK, you've been primed if not warned. Prepare to get your hands dirty. . . .

Rookwood Pottery

We're starting with the toughest pottery to evaluate, so, before losing hope, try to remember it gets easier after this one. Rookwood, as explained above, worked for many years in a variety of styles. To properly assess their product we must compare these particular styles with examples of their own kind as well as against pieces of another time or appearance.

We will work with the following, loosely delineated periods: early Victorian (1880 to 1895), later Victorian (1895 to 1905), Art Nouveau (1896 to 1910), and Modern (1915 to 1930).

This eight-inch, Iris-glazed vase was decorated by famed Rookwood artist Carl Schmidt. The Venetian harbor scene, a popular Rookwood subject, was painted in 1902. *(Photo courtesy of David Rago, Trenton)*

Early Victorian

Of all Rookwood's work, this remains the least appreciated and most undervalued. The work tends to be naive and confused (consider a vase with crabs and fishermen dancing around its surface), but it can be important, if for nothing more than historical consideration. The vases we'll compare will be decorated in the typical manner of the day, with wind-whipped bulrushes in black against a smeared brown ground and a flock of loosely defined crows flying overhead. Such pieces are usually under a clear high glaze (but not always) and date to about 1883 or 1884. While Rookwood often provided blanks for area clubs and home decorators, let's assume that our examples were painted by one of the permanent staff members such as Albert Valentien or Martin Rettig.

Vase 1 is the best painted of the three, with clearly defined rushes and a fair amount of depth between the foreground and background. The colors are a little more interesting, introducing some mahogany brown into the relatively drab scheme. The work encompasses the vase and is covered with a clear, shiny finish. It is worth about $600 to $800.

Vase 2 is almost identical in subject and quality, but the colors are lighter and the decoration is painted on a bisque field, which is considerably rarer. Also, the bisque treatment gives more depth to the work and adds a tactile sensation. It is worth about $750 to $1,000.

Vase 3 is of the same spirit, but the work is thicker, with less clarity and a coarser color selection. This is not a bad piece, but, unlike vase 1, it does not distinguish itself from most other examples you'll see from this period. It has a clear, shiny finish. It is worth about $400 to $600.

Later Victorian

Such pieces are distinguished by painted designs under deep brown glazes. Such decoration usually depicts flowers and plants, though Indians, historical figures, animals, and naked women occasionally surface. While the last may prove more interesting, we'll stick with flowers.

These pieces tended to be painted in a realistic manner, but the transparent brown overglaze itself created a murkiness that obscured the colors and sharpness. We will use two sets of examples, one with different artists and the other with different flowers.

Vase 1 of the first grouping was painted by Kataro Shirayamadani. The subject, as with all three of these vases, is nasturtium blossoms and leaves. Because of the vision of this artist, the natural slinky quality of the stems has been exaggerated so that a network of organic design covers most of the pot. The definition is excellent. This pot is worth $650 to $850.

Vase 2 is similar but painted by only a good, if capable, Fred Rothenbusch. His flowers are fine, but the inquisitiveness of the plant was never developed, and the blooms lack Shirayamadani's definition—$325 to $450.

Vase 3 was decorated by Clara Lindeman the day after she cracked her knee ice skating on the Ohio River. The flowers are clearly nasturtiums, but one would have a hard time believing they ever craved water—$275 to $375.

For the second grouping let's assume the quality of artwork is equal and all were brushed by Mr. Rothenbusch.

Vase 4 shows a ring of small-petaled daisies—$300 to $400.

Vase 5 depicts a nicely articulated cluster of lilac blossoms—$350 to $500.

Vase 6 bears a rich growth of fleshy and interesting orchids—$400 to $600.

Art Nouveau

This period probably saw Rookwood's best and most interesting work. They were on top of the painted pottery world and captured medals and ribbons from some of the world's toughest and most prestigious competitions. Further, the Art Nouveau style has remained the most favored by modern collectors of Rookwood pottery. The prices below will reflect this preference.

Vase 1 has a decoration painted by Kataro Shirayamadani identical to the first example in the Late Victorian section. However, it is under a clear shiny glaze (called "Iris glaze"), and the nasturtiums are vividly painted against a cream to mint green ground—$950 to $1,200.

Vase 2, again by Rothenbusch, is also under a clear, high glaze, though the background colors shade from cream to gray (almost all pieces in this style shade from lighter to darker colors)—$800 to $1,000.

Vase 3 is more of the same, but because of Lindeman's heavy hand, more obvious due to the truthful nature of a clear glaze, the flower is even less realistic than in the late Victorian version—$700 to $900.

Something that should be addressed at this point is crazing, or the light checking in the overglaze that looks like fracturing. Contrary to popular belief, this occurred during the glaze-firing process when the vase expanded more than the glasslike jacket that covered it.

Usually the crazing is light or not particularly distracting. Our examples above are all lightly crazed (not unlike some of the people who collect them). Occasionally, pieces were fired poorly, and the crazing is heavy, with small, tight squares of checking over the entire surface of the pot. For such examples one must deduct about 20 percent from the prices above. Rarely, pieces from this early period are found with no crazing. This is a major plus and perhaps as much as 30 percent can be added to the price of these.

One last word about crazing is that around 1915 Rookwood developed their clay bodies and glazes enough so that crazing became the exception rather than the norm. While an uncrazed example after 1915 is still preferable to the minority that did not fire perfectly, the disparity in price is not quite as great because, simply, they are more available.

Modern

Pieces from this later period were usually painted with strong, stylized designs under clear, uncrazed, glossy finishes. Assume that our examples below bear these traits. While such decoration still tended toward the representational, where an iris blossom was clearly an iris blossom, some element of the design usually was rendered in a slightly stylized, if not conventionalized, manner.

Vase 1 was painted by our aging friend Kataro Shirayamadani. Though his imagination had seen better days, he remained one of the company's top three artists until he left. This vase is decorated with yellow, star-shaped daffodils painted on a light blue to cream ground—$700 to $1,000.

Vase 2 was finished by the brush of Edward Diers, one of Rookwood's better and most consistent artists through his tenure there. His work was a cut below Shirayamadani's, though what he lacked in clarity he mostly supplemented with a style and sense of color clearly his own. This vase is decorated with white hydrangea blossoms on a dark green to yellow-green ground—$600 to $800.

Vase 3 was decorated by Flora King, one of the marginal decorators hired by Rookwood later on. Her work was distinguished by relatively flat painting in a bright palette such as a child would choose. Our third example shows unconvincing violet blossoms and leaves on an unshaded cream ground—$300 to $400.

A Rookwood plaque serves as a backdrop for two Grueby vases. While the size of the large Grueby vase is impressive, the lower bowl has the added distinction of having a second color applied to the alternating flowers. *(Photo courtesy of David Rago, Trenton)*

Grueby

Shifting gears, we'll now evaluate the prices of some of William Grueby's pottery, diametrically opposed to the sort of work produced by Rookwood. As described in the section that follows, Grueby worked with stylized designs under green matte finishes. Again, our comparison pieces will be eight inches tall and will bear similar green matte glazes. We will compare two different sets of vases to correspond with two levels of Grueby's production.

For the most part, decorated vases have tooled leaves and buds or flowers, applied to the surface of the thrown pot and then glazed. Grueby's choice of forms was crucial to the appearance of a piece, and subtle variations can make a drastic difference in scarcity and value.

Vase 1 is of a flaring cylindrical form with long, broad, vertical leaves reaching from top to bottom. It is classic Grueby in its simplicity and completeness and is worth about $650 to $850.

Vase 2 is identical to our first piece, but in addition to the leaves, simple bud forms alternate with the leaf points near the vase's mouth—$750 to $1,000.

Vase 3 is a bit broader in form with a swell in the center and a gentle flare at the opening. It does not have buds at the top, but the leaves overlap one another to form a rare and interesting pattern around the pot—$850 to $1,100.

Our second grouping is different in that each piece has a flower design tooled onto its surface that is glazed in a color that contrasts the green background. The most common second color is yellow, which will be our color of choice here.

Vase 1 is a bulging cylinder with long, spiked, green leaves and simple bud forms in yellow around the top. It is very much like Vase 2 in the first grouping except more colorful—$1,200 to $1,500.

Vase 2 is again of bulging cylindrical form, but tooled daffodils rather than buds accompany the green leaves—$2,250 to $2,750.

Vase 3 is a football shape with broad green leaves and colored iris blossoms, a flower somewhat rarer than daffodils. Also, the broader form allows for more surface on which to lay more decoration—$3,000 to $3,500.

Newcomb

Newcomb College was another Arts and Crafts producer working in two basic styles, with earlier, conventionalized designs under clear, shiny glazes, and later, carved work with matte finishes. The former are rarer and show a more varied range of decorative motifs. The latter were produced for a much longer period of time, and the designs tended to be repeated. We will start with the earlier work.

Vase 1 is decorated by Leona Nicholson, one of their best artists. It shows tooled iris blossoms in blue under a clear, high glaze. The leaves are green, and the background is cream with dark blue outlines—$2,250 to $2,750.

Vase 2 is decorated by one of any number of lesser decorators. Surface-painted dandelions are sketched in blue on a cream ground. The work is good but lacks the dimension of the first piece—$1,400 to $1,750.

Vase 3 is similar to our first vase, but tooled poppies are depicted in yellow and blue on a cream-and-green-banded ground. The introduction of a bright color such as yellow has a dramatic effect on the visual strength of the piece and ultimately on its value. The tooled surface, as on our first example, also adds to the dimension and contributes to the tactile quality of the pot—$3,000 to $4,000.

The pieces in this second grouping are all later, matte-glazed pieces and, for the sake of this comparison, bear a similar decoration of yellow daffodils on a blue ground.

Vase 1 shows decoration restricted to the top rim with moderate mottling of the vase's surface—$500 to $650.

Vase 2 has decoration that covers more of the surface, with the leaves stretching to the bottom of the pot. The carving is a little deeper and the coloration is a little stronger, with the blues deeper and a hint of green in the leaves—$650 to $900.

Vase 3 is the best of the grouping, with strong carving giving a good sense of depth to the flowers. The colors too are fine, with the blues deep, the green minty, and the yellow relatively vivid. This is an exceptional piece of matte period Newcomb—$900 to $1,300.

Teco

Teco Pottery is very much in vogue these days, perhaps because of their association with architect Frank Lloyd Wright and his use of certain pieces in his interiors. Covered almost exclusively in their distinctive, porous, green matte glaze, the best pieces show organic or architectural forms with handles, fins, and/or reticulations. Teco supposedly produced over thirteen hundred forms while in operation, and you can be assured that the boring, simple pieces far outnumber the vibrant, exciting ones.

We will compare the two main styles, architectural and organic, using fairly accessible forms, all under the green matte glaze. We will start with architectural.

Vase 1 is a corset form with straight, vertical handles starting at the flared base and ending at the flared rim. As with all such pieces, the lines are rectilinear and simple, relying on a visual strength resulting from the integration of individual components—$1,000 to $1,300.

Vase 2 is a straight-walled cylinder with simple, raised, vertical buttresses running the length of the pot. Though eight inches tall it is only about four inches wide—$600 to $800.

Vase 3 is a bulbous-bottomed vase with a wide, cylindrical neck buttressed with four broad, L-shaped handles joining the neck and the body. It is strong and massive for an eight-inch pot—$1,150 to $1,500.

Teco's organic forms are characterized by either curved or swirling, leaflike handles or embossed organic designs (such as corn kernels) over the pot's surface. While the overall appearance of these pots is striking, the individual elements of design are interesting in and of themselves.

Vase 1 is a bulbous-bottomed vase with a tapered neck and flared rim. Blades of grass are embossed up its neck, and the opening ends with raised nubs or spikes. There are no handles—$750 to $950.

Vase 2 has a thinner, bulbous bottom, a long, thin neck, and a flared rim. Four long, thin, curving handles extend from the bulbous bottom and end under the flared rim. This is an interesting form but not as rare or intense as better examples—$1,100 to $1,600.

Vase 3 is a cylinder with a flared rim. Twelve densely packed rows of leaves as handles come off the pot at its base and rejoin under its neck. The flared rim is spiked. This is a great compact piece—$4,500 to $5,500.

Marblehead

Marblehead is another New England–based Arts and Crafts pottery producer working with simple vase forms glazed in fine matte finishes and, when decorated, showing uncomplicated, conventionalized designs. Their ware was either plain or decorated, so we will compare examples of each. Remember that, for Marblehead, eight-inch pieces are far from common, especially if decorated.

Vase 1 is a bulging cylinder finished in a simple dark blue matte. This is one of the most common colors and perhaps the least valuable—$125 to $175.

Vase 2 is similar in form but in a medium to dark green, which is less common and more attractive—$175 to $225.

Vase 3 is a tapering cylinder with a gently flared rim, covered in a mocha brown matte, one of their rarest and most desirable colors—$275 to $375.

The second grouping compares three decorated pieces. Earlier pieces seldom bore more than two colors and usually depicted highly conventionalized, abstract geometric motifs. Middle-period pieces occasionally showed geometric designs but more often depicted curvilinear floral forms. Decoration could be either surface-painted or surface-painted and incised, the latter being preferable. Earlier pieces tended to be incised and painted, while later pieces were usually just painted.

Vase 1 is a tall, gentle corset form with dark green geometric designs tooled into a pea green ground. It is simple, striking, and austere—$1,500 to $2,000.

Vase 2 is a tapering cylinder with stylized trees in dark blue on a medium blue ground. The contrast could be better, and the lack of incising does not help. This is a sizable piece but not visually gripping—$1,150 to $1,650.

Vase 3 is a one-in-a-thousand pot with sweeping vines and berries in dark blue incised into a brown ground. The decoration is clear and in harmony with the form—$2,750 to $3,250.

Assuming for a moment that a small drill hole had been added to the side of any of the three last pieces, how much would that affect value? Such damage, visible and irrevocable, would drastically reduce a piece's worth and salability. However, Vase 3 would still be worth the most and would remain the easiest to sell. Unrestored, this pot would realize about $1,250 to $1,500. Vase 2, the least interesting of our grouping, would be worth about $600 to $800. And Vase 1, still worth owning, would bring about $800 to $1,100.

Although the severe mid-body twist dominates the appearance of this George Ohr vase, a close examination reveals very detailed technical work around the ruffled rim. This seven-inch vase was inscribed and dated 1898. *(Photo courtesy of David Rago, Trenton)*

George Ohr

George Ohr's work is the least predictable and probably the most difficult to evaluate because of the unique nature of each piece. Nevertheless, brilliance of color, intricacy of form, and the presence of the master's creative spark are distinctions that assist in determining the greatness of a piece.

Vase 1 is a corset form with a severe in-body twist at its center and a mottled, medium to dark green, high-gloss finish. It is an interesting form and, for Ohr, fairly large. However, the glazing is not vibrant and the form far from overpowering— $1,500 to $2,000.

Vase 2 has a bulbous bottom and a long neck ending in a severe flare. There are spaghetti handles on each side, looped and kinky. The glaze is medium green with red splotches and blue drips. Clearly a step up from Vase 1—$3,250 to $3,750.

Vase 3 is a tapering cylinder with applied, kinky spaghetti handles. It is covered with a light to medium blue high gloss

This unusual twelve-inch Fulper vase features four small buttresses and a blue flambé glaze. A second label indicated it had been displayed at the Panama-Pacific Exposition in San Francisco in 1915—an added bonus to its value. *(Photo courtesy of David Rago, Trenton)*

splotched with a vibrant orange glaze and drizzled with a bright pink. There are several deep in-body twists rippling through the body. This is one serious pot—$6,500 to $8,500.

Fulper

The Fulper Pottery produced a good-quality yet fairly affordable ware compatible with the Arts and Crafts interior. The glazes were good but limited to about fifteen colors and combinations. They sold through catalogs, and though variations certainly exist, the forms can be quite predictable. It is a good pottery for the serious beginner because fine examples can be had at relatively affordable prices. They were produced over a period of twenty-five years, until the mid-1930s, but we'll restrict ourselves to pieces dating until about 1922 for the sake of quality and consistency. These are pieces with either a rectangular, vertical, black ink-stamp mark or a vertical incised designation.

Vase 1 is a bulbous piece with a thick, cylindrical neck and a gently flared rim. The glaze, though early and rich, is a relatively common moss green dripping unevenly over a brick red matte—$275 to $350.

Vase 2 is a cylindrical form with embossed mushrooms around the base. Vases with embossed decoration are rare, and this is one of their more interesting examples. The glaze is a butterscotch brown flambé—$650 to $850.

Vase 3 is a bulbous, tapering cylinder vase with a creamy white, high gloss dripping unevenly over a fine mustard matte finish. This is a rare form with an excellent glaze—$1,000 to $1,500.

Please remember that the above examples are the estimated prices of imaginary pieces. These are rather accurate, based on today's market and will be even more helpful if augmented by the pieces pictured and evaluated in the following text. When in doubt, be conservative.

Ultimately, if one is to develop a sense of the potter's art, it is essential that the criteria designated at the beginning of this chapter are seen not as individual elements but rather parts of a single picture. The ability of the artist to harmonize the disparities between form, design, and technique is what distinguishes an average or a bad pot from a great one.

ARC-EN-CIEL POTTERY

Shopmark:
Impressed or imprinted *ARC-EN-CIEL* in arched outline of a rainbow

Principal Contribution:
Brief line of iridescent art pottery

Founders:
John Lessell, manager
Born: ca. 1871   Died: 1925

James Buckingham
Born: unknown   Died: unknown
Founded: 1903   Closed: 1907

Studios and Salesrooms:
Arc-En-Ciel Pottery Company
Zanesville, Ohio
1903–1905

The Brighton Pottery Company
Zanesville, Ohio
1905–1907

The firm exhibited its iridescent art pottery at the Louisiana Purchase Exposition in St. Louis in 1904, but a popular following failed to materialize. It was discontinued in 1905 when the firm switched to the production of household kitchenwares under the Brighton tradename.

Selected Prices

Due to the infrequency with which examples of this pottery appear on the market, establishing an in-depth price guide has not yet been possible. Until additional information is compiled, readers are advised to seek counsel from experienced collectors before either buying or selling important pieces.

AREQUIPA POTTERY

Shopmarks:
Incised or impressed letters *A* and *P* overlapping one another
Incised or impressed tree and jug with the words AREQUIPA/
CALIFORNIA
Paper label, again with tree and jug and words *AREQUIPA/
CALIFORNIA*
Any of the above in combination with the initials of the pottery
directors

Principal Contribution:
Decorated art pottery and tiles

Founders:
Dr. Philip King Brown and Henry E. Bothin, benefactors of the
Arequipa Sanitorium
Frederick H. Rhead, first director
Founded: 1911   Closed: 1918

Studios and Salesrooms:
Arequipa Pottery
Arequipa Sanitorium
Fairfax, California
1911–1918

"All the work is done by hand; everything, throwing the vase, drying, baking, decorating being done slowly, with individual interest. . . . The larger pieces are thrown by a man, but the rest of the work is done by the girls, who when they first come are not able to work more than an hour a day."

—*The Craftsman*
1913[1]

It is difficult not to compare the evolution and development of the art pottery produced at the Arequipa Pottery in Fairfax, California, with that of the Marblehead Pottery in Marblehead, Massachusetts, for several reasons. First, it was the success of the experiment begun in 1904 at Marblehead, in which crafts such as woodcarving, weaving, and pottery decorating were used as therapy for patients recovering from nervous break-downs, that inspired Dr. Philip King Brown and Henry E. Bothin to fund the Arequipa Sanitorium. Second, while other crafts were attempted, it was the pottery operation at both institutions that proved the most successful—artistically, if not financially.

Unfortunately, the Arequipa Pottery differed from the Marblehead Pottery in two significant ways, effectively preventing the California pottery from achieving the advanced and consistent quality represented by the Marblehead trademark.

At Marblehead the pottery operation quickly evolved into a separate entity from the medical institution, thus enabling its director, Arthur E. Baggs (1886–1947), to become its owner as well, ensuring consistent leadership and direction for the pottery. At Arequipa a similiar attempt was made, as the pottery was incorporated in 1913 while under the supervision of its first director, Frederick H. Rhead (1880–1942). Rhead had worked for the Jervis, Roseville, and Weller potteries before being contacted by Brown and Bothin, but problems with the transition from a workshop within the sanitarium to a separate business dependent on a work force of young female patients recovering from tuberculosis led to his departure only a few months later. Subsequently, a new director was named, and in 1915 the

---

1. Eloise Roorbach, "Making Pottery on the California Hills," *The Craftsman* (June 1913), p. 345.

corporation was dissolved, officially reverting responsibility for the pottery's management back to the sanitarium directors, who had always hoped that the "sale of the pottery would help finance [the patients'] hospitalization at the Arequipa Sanitorium."[2]

The pottery's second director, Albert L. Solon, improved the glazes being used on their wares and expanded both the number of young women working at the pottery and the sales network for their products. "Whereas Rhead had concentrated on matte glazes and raised 'squeeze-bag' decoration, Solon chose glossy glazes and carved decorations."[3] Like Rhead, Solon utilized California clays, most notably a bed of clay located on the grounds of the sanitarium; also like Rhead, Solon's efforts were hampered by the large turnover of patient-workers in the pottery. The time required for a young woman to become competent at decorating, carving, or glazing the pottery would often equal that required for her recovery, since the sanitarium was intended primarily for patients with mild cases of tuberculosis, and many stayed only four to five months.[4] As a result, the quality of the pottery produced at Arequipa varied considerably.

When Solon left in 1916 to accept a teaching position with what would later become known as California State University at San Jose, the directors chose Fred H. Wilde as his successor. Wilde brought considerable experience in both the development of new glazes and in tile production and had just begun to establish Arequipa Pottery's reputation as a source of quality interior tiles when "the war in Europe raised havoc with prices, and the pottery operation was brought to a close in 1918."[5]

2. Wendy Kaplan, ed., *The Art That Is Life: The Arts & Crafts Movement in America 1875–1920* (Boston: Museum of Fine Arts, 1987), p. 311.

3. Ibid.

4. Paul Evans, *Art Pottery of the United States* (New York: Charles Scribner's Sons, 1974), p. 19.

5. Ibid., p. 20.

While many examples of Arequipa pottery depended on their glaze and form for their effect, decorated pieces such as these three are the most sought-after of this California pottery's production. Examples decorated with Rhead's "squeeze-bag" technique stand at the top of Arequipa pottery. *(Photo courtesy of David Rago, Trenton)*

Selected Prices

Bowl: decoration folding over sides of low, square bowl, brownish semimatte glaze, 2″ × 10″, *$300–$350.*

Bowl: blue-green lava bubble glaze, 2″ × 8″, *$125–$150.*

Bowl: brown-purple glaze, 6″ × 8″, *$175–$200.*

Bowl: low, closed form with flaring sides, dark green matte glaze, *$125–$150.*

Vase: squat, bulbous form decorated with a tulip floral border in burnt orange on pale blue ground, 4″, *$225–$250.*

Vase: squat, square form with vertical ribs in cream glaze, 4″, *$225–$250.*

Vase: squat, bulbous form with high-gloss white finish over powder blue glaze, 6″ × 12″, *$275–$300.*

Vase: bulbous form in brownish burgundy matte, incised stylized leaf design circling the pot, 5" × 5", *$200–$225*.

Vase: white high-gloss glaze with stylized leaf decoration, 10" × 6", *$300–$350*.

Vase: cream-colored matte glaze with tulip decoration, 4" × 3", *$325–$375*.

Vase: brown matte glaze, impressed flower decoration, 2" × 6", *$300–$350*.

Vase: white and mottled green glaze, squeeze-bag decoration, 3" × 7", *$1850–$2100*.

Vase: yellow-green matte glaze with drip decoration, 7" × 3", *$345–$395*.

Vase: black-brown lava bubble glaze, 4" × 6", *$250–$275*.

Vase: dark gray matte glaze with brown speckled highlights, 3" × 2", *$175–$200*.

Vase: cucumber green matte glaze with leaf design, 6" × 2", *$275–$325*.

Vase: light gray-blue matte glaze over white, 4" × 3", *$175–$200*.

Vase: light gray-green drip glaze on bulbous form, 4", *$140–$165*.

Vase: medium blue glaze with leaf highlights, 8" × 4", *$300–$350*.

Vase: brown-purple drip glaze, 5" × 7", *$125–$150*.

Vase: light brown-gray, semimatte glaze, 6" × 5", *$110–$125*.

AVON POTTERY

Avon

Shopmark:
Incised *AVON*

Principal Contribution:
Small number of hand-thrown vases, mugs, and bowls

Founder:
Karl Langenbeck

Born: 1861   Died: 1938
Founded: 1886   Closed: 1888

Studios and Salesrooms:
Avon Pottery
Cincinnati, Ohio
1886–1888

Karl Langenbeck, a trained chemist, helped develop early production at Rookwood but was released in 1885. The following year he established the Avon Pottery. Although the pottery lasted only two years, it provided a basis for the careers of both Langenbeck and one of its apprentices, Artus Van Briggle. Langenbeck's line of art pottery featured "atomized colors and painted designs ... covered with a brilliant, untinted transparent glaze."[1] Van Briggle left in 1887 to work for Rookwood before organizing his own pottery. Langenback became a respected ceramic writer and worked in the management at Grueby Pottery.

1. Paul Evans, *Art Pottery of the United States* (New York: Charles Scribner's Sons, 1974), p. 23.

Selected Prices

Due to the infrequency with which examples of this pottery appear on the market, establishing an in-depth price guide has not yet been possible. The examples listed below are indicative only of the value of pieces of similiar form and decoration. Until additional information is compiled, readers are advised to seek counsel from experienced collectors before either buying or selling important pieces.

Vase: bulbous-bottomed with bulging neck and rolled rim, cobalt blue flowers and brown five-petal flowers, against gray-brown ground, incised curvilinear design on neck, 4″ × 6″, $225–$250.

Vase: bulbous top, collar rim, orange-red berries and green leaves on light green ground, 5″ × 5″, $175–$200.

EDWIN BENNETT POTTERY

Shopmarks:
Paper label with BRUBENSUL/EDWIN BENNETT POTTERY CO./BALTIMORE, MD. U.S.A.
Words *E.BENNETT POTTERY CO*, often with year and name of form, *ALBION*

Principal Contribution:
Commercial pottery and a brief line of art pottery vases

Founder:
Edwin Bennett

Born: 1818   Died: 1908
Founded: 1845   Closed: 1936

Studios and Salesrooms:
E. & W. Bennett
Baltimore
ca. 1845–1856

Edwin Bennett Pottery
Baltimore
1856–1938

Edwin Bennett had been a successful potter for more than fifty years when he decided to introduce a line of art pottery in 1894. Like his three brothers, Bennett had emigrated to the United States from England by 1841, when the three joined to form Bennett & Brothers in East Liverpool, Ohio, to produce the popular Rockingham ware using local clay. Edwin left in 1844 and by late the following year had established his own pottery in Baltimore.

The Edwin Bennett Pottery Company soon built a reputation for high-quality commercial earthenware and porcelain goods, including jugs, coffee- and teapots, vases, and, after 1869, tableware. Bennett may have been inspired by the exhibitions of art pottery at the 1893 Columbian Exposition in Chicago, for in 1894 his pottery introduced Brubensul. "This earthenware line, principally of jardinieres and pedestals, featured a combination of majolica-like glazes, especially of rich browns, orange, crimson, blue and green, which flowed and blended together in the firing."[1]

In 1895 Bennett introduced his second and last venture into art pottery production. Albion was Bennett's line of slip-decorated underglaze pottery. The body was often painted green, then decorated with slips of tinted clay to create desert or jungle scenes, including exotic animals, hunters, dancers, and riders.

1. Paul Evans, *Art Pottery of the United States* (New York: Charles Scribner's Sons, 1974), pp. 96–97.

Unfortunately, neither of Bennett's lines of art pottery proved financially successful, and after 1897 the experiment was dropped. Edwin Bennett lived until 1908, and his pottery remained in business until it too became a victim of the Great Depression.

Selected Prices

Due to the infrequency with which examples of this pottery appear on the market, establishing an in-depth price guide has not yet been possible. Until additional information is compiled, readers are advised to seek counsel from experienced collectors before either buying or selling important pieces.

BROUWER POTTERY
(Middle Lane Pottery)

Shopmarks:
Incised or impressed arch formed by two jawbones of a whale over the letter *M*
Incised in script, *FLAME*, and/or drawing of a flame
Incised script signature *BROUWER* (appears after 1903)

Principal Contribution:
Art pottery bowls and vases with rich glazes

Founder:
Theophilus A. Brouwer
Born: 1864   Died: 1932
Founded: 1894   Closed: 1946

Studios and Salesrooms:
Middle Lane Pottery
East Hampton, New York
1894–1902

Brouwer Pottery
West Hampton, New York
1903–1946

"With regard to the manner of my discovering this 'Fire Paint-ing,' I am frequently asked if it was by accident. It certainly was not, unless one considers seeing a bit of iridescent color on the bottom of a little sand crucible an accident. I saw this bit of color and determined to find out how it got there. It took me months of hard work, literally day and night before my muffle furnace door."

—*T. A. Brouwer*
1917[1]

Unlike the vast majority of the turn-of-the-century art potters, Theophilus A. Brouwer was seemingly unconcerned about the quantity of vases and bowls he produced. Brouwer essentially ran a one-man pottery, despite the fact that he had no formal training in glazes and served no apprenticeship under an experienced potter. The results of his experiments, however, revealed an artistic genius whose work, like that of fellow potter George Ohr or furniture designer Charles Rohlfs, created a new category of its own.

Brouwer's experiments concentrated more on glazes than forms or underglaze decoration, such as the technique of slip painting developed by Laura Fry at Rookwood. When ornament was applied, as in the case of leaves atop his vases, "they were formed separately, then crimped and light-heartedly applied."[2] Brouwer created glaze formulas designed to be fired at extreme temperatures for relatively short periods of time. "The pottery was exposed almost directly to the ultimate heat of the open furnace, the maturing and lustering of the piece taking place in

1. Frederick H. Rhead, *The Potter* (January 1917), pp. 43–49.
2. Martin Eidelberg, ed., *From Our Native Clay* (New York: Turn of the Century Editions, 1987), p. 68.

as little as seventeen minutes, once the process was refined."[3] Depending on the glaze formula and the particular firing technique, the pieces would emerge from their cooling stage with either a rich iridescence, a metallic luster, a crystalline formation, or any number of mottled colors encased in either a glossy or matte surface. One author has referred to them as "a series of rich, iridescent glazes with various textures and even with elusive suggestions of imagery."[4]

"Unlike the sober mat surfaces of Grueby and Merrimac," it has been noted in *From Our Native Clay*, "Brouwer's iridescent glazes are erratically colorful, much like the potter himself."[5]

Around 1900 Brouwer classified his work into five categories:

Fire Painting: His first and perhaps most famous process involved "the manipulation of the biscuit-fired, raw-glazed piece in what was practically an open reduction kiln."[6] The reaction between the glaze and the extreme heat would produce a variety of mottled colors under a high glaze.

Iridescent Fire Painting: Though similar in technique to Fire Painting, the result was a solid color with a rough texture, more iridescence, but fewer combined colors.

Kid Surface: The matte finish and solid colors (brown, white, blue, and gray) were the result of a roughly applied glaze.

Sea-Grass Fire Painting: The reaction between the glaze and the heat of the kiln produced "lines that look like sea grass . . . in green, brown, or gray on the plain glaze."[7]

3. Paul Evans, *Art Pottery of the United States* (New York: Charles Scribner's Sons, 1974), p. 174.

4. Robert Judson Clark, ed., *The Arts and Crafts Movement in America: 1876–1916* (Princeton, NJ: Princeton University, 1972), p. 128.

5. Martin Eidelberg, ed., *From Our Native Clay* (New York: Turn of the Century Editions, 1987), p. 68.

6. Paul Evans, *Art Pottery of the United States* (New York: Charles Scribner's Sons, 1974), pp. 173–174.

7. Ralph and Terry Kovel, *The Kovels' Collectors Guide to American Art Pottery* (New York: Crown Publishers, 1974), p. 7.

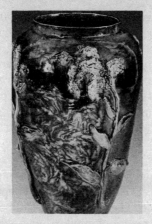

Black-and-white photographs cannot do justice to the Flame pottery of Brouwer. The orange and yellow goldenrod form a vivid contrast to a swirling brown background on a rare twelve-inch form. *(Photo courtesy of David Rago, Trenton)*

Gold Leaf Underglaze: Authentic gold leaf was applied between two layers of colored glaze before final firing.

Brouwer moved his pottery in 1903, designing, supervising, and building parts of his new three-building compound himself. Once settled into his new pottery, Brouwer went to work perfecting a technique and a line he called Flame Painting. "For this process only a hard body was used, and each piece of work was unique in concept as well as glaze treatment, the latter best described as catching and retaining 'the prismatic hues of the spectrum with a true rainbow iridescence.' "[8] Modern critics consider the results of his Flame Painting technique "the most successful and most visually dramatic of his eccentric and personal approaches to art pottery."[9] Accordingly, once Brouwer was satisfied with the results of the firing, he destroyed each mold.

8. Paul Evans, *Art Pottery of the United States* (New York: Charles Scribner's Sons, 1974), p. 175.
9. Martin Eidelberg, ed., *From Our Native Clay* (New York: Turn of the Century Editions, 1987), p. 96.

After 1911 Brouwer's interests widened, and his pottery pursuits occupied less and less of his time. Although a corporation that was formed in 1925 to promote his Fire Painted pottery was not dissolved until 1946, fourteen years after Brouwer's death, it does not appear that the project resulted in the production of any additional work by Brouwer or by anyone using his unorthodox techniques.

Selected Prices

Due to the infrequency with which examples of this pottery appear on the market, establishing an in-depth price guide has not yet been possible. The examples listed below are indicative only of the value of pieces of similar form and decoration. Until additional information is compiled, readers are advised to seek counsel from experienced collectors before either buying or selling important pieces.

Vase: Chinese shape with tapered foot and rim, iridescent magenta, medium blue and green-gold high glaze, 5″ × 5″, *$2250–$2750.*

Vase: bulbous bottom, long flaring cylindrical neck, glazed in iridescent brown and green-gold high glaze, 9″ × 5″, *$1500–$1750.*

Vase: bulbous bottom, long, flaring neck, glazed in violent orange and gold with green trillings, 7″ × 4″, *$1400–$1650.*

Vase: tall and bulging form with small collar rim, decorated with four applied yellow and brown goldenrod on stunning brown and gold iridescent flame-painted background, 12″ × 8″, *$7000–$8000.*

Vase: bulbous, with bulging rim and flame painted in iridescent yellow, orange, and brown, 8″ × 6″, *$2000–$2250.*

BUFFALO POTTERY

Shopmarks:
(Pre-1915) Stamped ink mark showing a grazing buffalo, plus the
words *BUFFALO POTTERY*, generally with the date
(Post-1915) Stamped ink mark with the words *BUFFALO
CHINA*, generally with the date until 1940

Principal Contribution:
Wide range of designs of tableware

Founder:
John D. Larkin

Born: 1845   Died: 1926
Founded: 1901   Closed: currently Buffalo
China, Inc.

Studios and Salesrooms:
The Buffalo Pottery Company
Buffalo, New York
1901–1956

"I was told the Company did not want to build a pottery, but
was forced to erect and equip one, to prevent delays in delivery,

and give its customers best quality by maintaining a fixed standard and protecting them from inferior workmanship."

—*"My Trip Through the Larkin Factory"*[1]
1913

At the age of thirty, John D. Larkin sold his interest in his
former employer's Chicago soap company and returned with his
new wife to his hometown of Buffalo, New York. Once they had
arrived, Larken immediately began looking for a small building
to house the soap factory he planned to establish. Before the
year had ended, the first bar of Sweet Home Soap had been
processed, wrapped, and sold. Before the decade had ended,
John D. Larkin had built a new three-story plant; and not long
after the century had ended, the John D. Larkin Company had
expanded into the production of perfumes, pharmaceuticals,
varnishes, packaged foods, clothing, oak furniture, and one of
the country's most successful potteries.

Larkin's incentive for establishing the Buffalo Pottery had nothing to do with the Arts and Crafts Movement. Pottery had become
one of the most popular items in the vast inventory of premiums
offered to the people who bought his soap products, and Larkin
soon realized that he could reduce his costs by producing his own
pottery rather than buying it from existing firms. In 1901 Larkin
offered the position of general manager to Louis Bown, a salesman
for the Crescent Pottery Company, one of the firms Larkin planned
to supplant. Bown brought in a team of experienced potters and
plant supervisors to design what was to become the "largest fire-
proof pottery in the world at that time . . . [and] the only pottery
in the world operated entirely by electricity."[2] An attractive piece-
work pay scale drew skilled potters and ceramic artists from across
the country. In 1903 the first dinnerware sets were pulled from
the factory's fifteen kilns, and less than seven years later Buffalo
Pottery was being sold in twenty-eight different countries.

1. Seymour and Violet Altman, *The Book of Buffalo Pottery* (New York:
Bonanza Books, 1969), p. 83.
2. Ibid., p. 21.

One of the men Bown brought with him to Buffalo was William J. Rea, who was named production superintendent. While the Buffalo Pottery was satisfying Larkin's desire both to reduce the cost of his products and to increase the efficiency of the Larkin Company, Bown "dreamed of an art pottery that would lend prestige to the company and also compete with the fine products of the English Staffordshire factories."[3] It would appear that around 1906 Bown asked Rea to begin experimenting with what would, by 1908, be called Deldare—a semiporcelain body distinguished by its olive green color. The famous decorative scenes painted on Deldare plates, platters, pitchers, bowls, and other forms became the responsibility of Ralph Stuart, a multitalented artist who had left Crescent Pottery at Rea's urging in 1903. Stuart was promoted to head of the art department and decorators, a position he held until he retired in 1942.

Stuart supervised the selection of appropriate scenes to be reproduced on each line of Deldare. In 1908 Fallowfield Hunt scenes were introduced and carried over into 1909; English village life and scenes from an English pub were the focus of some of the 1908 and 1909 Deldare pieces. The highly valued 1911 Emerald Deldare often featured humorous Dr. Syntax sketches and accompanying verse—a time-consuming addition that helps account for the scarcity of that particular year's issue. Each scene was hand-painted, using a transfer pattern to ensure strict adherence to the design and consequently producing uniform sets. The only freedom of expression permitted each artist was in the placement of the fluffy white clouds in the background.

According to authors Violet and Seymour Altman, "the bulk of the early Deldare was made in the years 1908 and 1909, only one design of Deldare being made in 1910. This was the 1910 calendar plate, of which an extremely small quantity was made. Today it is considered a choice collector's item. . . . All the early Deldare is plainly marked with the Deldare trademark, and most pieces are also dated with the year of manufacture."[4] A new

3. Seymour and Violet Altman, *The Book of Buffalo Pottery* (New York: Bonanza Books, 1969), p. 76.

4. Ibid., p. 77.

line of Deldare was introduced in 1911. Called Emerald Deldare, it has emerged as the most highly sought-after, not only because of the extremely high quality of the paintings but because it represents the last regular issue of Deldare made until 1923. In that year, in an attempt to regain its lost prestige, the firm began to reissue the Deldare line. The decision proved to be costly, and the line was dropped in 1925.

The other significant contribution to the art pottery movement made by the Buffalo Pottery, before switching the majority of its line to china dinnerware and commercial plates in 1915, was called Abino Ware. "Produced between 1911 and 1913, it was hand decorated; as far as is now known, no transfer prints were used."[5] While Abino Ware appears on the same forms as Emerald Deldare, the two lines bear little similarity to one another. Scenes for Abino Ware were inspired by Point Abino, not far from Buffalo on Lake Erie. Sailboats, a Dutch windmill, or on rare occasion, a pastoral scene, characterize Abino Ware, which was intended to replace Emerald Deldare as the firm's line of highly respected artware. Abino Ware is clearly marked, signed by one of three artists, and dated.

Selected Prices

Bowl, cereal: Deldare, Ye Olden Days, 6″, $250–$300.

Bowl, fruit: Deldare, Ye Village Tavern, 9″, $400–$450.

Bowl, nut: Deldare, Ye Lion Inn, 8″, $375–$425.

Bowl, sugar: Deldare, Scenes of Village Life, $165–$190.

Cup and saucer: Deldare, Dr. Syntax, $325–$375.

Cup and saucer: Deldare, Fallowfield Hunt, $200–$225.

Mug: Deldare, Ye Lion Inn, dated 1909, 4″, $275–$325.

Pitcher: Deldare, Emerald, Dr. Syntax, 9″, $700–$800.

Pitcher: Deldare, Fallowfield Hunt, The Death, 9″, $550–$650.

5. Paul Evans, *Art Pottery of the United States* (New York: Charles Scrinber's Sons, 1974), p. 36.

Pitcher: Deldare, Fallowfield Hunt, The Return, 8″, *$525–$575*.

Plate: Deldare, Emerald, Dr. Syntax, 9″, *$525–$575*.

Plate: Deldare, Fallowfield Hunt, Breaking Cover, 10″, *$225–$250*.

Plate: Deldare, Fallowfield Hunt, The Fall, 6″, *$100–$125*.

Plate: Deldare, Ye Lion Inn, 6″, *$100–$125*.

Plate: Deldare, Ye Village Streets, 7″, *$115–$140*.

Plate: Roycroft insigna, rust and spinach green geometric designs on cream ground, 9″, *$90–$100*.

Punch set: Roycroft insigna, large punch bowl and six mugs, all in brown high-glaze, *$250–$300*.

Tray, card: Deldare, Ye Lion Inn, 8″, *$275–$300*.

Tray: Deldare, Fallowfield Hunt, 8″, *$350–$400*.

Vase: Deldare, Ye Village Parson, 8″, *$700–$800*.

BYRDCLIFFE POTTERY

Shopmark:
Impressed pair of stylized wings over the name
BYRDCLIFFE, occasionally with artist's name, PENMAN
or HARDENBERGH

Principal Contribution:
Handmade pottery bowls and vases

Founders:
Edith Penman and Elizabeth R. Hardenbergh

Ralph Radcliffe-Whitehead[1]

Born: 1854   Died: 1929
Founded: 1903   Closed: ca. 1928

Studios and Salesrooms:
Byrdcliffe Pottery
Woodstock, New York
1903–ca. 1928

Ralph Radcliffe-Whitehead's Byrdcliffe Colony was intended as a haven for artists who wished to escape the industrialization of twentieth-century society. Although Byrdcliffe furniture shops failed, the pottery established by Edith Penman and Elizabeth R. Hardenbergh in 1903 received critical acclaim after exhibitions in New York and Boston and remained in operation through 1928. Entirely handmade, it featured unique color glazes over simple, undecorated forms. Some of their work was fired in the kilns of Charles Volkmar.[2]

Selected Prices

Due to the infrequency with which examples of this pottery appear on the market, establishing an in-depth price guide has not yet been possible. Until additional information is compiled, readers are advised to seek counsel from experienced collectors before either buying or selling important pieces.

---

1. See "Byrdcliffe Furniture" for additional information, p. 29.
2. Paul Evans, *Art Pottery of the United States* (New York: Charles Scribner's Sons, 1974), pp. 38–39.

CAMBRIDGE ART POTTERY

CAMBRIDGE

Shopmarks:
The conjoined letters *AP* encircled by the larger letter *C*, may
be encompassed by the outline of an acorn, all either stamped
or incised

On occasion the word *CAMBRIDGE, ACORN, GUERNSEY,*
or *OAKWOOD* may also appear

Principal Contributions:
Umbrella stands and jardinieres, followed by art pottery vases
and a line of kitchenware

President and Manager:
Charles L. Casey
Founded: 1900   Closed: 1933

Studios and Salesrooms:
Cambridge Art Pottery Company
Cambridge, Ohio
1900–1909

Guernsey Earthenware Company
Cambridge, Ohio
1909–1925

Atlas Globe China Company
Cambridge, Ohio
ca. 1926–1933

Among the various pottery firms that sprang up in southern Ohio as the demand for new art pottery forms continued to grow was the Cambridge Art Pottery in Cambridge, Ohio. Organized and first managed by Charles L. Casey in 1900, the firm immediately went into production of popular wares similar in form and glaze to those being marketed by Samuel Weller under the Louwelsa trademark, J. B. Owens's Utopia line, and Rookwood Pottery's Standard ware. The firm's rapid success was due in part to Casey's ability to attract experienced designers and artists, such as Charles B. Upjohn, to the pottery's new facility.

The Cambridge Art Pottery's first form of underglaze decoration was called Terrhea. It was followed by Oakwood, a less expensive line without any hand-applied underglaze decorations and, in 1903, by Acorn. All were formed from "local clays covered with glazes of high quality, notably in brown, deep purple, red and several blended shades."[1] What first began as an experiment in 1902 with "cooking utensils with an earthware brown body and a porcelain white lining,"[2] developed into a full line of kitchenware called Guernsey. From 1904 until 1906 the entire plant was geared for the production of the popular Guernsey line. The earlier three art wares were discontinued, and a feeble attempt in 1907 to initiate a new line, called Otoe, was dropped in 1908. As an indication of their intentions, the owners of the Cambridge Art Pottery changed the name of the firm to the Guernsey Earthenware Company in 1909.

Selected Prices

Due to the infrequency with which examples of this pottery appear on the market, establishing an in-depth price guide has not yet been possible. The examples listed below are indicative only of the value of pieces of similar form and decoration. Until additional information is compiled, readers are advised to seek

1. Elisabeth Cameron, *Encyclopedia of Pottery & Porcelain: 1800–1960* (New York: Facts on File Publications, 1986), p. 70.
2. Paul Evans, *Art Pottery of the United States* (New York: Charles Scribner's Sons, 1974), p. 43.

counsel from experienced collectors before either buying or selling important pieces.

Ewer: Terrhea, floral, squat form with bulbous bottom, 4″ × 5″, *$175–$200.*

Ewer: Terrhea, golden floral motif, 6″, *$185–$210.*

Tile: high-relief floral with majolica-type glaze, 6″ × 6″, *$20–$30.*

Vase: Terrhea, dog portrait, artist-signed, 9″, *$650–$750.*

Vase: Oakwood, brown and green, 8″, *$75–$85.*

CLEWELL

Shopmarks:
Impressed smaller letter *W* within larger letter *C*
Incised CLEWELL
Impressed CLEWELL METAL ART/CANTON, O.,
CLEWELL COPPERS or CLEWELL/CANTON, OHIO
On occasion the shopmark of the pottery firm providing the blank will also appear

Principal Contribution:
Line of bronze- or copper-coated pottery

Founder:
Charles Walter Clewell
Born: ca. 1876   Died: 1965
Founded: ca. 1906   Closed: 1965

Studios and Salesrooms:
Clewell Ware
Canton, Ohio
1906–1955

"A number of years ago, while visiting the Wadsworth Atheneum in Hartford, I saw a small bronze wine jug in the J. Pierpont Morgan Memorial Collection. The bronze had been found at Boscoreale during the excavations which led to the finding of the famous silver treasure of the Louvre, was accredited to the Romans and dated 200 B.C. It was blue; a wonderful blue varying from the very light tones through turquoise to almost black with flecks of green and rustlike brown and spots of bare darkened metal."

—*Charles W. Clewell*[1]

Unlike nearly all of the most respected craftsmen, artists, and designers associated with the art pottery movement in America, Charles Walter Clewell was not a potter. In truth, he was a metalsmith who developed a secret formula and technique for adhering thin layers of copper, silver, or bronze on the outside of fired earthenware vases, bowls, mugs, bookends, and similar wares.

The idea was not novel. Metalsmiths had for centuries applied copper, silver, and other metal overlays to pottery and ceramics, but according to Paul Evans, "Clewell's work appears to have been the first of the period to totally mask the ceramic body with a metal coating (a technique later employed in the production of Tiffany's Bronze Pottery)."[2]

Judging from the forms and marks, it appears that Clewell purchased biscuit wares (earthenware that has been fired once in the kiln) from a number of Ohio potteries, including Cambridge, Weller, and Owens. Using a process that has never been

1. Ralph and Terry Kovel, *The Kovels' Collectors Guide to American Art Pottery* (New York: Crown Publishers, 1974), p. 15.
2. Paul Evans, *Art Pottery of the United States* (New York: Charles Scribner's Sons, 1974), p. 57.

Charles Clewell's experimentation with copper-clad forms led to further development of an antique patina, giving his work the look of ancient metalware rather than twentieth-century pottery. *(Photo courtesy of David Rago, Trenton)*

revealed, Clewell would then deposit a thin coating of metal, either copper, bronze, or silver, over the entire exterior of the piece. As he perfected his technique, Clewell was able to duplicate both the hand-hammered effect that was popular during the Arts and Crafts movement and the appearance of metal rivets.

Not content with simply achieving a durable bond between the metal and the pottery, Clewell immediately initiated experiments that he continued throughout his career in an attempt to achieve a variety of natural-looking patinas on the metal. In referring to the bronze wine jug in the L. Pierpont Morgan Collection, Clewell added, "Seeing this little jug cost me more than two years of experimenting and a number of trips to Hartford to compare results, but finally the perfect blue appeared. It was a long hunt and particularly difficult; textbooks gave me no help."[3] The particular blue patina he had been seeking first began appearing on his bronze coatings after 1923, but he

3. Ralph and Terry Kovel, *The Kovels' Collectors Guide to American Art Pottery* (New York: Crown Publishers, 1974), p. 15.

continued to work at perfecting his techniques for both the bluish green patina on bronze and a matte green oxidation on copper.

Since he preferred to work alone and at his own pace, Clewell's production was quite limited. His technique and his patination formulas were, according to his wishes, destroyed at his death in 1965.

Selected Prices

Bowl: copper-covered red clay body, with lid, 6″ diameter, $350–$400.

Bowl: copper-covered with green patina, 7″ diameter, $175–$200.

Vase: copper-covered bulbous form with tapering rim, embossed, slip-decorated flowers, 5″ × 5″, $200–$250.

Candlesticks: model #380-2-6, deep rust and green patina on copper, 8″ pair, $375–$425.

Humidor: copper-covered form decorated with rivets, 9″, $600–$700.

Mug: copper-covered form with decorative rivets, 5″, $125–$150.

Vase: copper-covered bulbous form, green patina, 5″, $140–$165.

Vase: copper-covered with flared top, 5″, $140–$165.

Vase: copper-covered form with green base, metallic top, 10″, $325–$350.

Vase: copper-covered form over leaves in relief, 6″, $200–$225.

Vase: copper-covered, marked Owens, 6″, $140–$165.

Vase: copper-covered, green patina, gourd shape, 11″, $375–$400.

Vase: copper-covered form, 13″, $475–$525.

Vase: burnished copper with green patina, 10″ × 5″, $475–$525.

Vase: burnished copper with light greenish blue patina, 7″ × 4″, $250–$300.

Vase: burnished copper with green patina, 8″ × 6″, $350–$400.

Vase: burnished copper with burnt umber and green-blue patina, 7″ × 3″, $350–$400.

Vase: copper-covered form with heavy green patina, 5″, $200–$225.

Vase: copper over pottery form, three carved poppy buds standing up from the top edge, large stems raised from side of vase to bottom, large full poppy under the buds, two other poppy buds on back, reticulated openings around top running vertically, 13″, $2500–$3000.

Vase: copper-covered pottery with bluish green patina, bulbous bottom with flared lip, 7″, $200–$250.

CLIFTON ART POTTERY

 CLIFTON Cifton ℟

Shopmarks:
Incised or impressed CLIFTON or CLIFTON POTTERY/
NEWARK, N.J.
Indian ware may have reference to the location of the tribe from
which the form originated
Cipher marks (see illustration)

Principal Contribution:
Standard art pottery forms featuring clear glazes, underglaze decorations, or Indian motifs

Founders:
William A. Long
Born: 1844   Died: 1918
Fred Tschirner
(dates unknown)
Founded: 1905   Closed: 1914

Studios and Salesrooms:
Clifton Art Pottery
Newark, New Jersey
1905–1914

After having organized, operated, and sold Lonhuda Pottery,[1] William A. Long first went to work for J. B. Owens from 1896 until 1900, then moved to Colorado where he formed the Denver China and Pottery Company.[2] In 1905 he returned East, where the sixty-one-year-old Long and Fred Tschirner, a college graduate chemist, opened the Clifton Art Pottery.

From the very beginning of their partnership Long and Tschirner produced a line called Crystal Patina, which featured "a dense white body, resembling true porcelain, which was decorated with a pale green subdued-crystalline glaze; its likeness to the green oxidation of bronze suggested the line name."[3] In 1906 Long also created a number of vases, bowls, jugs, and jardinieres which were inspired by American Indian pottery forms. Although both Weller and Owens soon began creating similar lines, Long's Clifton Indian Ware marked the first significant production of this style. Using local New Jersey red clay for the body, Long incised native American Indian designs, which were then accented with colors but left unglazed for a realistic

1. See Lonhuda Pottery, p. 301.
2. See Denver China and Pottery, p. 268.
3. Paul Evans, *Art Pottery of the United States* (New York: Charles Scribner's Sons, 1974), p. 59.

appearance. The interiors of bowls and vases were generally treated with a glossy black glaze to make them waterproof.

Although their Indian Ware line and their other forms proved to be popular, Long and Tschirner chose not to expand their work force beyond the dozen assistants they had working in their small pottery.[4] In 1909 Long left their New Jersey pottery and moved back to Ohio, where he worked for Samuel Weller again, the Roseville Pottery Company, and the American Encaustic Tiling Company before his death in 1918 at the age of seventy-four. The Clifton Art Pottery Company produced decorated wares for only two additional years after Long's departure, gradually switching their emphasis to floor and wall tiles, which in 1914 led to changing their name to the Clifton Porcelain Tile Company.

Selected Prices

Bowl: Indian Ware, small neck and rim on squat, bulbous form, designed with dark brown hands on redware ground, design inspired by Four Mile Ruin, Arizona, 5″ × 8″, $150–$175.

Bowl: Indian Ware, 9″, $100–$125.

Bowl: Indian Ware, black, marked Florida, 2″, $50–$60.

Vase: Indian Ware, wide, short neck on squat, bulbous form, decorated with geometric Indian motifs, done in brown and beige glazes, derived from the Homolobi tribe, as indicated on underside, 8″ × 10″, $250–$300.

Vase: Indian Ware, angled rim and short neck on squat, bulbous form decorated with dark brown and beige band designs on dark brick red ground, designs based on Florida Indians, as indicated on the base, 10″ × 12″, $275–$325.

4. Elisabeth Cameron, *Encyclopedia of Pottery & Porcelain: 1800–1960* (New York: Facts on File Publications, 1986). p. 82.

Vase: Crystal Patina, decorated poppies, 1905, 6″, *$425–$475.*

Vase: Crystal Patina, bulbous base, cylindrical neck, 9″, *$200–$225.*

Vase: Crystal Patina, heavy crystalline pattern, green, 9″, *$200–$225.*

Vase: Indian Ware, bulbous bottom, black and red, 6″, *$100–$125.*

Vase: Indian Ware, black geometric pattern, Arkansas, 6″, *$185–$210.*

Vase: Indian Ware, thunderbird design, Homolobi, 8″, *$195–$220.*

Vase: with ivory stork surrounded by red and pale gray Japanese maple leaves, burnt red ground, 12″ × 7″, *$225–$250.*

Vase: Indian-style design in dark brown, light brown, on rust clay body, dark brown glass glaze inside, 3″ × 5″, *$85–$95.*

Vase: two loop handles, pale green crystalline glaze with light pinkish brown color, 3″ × 5″, *$60–$70.*

COOK POTTERY COMPANY

Shopmark:
The letter *C*

Principal Contribution:
Limited line of matte or metallic-glazed art pottery

Founder:
Charles H. Cook

Born: unknown   Died: unknown
Founded: 1894   Closed: ca. 1926

Studios and Salesrooms:
The Cook Pottery Company
Trenton, New Jersey
ca. 1894–ca. 1926

Production at the Cook Pottery concentrated on hand-painted granite wares (using transfers) at the close of the nineteenth century and by 1906 on commercial production of hotel china. For a few years in between, however, the firm produced approximately three lines of art pottery. The earliest featured underglaze decorations; of the latter two, Nipur ware "resembled pieces of pottery exhumed from the ruins of the ancient city of Nippur."[1] Metalline Ware took its name from a metallic glaze Harrold P. Humphrey developed.

Selected Prices

Due to the infrequency with which examples of this pottery appear on the market, establishing an in-depth price guide has not yet been possible. Until additional information is compiled, readers are advised to seek counsel from experienced collectors before either buying or selling important pieces.

1. Paul Evans, *Art Pottery of the United States* (New York: Charles Scribner's Sons, 1974), p. 63.

COWAN POTTERY

COWAN
POTTERY

Cowan Pottery

Shopmark:
(Early) Incised LAKEWOOD or COWAN POTTERY, often
with artist's initials or RC
(After 1920) COWAN or COWAN POTTERY stamped in black,
often above initials RC
(1927–1931) LAKEWARE

Principal Contributions:
Full range of commercial wares, including tiles, plus
line of art pottery

Founder:
R. Guy Cowan

Born: 1884   Died: 1957
Founded: 1913   Closed: 1931

Studios and Salesrooms:
The Cleveland Pottery and Tile Company
Cleveland, Ohio
1912–1917

Cowan Pottery Studio
Rocky River, Ohio
1920–1931

"It has left no room for time and effort to be put in on individual
work. Some of my friends feel that this is a great mistake and
that it is commercializing whatever ability we have. I have been
working, however, on the idea that in duplication of a good

design, it does not of necessity injure the product from an art standpoint."

—*R. Guy Cowan*
1929[1]

For R. Guy Cowan, pottery was his entire life. Born to a family of potters living in the clay-rich Ohio River Valley in the pottery town of East Liverpool, his father had taught him the potter's art before he had even finished high school. After graduation he studied under Charles Binns at the New York State School of Clayworking and Ceramics before returning to Ohio in 1908 to teach ceramics at the Cleveland Technical High School. Though a teacher by trade, Cowan continued his own education, spending his free time in the pottery studio of Horace Potter, "a popular gathering place for many of the Cleveland artists."[2]

Cowan soon constructed his own kiln and began entering examples of his pottery in small area exhibitions. With the encouragement of Horace Potter and support from the Cleveland Chamber of Commerce, whose members had seen his work on exhibit, Cowan was able to leave his teaching position and establish the Cleveland Pottery and Tile Company in 1913. Some of his earliest pieces bear the mark "Lakewood," named for the Cleveland suburb where he first worked. The Cowan pottery, as it was more casually called (Cowan never used the official name of his first studio in any of his marks, just as he never used his given name, Reginald), was growing larger year by year when World War I erupted; but in 1917 the thirty-three-year-old potter closed his small plant and enlisted in the army. In those four brief years, however, Cowan's work reflected the years of training and encouragement he had received. Both his tiles and art pottery of this period reveal the rapid development

1. Paul Evans, *Art Pottery of the United States* (New York: Charles Scribner's Sons, 1974), p. 71.
2. Ralph and Terry Kovel, *The Kovels' Collectors Guide to American Art Pottery* (New York: Crown Publishers, 1974), p. 18.

of a number of quality glazes, motivated, perhaps, by his desire "to cover the red clay body of the ware."[3]

When Cowan returned from duty in 1919, he reopened his former plant, but it soon became evident that neither the supply of natural gas for the three kilns nor the building itself was going to enable him to fulfill his plans for expansion. In the following two years Cowan constructed a nine-kiln plant in nearby Rocky River and returned to school at the John Huntington Polytechnic Institute in Cleveland in preparation for the large-scale commercial production he was about to undertake. Over the course of the next eight years the Cowan pottery rose to become one of the few potteries whose work was "both praised by art critics and [was] also commercially successful."[4] Mass production, even in special limited editions, required that molded forms take precedence over hand-thrown wares; Ohio red clays were replaced with the English clays required for their porcelain bodies. Nevertheless, Cowan continued to hire talented designers and chemists, who continued to produce a line of commercial art pottery with exceptional glazes throughout the decade.[5] Cowan tiles made from Ohio clay were purchased for numerous institutions, and their extensive line of figurines, lamps, ashtrays, dinnerware, and doorknobs, plus their last major line, Lakeware (an inexpensive line designed for florists and novelty stores), poured out of the kilns at an astonishing rate of 175,000 pieces per year.[6]

But even more swiftly, the stock market crash of 1929 brought it all to an end. Sales simply stopped, and less than two years later the Cowan Pottery Studio closed its doors. Guy Cowan accepted a position with the Onondaga Pottery Company in Syracuse, New York, where he worked until his retirement.

3. Paul Evans, *Art Pottery of the United States* (New York: Charles Scribner's Sons, 1974), p. 70.

4. Ibid., p. 71.

5. Ralph and Terry Kovel, *The Kovels' Collectors Guide to American Art Pottery* (New York: Crown Publishers, 1974), p. 19.

6. Elisabeth Cameron, *Encyclopedia of Pottery & Porcelain: 1800–1960* (New York: Facts on File Publications, 1986), p. 90.

Selected Prices

Bowl: blue luster glaze, 3″, *$25–$35*.

Bowl: copper glaze, flaring top, 8″, *$44–$55*.

Bowl: blue interior glaze, kneeling nude, 10″ diameter, *$250–$275*.

Candlestick: green matte glaze, 4″, *$30–$40*.

Candleholder: bulbous base, ivory glaze, pair, 4″, *$35–$45*.

Flower frog: mushrooms, ivory semigloss glaze, 5″, *$70–$80*.

Flower frog: single nude, ivory semigloss glaze, 7″, *$135–$145*.

Match holder: sea horse motif, matte green glaze, *$25–$35*.

Vase: green and blue, high glaze, 13″, *$40–$50*.

Vase: bulbous form, matte green glaze, 5″, *$60–$70*.

Vase: orange luster glaze, 6″, *$35–$45*.

Vase: flared rim, resting atop a stylized Chinese bird, medium to dark green high gloss, 11″ × 8″, *$175–$200*.

CRAVEN ART POTTERY

Jervis

Shopmarks:
Incised CRAVEN
Incised JERVIS

Principal Contribution:
Decorated and incised art pottery

Founders:
Albert L. Cusick and associates
Founded: 1904   Closed: 1908

Studios and Salesrooms:
Craven Art Pottery
East Liverpool, Ohio
1904–1908

The Craven Art Pottery was joined in 1905 by William P. Jervis, noted ceramics author and potter who formed his own company in 1908. Jervis designed a line of matte glazed pottery incorporating various colors on a single piece. Jervis's departure from the firm coincided with the plant's closing.

Selected Prices

Due to the infrequency with which examples of this pottery appear on the market, establishing an in-depth price guide has not yet been possible. Until additional information is compiled, readers are advised to seek counsel from experienced collectors before either buying or selling important pieces.

DEDHAM POTTERY and CHELSEA KERAMIC ART WORKS

Shopmarks:
(1875–1889) Impressed CHELSEA KERAMIC ART WORKS/ ROBERTSON & SONS or stacked letters *CKAW*, often with incised initials of decorators
(1891–1896) Paper label CHELSEA POTTERY/US/ TRADEMARK or impressed letters *C.P.U.S.* in cloverleaf
(1896–1928) Stamped mark of a resting rabbit beneath the words *DEDHAM POTTERY;* Volcanic Ware will have *DEDHAM POTTERY* incised along with initials *H.C.R.*
(1929–1943) Addition of the word *REGISTERED* beneath the stamped outline of the rabbit

Principal Contributions:
Early art pottery, crackle glaze tablewares, and Volcanic Ware

Founder:
Hugh Robertson
Born: 1844   Died: 1908
Founded: 1867   Closed: 1943

Studios and Salesrooms:
A. W. and C. H. Robertson
Chelsea, Massachusetts
1867–1872

Chelsea Keramic Art Works
Chelsea, Massachusetts
1872–1889

Chelsea Pottery U.S.
Chelsea, Massachusetts
1891–1896

Dedham Pottery
Dedham, Massachusetts
1896–1943

"Owing to the hand-made feature, there is usually a slight variance from the sizes of the pieces listed herein. Our firing is done in the old style kilns and there again is a slight variance in color, which adds rather than detracts from the appeal of the ware."

—*Catalog Introduction*
1938[1]

The Chelsea Keramic Art Works

The Robertson family was a family of proficient potters. James Robertson (1810–1880), the father of three potters (Alexander, Hugh, and George), had worked alongside his father in a small pottery in Scotland, rising to become the manager of a northern England firm before bringing his new family to America in 1853 and settling near Boston, where he once again served as a pottery superintendent.

All three of his sons followed him into the pottery profession, Alexander (1840–1925) forming his own pottery in Chelsea in 1865, where he was joined by Hugh (1844–1908) by 1867 and in 1872 by his father and brother George (1835–1914). The newly named Chelsea Keramic Art Works began offering a line of artware for sale in 1875, but it was discontinued shortly thereafter when the public failed to respond to their fine red earthenware designs, many of which were polished with boiled linseed oil in a unique process. In 1877, however, the Robertson family responded with a hand-thrown faience line "which brought Chelsea to the attention of connoisseurs of the day. Shapes were classically simple; glazes for the most part were soft in color and have proven remarkably free from crazing."[2] The elder Robertson died in 1880, but not before the Chelsea Keramic Art Works had begun to receive recognition for the

1. J. Milton Robertson, *Dedham Pottery Catalog* (1938), p. F. (Halifax, VA: Dedham Folio, 1987), reprint.

2. Paul Evans, *Art Pottery of the United States* (New York: Charles Scribner's Sons, 1974), p. 47.

many glazes that he and his sons had developed over his last fifteen years.

In 1878 John G. Low, a local artist who had joined the firm to learn ceramic techniques, left to form his own tile business, the Low Art Tile Works, also in Chelsea. George Robertson accepted Low's invitation to work for him in the building Low's father had financed. In 1884, four years after the death of James Robertson, Alexander decided to move to California, leaving management of the family firm to Hugh.

Robertson dedicated his efforts to the discovery of various new glazes; one in particular was inspired by a red Chinese glaze he had seen at the Philadelphia Centennial exhibition. As his grandson later described it:

> At the Centennial Exhibition in Philadelphia in 1876, Hugh saw the Korean Exhibit, including the Chinese Crackle and "Dragon's Blood" vases, which so intrigued him that on his return to Chelsea, he set out to produce this red. The final result was the production of Chinese Dragon's Blood, which was the same as the Ming Dynasty. The cost of these experiments left Hugh penniless, but during the stages of experimentation for the red color, he discovered the process of making crackle ware.[3]

Robertson preferred to work with undecorated forms, which would permit his "superb glazes and simple shapes to be appreciated unmarred. Glazes developed included sea-green, apple-green, mustard-yellow and turquoise, in addition to the rich and very successful oxblood, which was first obtained in 1885 and finally perfected in 1888."[4] It has been estimated that only three hundred examples of what Robertson considered authentic oxblood glazes were produced, although many of his near-successes have been touted as being equal to his greatest work.

While Robertson was diligently working with his award-winning glazes, the family pottery business was crumbling around him. In 1889, one year after he had perfected the "Robertson's Blood" glaze, the kilns sat cold. Without money for the

3. J. Milton Robertson, *Dedham Pottery Catalog* (1938), p. C. (Halifax, VA: Dedham Folio, 1987), reprint.

4. Paul Evans, *Art Pottery of the United States* (New York: Charles Scribner's Sons, 1974), p. 49.

fuel to fire them, Robertson was forced to end his experiments and close the pottery.

Chelsea Pottery U.S.

The closing of the Robertson pottery did not go unnoticed in Boston circles. Within a matter of months a group of local supporters had formed a board of directors to fund and oversee a new pottery by the name of Chelsea Pottery U.S. In 1981 Hugh Robertson was named manager, but "learning from the financial failure of his earlier pottery, Robertson and his directors decided that the firm should try making salable tablewares and avoid the expensive time-consuming art wares. Robertson remembered the crackleware glaze that he had achieved earlier on a few large vases. He worked on the process and within a few months after the formation of the new firm, he developed what is now the famous crackleware."[5]

The site of their pottery proved unsuitable, however, as smoke from nearby factories ruined several batches of tableware, and moisture from the Chelsea marshes affected the performance of the kilns. In 1895 one of the directors purchased a tract of land along a canal near Dedham, Massachusetts, and a new four-story pottery was constructed. With the move in 1896, the name of the firm was changed to the Dedham Pottery Company.

Dedham Pottery

The crackleware technique that Robertson had discovered years earlier and developed at the Chelsea Pottery provided the technical basis for an extensive line of dinnerware that served as the trademark of Dedham Pottery for nearly fifty years. Ironically, it was the popular success of his crackleware glaze that enabled Hugh Robertson to resume his work with various other glazes. While one of the plant's two new kilns was kept busy firing plates, cups, saucers, platters, bowls, and related

5. Ralph and Terry Kovel, *The Kovels' Collectors Guide to American Art Pottery* (New York: Crown Publishers, 1974), p. 31.

The wide assortment of Dedham pottery can only be hinted at by this photograph. The cup and saucer are in the popular elephant pattern, the five-inch cream pitcher illustrates the traditional Dedham rabbit, the twelve-inch dolphin platter is considered quite rare, and the five-inch lotus petal bowl, though less inspiring, remains practical. The Dutch Boy ashtray features a unique waterspout that must have amused a few proper Bostonians. *(Photo courtesy of Robert W. Skinner, Boston)*

tableware, the other was reserved for Robertson's experiments with his line of Volcanic Ware (1896–1899).[6] His new glaze technique involved a process in which a vase could conceivably be fired as many as twelve times, causing a thick glaze that had been applied around the top to run down the sides in unpredictable patterns. The failure rate was high and his experiments costly: Robertson died in 1908 from lead poisoning contracted from his lifelong work with pigments and glazes. William Robertson (1864–1929), his son, who had worked with him for years, took over the duties of plant superintendent, though he too had paid dearly for his profession. A kiln explosion in 1905 had permanently damaged both of his hands, leaving William incapable of designing pottery. As a result, the firm continued to use the dinnerware patterns designed by Hugh Robertson between 1891 and 1908. Despite the lack of new designs, the crackleware continued to grow in popularity through the 1920s and 1930s, but in 1943 J. Milton Robertson, the grandson of Hugh Robertson,

6. Martin Eidelberg, ed., *From Our Native Clay* (New York: Turn of the Century Editions, 1987), p. 96.

was forced to close down the famous kilns, citing a drop in sales and extensive repairs as the reasons for the firm's failure.

The line of Dedham crackleware designed by Hugh Robertson proved to be charming, artistic, and practical. The combination of the classic blue and white colors beneath a finely crackled glaze gave the dinnerware the appearance of being much older and much more fragile than it actually was. In fact, the "ware was fired at a high temperature so that a true porcelain was made."[7] Part of the closely guarded secret of the fine crazing in the final glaze was explained years later. The dinnerware was quickly removed from the hot kiln and rushed to the elevator that led to the top of the four-story building. As the cool air in the shaft enveloped the warm tableware, "a very audible crackling could be heard."[8] What captured the hearts of thousands, however, were the hand-painted Dedham borders: plump rabbits, parading elephants, outstretched butterflies, and graceful swans were among the two dozen patterns listed in the only catalog the firm released.[9] The drawing of the now-famous Dedham rabbit was submitted by a Boston art teacher in response to a contest Hugh Robertson sponsored in 1892 for a trademark for the newly formed firm. The Dedham rabbit pattern remained in production every year from 1892 until the plant closed in 1943.

As Marilee Meyer observed in her preface to the 1987 reprint of the original 1938 Dedham catalog, "purchases may be directed by motif, searching for various sizes and forms of one particular pattern, such as the Azalea or Butterfly. Others choose one specific form, perhaps the six inch plate, and collect several different patterns. Whatever the approach, the present collector has sparked an interest in Dedham pottery that is rapidly kindling in antiques shops, shows, and auctions throughout the country."[10]

7. Martin Eidelberg, ed., *From Our Native Clay* (New York: Turn of the Century Editions). p. 32.

8. Lloyd Hawes, *The Dedham Pottery* (Dedham, MA: Dedham Historical Society, 1968), p. 38.

9. J. Milton Robertson, *Dedham Pottery Catalog* (1938). (Halifax, VA: Dedham Folio, 1987), reprint.

10. Ibid., p. ii.

Selected Prices

Chelsea

Due to the infrequency with which examples of this pottery appear on the market, establishing an in-depth price guide has not yet been possible. The examples listed below are indicative only of the value of pieces of similar form and decoration. Until additional information is compiled, readers are advised to seek counsel from experienced collectors before either buying or selling important pieces.

Vase: two angled handles centering on a rolled rim and swollen cylindrical form, decorated with band of floral swags and petaled base, mottled blue-green glaze, 6″, $175-$200.

Vase: miniature pillow, narrow, short neck on flattened spherical form, mottled blue and cherry red glaze, 3″, $450-$500.

Vase: rounded rim and elongated neck on bulbous base, glazed in deep dragon's blood red iridescent glaze with both smooth and "orange peel"-textured areas, brilliant highlights, 8″, $1750-$2000.

Vase: bulbous bottom and cylindrical neck, covered in an oxblood finish, gold luster overglaze, 7″ × 4″, $1500-$1750.

Dedham

Ashtray: Dutch boy with shoulder yoke and hat drilled to facilitate water, drains onto oval shallow tray, 5″ × 5″, $400-$500.

Ashtray: elephant, stamped, 4″, $200-$225.

Bottle: sauce, pottery, short round neck on tall square form, blue script *G* on crackle ground, 8″, $225-$250.

Bowl: serving, square, rabbit pattern, stamped, 8″, $200–$225.

Bowl: elephant pattern, 3″ × 4″, $250–$300.

Bowl: lotus, repeating petals on outside highlighted with blue, 5″, $250–$300.

Creamer: grape pattern, 4″, $150–$175.

Cup and saucer: rabbit pattern in blue against white ground, 6″ (saucer), $125–$150.

Cup and saucer: seven polar bears on cup, with nine polar bears in blue and white on saucer, 6″ (saucer), $250–$300.

Cup and saucer: elephant pattern, 4″, $300–$350.

Cup and saucer: snowtree, 4″, $150–$175.

Cup and saucer: magnolia pattern, 4″, $150–$175.

Cup and saucer: azalea, demitasse, 5″, $150–$175.

Cup and saucer: azalea, stamped, 4″, $150–$175.

Dish: bonbon, rabbit pattern, 3″ × 4″, $225–$250.

Dish: celery, rabbit pattern, 5″ × 10″, $250–$257.

Humidor: brass screw-top handle holding flat cover on cylindrical form with white elephants on blue ground, 8″, $2000–$2250.

Jar: pottery, rabbit pattern, 5″, $150–$175.

Jar: spherical form, azalea pattern, 4″, $175–$200.

Pitcher: cylindrical, rabbit pattern, 5″, $175–$200.

Plate: eight stylized polar bears around edge in blue against white, 8″, $225–$250.

Plate: stylized ducks pattern, 8″, $175–$200.

Plates: rabbit pattern, 8″, $125–$150.

Plate: swan pattern, impressed mark, 7″, $225–$250.

Plate: swan pattern, stamped and impressed, 10″, $250–$275.

Plate: lily pattern, 6″, $150–$175.

Plate: turkey, 10″, $175–$220.

Plate: clover, impressed and stamped, 10″, $300–$350.

Plate: pineapple, stamped and incised, 10″, $225–$250.

Plate: snowtree, 10″, $150–$175.

Plate: lobster, stamped, 8″, $225–$250.

Plate: azalea, stamped and impressed, 7″, $150–$175.

Plate: lobster variation, signed HCR on front for Hugh Robertson, 8″, $550–$650.

Plate: moths with large tails alternating with star flowers, 6″, $125–$150.

Plate: clover pattern, 10″, $350–$400.

Plate: "Golden Gate San Francisco," central sunrise with poppy flower border, 10″, $2000–$2250.

Plate: turkey, 10″, $150–$175.

Platter: oval, dolphin, 12″, $700–$800.

Sugar and creamer: two small circular handles, with blue rabbit pattern on white, 5″ × 4″, $200–$225.

Tile: tea, square, rabbit pattern, 5″, $225–$250.

Tray: bacon, grape pattern, rectangular form, stamped and impressed, 10″ × 6″, $250–$300.

Vase: wide mouth on spherical form tapering toward base, iridescent red drip highlights on teal blue ground, 7″, $700–$800.

Vase: short neck on swollen cylindrical form tapering toward base, brown, green, and dark blue drip glaze, 7″, $225–$250.

Vase: short, cylindrical neck on bulbous form tapering toward base, mottled iridescent red glaze over rose-color ground, 4″, *$350–$400.*

Vase: dragon's blood, wide mouth on swollen cylindrical vase tapering toward base, 3″, *$500–$600.*

Vase: crackleware, wide mouth on bulbous form, tapering toward base, decorated with various sizes of flying cranes with outstretched wings, 7″ × 6″, *$1500–$1750.*

Vase: three-colored, elongated cylindrical neck on bulbous base, done with iridescent red, green, and taupe glazes, 8″, *$900–$1000.*

DENVER CHINA AND POTTERY COMPANY

Shopmarks:
Impressed DENVER over initials *L.F.* (Lonhuda Faience) in shield
Impressed DENVER over initials *C. & P. Co.*
Impressed DENAURA over arrow and DENVER

Principal Contribution:
Wide range of forms featuring underglaze decorations

Founder:
William A. Long
Born: 1844   Died: 1918
Founded: 1901   Closed: 1905

Studios and Salesrooms:
The Denver China and Pottery Company
Denver, Colorado
1901–1905

By the year 1900 William Long had started and sold one pottery company, had formed an ill-advised and short-lived partnership with Samuel Weller, and had revealed his technique of underglaze slip painting to both Weller and J. B. Owens.[1] It would not seem unusual for any man to then want to find a new home.

Long moved to Denver, where he started the Denver China and Pottery the same year that Artus Van Briggle opened his new pottery. Long continued to produce his Lonhuda line of underglaze decorated pottery as well as an inexpensive line of household pottery. In addition, he introduced a line called Denura, revealing an attraction for Art Nouveau designs "similar in concept to some of the early Van Briggle work"[2] and also for native Colorado flora. Many of his artware pieces were molded by his staff of approximately twenty workers. In 1905 the Denver China and Pottery Company merged with the Western Pottery Manufacturing Company, and Long moved to New Jersey, where he formed the Clifton Art Pottery.

Selected Prices

Due to the infrequency with which examples of this pottery appear on the market, establishing an in-depth price guide has not yet been possible. The examples listed below are indicative only of the value of pieces of similar form and decoration. Until additional information is compiled, readers are advised to seek counsel from experienced collectors before either buying or selling important pieces.

1. See Lonhuda Pottery, Weller Pottery, and J. B. Owens Pottery for additional information, pp. 301, 439, and 357, respectively.
2. Paul Evans, *Art Pottery of the United States* (New York: Charles Scribner's Sons, 1974), p. 88.

Vase: white matte glaze over decorated pine cones, 4″, $275–$325.

Vase: decorated with leaves and berries, medium green glaze, 6″, $300–$325.

Vase: gray-blue and green matte glaze, 4″ × 4″, $165–$190.

FRACKELTON POTTERY

Shopmark:
Incised initials *S.F.*, occasionally with year

Principal contribution:
Salt-glazed stoneware, occasionally with underglaze decoration

Founder:
Susan Stuart Frackelton
Born: 1848   Died: 1932
Founded: ca. 1882   Closed: ca. 1903

Studios and Salesrooms:
Frackelton Pottery
Milwaukee, Wisconsin
ca. 1882–ca. 1903

Susan Frackelton was a pioneer in the development of china painting, establishing the Frackelton China Decorating Works in 1893. She also experimented in salt-glaze stoneware, creating award-winning examples at numerous exhibitions. Unfortunately, she never possessed the necessary equipment or kilns to develop a line of art pottery; thus, examples of her work are considered quite rare. As a review in *The Craftsman* mentioned, "The product is small and no duplicates are made." The same author gave Mrs. Frackelton "the distinction of being the first American who has raised stoneware from the most common utilitarian uses to the rank of an artistic product."[1]

"At the same time," a modern observer recently noted, "Susan Frackelton was the first in a succession of pottery and china decorators to give up decorating for the lure of carving and modeling in wet clay. Her large, richly carved, and modeled 'Olive Jar' in saltglaze stoneware was exhibited in Chicago at the 1893 World's Columbian Exhibition to great acclaim."[2]

Selected Prices

Due to the infrequency with which examples of this pottery appear on the market, establishing an in-depth price guide has not yet been possible. Until additional information is compiled, readers are advised to seek counsel from experienced collectors before either buying or selling important pieces.

FULPER POTTERY

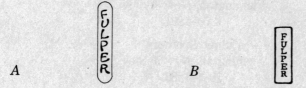

A   *B*

1. "The Frackelton 'Blue and Gray,' " *The Craftsman* (January 1903), p. 255.
2. Martin Eidelberg, ed., *From Our Native Clay* (New York: Turn of the Century Editions, 1987), p. 48.

Shopmarks:

(1909–1914) Ink-stamped circle VASEKRAFT/FULPER around potter at his wheel

(1909–ca. 1915) Ink-stamped vertical rectangle around vertical *FULPER* (see Shopmark *B* on p. 271)

(ca. 1915–1920) Ink-stamped vertical rectangle with rounded corners around vertical *FULPER* in Oriental-style lettering (see Shopmark *A* on p. 271)

(ca. 1915–1920) Smaller ink-stamped box around vertical *FULPER*

(1915–1925) Raised or incised vertical rectangle with rounded corners around vertical *FULPER*

(ca. 1922–1955) Impressed horizontal *FULPER* (no rectangle), generally with three- or four-digit number[1]

Principal Contributions:

Vases, bowls, and lamps utilizing a variety of quality glazes

Founder:

Samuel Hill

Born: 1793   Died: 1858
Founded: 1814   Sold: 1930

Studios and Salesrooms:

Samuel Hill Pottery
Flemington, New Jersey
1814–1860

Fulper Pottery
Flemington, New Jersey
1860–1881

Fulper Brothers
Flemington, New Jersey
1881–1889

Fulper Pottery, Inc.
Flemington, New Jersey
1889–1955

1. Robert W. Blasberg, *Fulper Art Pottery: An Aesthetic Appreciation, 1909–1929* (New York: The Jordan-Volpe Gallery, 1979), pp. 72–73.

This 56", high-back spindle oak side chair was designed by **Frank Lloyd Wright** in 1901 for the Ward W. Willits House in Highland Park, Illinois. It was featured at Christie's in New York in 1986, when it sold for $198,000. *(Photo courtesy of Christies, New York)*

Perhaps the most important copper and mica table lamp the firm produced, this 24″ high **Roycroft** lamp features six mica panels supported by a riveted copper shade. *(Photo courtesy of Christie's, New York)*

This inlaid mahogany **Greene and Greene** desk was designed for the Charles M. Pratt House in Ojai, California, in 1909, and features a gnarled fruit tree motif on both sides as well as the drop-front section. Height 48″, width 46¾″, diameter 22″. *(Photo courtesy of Christie's, New York)*

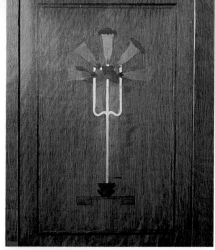

Above: This inlaid oak music cabinet was designed by **Harvey Ellis** and produced in **Gustav Stickley's Craftsman Workshops** in 1903. The inlaid door features copper and various woods; the cabinet is signed on the back with the earliest of the red "Als ik kan" decals, distinguished by the box around the name "Stickley." Height 57″, width 22″, diameter 14″. *(Photo by Ray Northway, Iowa City).* **Below:** The 5½″ **Overbeck** vase on the left features a cut-back design of white rams amid thorny vines and white birds; the early, high glaze **Newcomb College** 6″ vase in the center was decorated with incised flowers by Hattie C. Joor; the 4½″, **Saturday Evening Girls** covered bowl incorporates bees into the horizontal band, which gives it an Arts and Crafts flavor. *(Photo courtesy of David Rago, Trenton)*

Right: The **Fulper** mushroom table lamp with inset panels of stained glass, and the famous Fulper glaze, has also become an Arts and Crafts favorite. *(Photo courtesy of Christie's, New York)*

Below: The 8¾", corset-shaped **Marblehead** vase, decorated by Hanna Tutt, features the geometric designs that Arts and Crafts collectors have come to appreciate; the 6" vase was also decorated by Hanna Tutt, but in a conventionalized floral motif. *(Photo courtesy of David Rago, Trenton).*

Above: This 7½″ **Fulper** bowl features two ring handles around a flared rim, with the bulbous body set upon a pedestal vase. *(Photo courtesy of David Rago, Trenton)* **Below:** The 12″ **Roseville** Della Robbia vase on the left illustrates both the cut-back and incised techniques of decoration used by several art pottery firms. The dramatic 12″ "Flame" vase by **Brouwer** on the right is decorated with vertical goldenrod over an iridescent background. *(Photos courtesy of David Rago, Trenton)*

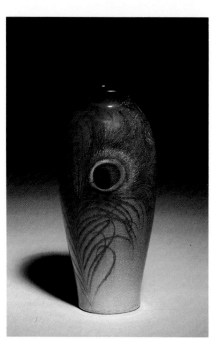

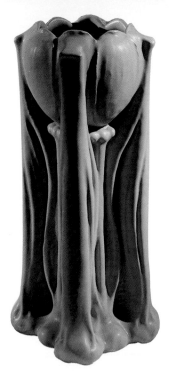

Above Left: This 8½″ **Rookwood** vase was decorated in 1900 by Carl Schmidt, with two navy and turquoise peacock feathers under the Rookwood Iris glaze. *(Photo courtesy of Christie's, New York)*. **Above Right:** This **Teco** vase was designed by sculptor Ferdinand Moreau in 1905 and was inspired by the lotus flower. *(Photo courtesy of the Struve Gallery, Chicago)*

Perhaps the best of the best, this 11″, hand-formed **Grueby** vase was designed by George P. Kendrick and features seven ribbed leaves separated by seven handles. *(Photo courtesy of Christie's, New York)*

Above: This delicate, 3½" **George Ohr** bowl was carefully crushed by the potter to create a totally unique form, but it also exhibits a fine Ohr glaze that collectors appreciate. *(Photo courtesy of David Rago, Trenton)* **Below:** The aesthetic value of an original finish and original leather upholstery is demonstrated in this pair of **L. & J. G. Stickley** dining chairs. *(Photo by Ray Northway, Iowa City)*

The soothing combination of mica and hammered copper has never been better demonstrated than in this 25½″ lamp designed and executed by **Dirk Van Erp** in 1910. *(Photo courtesy of Christie's, New York)*

"The use of natural clays, not over-refined, gives an element of
the unexpected, for the glaze 'steals' from the body in firing,
particles of mineral in the body, producing variations in color or
crystalline effects in the glaze."

—*Evelyn Marie Stuart*
1914[2]

In 1860 the Fulper family assumed possession of the pottery
that was to bear their name for nearly one hundred years. At
the outset they maintained the manufacture of a line of utility
household pottery and continued in this fashion under the management of three brothers: George W. Fulper, Edward B. Fulper, and William H. Fulper (1872–1928), who was largely
responsible for the introduction and development of Fulper's
art pottery production.

The Fulper entry into an already crowded art pottery market
came in the middle of the Arts and Crafts era. In 1909, utilizing
the same heavy New Jersey clay they had used for decades in
their commercial production, the Fulper brothers introduced a
line of art pottery by the name of Vasekraft. Recent research,
however, has revealed that experiments with various glazes for
the new line may have started as early as 1900, with experimental pieces being produced by 1906.[3] The new line was manufactured, according to a 1912 article, "from the same clay, in
the same factory, and in some cases by the same workmen that
are working on the more common articles."[4]

The wares developed at the Fulper Pottery for the Vasekraft
line ranged widely, from vases, jardinieres, and lamps to bookends, pitchers, clocks cases, and tiles. Although some required

2. Evelyn Marie Stuart, "Vasekraft—an American Art Pottery," *Fine
Arts Journal* (October 1913) p. 608; also quoted in Robert W. Blasberg's
Fulper Art Pottery.

3. Wendy Kaplan, ed., *The Art That Is Life: The Arts & Crafts Movement in America, 1875–1920* (Boston: Museum of Fine Arts, 1987), p.
262; and Paul Evans, *Art Pottery of the United States* (New York: Feingold & Lewis, 1987), p. 113.

4. Wendy Kaplan, ed., *The Art That Is Life: The Arts & Crafts Movement in America, 1875–1920* (Boston: Museum of Fine Arts, 1987), p.
262.

The glossy, high glaze on these Fulper vases (heights 5″–8″) have inspired unusual attention for a line of molded forms. The drip glazes on the vases at the far left and far right are among the most sought-after of this New Jersey pottery. *(Photo courtesy of David Rago, Trenton)*

hand-throwing, the majority were molded. While the heavy Fulper forms were open to criticism from early reviewers accustomed to Rookwood-inspired vases and ewers, the hundreds of quality glazes developed by William Fulper and his chemists have been credited with the popular and artistic success of the firm's art pottery.

Among the more successful and most popular of the Fulper glazes were the following:

Mirror—a high gloss glaze in either black, green, blue, ivory, or yellow

Wistaria—a flowing matte glaze in pastel colors, individually or combined

Flambé—unusual combinations of colors in a flame effect

Lustre—an iridescent glaze

Crystal—a crystalline glaze

Matte—textured dull glazes in a variety of colors, including shades of greens, yellows, and whites

Like Teco and Hampshire, the Fulper Pottery utilized a large number of molded forms to prevent production costs from driving the price of their pottery beyond the reach of their potential customers. Grueby, the symbol of hand-thrown art pottery, had entered the first stages of bankruptcy the same year that Fulper announced the introduction of Vasekraft, and it appears that the Fulper brothers were determined not to follow in their footsteps. Emphasis was placed on the development of dozens of unique glazes that, once perfected, could be applied to hundreds of classical, yet molded forms. The result was efficient production of a quality art pottery. As observed in the beautifully illustrated *From Our Native Clay*, "while Fulper produced its molded forms in large quantities, it made a point with its glazing techniques to encourage the fire in the kiln to give each piece unique markings."[5] Specific glazes were not generally assigned to specific forms but were used in alternative succession and, in many of the most spectacular wares, in combination with each other. One of the most highly valued of the many Fulper glazes is the crystalline, of which it was said that while "Teco has the distinction of producing the first microcrystalline glazes ... it was Fulper, a late entrant in the field of art pottery, who produced the more successful and more varied crystalline glazes. Because such glazes tend to flow irregularly, and the locations of the crystals cannot be predicted, such glazes were normally used on relatively simple, Oriental-inspired vessels."[6]

Among the many varied Fulper forms that are destined to become prized members of fine collections are those with deep, rich glazes. Unlike other potteries, which worked in numerous shapes but utilized only one or two particular types of glazes, the size and form of Fulper pottery is of less importance than the quality of their glazes. Dull, lifeless glazes can be found and should be recognized as such. Strong, well-distributed crystalline glazes, along with deep Mirror and rich Flambé, are among the most highly sought of the firm's many glazes.

One of the rarest of the Fulper glazes was the famous Famille Rose, which William Fulper may have first developed as an exhibition rather than a production glaze. "Fulper considered this the rediscovery of the ancient Chinese secret, and hence the

5. Martin Eidelberg, ed., *From Our Native Clay* (New York: Turn of the Century Editions, 1987), p. 99.
6. Ibid., p. 105.

glaze was applied to classical Chinese shapes."[7] The various red hues were time-consuming to duplicate, as reflected in both their rarity today and their original cost. At a time when an average worker was earning $10 a week, a fine example of Fulper's Famille Rose could cost as much as $100.

The now-famous Fulper mushroom lamps were first offered in 1910, coinciding perhaps with the arrival of Martin Stangl, who had created several new designs and numerous glazes by 1915. While stoneware lamp bases were not unusual, as Grueby, Tiffany, Teco, Hampshire, and Rookwood had all demonstrated, Fulper created a pottery shade as well, with as many as two dozen hand-incised openings for irregularly shaped pieces of stained glass. The lamps were praised for the "unity of base and shade in the same material, the utility of the lamp for reading, and the harmony of the glazes and forms within 'the general scheme of artistic home furnishing.' "[8] Like much of the Vasekraft line, lamp bases and even the pierced shades were often molded rather than hand-thrown, but the quality of the glazes and the relative rarity of the lamps ensured their popularity, not only between 1910 and 1920 but seventy years later as well.

Stangl's appointment as technical superintendent followed the retirement of George W. Fulper in 1911. Stangl oversaw the infusion of several new glazes into the Vasekraft line, which was awarded a medal at the 1915 San Francisco Exposition; but Stangl's departure that same year, coupled with a declining interest in art pottery, forced the company to accept a contract for the production of bisque doll heads, which were mass-produced under the Fulper trademark between 1918 and 1921 at a rate of nearly one thousand per day.[9] Stangl returned to the pottery in 1920 and purchased the business from the Fulper family in 1930, one year after a fire destroyed the main plant

7. Paul Evans, *Art Pottery of the United States* (New York: Feingold & Lewis, 1987), p. 110.

8. Wendy Kaplan, ed., *The Art That Is Life: The Arts & Crafts Movement in America, 1875–1920* (Boston: Museum of Fine Arts, 1987), pp. 262–263.

9. Paul Evans, *Art Pottery of the United States* (New York: Feingold & Lewis, 1987), p. 11.

The famous Fulper mushroom lamps have soared in recent months to astronomical prices, as Arts and Crafts collectors have shown their attraction to the glow of the light passing through the twenty-four pieces of stained glass set into the shade. In addition to being beautiful, Fulper mushroom lamps are also quite rare. *(Photo courtesy of David Rago, Trenton)*

and most of their inventory. Art pottery was produced on a reduced scale for five more years until 1935, when production was completely switched to dinnerware, ceramic gifts, and figurines. Although the name of the corporation was not changed until 1955, the production of important Fulper art pottery had, in effect, ended in the fire of 1929.

Selected Prices

Bowl: cream-green high-gloss glaze with polychrome treatment, blue crystal inside, 3″ × 11″, $90–$100.

Bowl: earthenware, blue-gray matte glaze, with green and gunmetal gray interior, 2″ × 5″, $40–$50.

Bowl: molded decoration of peacock feathers and eye of peacock feather in separate panels glazed with ivory, brown, and blue flambé glaze, green and blue around top, then blue, brown, and ivory streaked glaze inside, 5″ × 9″, *$250–$275.*

Bowl: scalloped edge, light and dark blue crystalline with brown, 9″, *$65–$75.*

Bowl and flower frog: green crystalline glaze with gray-brown mirror drip, flower frog in shape of scarab, 2″ × 8″ (bowl), *$100–$125.*

Bowl: effigy, brown and deep yellow, *$250–$300.*

Bowl: open, five fish jumping in and out of waves on interior, covered in high-glaze gold, rust, and sea green flambé, 3″ × 11″, *$750–$850.*

Bowl: closed form, alternating rows of overlapping, pointed leaves glazed in ivory to mahogany to metallic green high glaze, 6″ × 8″, *$550–$650.*

Bowl: low bulb bowl with brown flambé over yellow, 11″ diameter, *$40–$50.*

Candleholder: hooded, three leaded glass inserts above the opening in blue and cream, covered with metallic brown-gray crystalline flambé, 10″, *$900–$1000.*

Candleholder: hooded, three pieces of leaded glass in blue and cream set above the rectangular opening, glazed in deep blue and brown flambé, 10″ × 5″, *$800–$900.*

Candleholder: hooded, in antique green, three pieces of slag glass inset above the opening, 11″ × 6″, *$800–$900.*

Candleholders: three angular raised handles centering socket (on circular disks), glazed in shaded green with crystalline mottling, 1″ × 6″, *$85–$95.*

Cat: figural, mottled brown and cream glaze, 9″, *$250–$300.*

Cat: Siamese, sitting in poised position, tail curled around the front with gunmetal to buttermilk flambé covering body, 5″ × 10″, *$500–$600.*

Chamberstick: arched candle shield with loop handle on round shallow dish, 7″, *$90–$100.*

Lamp: #301, small conical shade with vertical pink glass panels on swollen cylindrical standard flaring toward foot, shaded celery green and slate gray drip glaze, 16″ × 9″ (price too volatile to predict).

Lamp: desk, leaded glass and ceramic, 24 pieces of yellow and cream leaded glass set into the shade, 14″ × 8″ (price too volatile to predict).

Lamp: table, with ceramic shade inset with 24 pieces of yellow and green slag glass, atop a flaring base, 17″ × 14″ (price too volatile to predict).

Vase: ribbed form, flared rim on baluster-shape form tapering toward base, decorated with white dripping to pale blue on green ground, 10″, *$350–$400.*

Vase: swollen cylindrical form flattened on seven sides, dark green dripping to brown dripping to sand glazes, 10″, *$250–$350.*

Vase: wide mouth centered by two loop handles on squat, bulbous form tapering toward foot, pale blue drip over matte rose ground, 9″, *$275–$300.*

Vase: squat, two-tiered form, with two angular handles and covered with a metallic blue flambé, ending unevenly over a medium to dark brown flambé, 6″ × 9″, *$400–$450.*

Vase: bulbous form, opening with short collar neck and flared rim, four large looping handles on high shoulder, blue glaze, 13″ × 10″, *$800–$900.*

Vase: two-handled, black glaze, with bulbous middle, flared foot, and flared opening, lightly streaked with silver crystals, 13″ × 7″, *$500–$600.*

Vase: bulbous bottom, cylindrical neck, and flared mouth, two small handles on either side, high-gloss seafoam green on bottom to yellow flambé, 11″ × 8″, *$300–$350.*

Vase: baluster, with flared foot and opening, copper-dust crystalline finish, 13″ × 8″, *$550–$650.*

Vase: bulbous, with buttressed, undulating rim, two large semicircular strap handles, cucumber green matte glaze, 9″ × 10″, *$450–$500.*

Vase: squat, bulbous bottom, flaring cylindrical neck, black, streaky glaze over silvery green flambé, 14″ × 7″, *$450–$500.*

Vase: bulbous, with two applied ring handles, green flambé at top, rose pink on rest of pit, 12″ × 9″, *$175–$200.*

Vase: high-gloss periwinkle blue streaking to dark brown over cream flambé, 10″ × 6″, *$175–$200.*

Vase: seven-sided, with bulging bottom and olive green, light blue, brown, orange, and yellow flambé high glaze, 10″ × 5″, *$225–$250.*

Vase: bulbous, with collar neck and flared rim in streaked iridescent gunmetal and powder blue high glaze, 9″ × 7″, *$225–$250.*

Vase: bulbous, squat, with mirrored brown, gray-green, and blue flambé, shaded to rose matte glaze, 8″ × 8″, *$250–$275.*

Vase: green crystalline glaze, two handles, touches of brown, 8″, *$100–$125.*

Vase: copper crystalline glazed, 4″, *$150–$175.*

Vase: caramel flambé glaze, gray-brown drip, raised ball design around neck, 7″, *$65–$75.*

Vase: two-handled, tapered neck and bulbous bottom, glazed at top in copper dust on aqua and silver high-gloss glaze, 10″ × 8″, *$200–$225.*

Vase: bulbous, with inward-curving rim, silvery green flambé on butterscotch luster at bottom, 6″ × 6″, *$200–$225*.

Vase: floor, with royal blue glaze, 17″ × 10″, *$200–$225*.

Vase: two-handled, Grecian, with mirrored gunmetal glaze over copper-dust finish, 15″ × 8″, *$500–$600*.

Vase: buttressed with light brown flambé and silver crystalline over green high glaze, 8″ × 6″, *$125–$150*.

Vase: three in-body handles at neck with leopard skin crystalline over green high glaze, 7″ × 5″, *$125–$150*.

Vase: two-handled, in blue-green high glaze over light green, 12″ × 11″, *$250–$300*.

Vase: buttress style, with pink and green semigloss glaze, 8″, *$110–$135*.

Vase: high-gloss mirror black with gray-black crystals, 8″ × 5″, *$200–$225*.

Vase: high-gloss, dark mirror black over apple green, 2″ × 5″, *$55–$65*.

Vase: light melon green, 4″ × 10″, *$175–$200*.

Vase: gray-green matte glaze over light green–yellow base of octagonal shape, 7″ × 7″, *$175–$200*.

Vase: famille rose glaze touched with blue and brown at bottom, 12″, *$200–$225*.

Vase: two handles, blue and olive flambé glaze, 6″, *$100–$125*.

Vase: dark and light blue mirror-like glaze with green, 9″, *$125–$150*.

Vase: handles at neck, purple and blue crystalline glaze, 9″, *$100–$125*.

Vase: cream, green, and brown streaked flambé glaze, 7″, *$125–$150*.

GRAND FEU ART POTTERY

GRAND FEU
POTTERY

L. A., CAL.

Shopmark:
Impressed GRAND FEU POTTERY/L.A., CAL.

Principal Contribution:
Simple forms of vases and bowls featuring high-quality glazes

Founder:
Cornelius Brauckman

Born: 1864　　　　Died: 1952
Founded: ca. 1912　Closed: ca. 1916

Studios and Salesrooms:
Grand Feu Art Pottery
Los Angeles
ca. 1912–ca. 1916

The relatively few numbers of examples of Grand Feu pottery that were produced and have survived have demonstrated that the firm ranks with the most highly regarded of all of the art pottery manufacturers. Grand Feu pottery exhibits exquisite glazes in a variety of colors; the decorative effect was left to the unique reaction of the glaze on each piece to the heat of the kiln. Unfortunately, the firm and its production remained small during the few years it produced art pottery.

Selected Prices

Due to the infrequency with which examples of this pottery appear on the market, establishing an in-depth price guide has not yet been possible. Until additional information is compiled, readers are advised to seek counsel from experienced collectors before either buying or selling important pieces.

GRUEBY POTTERY

GRUEBY POTTERY
BOSTON. U.S.A.

Shopmarks:
Impressed GRUEBY/BOSTON. MASS or GRUEBY POTTERY/BOSTON/U.S.A. or GRUEBY FAIENCE CO./ BOSTON/U.S.A., occasionally around outline of lotus plant
Paper label with lotus plant logo

Principal Contributions:
Hand-thrown art pottery vases, lamp bases, bowls, and tiles in matte glazes

Founder:
William H. Grueby

Born: 1867   Died: 1925
Founded: 1894   Closed: 1919

Studios and Salesrooms:
Grueby Faience Company
Boston
1894–1909

Grueby Pottery Company, Inc.
Boston
1907–1911

Grueby Faience and Tile Company
Boston
1909–1919

"Although for many years, dull-finished pottery has been produced by sand-blasting ware with a glossy finish, or by taking a piece of glazed pottery and treating it with acid to make it dull, the Grueby potteries were the first in the history of ceramics to make a dull finish pottery in their kilns. The surface thus obtained has a deep velvety look, unlike any other finish made."

—*The Craftsman*
1914[1]

For design pioneers such as Laura Fry, Gustav Stickley, and William Grueby, success proved to be a double-edged sword. No sooner had each developed a new, popular handcrafted design than a horde of competitors flooded the market with thousands of imitations. In each case the less-expensive imitations found a public excited about the new "look" but willing to sacrifice quality for a lower price. As many of their competitors prospered, the pioneers found themselves struggling not only for recognition but, especially in the cases of Stickley and Grueby, for a means of saving the company they each had founded.

As a young man William Grueby received his first extensive training with the firm of J. & J. G. Low Art Tile Works in Chelsea, Massachusetts. Grueby worked for over ten years with John G. Low (1835–1907) and his master glaze technician, George

1. Mary White, quoted in "The Potters of America," *The Craftsman* (December 1914), p. 302. Although scholars have since proved that the Grueby Pottery was not the first to develop a matte glaze, Miss White's statement remains as evidence of the respect accorded the Grueby pottery and their matte glazes. Recent research has led many historians to conclude that the Hampshire Pottery deserves recognition as being the first to develop a matte glaze, but it was the combination of the Grueby matte glaze and their hand-modeled forms that led to the widespread popularity of both their pottery and the matte glaze.

W. Robertson (1835–1914), both of whom had been trained by James Robertson at the Chelsea Keramic Art Works. In 1890 both Robertson and Grueby left the Low firm to establish individual businesses. While Robertson formed a new tile company with his brother Hugh in Chelsea, William Grueby moved to nearby Revere to begin manufacturing architectural terra-cotta, glazed bricks, and decorative tiles. A brief partnership intended to expand the market for his architectural products failed, and in 1894 Grueby reorganized his sole partnership under the name of the Grueby Faience Company.[2]

Grueby continued producing terra-cotta ornaments, but his interest in glazes (inspired, most likely, by George Robertson) soon led to experimentation with pottery forms, as he utilized the center portion of the kiln that grew too hot for the firing of the terra-cotta panels. In 1897 Grueby formally incorporated his firm to raise the capital necessary to expand into the lucrative, but risky, art pottery market. Two of his principal stockholders also became working partners: William H. Graves, a young architect from a prominent Massachusetts family, assumed the responsibilities of the corporation's business manager, while George P. Kendrick, a noted silversmith, became the chief designer of the Grueby Faience Company's early line of vases, lamp bases, and bowls. William Grueby remained the firm's general manager, but the addition of these two gifted individuals freed him to experiment with and develop a line of matte glazes.

Grueby's initial pottery experiments had utilized the same clay that had been ferried across from Martha's Vineyard for use in producing his terra-cotta ornaments. Although additional clay was shipped from New Jersey, the pottery produced by the newly organized firm retained some of the coarseness associated with their terra-cotta products—a circumstance that did not escape notice by at least one of their early critics.[3] Despite this questionable "flaw," the hand-thrown Grueby pottery garnered numerous awards and medals at major exhibitions in Boston, Paris, Russia, and St. Louis within the first seven years of its

2. "Faience" refers to any glazed earthenware or pottery, especially that of a fine quality with highly colored designs.

3. See *Keramic Studio* (February 1905), pp. 216–217.

The most famous of all of the Grueby forms is this gourd vase
(12″ × 7½″) with nine rows of alternating leaves beneath the
classic Grueby matte green glaze. Since each was hand-molded,
minute differences in the application of the leaves distinguish fine
examples from outstanding ones. *(Photo courtesy of David Rago,
Trenton)*

formal existence.[4] Their richly textured, flowing, matte green
glaze set in motion a trend that influenced the art pottery movement for years to come. "Immediately upon its appearance,"
the *Boston Globe* reported, "examples of the ware were bought
by museums around the globe from Philadelphia to Berlin to
Budapest to Tokyo."[5] Their immediate success, according to respected scholar Paul Evans, was due as much to the "shapes
[that] distinguished Grueby ware every bit as much as the glaze,
as they depended not on intricacy or elaborateness of design
and ornamentation, but rather on integrity and contour."[6]

In 1899, in an attempt to distinguish between their two principal lines, the firm established two loosely defined divisions.

4. The Grueby Faience Company shared a booth with Gustav Stickley
at the Pan-American Exposition in Buffalo, New York, in 1901. That
year and the next Stickley advertised small tables featuring "the now-
famous Grueby tiles" set in each top. Surviving examples are considered
both rare and extremely valuable.

5. Robert W. Blasberg, *Grueby* (Syracuse, NY: Everson Museum of Art,
1981), p. 17.

6. Paul Evans, *Art Pottery of the United States* (New York: Charles
Scribner's Sons, 1974), p. 119.

The Grueby Faience Company continued to manufacture terra-cotta, while the Grueby Pottery (formally incorporated in 1907) concentrated on art pottery. Despite the departure of chief designer George Kendrick in 1901, the pottery branch continued to excel. Addison B. LeBoutillier assumed design duties in 1901 and was succeeded years later by Julia H. Bradley. Although much of the decorating was assigned to female graduates of Boston area art schools, the quality and the forms remained consistent, for the decorative design of each vase, bowl, and lamp base was dictated by the chief designer and by William Grueby as operations manager. "One might wonder, though," Robert Ellison has speculated, "whether the lack of novelty and change did not ultimately lead to the pottery's downfall."[7]

In the process the designer would determine both the form of the hand-thrown vessel and the decoration—most often leaves or a simple flower—before turning the barely dry, though not yet fired, piece over to one of the assistants. The decorations would then be pressed into their appointed places, the piece fired, the glaze applied, and the piece returned to the kiln. The glazes included yellow, brown, blue, and white, but the most popular was the famous matte Grueby green—a color that inspired similar glazes at Teco, Van Briggle, Merrimac, and numerous other potteries. In rare instances a second or third color might also be applied to the tips of the leaves or the petals of the flowers; these have risen to become the most highly sought-after of all the Grueby designs.

In 1907, perhaps feeling the first effects of the flood of imitators that threatened to erode their hold on the art pottery market, the Grueby Pottery Company was incorporated and additional stockholders were brought in. The other branch, the Grueby Faience Company, entered into the first stages of bankruptcy two years later. In 1909 William Grueby turned management of the Grueby Pottery Company over to his associates, but within two years the art pottery line was brought to a close. After leaving Grueby Pottery, William Grueby formed a new Grueby Faience and Tile Company in an attempt to reestablish

7. Martin Eidelberg, *From Our Native Clay* (New York: Turn of the Century Editions, 1987), p. 66.

This Grueby vase features the characteristic leaves, which were shaped first and then applied to the moist clay body, but with an added touch: the petals of the flowers have been highlighted with yellow, making this a rare and highly desirable seven-inch vase. *(Photo courtesy of Don Treadway, Cincinnati)*

his name in the architectural wares business. As it was beginning to succeed, however, a disastrous fire in 1913 destroyed most of the plant. The factory was rebuilt, sales rebounded, and in 1919 the Grueby Faience and Tile Company was sold to the C. Pardee Works of New Jersey and moved there by 1921. Four years later, in 1925, William H. Grueby died.

Indicative of the respect accorded the Grueby pottery was the early agreement in which the L. C. Tiffany Company (along with several others) purchased Grueby bases for their prestigious line of stained-glass lamp shades at a time when Tiffany had his own art pottery factory. These lamps have since become the most highly sought-after of all of their type produced in this era. As another aspect of the pottery, Grueby tiles were produced at the same time as the art pottery and also fall into various value categories. An undamaged condition is crucial, and decorative scenes of animals or landscapes are firmly favored over undecorated tiles.

The Grueby Pottery, like its competitors, manufactured vases and bowls that, while always hand-thrown and individually modeled, were less expensive to produce than some of their more expressive and highly organic wares. These less-imaginative examples remain quite moderate in value, especially when compared to some of the more dynamic pieces. Just as not all Gustav Stickley furniture is as highly valued as the inlaid or spindle examples, not all Grueby pottery is as fervently collected as the two- or three-color examples. Grueby collectors continually seek expressive, organic vases demonstrating exquisitely tooled leaves or flowers covered with glazes rich in texture and color. Grueby offered several different glaze colors, but their famous matte green remains the most popular today. Although Grueby manufactured only hand-thrown pottery, the fact remains that some of his forms were not as expressive as others. Lifeless or unimaginative vases and bowls, regardless of their size, are less desirable than even small examples with crisp, vibrant decorations.

Although continued success escaped William Grueby and the firm he founded, the pottery he produced has endured as one of the most valued examples of art pottery produced during the Arts and Crafts movement, for as Robert Ellison has observed, "Grueby's sparse, austere ware were welcomed as a purifying concept in a market burdened with pottery that was either over-ornamented or full of dark, glossy painting."[8]

Selected Prices

Bowl: squat bulbous bowl in oatmeal glaze, undecorated, 4″, *$100–$125*.

Bowl: sculpted leaves surrounding piece, green matte glaze, 2″ × 6″, *$350–$400*.

Bowl: rolled rim on squat bulbous form molded with overlapping leaves, 2″ × 5″, *$300–$350*.

Lamp base: squat, cylindrical form with alternating tall blades and short leaves, matte green glaze, 11″, *$1000–$1250*.

Paperweight: scarab, mottled green glaze, 3″, *$125–$150*.

8. Martin Eidelberg, *From Our Native Clay* (New York: Turn of the Century Editions, 1987), p. 50.

Tile: matte green, undecorated, square, 6″, $75–$85.

Tile: incised Viking ship in white and brown on blue-green ground, 4″, $125–$150.

Tile: overlapping horses as part of a larger frieze, white on blue and green glazes, 6″, $300–$350.

Tile: black and beige Spanish galleon ship with white sails on slate blue ground, 8″, $300–$350.

Tile: molded grape pattern, square, 6″, $100–$125.

Tile: Spanish galleon on high seas decoration, 6″ × 6″, $90–$100.

Tile: prominent light brown tortoise beneath cluster of oversize green leaves, 6″ × 6″, $300–$350.

Tile: white polar bear against mottled, light blue matte ground, 5″ × 7″, $400–$450.

Vase: wide rolled rim and angled shoulder with repeating yellow flowers and molded leaves on bulbous form, 10″ × 8″, $2750–$3250.

Vase: elongated cylindrical neck on squat bulbous base with molded leaves, matte green, 7″, $350–$400.

Vase: slightly flaring rim and tapering neck on bulbous form with vertical repeating leaves, matte green, 6″, $250–$300.

Vase: two-color, elongated form, vertical green ribbed leaves over yellow ground, 9″, $1500–$1750.

Vase: cylindrical, vertical ribbing, 9″, $550–$650.

Vase: elongated, narrow neck on bulbous form, molded with overlapping leaves, mottled matte green glaze, 13″, $3000–$3500.

Vase: rolled rim and cylindrical neck on squat bulbous form with ridges, 4″, $250–$300.

Vase: elongated cylindrical neck on squat base angled at shoulder, mottled green, 8″, *$200–$250*.

Vase: wide mouth on swollen cylindrical form, molded with broad leaves alternating with closed buds suggesting yellow, green glaze, 11″, *$2500–$3000*.

Vase: two-color, short flared rim on swollen cylindrical form tapering toward base, decorated with six yellow buds alternating with broad leaves, deep green matte glaze, 10″, *$2500–$3000*.

Vase: flared rim and short neck on bulbous form, molded with classical discus thrower on one side and standing figure on reverse, matte green glaze, 10″, *$3000–$3500*.

Vase: flared rim and angled shoulder on cylindrical tapering form, decorated with buds alternating with leaves, 12″, *$1500–$1750*.

Vase: green matte oviform, with flaring rim, six long stylized leaves with rounded tips, alternating with six yellow buds on thin stems, 10″ × 7″, *$2000–$2250*.

Vase: bulbous tapering to long cylindrical neck, incised with eight elongated stylized leaves, in green matte glaze, 10″ × 3″, *$900–$1000*.

Vase: bulbous bottom, small pinched neck, and flared rim, ten incised vertical ribs with thick, mottled ochre matte finish, 4″ × 4″, *$350–$400*.

Vase: gourd, with nine rows of alternating leaves on body closing to swelling neck with nine short rows of leaves of a similar design, covered in green matte glaze, 12″ × 7″, *$5000–$6000*.

Vase: bulbous, with closed neck and flared rim, nine vertical melon ribs from top to bottom, glazed in green matte finish, 16″ × 10″, *$2500–$3000*.

Vase: white mottled glaze, 5″ × 4″, *$175–$200*.

Vase: burnt orange matte glaze, 3″ × 4″, $200–$225.

Vase: ovoid, with sculpted daffodils in yellow, mauve, and blue, and long spiked medium green leaves on darker green ground, 11″ × 6″, $3500–$4000.

Vase: squat, bulbous, with closed neck and flared rim, seven red buds alternating with seven broad green leaves on green matte ground, 6″ × 8″, $4500–$5000.

Vase: bulbous, squat bottom and long, thick, cylindrical neck, with seven crisply modeled trefoils in yellow at the top alternating with seven sharply rendered spade-shaped green leaves at the bottom, 12″ × 8″, $1500–$1750.

Vase: bulbous bottom tapering to cylindrical neck, with five tooled and applied trefoils alternating with five tooled buds rising from a triple overlapping row of leaves, 14″ × 8″, $1600–$1850.

Vase: three-lobed, leaves alternating with buds, under yellow-brown ochre matte glaze, 9″ × 5″, $350–$400.

Vase: green matte, round leaf design, 5″, 225–$250.

Vase: pale green matte glaze, 5″, $175–$200.

Vase: squat cylindrical form, with swollen base encircled with modeled stylized lotus leaves under green matte glaze, 5″ × 6″, $400–$500.

Vase: ovoid, with gently flared rim, three broad leaves, green matte glaze, 8″ × 4″, $650–$750.

Vase: bulbous, footed base, closed and flared rim, tooled leaves under green matte glaze, 9″ × 5″, $675–$775.

Vase: bulbous bottom tapering to a long, flaring neck, five white buds alternated with five short, broad leaves, fine green matte glaze, 7″ × 4″, $900–$1000.

Vase: bulbous bottom, squat, with tooled pointed leaves encircling base and part of flared neck, 5″ × 6″, $375–$425.

Even within the category of two-color Grueby vases, a special example will stand above all others. This mint-condition bulbous form (12″ × 8″) was decorated by artist Ruth Erikson in 1902. Featuring nine yellow narcissus on an even matte green ground, it still bore its original $30 price tag when it sold for $14,300 at a 1986 Rago auction in New York City. *(Photo courtesy of David Rago, Trenton)*

Vase: watermelon shape, mottled cobalt blue matte base with six incised vertical ribs and metal fitting, 7″ × 4″, $400–$450.

Vase: light blue matte glaze, low, with five precisely modeled leaves, 5″ × 4″, $400–$450.

Vase: green matte, carved panels around vase, 3″, $300–$350.

Vase: green matte glaze covering finely tooled leaves around bottom with stems and buds extending to top of vase, 8″, $600–$700.

Vase: thick green matte glaze, 3″, $200–$225.

HAMPSHIRE POTTERY

J.S.T. &CO.
KEENE. NH.

Hampshire
Pottery

Shopmarks:
Various combinations of the following: JAMES S. TAFT & CO./
J.S.T. & CO./ KEENE, N.H./HAMPSHIRE POTTERY/
HAMPSHIRE, printed, incised, or on a paper label.

Principal Contribution:
Matte glaze artware, including vases, bowls, and lamp bases

Founder:
James S. Taft

Born: 1844   Died: 1923
Founded: 1871   Closed: 1923

Studios and Salesrooms:
Hampshire Pottery Company
Keene, New Hampshire
1871–1923

"The 'Witch Jug' made by Hampshire for Daniel Low of Salem,
Massachusetts, and which can accurately be dated as produced
in 1892, was matt glazed and established the fact that Hampshire
was producing pieces thus glazed at least four years before
Grueby began operation."

—*Paul Evans*[1]

1. Albert Christian Revi, ed., *The Spinning Wheel Complete Book of Antiques* (New York: Grosset & Dunlap, 1972), p. 112.

In 1871, at the age of twenty-seven, James S. Taft purchased an abandoned building in Keene, New Hampshire, long known for its fine clay deposits, and with the help of his uncle transformed it into a budding pottery operation. Unfortunately, it burned down before the first piece of redware was produced. Less than two months later, however, a new building had been constructed, and the partnership had begun selling simple flowerpots produced from local clays. Within the next few years Taft and his uncle increased their line to include stoneware items, buying a neighboring pottery building to aid in their expansion, and by 1876 they were advertising flowerpots, vases, florists' supplies, and related items from one plant and jars, pitchers, jugs, pots, and similar household containers from the other.[2]

The turning point in the development of Keene pottery came in 1879, when Taft hired Thomas Stanley, an Englishman, to oversee the two plants and their continued expansion. Soon after arriving Stanley initiated a high-glaze majolica tableware that led to improvements in the quality of the firm's clay, decorations, glazes, and equipment. A gifted artist by the name of Wallace L. King was added to the growing staff; King oversaw the production of a Royal Worcester—style line of "plates, dishes, dressing table sets, etc. in a semi-porcelain body with a pink-tinged ivory matt surface"[3] and a popular line of souvenir plates and jugs with transfer-printed scenes, including "the famous Longfellow jug and the witch jug made to be sold in Salem, Massachusetts."[4] While the success of their transfer-decorated line paved the way for further expansion in their staff during the last decade of the nineteenth century, it also overshadowed an achievement in the field of matte glazes that has since been credited to the Grueby Faience Company. As the Kovels observed in their study, confirming Evans's earlier conclusion, the Hampshire pottery's "green matte finish was particularly popular. It is interesting that while Grueby was

2. Paul Evans, *Art Pottery of the United States* (New York: Charles Scribner's Sons, 1974), p. 129.

3. Elisabeth Cameron, *Encyclopedia of Pottery & Porcelain: 1800–1960* (New York: Facts on File Publications, 1986), p. 322.

4. Ralph and Terry Kovel, *The Kovels' Collectors Guide to American Art Pottery* (New York: Crown Publishers, 1974), p. 57.

The similarity between this Hampshire molded vase (10″ × 7″) and the hand-shaped Grueby line is unmistakable. This particular example had been drilled to accommodate a lamp cord and suffered in value as a result. *(Photo courtesy of D. J. Puffert, Sausalito)*

credited with making the first popular matte finished art pottery in America, the Hampshire Pottery used this glaze in 1883, four years before Grueby."[5]

Cadmon Robertson, Taft's brother-in-law, who joined the firm in 1904, proved to be a crucial addition to their management at a time when Wallace King, their forest artist, was nearing retirement. "A notable chemist, he introduced no fewer than 900 formulas and was responsible for the great variety of matt glazes from green and peacock (two-tone) blue, to old blue, gray, bronze, brown and yellow."[6] The good fortune of "New Hampshire's most successful commercial pottery"[7] seemed due to three factors: a durable clay body, a variety of affordable molded shapes, and quality matte glazes.

King's retirement in 1908 and Robertson's death in 1914 proved too much for the seventy-year-old Taft to overcome. Production continued to decrease until 1916, when the Hampshire Pottery Company was sold to George M. Morton, a former

5. Ralph and Terry Kovel, *The Kovels' Collectors Guide to American Art Pottery* (New York: Crown Publishers, 1974), p. 57.

6. Paul Evans, *Art Pottery of the United States* (New York: Charles Scribner's Sons, 1974), p. 130.

7. Albert Christian Revi, ed., *The Spinning Wheel Complete Book of Antiques* (New York: Grosset & Dunlap, 1972), p. 110.

potter at the Grueby Faience Company. Using the molds and glaze formulas included with the plant, Morton immediately fired more than one thousand of Hampshire pottery's most popular forms, but his planned infusion into the pottery market was halted by the onset of World War I. Afterward Morton switched Hampshire's focus to restaurant china and mosaic floor tiles, but in 1923 "the saga of the pottery . . . was drawn to a close with the death of the firm's founder, J. S. Taft, the dismantling of equipment and the destruction or scattering of the molds."[8]

In the years since, Hampshire pottery has languished in obscurity outside its home state, but the recent resurgence of interest in the Arts and Crafts movement and the sudden upswing in prices being paid for Grueby pottery has refocused attention on Hampshire pottery—particularly those pieces that have a Grueby-like appearance. Large matte-glazed examples with crisp, detailed features have developed a following of their own. Lamps and large vases in particular have found a new crowd of collectors who, like earlier admirers from their grandparents' era, are less concerned with the fact that Hampshire pottery was formed from molds than they are with its overall appearance—and its reasonable price.

Selected Prices

Bowl: blue matte glaze over darker blue, molded mushrooms design, 2″ × 5″, *$225–$250.*

Bowl: rolled rim molded with bud and lily pad leaves, matte green glaze, 10″, *$100–$125.*

Lamp base: five fingers on cylindrical standard flaring toward base with raised buds, 21″, *$200–$225.*

Lamp: oil, Handel shade, 16″ × 10″, *$600–$700.*

Pitcher: swollen cylindrical form with molded leaves curling to form spout and intertwined vines to form handle, mottled slate blue glaze with highlights of pink, 8″, *$125–$175.*

8. Paul Evans, *Art Pottery of the United States* (New York: Charles Scribner's Sons, 1974), p. 130.

This Hampshire pottery vase was designed and drilled as a lamp base in the factory. The sixteen-inch shade is unsigned, but similar examples were purchased from the Handel lamp company. The total height of the lamp is nineteen and one half inches. *(Photo courtesy of Robert W. Skinner, Boston)*

Vase: bulbous form tapering to base, molded overlapping leaf design and blue-green mottled matte glaze, 8″ × 8″, *$200–$225.*

Vase: green squat bulbous form with molded flowers, 5″, *$65–$75.*

Vase: squat form with rim and angled shoulder with broad leaves, blue glaze, 2″ × 5″, *$50–$60.*

Vase: repeating molded buds and broad leaves, 7″, *$100–$125.*

Vase: embossed with six long wide pointed leaves alternating with six buds on elongated stems, under green finish, 15″ × 9″, *$500–$600.*

Vase: bulbous form with flared neck, stylized embossed leaves encircling the pot, covered with thick, drippy, green matte glaze, 10″ × 8″, *$100–$125.*

Vase: bulbous bottom with long cylinder neck and flared rim in green matte finish, 8″, *$100–$125.*

Vase: #127, molded leaf design, glaze in green and brown, 8″, *$350–$400.*

Vase: light green mottled glaze with highlighted leaf design, 10″ × 7″, *$150–$175.*

Vase: small, green mottled glaze with red highlights, 3″ × 3″, *$65–$75.*

Vase: green matte glaze with stylized decoration, 2″ × 7″, *$75–$85.*

Vase: green matte glaze, molded flower and stem design, 7″, *$100–$125.*

Vase: green leaves on yellow ground, 7″, *$150–$175.*

Vase: tulip design around top, vines to bottom, green matte glaze, 9″, *$175–$200.*

Vase: thick brown and green drippy matte glaze, 7″, *$125–$150.*

JERVIS POTTERY

Shopmark:
Incised vertical JERVIS, occasionally wtih the letters *O* and *B* (Oyster Bay)

Principal Contribution:
Incised-decorated vases and bowls

Founder:
William Percival Jervis
(with initial assistance from Frederick H. Rhead)
Born: 1849   Died: 1925
Founded: 1908   Closed: ca. 1912

Studios and Salesrooms:
Jervis Pottery
Oyster Bay, New York
1908–ca. 1912

After having written about and worked for several potteries, William Jervis, assisted by his friend Frederick H. Rhead, whom he had worked with at the Avon Faience Company, opened a small pottery in 1908 in Oyster Bay, New York. Rhead may have designed some of Jervis's molds before leaving around 1910 to join the newly formed University City Pottery. Jervis preferred an incised form of decorative technique for his molded pottery; each piece was coated with a thin white clay slip, which, when dry, was carved with incised lines. The unwanted white slip was then peeled away, leaving the design intact on the redware body. The form would then most often be fired with a matte or, on occasion, a metallic glaze. The small pottery, with its limited output, closed around 1912 apparently on the retirement of William Jervis.

Selected Prices

Due to the infrequency with which examples of this pottery appear on the market, establishing an in-depth price guide has not yet been possible. The examples listed below are indicative only of the value of pieces of similar form and decoration. Until additional information is compiled, readers are advised to seek counsel from experienced collectors before either buying or selling important pieces.

Bowl: bisque royal blue glaze, band decorated around its rim with incised geometric pattern in pale blue and white, 3″ × 6″, *$475–$525*.

Mug: art pottery motto, slight flare to the otherwise cylindrical form with cut-out square handle, incised with motto "The joys that are to come" and flowers with leaf blades, green and white glaze on dark brown bisque, 6″ × 4″, *$250–$300*.

Pot: bulbous, with six carved, curving handles reaching from rim to base, tooled with stylized leaf forms, oval opening between handles to reveal a solid pot underneath, 8″ × 12″, *$2250–$2750*.

LONHUDA POTTERY

Shopmarks:
The word *LONHUDA* over the profile of an Indian chief's head, often with the year 1893
The word *LONHUDA* and the year, often with artist's initials

Principal Contribution:
Slip-decorated art pottery

Founder:
William A. Long
Born: 1844   Died: 1918
Founded: 1892   Closed: 1895

Studios and Salesrooms:
Lonhuda Pottery Company
Steubenville, Ohio
1892–1895

"Like its rival [Rookwood] it is somewhat costly and beyond the reach of many who may admire its worth, but good things are never cheap, and the Lonhuda is surely deserving of a rank among the best."

—*Pottery critic*
1892[1]

A Civil War veteran and small-town druggist, William A. Long may have seemed an unlikely candidate to become the founder of an influential art pottery, but Long was also a diligent chemist and a talented painter. After a trip to the Philadelphia Exposition in 1876, where he was introduced to various pottery forms, he began experimenting with a number of glazes in the rear of his Steubenville, Ohio, drugstore. "The records are confused, but either William Long developed a brown underglaze of the type used by Rookwood or he was licensed to use a process developed by Laura Fry in 1889."[2] In either event, by as early as 1889 Long had mastered the newly discovered underglaze technique of decorating pottery, and in 1892, after two years of experimentation in a small, homemade kiln, he was prepared to form a pottery company with the financial backing of two of his friends—W. H. Hunter, a local newspaper editor, and Alfred Day, an experienced potter. Their last names were combined with Long's to create the new company's name: Lonhuda.

The new firm moved rapidly, hiring Laura Fry, Helen Harper, Jessie Spaulding, Mary Taylor, and Sarah R. McLaughlin as artists. Laura Fry (1857–1943) had worked at the Rookwood Pottery in Cincinnati from 1881 to 1887. In 1884 Miss Fry made what many authorities have called the most important advance in the development of art pottery. She introduced a new method of applying underglaze decoration using a

1. *Pottery and Glassware Reporter* (December 15, 1892); also Paul Evans, *Art Pottery of the United States* (New York: Charles Scribner's Sons, 1974), p. 144.
2. Ralph and Terry Kovel, *The Kovels' Collectors Guide to American Art Pottery* (New York: Crown Publishers, 1974), p. 73.

"mouth-blown atomizer for spraying backgrounds of colored slip [resulting in] a smooth, harmonious ground with subtle, blended gradations of colors"[3] that the old brush method had been unable to achieve. The Rookwood firm incorporated her technique into what was to become one of its most popular—and most often imitated—lines, the Rookwood Standard. On leaving Rookwood, Miss Fry attempted to retain control over the use of her technique and was granted a patent in 1889. The Rookwood corporation, however, continued to teach the technique to its decorators, despite the threat of legal action. Miss Fry was an instructor at Purdue University in 1892 when asked to join the staff at Lonhuda Pottery. The following year, undoubtedly with Long's encouragement, Fry took legal action against Rookwood in an attempt to prevent them from using the technique she had developed, which at that time was also being utilized at Lonhuda. The case was not settled until 1898, when the court ruled in favor of Rookwood, explaining that although Laura Fry's patented technique had found "a new use for an old tool, the process was not a new one."[4]

In only its second year of existence, Lonhuda pottery was displayed at the Chicago World's Fair in 1893, where the relatively unknown pottery attracted a good deal of attention with its line of underglaze-decorated vases. Their artists used flowers, insects, fish, famous people, birds, and Indians as their motifs under quality high-gloss glazes on the traditional American Indian pottery forms that had inspired Long. One of the people attracted by Lonhuda pottery was Samuel Weller, who in 1894 convinced Long and his partners to sell him an interest in Lonhuda and to move their operation into one of Weller's Zanesville, Ohio, plants. Although the firm's pottery had garnered considerable artistic acclaim at the Chicago Exposition, the editor, the potter, and the former druggist had no experience in establishing an effective national sales campaign. Weller offered

3. Martin Eidelberg, ed., *From Our Native Clay* (New York: Turn of the Century Editions, 1987), p. 11.

4. Paul Evans, *Art Pottery of the United States* (New York: Charles Scribner's Sons, 1974), p. 142.

what the three men needed: additional capital and an established marketing network.

In 1895 the partners closed their small Steubenville operation, and Long moved to Zanesville to oversee the transition.
That same year Lonhuda Faience was put into full production
and was well received. Once Samuel Weller was assured of the
success of the new line and of the Lonhuda formula, his need
for Long dissipated, and within a year the partnership was dis-
solved. Understandably bitter, Long took his formula to Weller's archrival, the J. B. Owens Pottery, where it evolved into
that firm's first line of slip-decorated pottery, Utopian.

In 1896 Samuel Weller renamed his new line Louwelsa, combining the first three letters of his young daughter's name with
the first three letters of his last name plus the initials of his first
and middle names. Ironically, in 1909, at the age of sixty-five,
Long moved back to Zanesville, Ohio, where he went to work
for Samuel Weller.

Selected Prices

Due to the infrequency with which examples of this pottery
appear on the market, establishing an in-depth price guide has
not yet been possible. The examples listed below are indicative
only of the value of pieces of similar form and decoration. Until
additional information is compiled, readers are advised to seek
counsel from experienced collectors before either buying or selling important pieces.

Pitcher: glazed, slip-decorated with grapes on trailing
vine, 12″ × 5″, $200–$225.

Teapot: floral motif, high glaze, 5″, $375–$425.

Vase: floral motif, in green and brown high glaze, 8″, $250–
$300.

Vase: floral motif, bulbous form, 7″, $225–$275.

Vase: decorated maple leaves, pine glaze, 8″, $275–$325.

Vase: four-footed, pillow, grazing doe and stag on light

green to olive green to chocolate brown background, 11″ × 11″, *$1000–$1250*.

Vase: bisque oviform, with grayish blue grapes on pale green and rust vine, 9″ × 5″, *$200–$225*.

LOSANTI

Lo'santi

Shopmarks:
Incised initials *LMcL*, often overlapping *LOSANTI*, occasionally in Oriental lettering
Often the year and the mark of the pottery that produced the blank will appear

Principal Contribution:
Decorated porcelain vases

Founder:
Mary Louise McLaughlin
Born: 1847   Died: 1939
Founded: 1898   Closed: 1906

Studios and Salesrooms:
Mary Louise McLaughlin
Cincinnati, Ohio
active 1877–1906

"Miss McLaughlin, the President of the Club, is the discoverer of the method of decorating under the glaze that is still used as the foundation principle of the work at the Rookwood Pottery.

The same method was used at the other Art Potteries of Cincinnati during their existence."

—*Chicago World's Fair*
1893[1]

The verbal battle between Mary Louise McLaughlin, Thomas J. Wheatley, and Marie Longworth Storer over recognition as the first American to develop successfully the underglaze technique of decorating pottery with tinted clays (called slips in their creamy consistency) lasted from 1877 until at least 1893, when William Taylor, the president of Rookwood, bristled over the suggestion that his firm was indebted to McLaughlin for the technique that propelled Rookwood toward continued success. By that date Mary Louise McLaughlin had, for the most part, concluded her experiments with underglaze decoration—due in no small part to her eviction from the Rookwood Pottery in 1892 by Taylor.

McLaughlin's talents were eventually turned toward the challenge of creating (for the first time outside a major firm) a decorative porcelain. "The obstacles for Miss McLaughlin seemed overwhelming at times: no published technical instruction to follow, the necessity of adapting foreign formulas to American materials, [and] complaints from neighbors about the burning of coal in a backyard kiln,"[2] all of which contributed to an arduous trial-and-error beginning. Although her first public showing was in 1899, little more than a year after her experiments had begun, "it was not until about March 1901 that the best results were secured by a single firing at over 2500° F., wherein the native clay body and glaze matured together."[3]

McLaughlin continued to develop her technique, calling her new line of porcelain Losanti (Cincinnati had once been called

1. Herbert Peck, *The Book of Rookwood Pottery* (New York: Crown Publishers, 1968), p. 47.

2. Wendy Kaplan, ed., *The Art That Is Life: The Arts & Crafts Movement in America, 1875–1920* (Boston: Museum of Fine Arts, 1987), p. 250.

3. Paul Evans, *Art Pottery of the United States* (New York: Feingold & Lewis, 1987), p. 148.

Losantiville). Decorations included both painting and incising designs in the clay; the latter occasionally developed into pierced designs. Her particular style of carving is reflective of Art Nouveau motifs, as she "integrated her designs of gently swirling, conventionalized floral motifs . . . with the forms of the vases. Some leaf designs were carved so as to envelop and become the form of the vase itself, the irregular edges of the leaves jutting out to form the lip."[4] Soft, pastel glazes were used most often, although on rare occasions a bright, colorful glaze, such as red or even purple, will be found.

McLaughlin's experiments with porcelain were drawn to a close in 1906 as she moved on to conquer other challenges.

Selected Prices

Due to the infrequency with which examples of this pottery appear on the market, establishing an in-depth price guide has not yet been possible. The examples listed below are indicative only of the value of pieces of similar form and decoration. Until additional information is compiled, readers are advised to seek counsel from experienced collectors before either buying or selling important pieces.

Vase: porcelain, relief-decorated, short neck on bulbous form tapering toward base, carved with scrolled ferns, mottled maroon highlights on glossy green ground, 5", $5000–$6000.

Vase: squat, bulbous, painted and incised blue morning glory and dark green leaves, white porcelain ground, 2" × 2", $700–$800.

4. Martin Eidelberg, ed., *From Our Native Clay* (New York: Turn of the Century Editions, 1987), p. 50.

LOW ART TILE WORKS

Shopmark:
Name of firm incised or in raised letters on reverse of tile, often with CHELSEA, MASS. USA/ COPYRIGHT and the year

Principal Contribution:
Decorative tiles and art pottery vases

Founder:
John Gardner Low

Born: 1835   Died: 1907
Founded: ca. 1878   Closed: 1902

Studios and Salesrooms:
J. & J. G. Low Art Tile Works
Chelsea, Massachusetts
1878–1883

J. G. & J. F. Low Art Tile Works
Chelsea, Massachusetts
1883–1902

"The Lows never imitated other work, either domestic or foreign. They have never made hand-painted, mosaic, printed, encaustic, or floor tiles, and they have never employed men who were trained in other tile works. Consequently, their products are characterized by a marked originality, both in style and design, which has caused them to be extensively imitated, both at home and abroad."

—*Edwin Barber*
ca. 1904[1]

1. Ralph and Terry Kovel, *The Kovels' Collectors Guide to American Art Pottery* (New York: Crown Publishers, 1974), pp. 83–84.

Educated and trained in Europe as a landscape artist, John G. Low turned his talents to ceramics when it became apparent, at age thirty-five, that he was not going to be able to support himself through the sale of his paintings. Back in his hometown of Chelsea, Massachusetts, Low learned that a local pottery run by the Robertson family was in need of artists to decorate their new line of art pottery. Though inexperienced in this field, Low went to work for the Chelsea Keramic Art Works at the time that James Robertson, the father of the three famous pottery sons, "made what is believed to be the first pressed clay tiles produced in the United States."[2]

Low stayed with the Robertsons for more than a year, learning both the art pottery and the tile trade and experimenting with his own designs before leaving. Like many artists in 1876, Low journeyed to Philadelphia for the Centennial Exposition, returning with plans to form his own tile works. With the help of his father, John Low, the J. & J. G. Low Art Tile Works opened in 1878 in a new and fully equipped factory building. One of their first employees was George Robertson, the eldest son of James Robertson and an experienced glazer, whom John had come to know while working at the Chelsea Keramic Art Works. They produced tiles in a number of different sizes and a variety of colors, but most were either six or four inches square in natural tones of brown or green. Smaller tiles, especially the more common round tiles, were generally designed to decorate cast-iron stoves.

Although decorative tiles had long been produced in England, John G. Low was forced to learn the process through experimentation. The traditional means involved pressing damp clay dust under extreme pressure, using a metal plate decorated with the desired design. Afterward the tile would be glazed and then placed in the kiln to be baked. In another technique, wet clay was pressed into a mold that contained the desired design; it was then allowed to dry slowly, at which time it would shrink enough to permit it to be removed from the mold. After

2. Ralph and Terry Kovel, *The Kovels' Collectors Guide to American Art Pottery* (New York: Crown Publishers, 1974), p. 28.

additional air-drying, each tile was glazed and sent to the kiln. Low developed a process that he had first observed at the Robertson firm: actual plant forms, such as grass or leaves, were pressed into tiles, which were then used to form a matching tile with a corresponding raised design.

Another early employee was Arthur Osborne, a sculptor who stayed with the firm for more than fifteen years, working as an artist and designer. Osborne developed low-relief "plastic sketches,"[3] as Low called them—large square or rectangular tiles with sculpted scenes often depicting people from foreign countries, stories from mythology, animals, or plants, though studies of individuals were also popular. Most were signed with the artist's initials, the letter *A* inside the letter *O*.

Recognition came quickly for the young firm, as it received awards both in America and abroad for its fine tile work. A few years later, in 1883, the elder Low retired from the firm, making way for his grandson, John Farnsworth Low, and a new name for the business: the J. G. & J. F. Low Art Tile Works. The firm expanded into pottery, undoubtedly drawing on the experience brought to the firm by both Arthur Osborne and George Robertson. The Low Chelsea Ware shared much in common with the Oriental-inspired designs of Hugh Robertson: simple, undecorated forms with glazes that "ranged from dark cream to chocolate; delicate claret to a deep, almost oxblood red."[4] Paul Evans has speculated that "Low's firm was encouraged in the development of this line by Hugh C. Robertson after his Chelsea Keramic Art Works abandoned their similar efforts in favor of the crackleware and moved to Dedham."[5]

John Low also marketed a successful line of art tile soda fountains. Low had begun experimenting with tiles for a soda fountain around 1883, but his patent application was not approved until six

3. Elisabeth Cameron, *Encyclopedia of Pottery & Porcelain: 1800–1960* (New York: Facts on File Publications, 1986), p. 205.

4. Paul Evans, *Art Pottery of the United States* (New York: Charles Scribner's Sons, 1974), p. 152.

5. Ibid.

years later. In 1893 an elaborate twenty-foot-long, sixteen-foot-high model was displayed at the Columbian Exposition in Chicago. It helped spread the fame and the sales of Low art tile soda fountains across the country, but stiffer competition led to the end of both tile and art pottery production around 1902. Low's son, though a trained chemist and capable manager, was unable to save the firm, and in 1907—the year in which John Gardner Low died—the tile and pottery works was dismantled.

Selected Prices

Tile: plastic sketch, rectangular scene of sheep being herded through a European village street, glossy teal blue glaze, 18″ × 10″, *$400–$450*.

Tile: portrait, metal-framed plaque of Cordelia, blue-green glaze, 13″, $115–$140.

Tile: portrait, round frame with classical portrait, 4″, blue-green glaze, *$125–$150*.

Tile: portrait, man's head, brown glaze, 4″, *$65–$75*.

Tile: portrait, woman's head, green glaze, 6″ diameter, *$65–$75*.

Tile: portrait, man's head, signed by Arthur Osborne, brown glaze, 4″, *$140–$165*.

Tile: portrait, Grover Cleveland, green glaze, 6″, *$105–$130*.

Tile: stove (Quick Meal), green glaze, *$40–$50*.

MARBLEHEAD POTTERY

Shopmark:
Impressed outline of a ship and the initials *MP*, all enclosed in a circle, occasionally with initials *A.E.B.* (Arthur E. Baggs) and/or *H.T.* (Hanna Tutt)

Principal Contributions:
Hand-thrown vases, bowls, and tiles with conventionalized designs under a matte glaze

Founder:
Herbert J. Hall, M.D.
Born: unknown   Died: unknown

Director:
Arthur E. Baggs
Born: 1886   Died: 1947
Founded: 1904   Closed: 1936

Studios and Salesrooms:
Marblehead Pottery
Marblehead, Massachusetts
1904–1936

"The Marblehead Pottery stands for simplicity—all that is bizarre and freakish have been avoided. It stands for quiet, subdued colors, for severe conventionalization in design, and for careful and thorough workmanship in all details."

—*House Beautiful*
1912[1]

In 1904 the picturesque fishing village of Marblehead, Massachusetts, provided the overwrought patients of Dr. Herbert J. Hall with a relaxing environment in which they could recuperate. To aid them in their recovery, Dr. Hall established the Handcraft Shops, where each patient could, "under supervision, partake of certain occupational therapy in the form of arts and crafts."[2] As Dr. Hall explained in 1908, his intent was to provide his "nervously worn out patients the blessing and privilege of quiet manual work, where as apprentices they could learn again gradually and without haste to use their hand and brain in a normal, wholesome way."[3] Among the crafts with which they could experiment in the former clubhouse that served as the Handcraft Shops were metalwork, woodcarving, weaving, tiles, and pottery, the last inspired by the nearby Beverly Pottery (1866–1904).

To help organize and manage the pottery works, Dr. Hall contacted nineteen-year-old Arthur E. Baggs, who had been recommended by his former ceramics instructor Charles F. Binns (1857–1934). For the first three years Baggs and his patient-potters experimented with various forms and struggled to establish a studio and pottery operation with a consistent style and steady output. By 1908 production of "simple, well-designed shapes and severely conventional decoration,"[4] clearly reflective

1. Jonathan A. Rawson, Jr., "Recent American Pottery," *House Beautiful* (April 1912), p. 149; also quoted in Wendy Kaplan, ed., *The Art That Is Life: The Arts & Crafts Movement in America, 1875–1920* (Boston: Museum of Fine Arts, 1987), p. 257.

2. Albert Christian Revi, *The Spinning Wheel Complete Book of Antiques* (New York: Grosset & Dunlap, 1972), p. 104.

3. Wendy Kaplan, ed., *The Art That Is Life: The Arts & Crafts Movement in America, 1875–1920* (Boston: Museum of Fine Arts, 1987), p. 256.

4. Paul Evans, *Art Pottery of the United States* (New York: Feingold & Lewis, 1987), p. 157.

of both the philosophy of Charles Binns and the current Arts and Crafts movement, had reached nearly two hundred pieces per week.⁵ Realizing that the pottery's potential could only be hampered by tying it too closely to the sanitarium and its temporary patient help, Baggs began the weaning process by hiring a small staff of full-time designers, artists, and potters. Among them were Hanna Tutt, decorator; Maude Milner and Arthur Hennessey, designers; and Englishman John Swallow, potter; most remained with the pottery for several years. By 1915 it was apparent that Marblehead Pottery had outgrown its original intent, and it was agreed that Arthur Baggs would become its sole owner.

The simple forms and soft, matte-glazed decorations appealed to an Arts and Crafts–conscious public. While popular designs were often repeated, vases and bowls continued to be hand-thrown and individually decorated by the artists, ensuring their clients that no two items (with the exception of tiles and molded bookends) could ever be identical. Early designs occasionally featured incised Indian motifs over a red clay body, and early wares can often be distinguished by their wide foot rims and rough bottoms compared with the narrow, smooth bottoms of the later vases.

Other motifs found on Marblehead pottery include insects, flowers, birds, seashells, animals, fish, and sailing ships; but as Martin Eidelberg observed in 1972, "More important than the motif, however, is its treatment: the design is conventionalized into flat, abstract patterns. There is often an insistence on a rigid, vertical stem, and many of the patterns are purely geometrical."⁶ Fifteen years later Eidelberg went on to state that "typical of the new, sparse mode, Walrath and Marblehead shrank the design elements into linear, vertical or horizontal patterns and vastly increased the negative spaces of the ground. There was only one step left to take, and Baggs took it. He pushed past conventionalization into non-representational design through the use of geometric motifs."⁷

5. Elisabeth Cameron, *Encyclopedia of Pottery & Porcelain: 1800–1960* (New York: Facts on File Publications, 1986), p. 212.

6. Robert Judson Clark, ed., *The Arts and Crafts Movement in America: 1876–1916* (Princeton, NJ: Princeton University, 1972), p. 180.

7. Martin Eidelberg, ed., *From Our Native Clay* (New York: Turn of the Century Editions, 1987), p. 15.

This six-inch decorated Marblehead vase features stylized light brown trees against a matte green ground. In addition to the firm's impressed mark, it is signed by Hanna Tutt, one of their most important decorators. *(Photo courtesy of David Rago, Trenton)*

Essential to the Arts and Crafts style was the matte glaze popularized by Grueby, Hampshire, and Teco potteries prior to Marblehead's entrance. In contrast to Rookwood's version, the popular Vellum matte glaze, the matte glaze that Baggs and his associates developed, "is at once the color, the design, and the surface—fused by the kiln into an immutable whole, a three-dimensional object of uniform surface patterned with color and devoid of all depth, gloss, or visual trickery."[8]

While the undecorated Marblehead forms appeal to a wide range of collectors, Arts and Crafts enthusiasts have actively sought the decorated forms embellished with geometric designs and incorporating several colors. Like Walrath pottery, many times the colors are muted; those that reveal a distinct contrast between the colors have become very popular, as have those vases and bowls in which the form and decoration are in complete harmony. Collectors have also demonstrated a clear preference for those pieces in which the decoration utilizes a large portion of the clay body.

8. Martin Eidelberg, ed., *From Our Native Clay* (New York: Turn of the Century Editions, 1987), p. 15.

This grouping of Marblehead vases demonstrates the simple forms and restrained decoration that have made them popular with Arts and Crafts collectors. The nine-inch geometric vase is large for Marblehead pottery and surfaces less frequently than the three- to six-inch stylized plant forms. All were decorated by Hanna Tutt. *(Photo courtesy of David Rago, Trenton)*

With the help of a loyal staff, Baggs was able both to continue his own education and to teach at universities in New York and Ohio without jeopardizing the quality of the work at Marblehead. Even the undecorated ware that became more prevalent after 1920 still commands respect for its pure forms and quality glazes. Baggs's experiments with glazes both at Marblehead and with his friend R. Guy Cowan (1884–1957) at Cowan's pottery in Cleveland earned him the respect and admiration of colleagues across the country. Baggs closed the pottery at Marblehead during the Depression and served as professor of ceramic arts at Ohio State University until his death in 1947.

Selected Prices

Bookends: decorated with stylized cut-back and incised panel of a galleon on the sea, 5″ × 6″, *$120–$145.*

Bookends: light brown glaze, owl figure design, 6″ × 5″, *$185–$210.*

Bowl: shallow bowl angled on side, decorated with black spades and drip over dark green ground, 8″, *$275–$325.*

Jar: sloping shoulder on bulbous tapering form, decorated with a band of repeating galleons against a circle and scroll band, 7″, *$600–$700.*

Plaque: framed, dark green silhouettes of trees on lighter green ground, 6″ × 6″, *$900–$1000.*

Tile: white Spanish galleon in relief on blue ground, 7″ × 7″, *$200–$250.*

Tile: framed, decoration of green, blue, and purple flowers, *6″* × *6″*, *$175–$200.*

Tile: painted seascape with clouds and ship on horizon, impressed mark, 4″ × 4″, *$175–$200.*

Tile: stylized embossed design of dark blue peacock, with green leaves and red flowers against open blue ground with dark blue band border, 5″ × 5″, *$100–$125.*

Tile: stylized bouquet of flowers in a basket in blue, green, and yellow glazes on dark brown, 6″ × 6″, *$200–$225.*

Tile: four-color, masted ship cutting through the waves in blues, grays, and browns, 6″ × 6″, *$200–$225.*

Vase: green matte flaked with brown, incised brown designs, 4″, *$350–$400.*

Vase: two-color, cylindrical form with incised decoration, two horizontal bands around rim incorporating repeats of eight triangles with loop "handles" on three strong vertical stylized stems, forest green on dark blue ground, 9″ × 5″, *$2500–$3000.*

Vase: light blue matte glaze, incised with flower design band of three colors, 3″ × 5″, $400–$450.

Vase: three-color, wide mouth on squat cylindrical form, decorated with a repeating border of vines centering six corresponding medallions with berries, 7″ × 6″, $1250–$1500.

Vase: rolled rim on squat bulbous form swelling toward base, stylized bud and stem design in green on dark blue ground, 3″, $225–$250.

Vase: wide, rolled rim on cylindrical form swelling toward base, decorated with spades in repeating squares on long stems, brown glaze on green round, 6″, $600–$700.

Vase: medium blue matte glaze, 4″ × 6″, $85–$95.

Vase: wide, rolled rim on cylindrical form swelling toward base, decorated with band and squares with long stems, brown design on green ground, 6″, $500–$600.

Vase: wide mouth on cylindrical form, dark forest green glaze, 9″, $225–$250.

Vase: four-color, bulbous form swelling toward base, decorated with six repeating panels of stylized green leaves and blue berries outlined in brown on oatmeal yellow ground, 6″, $1000–$1250.

Vase: two-color, cylindrical form swelling toward base, olive green stylized tree with long trunk on lighter green ground, 6″, $700–$800.

Vase: bulbous body swelling toward base decorated with a wide band of conventionalize hanging flowers in light and darker blue on matte gray ground, 6″, $700–$800.

Vase: squat, bulbous, with large opening, four stylized, incised flowers in red and green, 3″ × 5″, $250–$300.

Vase: squat and bulbous, repeating, highly conventionalized panels, showing ochre sun and blue rays setting over stylized mountains, 3″ × 4″, *$600–$700.*

Vase: bulbous, open, finely decorated with incised red and green berries, dark blue leaves, medium blue ground, repeated eight times, 4″ × 5″, *$475–$575.*

Vase: cylindrical, with incised grapevine with pale green leaves and blue grapes encircling top portion of vase, 5″ × 3″, *$225–$250.*

Vase: slender oviform, with large opening, matte glazed in blue with black speckles, 7″ × 4″, *$100–$125.*

Vase: bulbous, stylized yellow roses, brown stems, green leaves, outlined in black, 4″ × 3″, *$275–$325.*

J. W. McCOY COMPANY

LOY-NEL-ART

McCOY

Shopmark:
Impressed *LOY-NEL-ART*, occasionally over the word *McCOY*

Principal Contribution:
Extensive line of commercial pottery and artware, plus a small amount of art pottery

Founder:
James W. McCoy
Born: unknown   Died: unknown
Founded: 1899   Closed: current

Studios and Salesrooms:
J. W. McCoy Company
Roseville, Ohio
1899–1911

Brush-McCoy Pottery Company
Roseville and Zanesville, Ohio
1911–1925

Brush Pottery
Roseville, Ohio
1925–current

"Little of the J. W. Brush-McCoy art lines was ever of a very high quality, and the mass-produced late lines can hardly be considered art pottery. Perhaps for this reason little of the work is ever found with marks."

—*Paul Evans*[1]

Like many of the Ohio art potteries, the history of the J. W. McCoy Pottery is both dominated and complicated by a number of devastating fires and corporate takeovers. The pottery first began in Roseville in 1899 with the production of an ever-expanding range of common housewares. The mass-production operation was churning out nearly five thousand pieces per day[2] when fire destroyed the entire pottery in 1903. But James McCoy soon had his plant rebuilt, his company incorporated, and his first lines entered into the art pottery market.

His first entry, Mont Pelee ware, was a "dull black lava-type pottery with some iridescence"[3] that had been inspired by ancient pottery discovered around that time by archeologists on the island of Martinique. Unfortunately, most of the inventory of Mont Pelee ware was destroyed in the 1903 fire. McCoy responded to the growing popularity of the line of matte green pottery being produced by William H. Grueby by introducing a similar version in 1906. His most artistic venture was a line of

1. Paul Evans, *Art Pottery of the United States* (New York: Charles Scribner's Sons, 1974), p. 156.

2. Ibid., p. 154.

3. Ralph and Terry Kovel, *The Kovels' Collectors Guide to American Art Pottery* (New York: Crown Publishers, 1974), pp. 92–93.

underglaze-decorated wares intended to compete with Weller's Louwelsa and Rookwood's Standard ware. Named after his three sons (Lloyd, Nelson, and Arthur), the 1908 Loy-Nel-Art vases represented McCoy's only significant contribution to hand-painted art pottery.

By that same year George S. Brush, who had been producing a line of molded housewares, saw his Zanesville, Ohio, plant destroyed by fire, which led to the formation of the Brush-McCoy Pottery Company in 1911 in McCoy's Roseville location. That firm then bought the Radford Pottery and took over the Owens Pottery building, including many of the Owens molds, in Zanesville. The Roseville plant continued to use many of the Owens molds as the basis of a large line of inexpensive artware, while the Zanesville employees produced household wares until a kiln fire eventually destroyed that plant as well. In 1925 the name of James McCoy was dropped, and the pottery became the Brush Pottery.

Selected Prices

Due to the infequency with which examples of McCoy art pottery (not commercial artware) appear on the market, establishing an in-depth price guide has not yet been possible. The examples listed below are indicative only of the value of pieces of similar form and decoration. Until additional information is compiled, readers are advised to seek counsel from experienced collectors before either buying or selling important pieces.

Vase: Loy-Nel-Art, iris decoration, 9″, *$115–$135.*

Vase: Loy-Nel-Art, with handles, decorated berries and leaves under brown glaze, *$200–$225.*

MERRIMAC POTTERY COMPANY

Shopmarks:
(1900–1901) Paper label, MERRIMAC CERAMIC COMPANY,
with drawing of a sturgeon
(1901–1908) Impressed or incised mark with *MERRIMAC* over
a sturgeon

Principal Contributions:
Decorative garden pottery, plus a line of art pottery featuring
quality colored glazes

Founder:
Thomas S. Nickerson
Born: unknown   Died: unknown
Founded: 1897   Closed: 1908

Studios and Salesrooms:
Merrimac Ceramic Company
Newburyport, Massachusetts
1897–1902

Merrimac Pottery Company
Newburyport, Massachusetts
1902–1908

"These pastes so pleasing to the eye, and withal so varied, since
they range from dull to highly vitrified surfaces, are left without
painted decoration: beauty, according to the modern principle,

being sought in a simplicity which embraces the entire work, extending to the form, as well as controlling the color."

—*The Craftsman*
1903[1]

Thomas S. Nickerson spent several years in preparation for the opening of his pottery in Newburyport, Massachusetts, in 1897. After study under Sir William Crookes in England and extensive experimentation at his home in picturesque Newburyport, Nickerson initiated production of florists' wares and glazed tiles under the name of the Merrimac Ceramic Company. Within the next three years Nickerson added a partner, increased the size and production of his plant, and began experimenting with forms of art pottery. His first offerings consisted primarily of flowerpots and vases with, according to Irene Sargent in 1903, "colors and glazes obtained by Mr. Nickerson [that] first attracted public attention: both having a wide variety."[2]

As Miss Sargent noted, Nickerson achieved a variety of colors, not through underglaze decoration but through a number of glazes, producing simple forms in greens, dull black, orange, brownish red, blues, and violet, some with an iridescence, others under a crackle surface. As recently observed, "Merrimac's dense mat glaze and leafy decoration suggest analogies with the work of the nearby Grueby Pottery, but the curling leaves are rhythmic when compared with Grueby's staid rigidity."[3]

In 1902 Nickerson and his partner, W. G. Fisher, changed the name of the company to the Merrimac Pottery Company as an indication to the public of their newly expanded range. His original line of garden pottery was not dropped, but instead the firm increased the quality, the variety of forms, and the total production to meet a growing demand. An additional line of

1. Irene Sargent, "Some Potters and Their Products," *The Craftsman* (July 1903), p. 249.

2. Ibid., p. 248.

3. Martin Eidelberg, ed., *From Our Native Clay* (New York: Turn of the Century Editions, 1987), p. 68.

Large examples of Merrimac pottery are considered rare. This eight-inch vase features hand-tooled swirling leaves under a medium matte green textured glaze. *(Photo courtesy of David Rago, Trenton)*

reproduction antique Roman pottery, called Arrhelian, produced from molds of authentic vases, was also added around 1902. In 1904 the firm exhibited at the Louisiana Purchase Exposition in St. Louis, returning home with a silver medal, indicative of the advances Nickerson had made in his development of the glazes that give the work "a cheerful, tender, bright, radiant character."[4]

For reasons yet unclear, Nickerson sold the Merrimac Pottery in 1908, possibly after production had ceased. Before the new owner had an opportunity to resume operations, however, a fire destroyed the plant and most of the inventory. It was never reopened.

4. Paul Evans, *Art Pottery of the United States* (New York: Charles Scribner's Sons, 1974), p. 169.

Selected Prices

Bowl: bulbous, closed form in green matte glaze, 4″ × 5″, $450–$550.

Bowl: modeled decoration, green matte glaze, with orange gloss interior, 8″, $200–$225.

Jar: baluster form, in splotched high-gloss brown glaze, 5″ × 4″, $125–$150.

Jardiniere: round, bulbous form with five conventionalized lily pads surrounding base, green metallic glaze, 5″ × 8″, $400–$450.

Jardiniere: textured forest green glaze, 7″ × 10″, $250–$300.

Vase: two-handled vase with bulbous bottom and cylindrical neck in splotched orange gold and dark green matte finish, 4″ × 3″, $175–$200.

Vase: bulbous closed-bowl form in splotched orange and pea green matte glaze, 4″ × 4″, $175–$200.

Vase: green semigloss glaze, feathering to brown glaze, 11″, $500–$600.

Vase: with handles, orange-red body under clear glaze, 8″, $150–$175.

Vase: wide mouth on cylindrical form with three open crocuses on slender stems, mottled green glaze, 4″ × 4″, $350–$400.

Vase: cylindrical, curled-in top and bottom rims and a slight waist at its center, crackled, frothy, white matte glaze ending over a medium blue semigloss finish, 4″ × 4″, $200–$225.

MATT MORGAN
POTTERY COMPANY

Shopmark:
Paper label, MATT MORGAN ART POTTERY/CINCINNATI
Incised oval mark, MATT MORGAN ART POTTERY CO./
CIN.O, often with initials of decorator

Principal Contribution:
Limited line of art pottery vases and plaques

Founder:
Matt Morgan
Born: ca. 1839   Died: 1890
Founded: 1883   Closed: 1884

Studios and Salesrooms:
Matt Morgan Art Pottery
Cincinnati, Ohio
1883–1884

Although the pottery concern of Mathew Morgan, an Englishman and an artist by trade, lasted but little more than a year,
it served as the springboard for two important artists: Mathew
Daly and N. J. Hirschfield, both of whom later worked at Rookwood. Production was limited, but the forms varied with both
an underglaze decorative line and examples featuring decorative gilt. After disagreements over the direction the pottery
should take, the firm closed in 1884, at which time the majority
of the molds and inventory were destroyed.

Selected Prices

Due to the infrequency with which examples of this pottery appear on the market, establishing an in-depth price guide has not yet been possible. The examples listed below are indicative only of the value of pieces of similar form and decoration. Until additional information is compiled, readers are advised to seek counsel from experienced collectors before either buying or selling important pieces.

Jar: blue body under clear high glaze, with lid, 5″, *$175–$200*.

Jug: red clay body, semigloss Limoges-style background in dark green and gold, cut-out design of flowers, leaves, and branches, high glaze on design in color of clay body, gold on top edge and handle, 6″, *$225–$250*.

Vase: decorated in Limoges style, with two birds, high glaze, 14″, *$600–$675*.

Vase: carved floral motif, decorated brown on green, 5″, *$200–$225*.

NEWCOMB POTTERY

NEWCOMB COLLEGE

Shopmarks:
(1894–1899) Words *NEWCOMB COLLEGE*
(1897–1948) Letter *N* within a larger letter *C*, often with date

Code: Letter *M*, mold form; letters *HB*, hand-built

Principal Contributions:
Decorated bowls, vases, candlesticks, mugs, and lamps in both high-gloss and matte glazes

Founders:
Ellsworth Woodward
William Woodward
Founded: 1895   Closed: 1939[1]

Studios and Salesrooms:
The Newcomb Pottery
The Sophie Newcomb Memorial College
(Tulane University)
New Orleans, Louisiana
1895–1939

"Our beautiful moss-draped oak trees appealed to the buying public but nothing is less suited to the tall graceful vases—no way to convey the true character of the tree. And oh, how boring it was to use the same motif over and over and over, though each one was a fresh drawing."

—*Sadie Irvine,*
decorator[2]

In New Orleans, as in Cincinnati, Chicago, Boston, and other American cities, the Arts and Crafts reform movement spawned an interest in improving the lives of young women by giving them training in weaving, leatherwork, metalsmithing, china decorating, and art pottery. As in other cities, clubs and organizations sprang up in New Orleans; but rather than developing into a private commercial enterprise, one such organization, the New Orleans Art Pottery, evolved into a school for pottery decorators at a recognized institution of higher education, the Sophie Newcomb Memorial College.

1. In 1940 the Newcomb Guild was established and continued to use the Newcomb Pottery shopmark until 1948.
2. Paul Evans, *Art Pottery of the United States* (New York: Charles Scribner's Sons, 1974), p. 187.

With the Rookwood Pottery as a model, the president of Newcomb College, acting on a proposal submitted by two members of the art faculty, brothers William and Ellsworth Woodward (both of whom had been involved with the New Orleans Art Pottery), had thrown his wholehearted support behind the project by 1895. Mary Sheerer was persuaded to leave Cincinnati to oversee the pottery decoration department; Joseph Meyer, a friend of the Woodwards and a potter at the New Orleans Art Pottery, assumed responsibility as head potter in 1896, a position he was to retain until he retired in 1927. The early days of "big heartbreaks and bigger dreams"[3] gradually gave way to repeated success. The veteran Meyer was adept at throwing the forms requested by the designers and providing practical experience with glazes, while Miss Sheerer guided the decorators in their quest for both artistic expression and practical skills. Although the pottery may never have been an outstanding commercial success, income from the sale of their work encouraged the young decorators and ensured continued support by the college.

Work from the early period of Newcomb (1895–1901) was marked by a great deal of experimentation with types and colors of decorations, including underglaze slip painting, but in a distinctive style—"favoring bright, clear tones, covered with a clear transparent glaze"[4]—totally unlike that being popularized at Rookwood. Since the goal of the pottery was to train young decorators rather than potters, both the shapes of the pieces and the clear, high-gloss glaze remained relatively consistent, whereas the artwork revealed a good deal of experimentation. Eventually, though, naturalistic Southern motifs in lively blue and green colors emerged as the most popular of the Newcomb Pottery line. Their exhibit at the Pan-American Exposition in Buffalo in 1901 garnered a silver medal and vital national exposure; numerous sources were soon reporting that the student decorators at the pottery could not keep up with the large numbers of orders that were coming in from all parts of the country.

3. Jessie Poesch, *Newcomb College: An Enterprise for Southern Women, 1895–1940* (Exton, PA: Schiffer Publishing, 1984), p. 18.
4. Ibid., p. 20.

Earliest examples of Newcomb College pottery are often coated with a high-gloss glaze considered rare by collectors. This six-and-one-half-inch vase is decorated with incised flowers in blue and green. It was thrown by Joseph Meyer and decorated by Leona Nicholson. *(Photo courtesy of David Rago, Trenton)*

The second period (1902–1910) in the development of Newcomb pottery was ushered in with a series of awards at national exhibitions. The number of student decorators was increased from ten to fifteen for a brief time, perhaps indicative of their involvement in several expositions, but the temptation to expand into a manufacturing concern never seems to have been a serious topic of discussion at the college. Content to serve as a model for other institutions and encouraged by their artistic recognition and popular success, the pottery entered a period of combined creativity and continued refinements. Clearly defined incised designs under light blue or green glazes emerged, as well as the rare red glazes experimented with between 1903 and 1907. Relief modeling and more subtle incising led a "movement toward a softer, more romantic handling"[5] after 1908.

The third era (1910–1918) was initiated with the arrival of Paul Cox (1897–1968), who developed a matte glaze in his first year at Newcomb Pottery, and the emergence of Sadie Irvine (1887–1970) as perhaps the pottery's single most important decorator. The matte glazes made popular by Grueby, Hampshire,

5. Jessie Poesch, *Newcomb College: An Enterprise for Southern Women, 1895–1940* (Exton, PA: Schiffer Publishing, 1984), p. 53.

These two vases illustrate the development in the style of decorating at Newcomb College. The upper vase is an early highglaze, while the lower is the more common matte-glazed, mossdraped oak scene associated with artist Sadie Irvine and the post-1910 period. *(Photo courtesy of David Rago, Trenton)*

and Teco could not simply be applied to the decorated Newcomb wares; it was left to Cox to adapt and perfect a matte glaze that would please both the public and the pottery's decorators. Sculpted low relief continued to take precedence over the earlier sharply defined incised lines; and the misty, almost mysterious Southern landscapes were complemented by Cox's matte and semimatte glazes. Sadie Irvine had been a student decorator in 1903 and remained with the pottery until she retired in 1952. Credited with the famous bayou scene depicting a moss-draped oak tree illuminated by a full moon, she served as the backbone of the decorating department for more than two decades.

While the year 1919 is used to mark the departure of Paul Cox and the beginning of the third period of development of the pottery, it coincides with the general decline in interest in the Arts and Crafts movement. The public still responded enthusiastically to Newcomb pottery, but the experimentation and enthusiasm that characterized the earlier periods was largely replaced by standardized forms and decorations (though still done by hand) that dominated production in the 1920s and 1930s. In 1939 the college changed the emphasis from commercial production to instruction, in effect bringing to a close not only the third period in its development but the Arts and Crafts era of the Newcomb Pottery. The change was marked also by the announcement of the formation in 1940 of the Newcomb Guild, which, while still serving as a pottery outlet for students and staff, was but an echo of its former self.

Although Newcomb collectors dream of someday discovering a rare experimental piece of red Newcomb pottery, most are also quite pleased if they discover a highly valued example of the early high-gloss glaze. Regardless of whether they are early or later, vases and bowls with crisp carving, clear definition, and a rich, warm blend of colors are the most popular among Arts and Crafts collectors. While the Sadie Irvine "moonlight and moss" motif is among their most common, it remains representative of the pottery's work and for that reason alone is popular with all art pottery collectors. Advanced Newcomb collectors distinguish between different treatments of this same motif on the basis of how well it fits the particular pottery shape, the depth and dimension of the decoration, and the crispness of the details.

Selected Prices

Bowl: wide and with curled rim ending in four points, with cut-back white flowers and green leaves on medium blue ground, 3″ × 8″, *$250–$300.*

Bowl: gray-blue matte glaze, floral decoration band around top, 4″ × 8″, *$550–$650.*

This fine example of an early high-glaze Newcomb College vase illustrates the use of incised lines to highlight the decoration. *(Photo courtesy of Don Treadway, Cincinnati)*

Coaster: decorated with repeating lily-of-the-valley, green border on matte blue, 4″ diameter, $175–$200.

Mug: high-glaze, cylindrical body flared slightly at base, decorated with repeating motif of yellow sunflowers with intertwined green stems, black outlines and handle, 4″, $1000–$1250.

Mug: tapering cylindrical body, applied curing handle, band of cut-back oak trees in green-blue outlined in cobalt, with cream ground, 5″ × 5″, $900–$1000.

Pitcher: high-glaze, with handle, deeply incised yellow rosebuds and green leaves and stems on light blue and dark blue banded ground, flaring bottom glazed in mottled medium to dark blue, 7″ × 4″, $2000–$2250.

Vase: short neck on bulbous form with a collar of carved flowers on matte blue, 6″, $225–$250.

Vase: wide mouth on squat, bulbous form decorated with Spanish moss and full moon, matte, 5″, $250–$300.

Vase: swollen cylindrical form, decorated with opening

crocus with joining leaves banding in blues and greens, marked TT 40, X, 6″, *$1250–$1500*.

Vase: matte, Spanish moss, wide mouth on squat, bulbous form, relief-decorated with clearly defined repeating trees against a pink blush, 4″ × 3″, *$500–$600*.

Vase: squat, bulbous form with four spaced handles enclosing border decoration of clusters of pink flowers, muted blue matte ground, 4″ × 5″, *$350–$400*.

Vase: baluster form, stepped-in neck, and wide collar rim, with carved pale blue grapes hanging from a thick green vine encircling the top of the rim, 8″ × 4″, *$500–$600*.

Vase: baluster form, with clusters of small, light blue daffodils with long green leaves and stems encircling the pot, 8″ × 4″, *$550–$650*.

Vase: squat and bulbous, with cut-back oak trees with hanging Spanish moss in blue and green against pale pink sky, 2″ × 3″, *$450–$500*.

Vase: Clusters of small, light blue flowers with long green leaves against a medium blue ground, 7″ × 4″, *$900–$1000*.

Vase: bulbous, with small opening, sculpted, stylized leaves in pink and purple, on purple ground, 4″ × 5″, *$425–$475*.

Vase: high-glaze, squat, bulbous, with eight yellow flowers with green-blue leaves and thick stems, outlined in dark blue, 6″ × 4″, *$2000–$2250*.

Vase: blue trees and Spanish moss over a cream sky, blue horizon, 6″ × 9″, *$1000–$1250*.

Vase: squat and bulbous, with cut-back blue bellflowers with yellow centers and green leaves, medium blue ground, 4″ × 4″, *$350–$400*.

Vase: bulbous bottom with cylindrical neck, blue leaves

ending in four pierced, ring handles, green leaves on neck with white blossoms, 7″ × 4″, *$600–$700.*

Vase: flaring cylindrical form, collared rim, carved bayou scene and full moon, in shades of blue, 8″ × 4″, *$1400–$1600.*

Vase: bayou scene with sharply detailed trees in blue and green, long running fence in blue, light pink sunset, 6″ × 5″, *$1000–$1200.*

Vase: cut-back blue trees with overhanging Spanish moss against pale blue sky and white moon, 6″ × 3″, *$550–$600.*

Vase: cut-back oak trees and hanging moss in blue and pale green matte glaze, 6″ × 3″, *$475–$525.*

Vase: moonlight through moss scenic, 6″ × 3″, *$400–$500.*

Vase: blue-green semimatte glaze with floral decoration, overall crazing, 6″ × 4″, *$300–$350.*

Vase: blue matte glaze with floral band of cut-back flowers, 4″ × 5″, *$300–$350.*

Vase: blue matte glaze, tricolor incised flower design with precise detail, 4″ × 4″, *$450–$500.*

Vase: floral decoration of honeysuckle surrounding vase, green leaves, 5″, *$450–$500.*

Vase: floral motif, matte blue with deeper blue band around top edge with white flowers, green leaves, 4″ × 6″, *$275–$325.*

Vase: solid deep blue matte glaze with green drip, ribbed body, 5″, *$225–$250.*

Vase: floral motif, blue with green leaves, white and pink flowers between leaves at top, touches of pink all around top, 6″, *$350–$400.*

Vase: oak trees with hanging moss against a red sky, 6″, *$1100–$1350.*

Vase: blue matte, decoration of deep pink honeysuckle and green leaves, 3″, *$275–$325*.

Vase: floral matte, dark blue background, wide green-blue leaves, pale blue flowers, yellow centers, 5″, *$325–$375*.

Vase: high-glaze floral, light green leaves from bottom, pale blue flowers with white, dark blue in background, 6″, *$1000–$1100*.

Vase: dark blue scenic with trees and moss, medium blue background, yellow moon, 4″ × 5″, *$575–$675*.

NILOAK POTTERY

NILOAK

Shopmarks:
(1910–1928) Impressed NILOAK
(After 1928) Impressed NILOAK and patent number
Paper label, NILOAK POTTERY in a circle
Paper label, FROM THE NILOAK POTTERIES AT
BENTON, ARKANSAS
(Later) Raised letters, NILOAK

Principal Contribution:
Wide range of marbleized art pottery forms

Founder:
Charles Hyten
Born: 1887   Died: 1944
Founded: 1909   Closed: 1946

Studios and Salesrooms:
Niloak Pottery Company
Benton, Arkansas
1909–1946

"There have been numerous attempts to imitate the Mission ware.... All, however, are inferior copies in comparison to Niloak's Mission ware, which occupies a distinctive place in the art pottery movement."

—*Paul Evans*[1]

After their father's death, their mother's remarriage, and her subsequent move to Ohio in 1895, Charles Hyten and his two brothers elected to remain in Benton, Arkansas, to continue the operation of their father's Eagle Pottery. Eventually, two small businesses were formed; in addition to the Eagle Pottery, which continued to produce commercial stoneware such as crocks, churns, and jugs for more than three decades, the Hyten Brothers Pottery was organized and later renamed the Niloak (nī′ lōk) Pottery.

Around 1909 Charles Hyten began experimenting with several different colors of local clay on the potter's wheel at the same time. The result was a multicolor, swirling effect that was striking in appearance but that did not come without its own problems. Different types of clay dry and shrink at different rates, and Charles spent several years perfecting a process and a formula that would permit him to utilize several different clays in each vessel.

The first pieces were produced in 1910, and their immediate popularity led to formal organization and naming of the Niloak Pottery Company in 1911. Their new name came from the word *kaolin*, a fine white clay that has been used for centuries in the manufacture of quality Chinese porcelain; spelled backward it becomes Niloak. Ironically, kaolin may not have been used in the production of Niloak's most famous line, Mission,[2] but the effect was not lost. "Forms, pre-dominantly classical or

1. Albert Christian Revi, ed., *The Spinning Wheel Complete Book of Antiques* (New York: Grosset & Dunlap, 1972), p. 108.
2. Wendy Kaplan, ed., *The Art That Is Life: The Arts & Crafts Movement in America, 1875–1920* (Boston: Museum of Fine Arts, 1987), p. 387.

Perhaps the most common of any hand-thrown pottery of the period, no two pieces of Niloak are ever identical. The pottery became an attraction for tourists wishing to watch the potters combine several different colors into a single, swirling form. *(Photo courtesy of David Rago, Trenton)*

Oriental, included small bowls, candlesticks, pitcher and tankard sets, steins, punchbowl and cup sets, fern dishes, clocks, and vases made in a variety of sizes adaptable as lamps."[3]

Some of their early experimental pottery had a glaze applied to both the inside and the outside of the piece, but Charles soon instituted the classic Niloak style, in which the marbleized pieces were glazed only on the inside, making them suitable to hold water but leaving the outside with a natural clay texture. The colors that appeared depended on the types of clays being used at any particular time and the skill of the potter. The later pieces tend to be more colorful than the early examples, perhaps reflective of Charles's experiments with colored pigments and the refinement of his patented mixing and drying process.

The incorporation of the Niloak Pottery enabled the brothers to sell the stock necessary to raise the capital to build a new

3. Wendy Kaplan, ed., *The Art That Is Life: The Arts & Crafts Movement in America, 1875–1920* (Boston: Museum of Fine Arts, 1987), p. 386.

and larger plant. The unique pottery quickly became popular, first in Benton, then spreading across the country, as the firm employed salesmen as well as additional potters. Production rose to as many as seventy-five thousand pieces per year as seven potters turned out the swirling shapes, no two of which were identical in either color or form, often before a crowd of admiring tourists.[4] By 1918 Charles was able to buy back most of the stock they had issued in 1911, thus acquiring complete control of the pottery. Soon Niloak pottery was being sold in Europe and the Far East, as well as across the United States and Canada.

The Depression, however, cut into sales of the handmade pottery, leading Charles to introduce a line of molded, less expensive pieces marked Hywood. The new line failed to stave off serious financial problems; Charles soon lost control of the property and the Niloak Pottery and was reduced to being a salesman for the firm he had founded. He died in 1944, two years after the last piece of marbleized Niloak was made and two years before the Niloak Pottery Company finally closed.

Selected Prices

Bowl: low open form of swirling clays, 3″ × 6″, $40–$50.

Candlestick: Mission ware, with saucer-style base, 4″, $90–$100.

Candlestick: Mission ware, 8″, $100–$110.

Lamp base: Mission ware, swirled clay body, 7″, $150–$175.

Pitcher: cylinder, handled, marbleized mixture of light blue, cream and terra-cotta-colored clays, 10″ × 6″, $225–$250.

Vase: corset form of marbleized mixture of terra-cotta, blue, and cream clays, 6″, $50–$60.

4. Paul Evans, *Art Pottery of the United States* (New York: Charles Scribner's Sons, 1974), p. 191.

Vase: Mission ware, dark brown swirl, 9″, *$95–$110*.

Vase: rolled rim and colored with swirled brown, blue, and cream clays, 11″ × 8″, *$125–$150*.

Vase: Mission ware, earth tones, flared lip, 6″, *$75–$85*.

Vase: Mission ware, collar neck, 8″, *$105–$115*.

Vase: pale cream, blue, and gray matte in the Mission ware style, 8″ × 4″, *$85–$95*.

Vase: pale blue, gray, and brown matte in the Mission ware style, 10″ × 6″, *$100–$110*.

Vase: pale blue, cream, and gray matte, in the Mission ware style, 8″ × 4″, *$85–$95*.

NORSE POTTERY

Shopmark:
Impressed NORSE, with the last four letters within the large letter *N*

Principal Contribution:
Household pottery finished with a matte metallic glaze to imitate antique bronzes

Founders:
Thorwald P. A. Samson
Louis Ipson
Born: unknown   Died: unknown
Founded: 1903   Closed: 1913

Studios and Salesrooms:
Norse Pottery
Edgerton, Wisconsin
1903–1904

Norse Pottery Company, Inc.
Rockford, Illinois
1904–1913

Inspired by antique bronze bowls excavated in Sweden and Denmark, Thorwald P. A. Samson and Louis Ipson, former potters at Pauline Pottery in Edgerton, Wisconsin, formed a small company to produce and distribute replicas made from local clay in 1903. Hindered by a lack of capital, the pair sold their designs to A. W. Wheelock, who had been their major distributor. Wheelock moved the firm and its two founders to Rockford, Illinois, where he had built a new plant. Between 1904 and 1913 the Norse Pottery Company produced a large number of examples, decorated with incised lines and painted, then "decorated with a dull metallic glaze with highlights in the effect of verdigris in the corners, crevices and sunken lines of the etchings."[1]

Selected Prices

Due to the infrequency with which examples of this pottery appear on the market, establishing an in-depth price guide has not yet been possible. The examples listed below are indicative only of the value of pieces of similar form and decoration. Until additional information is compiled, readers are advised to seek counsel from experienced collectors before either buying or selling important pieces.

Bowl: incised design with serpent-head handles, 6″, $175–$200.

---

1. Paul Evans, *Art Pottery of the United States* (New York: Charles Scribner's Sons, 1974), p. 194.

Bowl: low, open form with incised geometric design, 6″, $125–$150.

Candlesticks: with snakes around base, pair, 12″, $100–$125.

Mug: incised decoration, bronzed over black, 5″, $125–$150.

Vase: incised geometric design, black and gold, 5″, $125–$150.

Vase: incised geometric design, black and gold, 9″, $175–$200.

Vase: black with incised line and dot design filled in with green, 9″, $175–$200.

NORTH DAKOTA
SCHOOL OF MINES

Shopmark:
Incised cobalt blue circle UNIVERSITY OF NORTH DAKOTA/GRAND FORKS, N.D./MADE AT SCHOOL OF MINES/N.D. CLAY, also with glaze number

Principal Contribution:
Art pottery produced from North Dakota clays

Founder:
University of North Dakota
Founded: ca. 1892   Closed: current

Studios and Salesrooms:
North Dakota School of Mines
University of North Dakota
Grand Forks, North Dakota
ca. 1892–current

The pottery studio at the North Dakota School of Mines was developed from a study of the suitability of clays found within state boundaries for use in pottery production. After a successful exhibition at the 1904 Louisiana Purchase Exposition in St. Louis, the university continued to hire experienced potters to instruct and train students in throwing, molding, decorating, and glazing pottery. As a result, the shapes, styles, and quality of the pottery bearing the ink trademark varies considerably, although the tenure of Margaret Kelley Cable, who remained with the pottery from 1910 until 1949, provided the stability and direction required for the production of quality pottery. The university has maintained a detailed record of the glaze numbers often found on the pottery, which can help pinpoint the year of production.

Selected Prices

Bowl: undecorated, brown matte glaze, 6″ diameter, $100–$125

Bowl: dark blue under high-gloss glaze, 5″ diameter, $100–$125.

Bowl: carved turkey motif, in greens and browns, artist signed, $325–$375.

Tile: incised girl, 5″, $95–$115.

Vase: black and green matte glaze, 8″, $100–$125.

Vase: carved Indian motif, artist signed, 9″, $425–$475.

Vase: incised leaf motif, 7″, $300–$350.

Vase: turkey motif, with greens and browns, artist signed, 3″, $300–$350.

Vase: squat, bulbous, with cut-back panel decoration of an ox pulling a covered wagon, in green on a brown ground, repeated four times, 4″ × 6″, $300–$350.

Vase: brown matte glaze with six daffodil-decorated panels, 7″ × 6″, *$600–$700.*

Vase: brown-green monochromatic matte glaze with stylized flower decoration, 6″ × 5″, *$750–$850.*

GEORGE OHR POTTERY

GEO. E. OHR
BILOXI, MISS.

Shopmark:
Impressed or incised script signature or G.E. OHR, BILOXI or
GEO. E. OHR/BILOXI, MISS.

Principal Contribution:
Bowls and vases in bizarre forms and twisted shapes under
quality glazes

Founder:
George E. Ohr

Born: 1857   Died: 1918
Founded: ca. 1883   Closed: ca. 1909

Studios and Salesrooms:
Biloxi Art Pottery
Biloxi, Mississippi
ca. 1883–ca. 1909

"I send you four pieces, but it is as easy to pass judgment on my productions from four pieces as it would be to take four lines from Shakespeare and guess the rest."

—*George Ohr*
1905[1]

1. Paul Evans, *Art Pottery of the United States* (New York: Feingold & Lewis, 1987), p. 29.

While George Ohr certainly had no problem using Shakespeare to illustrate his work, most of his contemporaries—especially some of his fellow potters—would never have predicted that his bizarre and often grotesque vases and bowls would someday become prized additions to the collections of major museums around the world. "He is ever making," a visitor reported in 1900, "and as comparative few are buying, he is accumulating a vast quantity of pottery, having upwards of 6,000 or 7,000 pieces, no two of which are just alike in shape and decoration; and every one of these, he is quite satisfied in his own mind, will some day be worth its weight in gold."[2]

Ounce for ounce, the best work of George Ohr is now worth more than its weight in gold, but several years before his death in 1918, George Ohr, frustrated at the public's failure to respond favorably to his life's work, packed his inventory of pottery in boxes and retired. Most of it remained untouched until 1972, when an astute collector managed to buy nearly the entire inventory from the potter's family. Since that time both the works and the reputation of the infamous "mad potter of Biloxi" have spread across the country.

While many of Ohr's contemporaries did not like him or his pottery, none could ignore him. Ohr managed to offend and confuse the austere Arts and Crafts reformers as carelessly as their staunch Victorian predecessors. Early historian E. A. Barber described his work as "twisted, crushed, folded, dented and crinkled into grotesque and occasionally artistic shapes."[3] For many, Ohr's eccentric behavior and his bizarre forms overshadowed the technical aspect of his pottery. Using local clay he dug by hand from a nearby riverbank and hauled to his pottery in a wheelbarrow, Ohr was able to create eggshell-thin vessels of extraordinary quality, but, dissatisfied with their static silhouettes, he proceeded to "dig his fingers into the moist, plastic clay of his perfectly executed, wheel-thrown vessels . . . twisting, crinkling, indenting, folding, ruffling, lobing, off-centering,

2. Paul Evans, *Art Pottery of the United States* (New York: Feingold & Lewis, 1987), p. 28.

3. Robert Judson Clark, ed., *The Arts and Crafts Movement in America: 1876–1916* (Princeton, NJ: Princeton University, 1972), p. 135.

While his twisted and crumpled forms have captivated a modern audience, Ohr collectors know that his technical skill in glazes and at the wheel were equal to his artistic ability. The eggshell-thin wall of the cup at the right demonstrates the dexterity of the "mad potter of Biloxi." *(Photo courtesy of David Rago, Trenton)*

and conjoining"[4] until he had created forms never before imagined, let alone seen by most people.

Ohr's creations, however, while reflections of a rebellious nature, were the work of a genius rather than a huckster promoting a gimmick. Scholars in search of a source for his inspiration have attributed it to nearly everything from Pennsylvania folk art to Victorian glassware to the pottery of the American Indians;[5] a study in frustration, it is a reflection not so much of

4. Martin Eidelberg, ed., *From Our Native Clay* (New York: Turn of the Century Editions, 1987), p. 54.

5. See Wendy Kaplan, ed., *The Art That Is Life: The Arts & Crafts Movement in America, 1875–1920* (Boston: Museum of Fine Arts, 1987), p. 252; also Kirsten Hoving Keen, *American Art Pottery, 1875–1930* (Wilmington, DE: Delaware Art Museum, 1978), p. 44.

their efforts as of Ohr's unbridled creativity. Less concerned than scholars with the inspiration for his work, Ohr was relentless in his task. "No two pieces alike,"[6] he declared at exhibitions where he turned, twisted, and fired vases in a portable kiln before an audience of curious bystanders. Their failure to support his unusual pottery prompted him to declare toward the end of his career, "If it were not for the housewives of Biloxi who have a constant need of flowerpots, water coolers, and flues, the family of Ohr would often go hungry."[7]

At least one reviewer found Ohr's pottery to be a sincere and refreshing change from the outpouring of pottery from hundreds of Ohio kilns. ". . . unlovely as they are," the *Clay Worker* reported of Ohr's pottery in 1905, "they appeal more strongly to the person who is genuinely interested in the art of pottery than all the smooth shapes, molded with exasperating mechanical accuracy, which the so-called 'art potteries' turn out by the million to sell to the pseudo-artistic public of our day."[8] Seventy years later, as the Arts and Crafts revival began to sweep the country, the pottery of George Ohr literally came out of the attic to find a receptive and appreciative audience.

The unique nature of Ohr's work has made it difficult for modern collectors to make comparisons between pieces or draw conclusions that will enable them to distinguish between a highly desirable example and one that is less apt to inspire widespread interest. While generalizations are dangerous when applied to an artist as imaginative as George Ohr, most advanced collectors agree that the twisted, tortured forms are among the most sought-after of his work. Reflective, perhaps, of his personality, the colorful, vibrant glazes are clearly favored over flat blacks or solid browns. Examples with outlandish handles, spikes,

6. Kirsten Hoving Keen, *American Art Pottery, 1875–1930* (Wilmington, DE: Delaware Art Museum, 1978), p. 44.

7. *Crockery and Glass Journal* (December 30, 1909) p. 50; also quoted in Wendy Kaplan, ed., *The Art That Is Life: The Arts & Crafts Movement in America, 1875–1920* (Boston: Museum of Fine Arts, 1987), p. 252.

8. Kirsten Hoving Keen, *American Art Pottery, 1875–1930* (Wilmington, DE: Delaware Art Museum, 1978), p. 46.

The nine-inch vase, while devoid of any in-body twists, is decorated with a pair of Ohr handles; the four-inch indented vase was coated with a bright yellow high-gloss glaze and green speckles. Although both are fine examples, neither approaches the desirability of the six-inch double-gourd vase on the right, which combines a dimpled base, an in-body twist, and a ruffled rim beneath a fine metallic brown-lustre flambé glaze. *(Photo courtesy of David Rago, Trenton)*

spouts, and snakes—especially when combined with multicolored glazes—have collectors scrambling for an opportunity to add one to their collection. The new enthusiast may find the prices paid for premium Ohr as startling as his designs but can rest assured that less colorful, less imaginative Ohr pottery can still be found on the market.

Selected Prices

Because of the unique nature of George Ohr's forms and glazes, collectors are advised that minute differences can affect the value of two similar forms in dramatic fashion. For that reason, it is best to seek additional information before buying or selling important pieces.

Bowl: crimped snake on spherical ribbed form, glossy brown glaze, 3″ × 4″, $300–$350.

Bowl: bulbous, open, with splotches of black and brown on gray ground, 3″ × 4″, $225–$250.

Bowl: crimped, wide-mouthed, shallow form with folded, ruffled interior and crimped edge, mottled brown and purple glaze, 5″, $600–$700.

Bowl: bisque-fired open form with severe in-body twist and notched rim, 3″ × 5″, $325–$375.

Candleholder: bisque-fired, double-handled, one a loop and the other a double-kinked band from the base to neck, pink-orange to cream-clay color, 5″ × 5″, $250–$275.

Pitcher: slight serpentine to stretched rim, bulbous form with flattened back and cutout forming handle, glossy blue glaze, 4″, $600–$700.

Pitcher: folded handle on bulbous form, angled shoulder incised with triangles and diagonals over a scenic panel with mountains, lake, and a boat, reverse decorated with incised floral motif with butterflies, mottled glossy teal blue glaze, 6″, $2000–$2500.

Pitcher: thin-walled, handled cream pitcher with gunmetal gray metallic, glazed, sandy finish, 4″, $225–$250.

Pitcher: swirling form with ruffled rim, pinched and folded handle, in orange-pink to light orange clay, 4″ × 5″, $375–$425.

Pitcher: bulbous, with squeezed cut-out handle, royal blue matte exterior, yellow-brown interior, 3″ × 4″, $475–$575.

Pitcher: thin spout, double-curled handle, glazed with a sponged brown and spinach green over an orange ground, 8″ × 4″, $900–$1000.

Pitcher: severely twisted neck and fully dimpled lower section, orange-pink and cream clay, bisque, 3″ × 4″, *$325–$375*.

Shell: conch replica, with wide opening and rows of spikes, under high-glaze finish, 5″ × 9″, *$1500–$1750*.

Vase: mottled blue and green glaze on pear-shaped form, 4″, *$200–$225*.

Vase: bulbous, elongated neck with a twist on short, squat base, mottled brown-green glossy glaze, 4″, *$600–$700*.

Vase: angular bottom, with bulbous, rounded top, light clay, 5″ × 4″, *$165–$190*.

Vase: footed, cylindrical, seven vertical flutes ending in piecrust opening, cobalt blue glaze, 4″ × 4″, *$900–$1000*.

Vase: bulbous bottom and collar neck, in-body twist at bottom, metallic black and brown glaze, 3″ × 4″, *$450–$550*.

Vase: bulbous bottom, flaring rim folded inward and pleated, apple green glaze, 4″ × 4″, *$800–$900*.

Vase: bulbous, with tightly crimped rim and fully indented body, covered with mottled brown and speckled green flambé covered with mirrored, gunmetal high glaze, 6″ × 6″, *$3000–$3500*.

Vase: hourglass shape with bulging bottom and completely pinched, flaring neck, under gunmetal high glaze, 4″ × 3″, *$1000–$1250*.

Vase: bulbous, 13 oval indents encircling the body, with ruffled rim and covered with mauve blister glaze, 5″ × 4″, *$1500–$1750*.

Vase: bulbous bottom, long cylindrical neck, in-body twist and flanked by two ear-shaped handles with double kinks in each, 6″ × 5″, *$2500–$3000*.

Only George Ohr could take a traditional vase form, add a series of indentations, an in-body twist, and a metallic flambé glaze, and create an entirely new fashion. Unfortunately, it took sixty years for it to catch on. *(Photo courtesy of David Rago, Trenton)*

Vase: bisque, bulbous bottom, tapering neck, ending in ruffled rim, 6″ × 4″, *$325–$375.*

Vase: bulbous, open vase-bowl form, deeply manipulated ridges and dimples under purple over pink high glaze, 4″ × 5″, *$1200–$1400.*

Vase: squat, bulbous, with one compressed and deeply pinched end, light blue glaze splotches over feathered and speckled dark blue and green over tan ground, *$900–$1000.*

Vase: bulbous form with large dimple on either side and a lip above each dimple, glazed in medium to spinach green, with sponged dark blue-green overglaze, 5″ × 4″, *$400–$450.*

Vase: bisque-fired, wide, angular, bulbous bottom, footed base, and bulbous top ending in a crimped opening, incised into base: "Mary had a little lamb. Ohr has a little pottery. That's no joke," 7″ × 6″, *$350–$400.*

Vase: bulbous, with collar rim, dark green splotches with dark blue centers, 4″ × 3″, *$250–$300.*

Vase: cylindrical bottom, pinched-in waist, and flared rim in feathered green and metallic brown glaze, 6″ × 2″, *$400–$500.*

Vase: bulbous, with collar rim and pinched-in walls, dark brown high-gloss glaze, 6″ × 6″, *$450–$550.*

Vase: glazed in purple, yellow, brown, and blue, 4″, *$300–$350.*

Vase: bisque-fired, bulbous, squat form with in-body twist, incised "Mud from N.O. Street" and "1905," 5″ × 5″, *$225–$250.*

OVERBECK POTTERY

Shopmarks:
(Pre-1937) Impressed joined letters *O B K*, occasionally over the letter *E* (design by Elizabeth), *H* (decoration by Hannah), and/ or *F* (decoration by Mary F.)
(Post-1937) Impressed joined letters *O B K*, on occasion over the initials MF (Mary F. Overbeck)
Dating key: *H*, pre-1931; *E*, 1911–1935; *F* or *MF*, 1911–1955

Principal Contributions:
Decorated vases, bowls, candlesticks, and figurines

Founders:
Margaret Overbeck
Born: 1863   Died: 1911

Hanna Overbeck
Born: 1870   Died: 1931

Elizabeth Overbeck
Born: 1875   Died: 1936

Mary Overbeck
Born: 1878   Died: 1955
Founded: 1911   Closed: 1955

Studios and Salesrooms:
Overbeck Pottery
Cambridge City, Indiana
1911–1955

"They lived unto themselves, with commitment only to themselves and their desire to create."

—Kathleen Postle[1]

For the Overbeck sisters, 1911 was a year of both triumph and tragedy. After two years' study under noted ceramics instructor Charles F. Binns, Elizabeth Overbeck had returned to the family home in Cambridge City, Indiana, to help her three sisters form the Overbeck Pottery. Their sprawling two-story house was transformed into an active pottery, with a basement workshop, a first floor studio, and a kiln in a nearby building. Before the young pottery could celebrate its first anniversary, however, Margaret Overbeck, the oldest of the sisters and

1. Kathleen Postle, *The Chronicle of the Overbeck Pottery* (Indianapolis, IN: Indiana Historical Society, 1978), p. 27.

characterized as the guiding spirit of the founding, died from injuries sustained in an automobile accident the year before.

The management of the firm fell upon the shoulders of Elizabeth and her two artistic sisters: Hannah, who had suffered all her life from a debilitating form of neuritis, and Mary Frances, who, like her oldest sister Margaret, had studied under Arthur W. Dow at Columbia University before teaching art in the public school system. Hannah, an accomplished watercolorist, took charge of the Overbeck Pottery design and decoration, while Mary Frances assisted her and created many of the pottery's glazes. Elizabeth, in addition to developing glazes, oversaw the technical production, mixing clays shipped from Tennessee, Delaware, and Pennsylvania and working on the potter's wheel.

From the beginning, Overbeck pottery was distinctively unique. Although molds were made, they were not used until after 1936, when Mary Frances became the sole Overbeck potter. "The pottery was built upon a definite philosophy, with an aim to achieve not quantity, but quality from both technical and aesthetic standpoints."[2] Vases, candlesticks, bowls, tiles, and tea sets (with molded cups and saucers) constituted much of their early production; ceramic sculpture was undertaken later. Decorations consisted of carving or glaze inlay: matte during the Arts and Crafts period, evolving into brighter colors as public tastes changed.

Overbeck admirers generally prefer the early work executed during the Arts and Crafts period. Abstract examples with limited, subdued color but crisp design often seem austere to observers of other eras but are considered most desirable by advanced Overbeck collectors. Keen carving on simple forms, highlighted with a matte glaze, characterize some of their most sought-after work. Undecorated forms, although attractive, are not as highly valued.

The well-known Overbeck figurines were initiated sometime before the death of Elizabeth in 1936 and continued for several years thereafter. Often molded and generally less than five

2. Kathleen Postle, *The Chronicle of the Overbeck Pottery* (Indianapolis, IN: Indiana Historical Society, 1978), p. 51.

Overbeck Pottery often featured cut-back designs, such as the rabbits and flowers on this eight-inch vase and the rams and vines on the five-and-one-half-inch version with a flared collar rim. *(Photo courtesy of David Rago, Trenton)*

inches high, "these figurines included ladies and gentlemen in old-fashioned costumes, grotesque and humorous figures of people, animals and birds."[3] Many were uniquely original and are highly valued today. Multifigured scenes were executed on rare occasion and rank among the most treasured by Overbeck collectors. After 1936, when responsibility for the operation fell to Mary Frances, production gradually slowed, and reliance on molded forms increased until, at her death in 1955, the family pottery was closed.

Selected Prices

Due to the infrequency with which early examples of Overbeck pottery appear on the market, establishing an in-depth price guide has not yet been possible. The examples listed below are

3. Paul Evans, *Art Pottery of the United States* (New York: Charles Scribner's Sons, 1974), p. 204.

indictive only of the value of pieces of similar form and decoration. Until additional information is compiled, readers are advised to seek counsel from experienced collectors before either buying or selling important pieces.

Bowl: five incised and painted robins in red and beige, perched on flowering branches, mottled green ground, 3″ × 5″, *$700–$800.*

Candleholders: high-glaze, with stylized pink 'Spiral" flowers, blue stems, and pale green leaves against a mottled gray-green ground, 3″ × 3″, *$175–$200.*

Figure: funky dog with turquoise body with large black polka dots, lavender ears, and big paws, 2″ × 3″, *$175–$200.*

Figure: large woman dressed in Old South Southern Belle attire, with pink wide-brimmed hat, golden locks, a white dress with pink polka dots, and four layers of ruffles, carrying a bouquet, 7″ × 5″, *$225–$275.*

Figurine: country girl in pink bonnet and blue and white gingham dress, with large duck, on green grass with flowers, 4″ × 4″ × 3″, *$250–$300.*

Figurine: quacking white duck with large, black eyes, an orange bill, and exaggerated webbed feet, 2″ × 4″ × 4″, *$175–$200.*

Vase: bulbous, with collar rim, cut-back design of white rams with yellow antlers, small white birds with yellow tails, lavender and blue thorny vines with clusters of yellow berries, lavender and blue rocks, all against a lime green ground, 5″ × 4″, *$2250–$2750.*

Vase: bulging cylindrical form, with small collar rim, decorated with pale green matte cut-out pattern of rabbits amid angular flowers and leaves, 8″ × 5″, *$2000–$2250.*

Vase: bulbous, pink matte glaze, three cut-back panels of

stylized trees in pink on light brown ground, 5″ × 4″, $800–$900.

Vase: bulbous, with wide flared neck in matte olive green, wide band of light olive green fish and sea plants, 5″ × 5″, $1000–$1250.

Vase: cylinder, with three cut-back panels of stylized flowers, stems and leaves encircling its body, fawn brown finish, 7″ × 3″, $750–$850.

Vase: cylindrical with rolled rim and curved base, five cutback mystics with starred robes, in pink, 12″ × 6″, $2250–$2500.

J. B. OWENS POTTERY COMPANY

OWENS
UTOPIAN

Shopmark:
Impressed OWENS or J. B. OWENS and name of form
(After 1906) Impressed OWENSART, often with artist's
initials and production numbers

Principal Contributions:
Commercial household wares and art pottery vases

Founder:
J. B. Owens

Born: 1859   Died: 1934
Founded: ca. 1885   Closed: 1929

Studios and Salesrooms:
J. B. Owens Pottery Company
Roseville, Ohio
ca. 1885–1891

Zanesville, Ohio
ca. 1891–1929

"The arch-rivalry among Zanesville's Big Three—Owens, Weller and Roseville—was responsible for the offering of a great many lines of each. Many were out-and-out imitations of another's successful line, while others were skillful design and decorative achievements."

—Paul Evans[1]

Characterized by one of his rivals as a "natural," J. B. Owens had established a reputation as a prolific pottery salesman when he decided, in 1885, to leave the road and establish his own stoneware and pottery factory in Roseville, Ohio. By 1891, though, he had decided to relocate his growing flowerpot operation in nearby Zanesville, where he quickly expanded his factory and his line of pottery, hiring a number of skilled potters and talented artists. Karl Langenbeck, who had worked with the famed Rookwood artist Maria Longworth Nichols, was hired as head chemist that first year in Zanesville. Among the many talented artists and designers was W. A. Long; he had created the Lonhuda Pottery before sharing the secret of his technique with Samuel Weller, who promptly renamed it Louwelsa. Long created a similar line for Owens during the time he worked at Zanesville (1896–1900). Called Utopian, it was "painted with flowers, animals, or portraits, notably of American Indians, in slip, usually against a dark background under a high-gloss glaze."[2]

1. Paul Evans, *Art Pottery of the United States* (New York: Charles Scribner's Sons, 1974), p. 206.

2. Elisabeth Cameron, *Encyclopedia of Pottery & Porcelain: 1800–1960* (New York: Facts on File Publications, 1986), p. 253.

Owens continued to expand, despite a disastrous fire in 1902, eventually adding a plant in New York City and offering several hundred items in his sales catalog. Production was spurred by the development of a continuous kiln that both increased the daily number of finished pieces and reduced the number of kiln failures. In addition to being a popular success, the Owens art pottery displayed at the Lewis and Clark Exposition in Oregon in 1905 won four gold medals for excellence.

That same year, however, J. B. Owens made a drastic change in the focus of his operation. He completely dropped the highly successful line of inexpensive molded pottery and replaced it with a large tile operation that was so effective in undercutting the prices of all of his competitors that a consortium of tile manufacturers offered to buy his tile works. Owens agreed, and in 1907 the plant changed hands and was promptly shut down. At the same time that he was getting into tile production, Owens began placing even greater emphasis on a new line of art pottery, called Owensart. Additional lines of art pottery, most notably Soudanese, Aqua Verdi, Lotus, Parchment Lotus, and Brushmodel Lotus, were produced in a popular matte glaze.[3]

These lines were all introduced between 1905 and 1907 and, along with several other new art pottery forms, were exhibited at the Jamestown (Virginia) Tercentennial Exposition in 1907. For whatever reason, though, Owens ceased production of his art pottery that same year. Once again he created a successful tile operation that continued to expand every year until a fire in 1928 destroyed his main plant. Against the advice of his friends, Owens rebuilt the factory, which he lost during the ensuing Depression.

Selected Prices

Mug: Utopian, underglaze decorations of berries, artist signed, 4″, *$125–$150.*

3. Paul Evans, *Art Pottery of the United States* (New York: Charles Scribner's Sons, 1974), p. 209.

Pitcher: Lotus, underglaze-decorated sandpiper motif, 8″, $375–$400.

Pitcher: Utopian, floral design, artist signed, 12″, $375–$425.

Vase: Utopian, roses motif, artist signed, 11″, $250–$300.

Vase: Soudanese, bulbous bottom, wide cylindrical neck, violet and purple iris blossom, green leaves on black ground, 8″ × 4″, $250–$300.

Vase: Lotus, floral design with purple on gray, 14″, $375–$425.

Vase: Lotus, vellum glaze, berries and leaf motif, 4″, $100–$125.

Vase: matte Utopian, floral motif, in purple and gold, 5″, $225–$250.

Vase: matte glaze bottle, slip-decorated with grayish blue and light brown flowers on a grayish blue and light brown ground, 10″ × 5″, $100–$125.

Vase: Utopian, decorated berries, on twisted form, 4″, $125–$150.

Vase: Utopian, daisy motif, 11″, $175–$200.

Vase: Utopian, bulbous form, high glaze, 11″, $225–$250.

Vase: Utopian, floral motif, 4″, $85.

Wall pocket: bamboo shape, in matte green glaze, 10″, $150–$165.

PAULINE POTTERY

PAULINE
POTTERY

Shopmarks:
Incised outline of a crown, with the letter *P*, *O*, or *C* in the
center; addition of *TRADE MARK* after 1891
Incised PAULINE POTTERY, often with decorator's initials,
year or model number (the lower the number,
the older the piece)

Principal Contribution:
Decorated art pottery, including vases, candlesticks,
teapots, and bowls

Founder:
Pauline Jacobus
Born: 1840   Died: 1930
Founded: 1883   Closed: 1909

Studios and Salesrooms:
Pauline Pottery
Chicago
1883–1893

Edgerton, Wisconsin
1902–1909

"PAULINE POTTERY, near Edgerton, Wisconsin, study and
recreation combined, summer school during July for practical

instruction in art of Pottery. Number of pupils limited, for rates and further particulars address Mrs. Pauline Jacobus."

—*Magazine advertisement*
1906[1]

Pauline Jacobus was an amazing woman. While a student at the Art Institute in Chicago in the early 1880s, she decided that she was going to establish her own art pottery studio. To learn the craft, she enrolled in Maria Longworth Nichols's Cincinnati studio, Rookwood, where she was exposed to the wide range of skills required to make, decorate, and fire pottery. While still studying in Cincinnati, however, she received word from her husband "that there was a group of women who planned to open an art pottery studio in Chicago."[2]

Mrs. Jacobus immediately left Rookwood, hired the services of John Sargent, who was a renowned kiln maker, and in 1883 announced her first showing in a small Chicago shop. The name of the new pottery was suggested by her husband, a wealthy member of the Chicago Board of Trade. Her first employees were art students hired to decorate her wares, but as recognition and orders began to come in, they were soon replaced by full-time artists. "Artware with a yellow earthenware body decorated either with underglaze or monochrome glazes was produced, as was an incised and gilded redware."[3]

From the beginning, Mr. Jacobus had shown a sincere interest in his wife's venture, and it was he who first heard about a vein of high-quality yellow clay 125 miles away in Edgerton, Wisconsin. Until then her clay had been shipped by rail from Ohio, and the opportunity to eliminate that cost and move to larger quarters close to a new source of clay was tempting.

1. Ralph and Terry Kovel, *The Kovels' Collectors Guide to American Art Pottery* (New York: Crown Publishers, 1974), p. 162.

2. Ibid., p. 160.

3. Paul Evans, *Art Pottery of the United States* (New York: Charles Scribner's Sons, 1974), p. 217.

Mr. Jacobus set to work contacting investors and securing rights to both the clay and an empty building in Edgerton. As a result of his efforts, "the Pauline Pottery was incorporated on February 14, 1888 with capital stock of twenty thousand dollars."[4] Within a matter of weeks Mr. Jacobus had moved his business into the first two floors, and Mrs. Jacobus and Pauline Pottery were occupying the third, with six adjacent kilns. With retail outlets such as Tiffany's in New York, Kimball's in Boston, and Marshall Field's in Chicago, her staff soon rose to more than thirty, with "thirteen ladies hired to decorate the art pottery."[5] Most of the decorating was done by brush from designs drawn by Mrs. Jacobus; her decorative designs reveal an interest in flowers and plants.

In 1893, however, Mr. Jacobus died, and financial complications led to the closing of both his business and that of Pauline Pottery. Mrs. Jacobus was not about to admit defeat. Although the major stockholders had decided to liquidate all of the pottery equipment at auction, she purchased the remaining clay and one of the brick kilns. The clay was shipped to the family home in Edgerton, while she and an assistant numbered each brick in the kiln, carefully dismantled it, transported it back to her house, and reassembled it in her backyard. In 1902 she was back in business, housing student decorators in her boardinghouse while making pottery in her basement and firing it in her backyard kiln.

"During the years she worked with clay she washed, molded, threw, cast, decorated, and filled and fired the kiln. The heavy manual labor required to fill and lift the saggars and to seal and brick the kiln was quite an accomplishment for a woman."[6] Much of the pottery she produced during this time featured "low-fired crackle glazes used on a white body, and blended glazes, notably a 'peacock' combination of deep blue and green."[7]

4. Ralph and Terry Kovel, *The Kovels' Collectors Guide to American Art Pottery* (New York: Crown Publishers, 1974), p. 161.

5. Ibid.

6. Ibid., p. 163.

7. Elisabeth Cameron, *Encyclopedia of Pottery & Porcelain: 1800–1960* (New York: Facts on File Publications, 1986), p. 172.

Mrs. Jacobus decided to close Pauline Pottery in 1909. Two years later a fire destroyed her house, her studio, and all but a few of her remaining artwares. After the fire Mrs. Jacobus went to live with her children and passed away in 1930.

Selected Prices

Due to the infrequency with which examples of this pottery appear on the market, establishing an in-depth price guide has not yet been possible. The examples listed below are indicative only of the value of pieces of similar form and decoration. Until additional information is compiled, readers are advised to seek counsel from experienced collectors before either buying or selling important pieces.

Jug: bulbous, two spouts on either side of a handle at the top center with metallic gold bamboo reed design against cobalt blue high glaze, 9″ × 9″, *$250–$300.*

Pitcher: underglazed decoration, morning glory motif, 11″, *$550–$650.*

Tile: Limoges style, fish and underwater vegetation, 6″, *$300–$350.*

Vase: squat, bulbous, four indents forming a quatrefoil opening at the top, stylized flowers and falling petals of light gold and burgundy are outlined in black, against a cream-to-yellow ground, dark blue crown atop, 4″ × 5″, *$250–$300.*

PETERS AND REED
POTTERY COMPANY

Shopmark:
Peters and Reed—none.
The Zane Pottery Company—the letters *Z.P.Co* over the words
ZANE WARE/MADE IN USA

Principal Contributions:
Line of flowerpots and jardinieres, plus molded art pottery

Founders:
John D. Peters and Adam Reed
Born: unknown   Died: Adam Reed, 1922
Founded: 1898   Closed: 1920
(renamed The Zane Pottery Company)

Studios and Salesrooms:
Peters and Reed Pottery Co.
South Zanesville, Ohio
1897–1920

The Zane Pottery Company
South Zanesville, Ohio
1921–1941

"Moss Aztec offers ... the quiet effect of the rich red brown
tones of the Historic Aztec Indians coupled with the apparent
mossy deposit of nature."

—*Catalog description*
1921[1]

When Samuel Weller discontinued his line of flowerpots in 1897
to concentrate on the popular underglaze art pottery, two of his
employees, John Peters and Adam Reed, saw an opportunity to
start a business of their own. The two men rented a former
stoneware building in Zanesville, Ohio; but before they had an
opportunity to establish themselves, the property was purchased by the Roseville Pottery and the entrepreneurs were
forced to move. Peters and Reed soon found a building in South
Zanesville and started producing red earthenware flowerpots.
By 1900 they were able to incorporate and had added a line of
decorated jardinieres. Although it appears that Adam Reed began experimenting with an art pottery line as early as 1901,[2]
the pair concentrated on building a clientele for their growing
line of flowerpots and kitchenware.

Around 1905 Frank Ferrell, a designer at Weller Pottery,
left that firm to work for Peters and Reed as both a designer
and a salesman, staying until 1917, when he resigned to work
for Roseville Pottery. It may have been Ferrell's arrival that
prompted Peters and Reed to drop production of their three-
year-old kitchenware line and in 1907 to enlarge their line of
"inexpensive jardinieres with hand-painted decorations on a
glazed surface ... in matt green, high-gloss red, green and
blended glazes."[3]

1. Ralph and Terry Kovel, *The Kovels' Collectors Guide to American
Art Pottery* (New York: Crown Publishers, 1974), p. 168.
2. Paul Evans, *Art Pottery of the United States* (New York: Charles
Scribner's Sons, 1974), p. 222.
3. Ibid.

The firm's first extended offering of art pottery was designed by Frank Ferrell shortly before 1912 and named Moss Aztec. Under his direction, the "pieces were molded in local red clay and coated in a finish which was then wiped off the raised portions of relief decoration, leaving a mossy effect in the recesses."[4] Additional lines followed, each with a molded form and matte finish.

John Peters retired from the firm in 1920, leaving Adam Reed as president. The following year Reed changed the name of the firm to The Zane Pottery Company. He died in 1922, but the Zane Pottery Company continued under the direction of Harry S. McClelland, who had worked for the firm since 1903. Many of the molds designed during the tenure of Peters and Reed were used for several years thereafter. Distinguishing the later pottery from that produced prior to 1920 was made possible by the incorporation of a trademark—the letters *Z.P.Co.* over the words *ZANE WARE/MADE IN USA*—by the South Zanesville company. The pottery was sold to the Gonder Ceramic Art Pottery Company in 1941.

Selected Prices

Bowl: Moss Aztec, pine cone design, artist signed, 6″, *$75–$85*.

Bowl: decorated in vines and berries with brown and green glaze, 3″ × 8″, *$45–$55*.

Bowl: decorated in swirling blue and gray, 6″ × 2″, *$45–$55*.

Hanging basket: Moss Aztec, with roses motif, *$35–$45*.

Jardiniere: Moss Aztec, grape design on border, artist signed, 9″, *$85–$95*.

Mug: decorated with applied grapes, 6″, *$65–$75*.

Vase: chromal scenic design with stylized decoration, 7″, *$175–$200*.

4. Elisabeth Cameron, *Encyclopedia of Pottery & Porcelain: 1800–1960* (New York: Facts on File Publications, 1986), p. 258.

Vase: chromal scenic design of cabin in woods, 8″ × 6″, $175–$200.

Vase: Moss Aztec, floral motif with cone shape, artist signed, 8″, $55–$65.

Wall pocket: Moss Aztec, 7″ $50–$60.

PEWABIC POTTERY

Shopmark:
Impressed PEWABIC/DETROIT, often below line of oak leaves or with initials *MCP*

Principal Contributions:
Art pottery vases and architectural tiles

Founders:
Mary Chase Perry
Born: 1867   Died: 1961
Horace J. Caulkins
Born: 1850   Died: 1923
Founded: 1903   Closed: 1965

Studios and Salesrooms:
Pewabic Pottery
Detroit
1903–1965

"One of the chief prides of the Pewabic operation in addition to its work was that the methods of big business never overtook the intimacy of the pottery. The creative work was kept consistently in the hands of the artist, and the technical end of the operation was achieved with the simplest equipment needed for the job."

—*Paul Evans*[1]

Among the most important of the women who were active in Arts and Crafts ceramics was Mary Chase Perry—"an adventurous artist with a love of color and experiment."[2] Trained as an artist at the Cincinnati Art Academy from 1887 until 1889 (where she met Maria Longworth Nichols and Kataro Shirayamadani) and later with the renowned ceramic teacher Charles Binns, she returned to Detroit, where her mother lived, and, like many women artists of the period, engaged in china painting.

By 1900, however, she was experimenting with clay sculpture, having outgrown overglaze decorations and instead turning to creating her own ceramics, using her neighbor Horace Caulkins's dental kiln to fire her first pieces. Working together, "they developed the Revelation kiln, a portable, kerosene-burning, muffle kin that became standard for the china painting movement and was used by many of the leading art potteries."[3] As Anthea Callen observed in her work on women artists in the movement, "Her early work displayed the influences of William H. Grueby, who was responsible for introducing matt glazes into American art pottery, and of European Art Nouveau ceramics, often through the intermediary exponents of the style such as Louis Tiffany."[4]

In 1903 Perry and Caulkins formed a pottery company, taking the name Pewabic from a nearby river. Ironically, "it was only after many years that Miss Perry learned Pewabic meant

1. Paul Evans, *Art Pottery of the United States* (New York: Charles Scribner's Sons, 1974), p. 227.

2. Garth Clark and Margie Hughto, *A Century of Ceramics in the United States: 1878–1978* (New York: E. P. Dutton, 1979), p. 46.

3. Ibid.

4. Anthea Callen, *Women Artists of the Arts and Crafts Movement: 1870–1914* (New York: Pantheon Books, 1979), p. 86.

'copper color in clay.' "[5] Miss Perry also developed a fascination with glazes. Joseph Herrick, a potter, was hired to throw the forms on the wheel, working from drawings Miss Perry provided, while she took charge of the decorating and the glazes. "Her [early] vases were decorated with conventionalized natural forms and matt glazes, but gradually her interest centered on the effects of glazes, and of necessity the forms of her pots became simpler in order to show off the rich colors and lusters."[6] As a result of her personal preoccupation with glazes, "the forms lacked the evolution and continuity of Binns and Robineau. Nonetheless she produced a few masterpieces whose beauty derives largely from her range of extraordinary glazes, from elusive, iridescent glazes to cloudy, rich inglaze lusters."[7]

Clay was shipped to their basement studio from four different states, plus England, to form a durable, near-white body after it had been fired at high temperatures in their kiln. Miss Perry soon developed a formula for an iridescent glaze that became a staple of Pewabic production. "She evolved deep blues and burning gold, among many others, and her late work is characterized by subtle overlays of dripping color and a sparkling iridescence that made her glazes quite original for the period, and ensured her importance in the development of American ceramics."[8]

Perry and Caulkins enlarged their operation in 1907. Even while their works were being turned out in the basement of Horace Caulkins's house, they were receiving national recognition. In addition to their famous glazed vases, the pair began producing architectural tiles. Her friend and patron, Charles L. Freer, was responsible for introducing Miss Perry and Pewabic art tiles to leading architects in Detroit. Their first major commission, for St. Paul's Cathedral, was completed in 1908 and led

5. Ralph and Terry Kovel, *The Kovels' Collectors Guide to American Art Pottery* (New York: Crown Publishers, 1974), p. 170.

6. Anthea Callen, *Women Artists of the Arts and Crafts Movement: 1870–1914* (New York: Pantheon Books, 1979), p. 86.

7. Garth Clark and Margie Hughto, *A Century of Ceramics in the United States: 1878–1978* (New York: E. P. Dutton, 1979), p. 47.

8. Anthea Callen, *Women Artists of the Arts and Crafts Movement: 1870–1914* (New York: Pantheon Books, 1979), pp. 86–87.

Three classic Pewabic pottery forms: a thirteen-inch tapered-neck vase with a dual flowing glaze, a squat five-inch vase with a high glaze, and an eight-inch vase with a collar rim. Like most Pewabic pottery, each is clearly marked. *(Photo courtesy of David Rago, Trenton)*

to both critical and popular acclaim, plus additional commissions from architects Cass Gilbert, Greene and Greene, and others.[9]

In 1918, at the age of fifty-one, Miss Perry married William B. Stratton. Her associate, Horace Caulkins, died in 1923, but she continued to run Pewabic Pottery alone, even through the Depression had closed the doors on so many other firms. Two major tile commissions, the National Shrine of the Immaculate Conception, Washington, DC (1923–1931), and the Detroit Institute of Arts (1927) helped ensure her continued success through tough times. In 1938 her husband was killed in a tragic streetcar accident, but Mary Perry remained undaunted. With the assistance of Ira and Ella Peters, she continued to run the Pewabic Pottery until her death in 1961 at the age of 94. Pewabic Pottery remained in operation until 1965, at which time

9. Garth Clark and Margie Hughto, *A Century of Ceramics in the United States: 1878–1978* (New York: E. P. Dutton, 1979), p. 47.

it became a museum under the direction of Michigan State University.

Selected Prices

Bowl: wide conical form tapering toward base in copper and green striations, 2″ × 5″, *$100–$125.*

Vase: squat and bulbous with sky blue and black speckled glaze, 4″ × 4″, *$250–$350.*

Vase: flaring rim on tapering form in blue, 3″ × 4″, *$90–$100.*

Vase: bulbous, with collar neck and rolled rim with iridescent gray to brown glaze, 10″ × 6″, *$300–$350.*

Vase: closed bowl form, bulbous, with collar rim, gray-blue flambé, 6″ × 6″, *$325–$375.*

Vase: bulbous bottom with cylindrical neck and flared rim, iridescent blue and gold flambé, 4″ × 3″, *$250–$300.*

Vase: bottle form with iridescent gold glaze dripping unevenly over midnight blue iridescent finish, 15″ × 6″, *$1000–$1250.*

Vase: flaring to a bulbous top and heavily carved, stylized flowers and leaves, turquoise matte glaze, 10″ × 6″, *$1000–$1250.*

Vase: bulbous, with flared neck in iridescent red glaze, 5″ × 4″, *$225–$250.*

Vase: bulbous, with flared rim, iridescent copper flambé over mottled turquoise blue high glaze, 6″ × 5″, *$225–$275.*

Vase: blue iridescent glaze with pink and gold highlights, 4″, *$225–$250.*

Vase: high-glaze, cream-gray bold with matte and iridescent glaze on outside, turquoise blue inside, 4″ × 4″, *$125–$150.*

Vase: high-glaze, silver-gray glaze, highly iridescent, 2″ × 2″, *$75–$85.*

Vase: high-glaze, yellow-green iridescent glaze with gray patches, 5″ × 9″, *$350–$400.*

Vase: iridescent greenish gray with pink highlights on bottom, turquoise drip from top, 4″, *$200–$225.*

Vase: bright blue with pinkish gray drip around top, 5″, *$225–$250.*

PAUL REVERE POTTERY
and
SATURDAY EVENING GIRLS

P·R·P   S·E·G·

Shopmarks:
(Pre-1915) Paper label or painted, BOWL SHOP/S.E.G./
18 HULL ST./BOSTON, MASS
Impressed mark of Paul Revere on horseback over words *THE
PAUL REVERE POTTERY/BOSTON*
Letters *S.E.G.* or *P.R.P.*, often with year

Principal Contributions:
Art pottery, children's dishes, and tiles

Founders:
Edith Brown and Mrs. James Storrow
Founded: 1906   Closed: 1942

Studios and Salesrooms:
Paul Revere Pottery
Boston
1906–1915

Brighton, Massachusetts
1915–1942

"To Miss Edith Brown is due a large part of the credit for the quality of the work produced. A distinctive character has been maintained both in design and technique, and too high praise can scarcely be awarded to the wares."

—*C. F. Binns*
1916[1]

The Paul Revere Pottery grew out of the concerns of two women—Edith Brown and Mrs. James J. Storrow—for the growing number of young immigrant women living in turn-of-the-century Boston. Miss Brown and Edith Guerrier, a Boston librarian, conceived the idea of having a group of young girls who met each week at the Saturday Evening Girls Club decorate pottery that would then be sold to help support their settlement house activities. The girls set about learning the basics of ceramics, and in December 1906 Mrs. Storrow purchased a small kiln and hired an experienced potter to teach the young women how to glaze and fire their wares.

The Saturday Evening Girls Club had started their pottery experiment in 1906 in what little spare space their settlement house offered, and it soon became evident that the pottery was going to have to move to larger quarters if it ever hoped to sustain itself. Mrs. Storrow stepped forward once again, as she was to do for several years hence, and in 1908 provided a four-story brick structure for the girls and the pottery's director, Edith Brown. The building stood not far from the Old North Church; thus, the growing pottery took on a new name in honor of the revolutionary war hero who had taken the cue for his famous ride not far from their site.

1. Anthea Callen, *Women Artists of the Arts and Crafts Movement: 1870–1914* (New York: Pantheon Books, 1979), p. 91.

This Saturday Evening Girls decorated bowl (5″ × 11½″) features eight repeating white geese on a blue and green ground. In addition to the *S.E.G.* mark, it is dated "7-15." *(Photo courtesy of Robert W. Skinner, Boston)*

The Saturday Evening Girls Club continued to provide the decorators for the pottery, and it is estimated that "over two hundred girls worked on the pottery, although only about ten were active at any time."[2] Most worked five days a week, plus half of Saturday in what has been described as ideal working conditions for sculpting and painting pottery. "The decorators at Paul Revere were girls just out of school, who after a year's training were able to undertake the more skilled aspects of the work such as the incising of designs on the ware in the biscuit stage or the application of colors."[3] The natural turnover in the staff required a great deal of training time, which served one purpose of the pottery—to train young women—but also helped to defeat another, that being to become and remain profitable. "The pottery in the next few years developed rapidly and grew steadily, but instead of making money it required thousands of dollars to subsidize it."[4]

2. Ralph and Terry Kovel, *The Kovels' Collectors Guide to American Art Pottery* (New York: Crown Publishers, 1974), p. 189.

3. Paul Evans, *Art Pottery of the United States* (New York: Charles Scribner's Sons, 1974), pp. 213-214.

4. Ibid.

Saturday Evening Girls decorated plates were popular in Boston during the Arts and Crafts era. The eight-and-one-half-inch example with eight pigs around the border features the initials *H.O.S.* in the center for Helen Osborne Storrow, their benevolent patron. Her initials can also be found on the rims of the plate and bowl on the right. *(Photo courtesy of Robert W. Skinner, Boston)*

In 1915 another major expansion was required. A new building was designed by Edith Brown and modeled after the Rookwood factory in Cincinnati. Once again, Mrs. Storrow came forth with the funds to finance the new structure and equipment in Brighton. The new pottery building allowed an increase in the number of employees to nearly twenty and in the number of kilns to four. As the size of the staff and facility increased, so did their line of pottery. Vases, lamps, bookends, paperweights, and candlesticks were complemented with dinnerware sets and tiles, including a popular series illustrating the ride of Paul Revere. "Most popular of all, however, were the children's breakfast sets, which consisted of a pitcher, bowl and plate, all decorated with popular juvenile motifs of chicks, rabbits, ducks and the like. Upon special order, monograms or initials could be incorporated in the design of these sets."[5]

Under the firm hand of Edith Brown and the benevolence of Mrs. Storrow, the pottery continued to produce high-quality

5. Paul Evans, *Art Pottery of the United States* (New York: Charles Scribner's Sons, 1974), pp. 213–214.

wares, but the expenses involved in the hand-decorating process prevented it from ever surviving on its own. Edith Brown died in 1932, but not even a change in leadership could prevent the economic depression that paralyzed the country from closing the Paul Revere Pottery. The kilns remained in reduced operation until finally, in 1942, two years before the death of its patron, Mrs. Storrow, the pottery closed.

Some of the art pottery produced at the Paul Revere Pottery features incised lines and painted decorations similar to that of Newcomb pottery. "The design was outlined in black and filled in with flat tones in the manner of the period's illustrational style. Soft in color and texture, pieces most often were glazed in the popular Art Nouveau matt shades of yellow, blue, green, gray, white and brown. A number of pieces were also decorated with a high-gloss glaze, in colors ranging from jade to metallic black."[6]

Selected Prices

Paul Revere Pottery

Bowl: shallow blue form, pale band centering medallion with cottage and trees, 7″ *$300–$350.*

Bowl: dark and light green with brown, decorated with oak tree design, 2″ × 5″, *$400–$500.*

Cup: egg, blue and white decorated, 2″, *$65–$75.*

Cup: egg, blue and white with acorn design, 2″, *$75–$85.*

Cup and saucer: light blue band centering tree medallion on blue ground, 6″, *$100–$125.*

Luncheon set: six tea cups, five saucers, bouillon cup, three bowls, creamer, turquoise interior, cherry red exterior, *$100–$125.*

Pitcher: wide-mouth form, wide band of trees on yellow ground, 4″ × 4″, *$100–$125.*

6. Paul Evans, *Art Pottery of the United States* (New York: Charles Scribner's Sons, 1974), p. 216.

Pitcher: wide mouth on squat tapering form, stylized green and blue drip glaze band on blue ground, 7″ × 6″, *$125-$150.*

Plate: white and yellow hands centering owl in a tree, 8″, *$150-$175.*

Plate: incised landscape band with trees and house on a lake, centering a flying goose monogrammed medallion, blue and green border on yellow, 8″, *$350-$400.*

Plate: light and dark blue bands centering tree medallions, 8″, *$175-$200.*

Plate: decorated with pine cones, 10″, *$200-$225.*

Plate: white band with initials *H.O.S.*, centering rooster medallion on forest green ground, 8″, *$400-$500.*

Vase: rolled rim on squat, bulbous form decorated with Greek key border in browns and yellows, 4″ × 5″, *$200-$225.*

Saturday Evening Girls

Bowl: open form, incised and decorated with a border of green trees, with green mountains and blue sky, all outlined in black on green ground, 3″ × 8″, *$450-$550.*

Bowl: open form, glazed in pea green semigloss, covered with copper lid showing an enameled red and orange peony on a blue ground, 2″ × 4″, *$300-$350.*

Bowl: band of white roosters on green ground, interior motto: "Harriet—early to bed and early to rise makes a child healthy, wealthy and wise," 5″, *$550-$650.*

Bowl: cereal, decorated with a band of repeating squirrels on green band and white ground, 6″, *$550-$650.*

Bowl: stylized green trees and blue sky against dark gray ground, 2″ × 8″, *$350-$400.*

Bowl: repeating trees on blue and brown band, green ground, 11″, *$800–$900.*

Bowl: flared, turquoise interior, gunmetal gray exterior, 6″ × 12″, *$100–$125.*

Bowl: repeating yellow roosters facing each other on white ground, 6″, *$600–$700.*

Bowl: blue stylized lotus on white band, 2″ × 4″, *$200–$225.*

Bowl: incised decoration of eight repeating white geese and vegetation on a blue and green ground, 5″ × 11″, *$750–$850.*

Breakfast set, child's, includes bowl, plate, and pitcher, decorated with blue band of repeating chicks on white ground, 6″, *$225–$275.*

Casserole: oval form with green tree band on blue ground, small loop handles, 11″ × 7″, *$225–$275.*

Mug: souvenir, blue band with Greek key band over dedication "M.I.T. '91 Osterville 1911," white ground, 5″, *$150–$175.*

Mug: with large handle and with three incised Viking ships in brown with green sails on blue and white water against a cream sky, top and bottom banded in marine blue, design outlined in black, 5″ × 6″, *$1250–$1500.*

Pitcher: handled, bulbous bottom, in cream matte with Greek key design in blue and green, outlined in black, around the top rim, 5″ × 4″, *$300–$325.*

Pitcher: wide mouth and handle on ovoid body, decorated with a triple repeat of Viking ships in green and brown on a pale blue background, 10″, *$900–$1000.*

Pitcher: bulbous form with angled handle, circular medallion with initials *E.L.C.* on blue ground, 7″, *$150–$175.*

Pitcher: pear-shape form with applied handle, white band

of tortoise and hare decoration on blue ground, motto "Slow but Sure" around neck, 4″, *$600–$700.*

Plate: eight squealing pigs with curly tails on brown and yellow border, central monogram *H.O.S.* for Helen Osbourne Storrow, 8″, *$800–$900.*

Plate: running rabbit medallion centered by yellow and pale green band, 7″, *$200–$250.*

Plate: blue and beige tree border on forest green glaze, central monogram *TMO* for Thomas Mott Osborne, 8″, *$250–$300.*

Plate: beige and green band of repeating chicks and wheat shafts on white ground, 8″, *$250–$300.*

Plate: incised lotus border in white on blue ground, 8″, *$200–$225.*

Plate: white hen and chick border on blue band with motto, "O Don't bother me said the hen with one chick," 6″, *$700–$800.*

Tile: round, incised stand of green trees on a blue lake, 6″, *$250–$300.*

Tile: white goose with elongated neck against stylized green and blue landscape and blue border, 5″, *$200–$225.*

Trivet: square, with simple olive green geometric border, outlined in black, around a light green matte center, four corner feet, 5″, *$250–$300.*

Trivet: square, with incised geometric bands in green, brown, and blue overlaping squares, 5″, *$150–$175.*

Vase: bulbous form, with band of stylized water lilies and leaves in light blue and green, outlined in black, 7″ × 6″, *$450–$550.*

Vase: high-glaze dark blues and greens, 6″, *$100–$125.*

RHEAD POTTERY

Shopmark:
Impressed design or paper label, potter sitting at his wheel,
with words *RHEAD POTTERY/SANTA BARBARA*

Principal Contributions:
Decorated household vases, large garden ornaments

Founder:
Frederick H. Rhead
Born: 1880   Died: 1942
Founded: 1913   Closed: 1917

Studios and Salesrooms:
Rhead Pottery, Inc.
Santa Barbara, California
1913–1917

Frederick H. Rhead came to America in 1902 after training
with his father in England to become a potter. Over the course
of the next ten years he served as an artist and art director for
the Avon Faience Company, Weller Pottery, Roseville Pottery,
the Jervis Pottery, and the Arequipa Pottery, designing important lines for each. In addition, he wrote and taught extensively.

Rhead and his wife left the Arequipa Pottery in 1913 after a
disagreement with the sanitarium directors. They moved to

Santa Barbara, where Rhead established his own pottery firm. Two potters turned out large garden wares and small vases and bowls designed by Rhead that reveal a strong Oriental influence; the clay was native of California. Much of Rhead's fame came from his development of fine glazes, in particular a number of "black glazes of Chinese inspiration which resulted from fifteen years of personal research."[1] Like the pottery forms, decorations were designed by Rhead but often applied by assistants.

Unfortunately, Rhead's business ability did not equal his artistic powers. The small concern closed in 1917, but Rhead remained active in research, education, and the encouragement of new potters.

Selected Prices

Due to the infrequency with which examples of this pottery appear on the market, establishing an in-depth price guide has not yet been possible. Until additional information is compiled, readers are advised to seek counsel from experienced collectors before either buying or selling important pieces.

ADELAIDE ALSOP ROBINEAU

Shopmark:
Incised initials *R P* (Robineau Pottery) within a circle
(Early) Incised initials *A-R*
After 1908 the year generally is also found

1. Elisabeth Cameron, *Encyclopedia of Pottery & Porcelain: 1800–1960* (New York: Facts on File Publications, 1986), p. 276.

Principal Contribution:
Small number of decorated porcelain wares exhibiting quality matte and crystalline glazes

Founder:
Adelaide Alsop Robineau

Born: 1865   Died: 1929

Founded: ca. 1904   Closed: ca. 1916

Studios and Salesrooms:
Robineau Pottery

Syracuse, New York

ca. 1904–ca. 1916

"I have seen the Scarab Vase in all its stages of construction, and I know the labor and patience involved. Many times during the carving, Mrs. Robineau would work all day, and on an otherwise clean floor there would be about enough dry porcelain dust to cover a dollar piece, and half an inch more carving on the vase."

—*F. H. Rhead*
1917[1]

The significance of the contribution of Adelaide Alsop Robineau to the development of the art of porcelain design and glazes cannot be overstated or adequately summarized. Her life, her work, and her techniques are as complex as the design on the famous Scarab Vase. All contributed, as one study has been subtitled, to her "Glory in Porcelain."[2] Unfortunately, her output was extremely small; a true studio potter, she never entered into pottery production, preferring instead to invest innumerable hours in each work, bringing it as close to perfection as humanly possible before selling it directly to a major museum.

The initial outlet for young Adelaide Alsop's artistic abilities was china painting, deemed an acceptable profession for young women of her day. Her marriage to Samuel Robineau in 1899

1. Peg Weiss, ed., *Adelaide Alsop Robineau: Glory in Porcelain* (Syracuse, NY: Syracuse University Press, 1981), p. 215.

2. Ibid.

While all porcelains by Adelaide Alsop Robineau are rare, collectors are more apt to encounter one of her smaller vases, such as the two-inch streaked-glaze example on the right, than even the four-inch blue crystalline glaze example on the left. The nine-inch porcelain vase in the center was designed by Emile Diffloth at University City. *(Photo courtesy of Christie's, New York)*

spurred the realization of her dream of establishing a magazine dedicated to the artistic and technical aspects of china decorating. The first issue of *Keramic Studio* appeared in May of that same year and proved an immediate success; over the course of her career it provided artists and designers with articles from noted potters such as Charles Volkmar, F. H. Rhead, Charles Binns, and Mary Chase Perry, news of exhibitions, technical information, and color illustrations of important works. For Adelaide Robineau, it eventually provided her with the inspiration and financial freedom to establish her own small pottery.

Her early experiments led to a display of seven vases at Gustav Stickley's March 1903 Arts and Crafts Exhibition in his Syracuse showroom (the Robineau home included furniture from the Stickley workshops). With her husband's assistance, Adelaide continued to experiment, "eventually developing the unusual range of glazes both fixed and flowing, crystalline and matte, for which she is known."[3] Her tenacity and skill led to

3. Peg Weiss, ed., *Adelaide Alsop Robineau: Glory in Porcelain* (Syracuse, NY: Syracuse University Press, 1981), p. 19.

numerous awards for her porcelains and recognition as a leading authority. She experimented successfully in a number of different styles: Arts and Crafts, Art Nouveau, Oriental, and Art Deco. Though her limited production and enormous personal investment dictated that her rewards would arrive in forms other than monetary, she continued to experiment, teach, edit, write, and raise three children—even addressing the problem of women artists in 1913 by declaring: "It is because of the children and the home that we cannot and will not give up, that the woman can never hope to become as great in any line as man. Art is a jealous mistress and allows no consideration whatever to interfere with her supremacy."[4]

Adelaide Robineau continued to work on her pottery until her death in 1929. As Martin Eidelberg observed, "For Robineau, the perfection of all-over excising became a foremost goal. In the compulsive realm of her thinking, time was her commodity to squander."[5] The famous Scarab Vase that she labored over at University City pottery in 1910 consumed over one thousand hours of her time. While critics may enjoy debating which among her many accomplishments was her most significant, all agree on one point: because of the extraordinary degree of skill it exhibits, every surviving example of her work is highly valued today.

Selected Prices

Due to the infrequency with which examples of Robineau porcelain appear on the market, establishing an in-depth price guide has not yet been possible. Until additional information is compiled, readers are advised to seek counsel from experienced collectors before either buying or selling important pieces.

4. Adelaide Alsop Robineau, *Keramic Studio* (May 1913), p. 1; also quoted in Peg Weiss, ed., *Adelaide Alsop Robineau: Glory in Porcelain* (Syracuse, NY: Syracuse University Press, 1981), p. 29.

5. Martin Eidelberg, ed., *From Our Native Clay* (New York: Turn of the Century Editions, 1987), p. 52.

ROBLIN ART POTTERY COMPANY

ROBLIN

Shopmark:
Impressed figure of a bear and/or *ROBLIN*
Occasionally with the initials *A.W.R.* and date
Occasionally with Linna Irelan's name or initials and her personal mark: a spider and its web

Principal Contribution:
Art pottery vases

Founders:
Alexander W. Robertson
Born: 1840   Died: 1925

Linna Irelan
Born: unknown   Died: unknown
Founded: 1898   Closed: 1906

Studios and Salesrooms:
Roblin Art Pottery Company
San Francisco
1898–1906

"California is the only state in the Union that has all the clays necessary for the production of the finest grades of pottery."

—*Alexander Robertson*
1905[1]

1. Paul Evans, *Art Pottery of the United States* (New York: Charles Scribner's Sons, 1974), p. 250.

The Roblin Art Pottery traces it beginnings back to Chelsea, Massachusetts, where James Robertson and his three sons, George, Alexander, and Hugh, were all active in the pottery business. In 1865 Alexander started his own pottery in Chelsea, producing a plain brown-glazed earthenware; brother Hugh joined him a few years later, forming the A. W. & H. C. Robertson Pottery Company in 1868. While the brothers may have experimented with early art pottery, the firm survived by manufacturing both simple and fancy flowerpots. In 1872 their father and their younger brother George joined them, and under the inspiration and guidance of James Robertson, the new firm—Chelsea Keramic Art Works—soon began producing important art pottery and accompanying glazes.

The Robertsons continued to manufacture a commercial line of pottery, even selling undecorated, yet occasionally marked pottery blanks to other artists and experimenting with decorated tiles. George Robertson left the firm in 1878 to work with John G. Low at his fledgling tile works, and in 1880 James Robertson passed away. Alexander and Hugh continued to work together for the next four years, but in 1884 Alexander decided to move to California.

While it seems that Alexander Robertson went to California intent on opening a new pottery, it was not until he met Linna Irelan in 1891 that first serious steps were taken toward that end. The pair shared an unbridled enthusiasm for California clays and twice made unsuccessful attempts to establish a pottery that would rely on and promote native California minerals and materials. Finally, in 1898 the Roblin Art Pottery Company—the name representing the first three letters of Robertson's and Linna Irelan's names—was established in a small house in San Francisco.

The firm's output revealed the impact the Robertson family's Chelsea pottery had on Alexander. "Red, buff and white clays were used for the body, and all pieces were thrown by Robertson in shapes reminiscent of those he had produced at Chelsea. Often the vases were left in bisque or with only the interior glazed. Others were glazed, again using only native California materials."[2] Unafraid to experiment, the pair produced forms involving a wide variety of decorative techniques. Linna Irelan was primarily responsible for the decorating, including incising and carving the clay—"sometimes to an extreme. . . . Robertson's own tastes were far more severe and classical, and frequently the only embellishment he would employ was finely executed handles, beading or application of a high-gloss glaze of a quality equal to the finest produced anywhere."[3]

While plans to dramatically expand the small, quality operation seemed continually in the works, none had materialized by the time the San Francisco earthquake leveled much of the city. The Roblin Art Pottery was not spared, and at age sixty-six Alexander Robertson chose not to rebuild. He moved to Los Angeles with his son, Fred H. Robertson (1880–1952), who had joined the firm a few years earlier. He continued to research and experiment with California clays and glazes until retiring in 1915.[4]

Selected Prices

Due to the infrequency with which examples of this pottery appear on the market, establishing an in-depth price guide has not yet been possible. The examples listed below are indicative only of the value of pieces of similar form and decoration. Until additional information is compiled, readers are advised to seek counsel from experienced collectors before either buying or selling important pieces.

Vase: bulbous body, with short neck collar, bisque body, 3″, $250–$300.

Vase: undecorated, with brown glaze, 6″, $225–$250.

2. Paul Evans, *Art Pottery of the United States* (New York: Charles Scribner's Sons, 1974), pp. 250–251.

3. Ibid., p. 251.

4. Elisabeth Cameron, *Encyclopedia of Pottery & Porcelain: 1800–1960* (New York: Facts on File Publications, 1986), p. 280.

ROOKWOOD POTTERY

Shopmarks:
(ca. 1880) Painted *ROOKWOOD* and initials *M.L.N.*
(1881–1882) Variety of forms incorporating words *ROOKWOOD POTTERY*, often with year 1881 or initials *M.L.N.*
(1882–1885) Word *ROOKWOOD* and the year
(1886) Monogram *RP*
(1887–1900) Monogram *RP* with one flame added each year
(1901–1967) Monogram *RP* with fourteen flames over Roman numeral for the year

Principal Contributions:
Underglaze-decorated vases, bowls, lamps, and tiles in high-gloss and matte glazes

Founder:
Maria Longworth Nichols (Storer)
Born: 1849   Died: 1932
Founded: 1880   Closed: 1967

Studios and Salesrooms:
Rookwood Pottery
Cincinnati, Ohio
1880–1967

"A vase made at Rookwood under the conditions existing there is as much an object of art as a painted canvas or sculpture in marble or bronze. And the artist's signature upon the vase is as genuine a guarantee of originality."

—*Rookwood catalog*
1904[1]

Just as the Grueby Pottery was not the first to develop the matte glaze but has often been credited with its invention, the Rookwood Pottery was not the first to develop underglaze slip decorations; yet no other pottery in the Art Nouveau or Arts and Crafts era was able to develop it as artistically and promote it as successfully as this Cincinnati company.

While most art potteries of this era were founded with more artistic ability than firm financial footing, the Rookwood Pottery was built on money. At the time she was born, Maria Longworth's grandfather owned much of downtown Cincinnati; her father extended the family's real estate holdings into the spreading suburbs. Described as "vivacious, attractive, ambitious for personal success, and . . . a careless money manager,"[2] by 1875 the twenty-six-year-old Maria Longworth Nichols had discovered china painting and was preparing to begin experimenting with her own pottery. Five years later her father gave her both a building and the capital to buy equipment and hire a staff. Even the Rookwood name came from her father, as it was also the name of his country estate.

As the number of vases, pitchers, bowls, and household wares increased after 1880, so did the staff and the building. Among the first decorators were Albert R. Valentien and Laura Fry, who added several new shapes to the growing line. Were it not for the continued patience and generosity of Mrs. Nichols's father, however, the pottery could not have continued beyond the first or second years, let alone expanded. In 1883, perhaps at her father's suggestion, William W. Taylor was hired as business manager. Although (or perhaps because) he had no pottery experience, he quickly instituted a number of cost-cutting

1. *Rookwood 1904 Catalog.*

2. Herbert Peck, *The Book of Rookwood Pottery* (New York: Crown Publishers, 1968), p. 2.

measures, including discontinuing slow-selling shapes and revoking the kiln privileges of Louise McLaughlin and the Pottery Club; and by the end of the next year the improvement was evident. That same year Laura Fry discovered a new use for the mouth-blown atomizer that led in 1885 to the development of the first airbrush technique for applying underglaze decorations. As Martin Eidelberg aptly illustrated in *From Our Native Clay*, "The earlier vases show a heavily charged brush and rich impasto, while the later Rookwood Standard ware is finely rendered in thinned slips with subtle airbrushed transitions of background color. Although Japanese motifs and styles continued to play a part in Rookwood's output . . . , we can note how sophisticated it became and, by contrast, how charmingly naive it was at first."[3] By 1888 the pottery was showing a substantial profit, but Mrs. Nichols had remarried soon after the death of her first husband in 1885 and ever since had begun to lose interest in the venture. Finally, in 1890 her financial interest in the Rookwood Pottery was transferred to William Taylor.

Under Taylor's leadership a new pottery was built in 1891 atop Mt. Adams overlooking downtown Cincinnati. Senior decorators, such as Artus Van Briggle, Matt Daly, Kataro Shirayamadani, Albert and Anna Valentien, and William McDonald, were given private studios. Visitors were encouraged but controlled, affording the pottery valuable exposure and free publicity without disrupting the artists' work. "Most visitors were impressed," Herbert Peck related, "when it was explained that a single piece of Rookwood might pass through the hands of as many as twenty-one people before it reached perfection as a finished piece."[4] Floral decorations in rich, dark colors dominated as the most popular and the most prevalent motif in Rookwood Standard ware, which was awarded several medals at national and international expositions in 1892 and 1893.

While Taylor brought efficiency to Rookwood, he also encouraged experimentation. In 1892 the Gorham Manufacturing

3. Martin Eidelberg, ed., *From Our Native Clay* (New York: Turn of the Century Editions, 1987), p. 23.

4. Herbert Peck, *The Book of Rookwood Pottery* (New York: Crown Publishers, 1968), p. 45.

Company began applying silver overlay to selected Rookwood wares. By 1894 three additional high-glaze styles to complement Rookwood Standard had been introduced: Iris, Sea Green, and Aerial Blue. Two years later the first experiments with a matte glaze were being carried out by decorator Artus Van Briggle, whom Rookwood had sent to Paris to study for more than two years. Production for most of Taylor's tenure grew to an average of ten thousand to fifteen thousand pieces of art pottery per year in over two thousand different shapes.[5] The vast majority were hand-thrown and hand-decorated by potters and artists who were described as a "close, happy, spirited group who thoroughly enjoyed their work and their play."[6]

In 1904 the Rookwood Pottery published a detailed catalog in an unsuccessful attempt to motivate mail order sales. In it eight different styles were described and illustrated, including the following:

Standard—"noted for its low tones, usually yellow, red and brown in color, with flower decoration, characterized by a luxuriant painting in warm colors under a brilliant glaze."

Sea Green—"characterized by a limpid, opalescent sea green effect. A favorite decoration is a fish moving under water."

Iris—"a light type with deliciously tender and suggestive color effects under a brilliant white glaze."

Vellum—"devoid of lustre, without dryness, it partakes both to the touch and to the eye of the qualities of old parchment."[7]

William Taylor also introduced Rookwood tiles in 1901 in anticipation of an eventual decline in art pottery sales and a growing

5. Herbert Peck, *The Book of Rookwood Pottery* (New York: Crown Publishers, 1968), pp. 70–97.

6. Ibid., p. 65.

7. *Rookwood 1904 Catalog;* also Herbert Peck, *The Book of Rookwood Pottery* (New York: Crown Publishers, 1968), pp. 74–91.

This assortment of Rookwood vases and bowls was produced between 1913 and 1920, when hand-decorated wares were beginning to give way to these less-expensive, molded production
artwares. The circular tile in the foreground is by California Faience. *(Photo courtesy of D. J. Puffert, Sausalito)*

need for architectural faience. The tile department developed
slowly and proved to be a drain on Rookwood resources for
several years, despite important commissions from major hotels
and the New York City subway expansion program. The pottery was shaken when Taylor died unexpectedly in 1913, but
due to his foresight and the program he had established, it continued to prosper. By 1920 the pottery boasted fifteen kilns and
more than two hundred employees; while the demand for expensive hand-decorated art pottery dwindled, their line of
molded artwares proved popular.

The Depression, however, brought an end to prosperity at
Rookwood. In 1932, staggered by an adverse Internal Revenue
Service judgment, extensive boiler repairs and plummeting
sales, the directors laid off nearly all of the decorators; despite
additional drastic measures, in 1941 the Rookwood Pottery
Company declared bankruptcy and was sold several times over
the course of the next thirty years before production was finally
halted.

Rookwood Decorators and Their Marks

Over the course of its lengthy history the Rookwood Pottery
employed more than 110 decorators.[8] While each piece of Rookwood pottery must be judged on its individual merits (see David

8. Herbert Peck, *The Book of Rookwood Pottery* (New York: Crown
Publishers, 1968), pp. 138–148.

Rago's introductory remarks), certain decorators have emerged as among the most important decorators of the Arts and Crafts era (see Table 1).

Table 1

Artist	Years at Rookwood	Mark
Matthew Daly (1860–1937)	1882–1903	M.A.D. M A Daly
Laura Fry (1857–1943)	1881–1887	L.A. (conjoined)
William Hentschel (1892–1962)	1907–1939	W.E.H.
Edward Hurley (1869–1950)	1896–1948	E.T.H.
Elizabeth Lincoln (1880–1957)	1892–1931	L.N.L.
William McDonald (1865–1931)	1882–1931	W.McD.
Charles (Carl) Schmidt (1875–1927)	1896–1927	C.S. (conjoined in circle)
Kataro Shirayamadani (1865–1948)	1887–1915 1925–1948	K.S. (or name in Japanese)
Sara Alice Toohey (unknown)	1887–1931	S.T. (conjoined)
Albert R. Valentien (1862–1925)	1881–1905	A.R.V.
Artus Van Briggle (1869–1904)	1887–1899	A.vB. [sic]
John Wareham (1871–1954)	1893–1954	J.D.W.
Grace Young (1869–1947)	1886–1904	G.Y. (conjoined)

Selected Prices

Bowl: wide mouth with ruffled rim on straight-sided shallow form, decorated with apple blossoms on shaded pink to brown ground, 2″ × 8″, *$175–$200.*

Ewer: bisque-painted, with white blossoms and green leaves in slip-relief against olive green ground, gilded neck, 9″ × 5″, *$300–$350.*

Ewer: with overlay, pinched silver rim and loop handle on elongated neck and bulbous body decorated with yellow primroses, standard glaze ground, initialed *S.E.C.* for Sallie Elizabeth Coyne, 6″, *$1750–$2000.*

Ewer: bisque, pale blue to light pink, delicate Oriental-style decoration of white and blue and gold flowers with gold stems and leaves, white moon behind decoration, gold around neck, top, and handle, 7″, *$400–$500.*

Humidor: standard glaze, covered cylindrical form decorated with pipes and cigars on shaded ground, 7″, *$200–$225.*

Jar: bulbous, covered, with squeeze-bag design of stylized leaves in an olive brown and dark blue matte glaze, 18″ × 12″, *$1250–$1500.*

Lamp: "Gone with the Wind," milk glass shade and chimney fitting onto spherical form decorated with thistles and bees on blue matte ground, mounted on bronze base, 22″, *$600–$700.*

Lamp base: short neck on swollen cylindrical form tapering toward base, central landscape in greens and purples on slate gray ground shaded with pink, 11″, *$650–$750.*

Loving cup: cylindrical form decorated with moonlit landscape centered by three loop handles, 7″ × 6″, *$800–$900.*

Loving cup with fairies: standard glaze, wide mouth, and

three sides with cherubic figures playing and picking grapes in a vineyard, 8″, *$500–$650.*

Mug: with overlay, silver rim, pierced scroll design, and loop handle on cylindrical form decorated with yellow daffodils on green ground, 6″, *$900–$1000.*

Paperweight: "Potter at the Wheel," light green matte glaze, 3″, *$100–$125.*

Pitcher: short neck and angled handle on swollen cylindrical form tapering toward base, incised blue dogwood blossoms on white ground, 7″, *$225–$250.*

Pitcher: trefoil rim and loop handle on elongated neck and squat base with angled shoulder, decorated with spider and marsh grasses in black, white moon and accents in dark brown glaze, gilt highlights, impressed in block letters, *ROOKWOOD 1882,* 6″, *$600–$700.*

Pitcher: miniature, Iris-glazed, with handle, painted cream and yellow phlox and green leaves on pink to cream ground, 3″ × 2″, *$325–$375.*

Plaque: Vellum, muted landscape scene of a river and plush trees in the foreground, a barn along the bank in the background against a violet and pink sky, 4″ × 8″, *$675–$775.*

Plaque: Venetian sailboats on the Aegean with tall, striped posts in the foreground and silhouette of St. Mark's Square in the background, 12″ × 9″, *$2000–$2250.*

Plaque: white birch trees and green foliage on rolling green ground against violet-purple sky, 7″ × 6″, *$700–$800.*

Plaque: Vellum glaze, track-covered road vanishing into a royal blue horizon, with full foliated trees on either side, 8″ × 6″, *$675–$775.*

Plaque: Vellum glaze, rectangular, with black and green

trees, blue lake and horizon, blue and white clouded sky, 9″ × 14″, *$1250–$1500*.

Plaque: Vellum, tall thin birch trees against a pale pink snow-covered ground, 6″ × 8″, *$900–$1000*.

Teapot: Standard glaze, button finial on cover fitting into tapering form with loop handle and curved spout, decorated with yellow daffodils, 7″, *$300–$350*.

Tile: dark aqua blue matte background with incised yellow-brown ship, 8″ × 8″, *$225–$250*.

Tile: landscape, with tall brown trees and dark green leaves, 12″ × 12″, *$450–$550*.

Tray, pin: round, shallow edge with slight flute, decorated with yellow mouse on Standard glaze brown, 7″, *$175–$200*.

Trivet: round, smooth back, scene of entrance to Rookwood on front, light green matte glaze, 6″, *$175–$200*.

Vase: Standard glaze, wide flaring rim on bulbous base, painted with orange flowers on brown glaze, 5″, *$100–$125*.

Vase: swollen cylindrical form tapering toward base, decorated with pale blue iris on shaded ground, 7″, *$175–$200*.

Vase: Standard glaze, flared rim on elongated neck and bulbous body, decorated with violets on yellow ground, 6″, *$150–$175*.

Vase: bisque, wide short neck with gilt punch decoration on swollen cylindrical form tapering toward base, decorated with whimsical enameled frogs being chased by several ducks in greens, blues, and brown highlights, repeating gilt punch-decorated lower band, 20″, *$2250–$2750*.

Vase: short neck on bulbous form tapering toward base,

decorated with blowing milkweed in green and white on shaded gray ground, 8″, $900–$1000.

Vase: sgraffito-decorated, wide mouth and elongated neck with repeating designs of orange scrolls and yellow circles on angled shoulder and bulbous tapering base, glossy brown glaze, 10″, $600–$700.

Vase: wax matte, cylindrical form tapering toward base, decorated with panels of floral bouquets in lavender on mottled aqua ground, 5″, $175–$200.

Vase: Standard-glaze, concave rim on flattened spherical form, tapering toward base decorated with honeysuckle and bellflowers on leafy stems, shaded gold ground, 14″ × 12″, $800–$900.

Vase: jeweled porcelain, flared rim, elongated cylindrical neck on baluster form tapering toward base, solid blue glaze to shoulder over Persian floral pattern of blue and green on turquoise, 18″, $400–$450.

Vase: Standard glaze, flat broad lip on swollen bulbous form tapering toward base, decorated with golden nasturtiums on burnt orange and brown glaze, 7″, $300–$375.

Vase: sterling silver overlay, wide mouth on cylindrical form tapering toward base, silver rim with elongated pierced strapwork in Art Nouveau style, framing yellow tulips and green leaves on standard-glaze ground, 7″, $1250–$1500.

Vase: cylindrical body with crisp mountainous scene fully extending around vase, unusual shading from blue to white, lavender and purple, to green foreground, 8″, $700–$800.

Vase: short neck and angled shoulder on tapering form molded with poppies, done in matte green glaze, 12″, $250–$300.

Vase: floor, with branches of white flowers in slip-relief

against a mottled sky in gold, blue, and green, two large swallows in the foreground, 24″ × 14″, *$2250–$2500.*

Vase: production, in matte blue-green, with wide band of incised stylized flowers, 12″ × 9″, *$100–$125.*

Vase: impasto, bulbous form, with long cylindrical neck and bough of white wild roses against dark gray ground, 11″ × 6″, *$350–$450.*

Vase: light blue, bulbous jewel porcelain, with collar neck and faintly incised melon ribbing in dark blue, 13″ × 12″, *$250–$300.*

Vase: floor, bulbous form ending in flared, collar neck, fleshy poppy blossoms and stems in slip-relief, 22″ × 8″, *$2750–$3250.*

Vase: Vellum, with carved and painted stylized peacock feathers in light green, burgundy, and dark blue on a rose-pink ground, 10″ × 5″, *$1200–$1400.*

Vase: bulbous, with closed neck and flared rim, embossed decoration of deer and trees, under burgundy high glaze, 8″ × 6″, *$200–$250.*

Vase: tapering with gently flaring neck, three large rectangular scenic panels, one a swamp scene with geese, the second a village scene with cottages, and the third a tropical harbor scene with boats, 15″ × 6″, *$1250–$1500.*

Vase: glazed with single large rook perched in a fir tree against a large full moon on a light blue, uncrazed ground, 8″ × 4″, *$1750–$2000.*

Vase: Vellum, with pink and white apple blossoms and green leaves stretching across medium blue to light green ground, 11″ × 6″, *$700–$800.*

Vase: Iris glaze, with pink poppies and green with whiplash stems painted against olive to cream ground, 8″ × 4″, *$750–$850.*

Vase: Standard glaze of bulging cylinder form with collar

The seven-inch Vellum seascape vase on the left was painted by Sallie Coyne; the large Vellum landscape vase was the work of Edward T. Hurley, another Rookwood artist; the rare seven-inch Iris-glazed vase on the right features a peacock feather painted by Carl Schmidt. *(Photo courtesy of Don Treadway, Cincinnati)*

neck and flared rim, golden sunflowers with light green and gold leaves, 24″ × 10″, *$1750–$2250.*

Vase: Iris glazed, band decorated with branch of pink wild flowering roses and buds, against gray background, 8″ × 4″, *$450–$500.*

Vase: wax matte, deep blue and pink touched with yellow, red flowers, and green leaves, 7″, *$300–$350.*

Vase: floral Vellum, deep grayish blue to orange to brown, pink roses, pale green leaves, 7″, *$200–$225.*

Vase: wax matte, orange and brown, pale green, orange and blue flowers, green and rust colored leaves, 5″, *$200–$225.*

Vase: wax matte with blue rim, yellow flowers and green leaves outlined in brown against a greenish yellow ground, 7″ × 4″, *$175–$200.*

Vase: wax matte, with crimson berries with greenish yellow leaves on a branch that entwines around the vase against a crimson ground, 6″ × 4″, *$175–$200.*

Vase: wax matte, pink touched with yellow and green, flower and leaf decoration in orange, yellow, and shades of green, 6″, *$225–$250.*

ROSEVILLE POTTERY COMPANY

Shopmark:
Numerous variations, including:
(Pre-1904) Impressed ROZANE/RPCo or RPCo.
(Pre-1904) Impressed AZUREAN/RPCo
(After 1904) Paper label or impressed mark, ROZANE WARE, enclosed in circle, over name of individual design

(After 1905) Ink stamp ROZANE OLYMPIC POTTERY or ROSEVILLE POTTERY CO./ZANESVILLE,O. or FUJIYAMA

(After ca. 1910) Ink stamp of large letter *R* encompassing small letter *V*

Principal Contributions:
Decorated art pottery and commercial artware

Principal owner:
George F. Young
Born: 1863   Died: 1920
Founded: 1890   Closed: 1954

Studios and Salesrooms:
Roseville Pottery Company
Roseville, Ohio
1890–1910

Zanesville, Ohio
1898–1954

"We first went to the Roseville potteries, which occupy a large group of buildings, wherein is manufactured a great variety of wares, including washstand sets, jardinieres, and art ware. Over three hundred persons are employed at this plant, and about five thousand pieces of finished ware are turned out every day."

—*A reporter*
1905[1]

First organized in 1890 to produce utilitarian stoneware, the Roseville Pottery began a rapid expansion under the leadership of George F. Young in 1892. As sales increased, Young added more employees and, in 1898, two additional plants, one in Roseville, Ohio, and the other in Zanesville, Ohio. By 1901 a second factory in Zanesville had been purchased, paving the way for consolidation in 1910 of the firm's entire production in Zanesville, where abundant supplies of both quality clay and inexpensive natural gas needed to fire the kilns had attracted a number of potteries.

Competition among the firms was fierce and their tactics ruthless. Laura Fry at Lonhuda Pottery unsuccessfully sued Rookwood in 1893 for infringement on her patented decorating technique. Samuel Weller took a different approach. He lured Lonhuda founder William Long to Zanesville to learn the technique, then broke with him. Weller renamed Long's pottery Louwelsa, which soon proved popular. In 1900, after the courts refused to uphold Laura Fry's patent claim, George Young hired designer Ross C. Purdy to duplicate Fry's technique in a line that would compete against Weller's Louwelsa. The new line

1. Ralph and Terry Kovel, *The Kovels' Collectors Guide to American Art Pottery* (New York: Crown Publishers, 1974), p. 239.

was introduced shortly thereafter—Rozane, taking its name from the first two letters of the company name and the first four from the site at which it was produced.

Roseville's new Rozane line entered an already crowded field of underglazed, slip-decorated art pottery: Weller's Louwelsa, Long's Lonhuda, Owens's Utopian, and Rookwood's Standard were already established, but the combination of Young's organizational skills and a group of talented designers enabled Roseville's entry to battle successfully for public recognition and sales. "Originally marketed as Rozane, it later became available with light or dark ground and was produced until 1919 under the title Rozane Royal."[2] A steady stream of variations on the original Rozane Royal rolled out of the Roseville kilns for the next eight years, including the following:

Azurine (ca. 1902)—blue and white underglaze decoration, often of ships, portraits, or flowers, on blue and white background, with high glaze

Rozane Crystalis (1907)—crystallized flowing glaze

Rozane Egypto (ca. 1905, designer John Herold)—relief-decorated vases in Egyptian forms, covered with matte green glaze

Rozane Fudji (ca. 1905, designer Gazo Fudji)—incised stylized decorations of insects or geometric designs, similar in style to Rozane Woodland but without the background dots

Rozane Mara (ca. 1904, designer John Herold)—a metallic luster similar to Weller's Sicardo

Rozane Mongol (ca. 1900–1904, designer John Herold)—a high-gloss oxblood glaze, also called Chinese Red

Rozane Woodland (ca. 1905, designer Gazo Fudji)—a matte finish over incised floral designs, small dots in the background.

2. Paul Evans, *Art Pottery of the United States* (New York: Charles Scribner's Sons, 1974), p. 265.

Considered one of the finest examples of Roseville art pottery, this nineteen-and-one-half-inch Rozane Fujiyama floor vase displays an Art Nouveau motif of a woman surrounded by flowing green and red enamel-like decorations on a bisque ground. *(Photo courtesy of David Rago, Trenton)*

Among the most noteworthy of the art pottery designs produced during this time was Della Ròbbia, which was designed by Frederick H. Rhead, art director at the pottery from 1904 to 1908. By means of a special technique he devised, background clay was cut away using "specially ground darning needles set in handles with the incised clay coming out the eye of the needle, then chiseling out the background to the second layer of color, and then painting in colored slips where additional color was desired."[3]

Rhead's departure in 1908 signaled the end of the era of hand-decorated art pottery at Roseville. Decorations were designed to be applied by ordinary workers rather than artists; it was reported that "an artist-decorator who previously might have spent a day on a piece was then expected to finish more than 300 items a day."[4] By 1918 Roseville Pottery boasted of being

3. Elisabeth Cameron, *Encyclopedia of Pottery & Porcelain: 1800–1960* (New York: Facts on File Publications, 1986), p. 287.

4. Paul Evans, *Art Pottery of the United States* (New York: Charles Scribner's Sons, 1974), p. 266.

This seven-inch Della Robbia–line Roseville vase was decorated by using darning needles to incise and remove the clay around the design. Background colors were often applied to provide the necessary contrast. *(Photo courtesy of David Rago, Trenton)*

one of the first art pottery factories to install a continuous tunnel kiln. At this time, Paul Evans concludes, "Roseville must definitely be considered a producer of industrial artware rather than of art pottery—a distinction which should be carefully drawn."[5]

Selected Prices

Jardiniere: Rozane Royal, Sylvan, and pedestal, with panel of animals around the top, embossed in bone white, with traces of green and bright autumn leaves, 33″ × 15″, $225–$250.

Jardiniere: bulbous form with indented rim and four loop handles on stand flaring toward base, squeeze-bag-decorated with flying geese, circular trees, and landscape, 44″ × 20″, $600–$700.

Pitcher: handled, wide, flaring rim and short spout,

5. Paul Evans, *Art Pottery of the United States* (New York: Charles Scribner's Sons, 1974), p. 267.

three-footed base, covered with gold-to-cream flambé, 7″
× 6″, *$700–$800.*

Umbrella stand: modeled and slip-decorated with cobalt
blue, pale olive, and gold peacock perched in brown and
green tree, blue vine around base and rim, 20″ × 10″,
$800–$900.

Vase: Mostique, wide mouth on tapering cylindrical form
with two handles, incised design with orange square and
white triangles on blue bands forming panels, mottled gray
ground, 9″, *$75–$85.*

Vase: narrow neck flaring to ball-shaped center on pedestal floor, glossy glaze over pale green sgraffito and
carved decoration with entwined vines and grape clusters
on a chip-carved textured ground, geometric border sur-
rounds pedestal base, 10″, *$700–$800.*

Vase: Fudji, bulbous bottom with bulging cylindrical neck,
decorated in a squeeze-bag high glaze, Alhambraesque design in gold, turquoise, and blue, 8″ × 5″, *$800–$900.*

Vase: Della Robbia, cut-back incised and painted grapes,
olive green, dark green and brown grape leaves, cream
and light blue ground, 12″ × 4″, *$2000–$2250.*

Vase: elongated, corset-shape form, highly glazed, incised
gold and rust flowers, green stems, bisque ground, 11″ ×
4″, *$450–$550.*

Vase: Rozane Royal, thin, with elongated neck and flared
rim, slip-painted with large blue flower surrounded by olive green leaves against brown high glaze, 18″ × 6″, *$225–*
$275.

Vase: Chloron, matte green glaze, in tapered form, 12″,
$250–$300.

Vase: red, Silhouette, Art Deco-style decoration of nude
in panel, 7″ × 9″, *$125–$150.*

Vase: Futura, gunmetal with green flambé drip, 11″, *$325–$375.*

Vase: Silhouette fan, green glaze, nude in panel, 7″ × 7″, *$125–$150.*

Vase: Imperial II, green with green and white drip, yellow design around neck, 7″, *$125–$150.*

SHAWSHEEN POTTERY

Shopmark:
Imprinted or incised outlines of the overlapping letters *SP*

Principal Contributions:
Vases, bowls, and jardinieres

Founders:
Edward Dahlquist
Born: 1877   Died: 1972
Elizabeth Burnap Dahlquist
Born: 1875   Died: 1963
Founded: 1906   Closed: 1911

Studios and Salesrooms:
Shawsheen Pottery
Billerica, Massachusetts
1906–1907

Mason City, Iowa
1907–1911

After a promising beginning in Billerica, Massachusetts, Edward and Elizabeth Dahlquist moved their family pottery to Mason City, Iowa, in 1907, where they continued to teach ceramics while producing a limited line of relief-decorated pottery. Their early work was hand-coiled and "described as a warm black, with tones of bronze and copper on it, rich in effect and recalling the Etruscan potteries and bronzes seen in museums."[1] In Iowa they also produced hand-thrown pottery and, in conjunction with their teaching, fired works of student potters as well.

The pottery closed around 1911, when the couple moved to Chicago. In addition to their teaching, the Dahlquists also opened an art gallery, where it is reported that most of their earlier—and most desirable—work was sold.[2]

Selected Prices

Due to the infrequency with which examples of this pottery appear on the market, establishing an in-depth price guide has not yet been possible. The example listed below is indicative only of the value of pieces of similar form and decoration. Until additional information is compiled, readers are advised to seek counsel from experienced collectors before either buying or selling important pieces.

Vase: incised, cylindrical neck on bulbous base, matte green glaze, 6", $250–$300.

1. Paul Evans, *Art Pottery of the United States* (New York: Charles Scribner's Sons, 1974), p. 269.
2. Ibid., p. 271.

STOCKTON ART POTTERY

MARIPOSA POTTERY
STOCKTON
CALIFORNIA

Shopmarks:
Impressed circle containing STOCKTON/CALIFORNIA/
S.A.P.Co. above word *REKSTON*
Painted under glaze, MARIPOSA POTTERY/STOCKTON/
CALIFORNIA

Principal Contributions:
Molded underglaze-decorated vases, bowls, and pitchers

Founder:
Stockholders, including Arthur C. Hopkinson, manager;
Thomas W. Blakey and John W. Blakey, superintendents
Founded: 1894   Closed: 1900

Studios and Salesrooms:
Stockton Terra Cotta
Stockton, California
1894–1895

Stockton Art Pottery
Stockton, California
1896–1900

Although marked examples of Stockton art pottery are rare, those that have surfaced have confirmed the development of blended underglaze slip painting in California as early as 1895. The company was hampered by a series of economic recessions in California that ended production of decorated art pottery at the Stockton firm soon after it began. Although most forms were molded, several examples of the Rekston line with its underglaze decorations of plants and flowers are considered as fine as much of that produced at Weller, Owens, and Roseville.

Selected Prices

Due to the infrequency in which examples of this pottery appear on the market, establishing an in-depth price guide has not yet been possible. Until additional information is compiled, readers are advised to seek counsel from experienced collectors before either buying or selling important pieces.

TECO POTTERY
(The Gates Potteries)

Shopmark:
Impressed TECO, with the letters arranged vertically

Principal Contribution:
Art pottery with strong architectural or organic qualities in solid-color glazes

Founder:
William D. Gates
Born: 1852   Died: 1935
Founded: ca. 1886   Closed: 1930

Studios and Salesrooms:
American Terra Cotta and Ceramic Company
Terra Cotta, Illinois
1886–1930

"It is my earnest desire to put in each and every home a vase of
my own make to become part of the home, and that I can so feel
that I have in this way done something lasting, and have contributed to the homes and happiness of my generation."

—*William D. Gates*[1]

While many of the important figures in the art pottery movement descended from pottery families, William Day Gates was
originally a practicing attorney in Chicago. And while many artistic potters of this era failed to manifest the business sense
necessary to develop and maintain a profitable enterprise, Gates
brought to his pottery the rare combination of necessary artistic
and practical temperaments required to build a successful pottery business.

Gates opened the American Terra Cotta and Ceramic Company in 1886 in Terra Cotta, Illinois, forty-five miles northwest
of Chicago, with initial production focused on manufacturing
decorative bricks, drainpipes, and architectural terra-cotta. The
plant was organized in an old grist mill built on the banks of a
picturesque lake in hopes that the serene environment would
serve as an inspiration to his potters. Gates's contribution to
the art pottery market evolved slowly. As his experiments in-
tensified, he built additional kilns and hired more chemists and
designers, including two of his sons, but not, however, at the
sacrifice of his profitable architectural terra-cotta work. Although the name of his new art pottery line had been registered
and experimental pieces made as early as 1895, it was not until
1901—twenty years after he arrived in Terra Cotta—that Gates
introduced his first line of art pottery to the public. He called it
Teco pottery, taking its name from the initials of the community
in which it was produced.

From the beginning the majority of Teco pottery was made
from molds, which Gates recognized as critical to the commercial production and profitability of the line. Not only did Gates
refuse to apologize for producing molded forms, he advocated
the technique, in a manner similar to that in which Frank Lloyd

---

1. *Gates Pottery catalog* (n.d., n.p.).

Wright and Gustav Stickley embraced the role of the machine
in furniture production—as a means of providing the public with
artistic wares at affordable prices. Gates designed some of the
most elaborate of the early vases himself; to set his pottery
apart from the others, he also commissioned designs from several prominent artists and architects, including Hugh Garden,
Fritz Albert, W. K. Fellows, and Max Dunning, many of whom
may have been at Gates's pottery arranging for terra-cotta ornaments for their building projects. As Robert Ellison has noted,
"Gates and some of his architect friends contributed designs
with geometric, three-dimensional architectural elements, while
the European-trained sculptors Fernand Moreau and Fritz Albert executed designs that were voluptuously organic or dy-
namically swirling.[2]

Some of the earliest Teco forms featured subtle red, tan, and
yellow glazes, but when Grueby Pottery and its famous matte
green glaze began to attract widespread attention around 1904,
Gates introduced a similar green glaze that would dominate Teco
production until 1912. (Ironically, the chemists at Gates's pottery were the first in America to develop a crystalline glaze,[3]
but Gates apparently chose not to pursue it after the Louisiana
Purchase Exhibition in St. Louis in 1904.) Sensing that the public would not distinguish (or could not afford to distinguish) between the expensive, hand-thrown Grueby and the inexpensive,
molded Teco—both artistically pleasing and in similar green
matte glazes—Gates gambled with his "Teco green" and won.
In 1911, the year in which the financially troubled Grueby Pottery ceased production of its acclaimed art pottery, the Gates
operation was at the zenith of its production, advertising more
than five hundred different varieties of Teco.

Like William Grueby, however, William Gates generally refrained from utilizing underglaze decorations on his pottery. He
preferred to let the form provide the decoration and the glaze

2. Martin Eidelberg, *From Our Native Clay* (New York: Turn of the
Century Editions, 1987), p. 54.
3. Ibid., p. 98.

Each of these three Teco pieces was designed around 1905. The thirteen-inch vase in the center and the eight-and-one-half-inch example on the right reveal the architectural qualities that made this pottery popular with Frank Lloyd Wright, as well as with many of today's Arts and Crafts collectors. The unusual six-inch bulbous form on the left features twelve pierced openings, plus a vertical floral motif around the body. *(Photo courtesy of David Rago, Trenton)*

determine the color. As the demand for both "Grueby green" and "Teco green" declined around 1910, Gates introduced additional glaze colors: rose, yellow, blue, purple, and several shades of brown. Grueby and Teco were both familiar subjects to readers of Gustav Stickley's magazine, *The Craftsman.* In observing the ads that Gates began placing in the magazine in 1904, Paul Evans remarks that "it is interesting to study the objects illustrated and see what started out with creative artistry steadily decline, like so many of its rivals, into mass-produced containers of uninspired design."[4]

4. Paul Evans, *Art Pottery of the United States* (New York: Charles Scribner's Sons, 1974), p. 280.

Pierced openings are characteristic of some of the most popular Teco pottery today. This eleven-and-one-half-inch vase features twelve fully reticulated leaves beneath a matte green glaze. *(Photo courtesy of David Rago, Trenton)*

Interest in even the later, less-interesting forms kept the Teco line in production until 1922. From then until 1930, when William Gates sold the Gates Potteries, production dwindled as the demand for art pottery, architectural terra-cotta, and garden ornaments declined. The new owner changed the name of the pottery but may have continued to use the Teco trademark for some years thereafter.[5]

Most of today's Teco collectors prefer the early, strong, architectural pieces with rectilinear and geometric forms to the later, plainer, and smaller examples adapted for ease in production. Vases with handled buttresses, reticulated leaves, and pierced openings are highly sought-after, as are early forms that took their inspiration from natural plant forms. As one Teco catalog states, "Most happiness comes from the perception of the beautiful . . . and arises from either form or color. Both are exemplified in the highest degree in Teco pottery."[6]

5. Ralph and Terry Kovel, *The Kovels' Collectors Guide to American Art Pottery* (New York: Crown Publishers, 1974), p. 262.
6. *Gates Pottery catalog* (n.d., n.p.).

Selected Prices

Bowl: circular, with embossed geometric design and matte green glaze, 2″ × 10″, *$150–$175.*

Bowl: green matte glaze, 1″ × 4″, *$95–$120.*

Bowl: light green matte glaze, 2″ × 7″, *$125–$150.*

Bowl: molded, mustard color, wide flattened form swelling at base molded with stylized roots, 2″ × 8″, *$275–$325.*

Chamberstick: green matte, molded leaf design around neck, small leaves around top, curved handle, 10″, *$225–$250.*

Lamp: footed Alladin's, with loop handle and spout, purple and orange adventurine semigloss finish, 3″ × 5″, *$150–$175.*

Pitcher: shaped rim extending to curving handle on cylindrical form tapering toward base, 9″, *$175–$200.*

Pitcher: metallic glaze, solid mahogany brown with sparkles overall, 4″, *$250–$300.*

Vase: green matte, touch of gray in glaze, 7″, *$350–$400.*

Vase: dark brown matte glaze, with handles, specks of black in glaze, 8″, *$700–$800.*

Vase: green matte, slight ruffled top, 5″, *$100–$125.*

Vase: yellow bud, flared rim, and narrow neck on squat onion shape flaring toward base, 4″ × 5″, *$300–$350.*

Vase: elongated cylindrical neck on bulbous, molded base divided into three segments with splayed feet, 16″, *$350–$400.*

Vase: flared rim and narrow neck on angled shoulder and tapering form, two strong, angular handles continuing to buttress feet, green glaze, 7″, *$300–$350.*

Vase: brown matte glaze, squared handles at top, 4″, *$250–$300.*

These three Teco vases are typical of the firm's work around
1910. Buttress handles and pierced openings give the molded
seven-inch-high bodies a hand-sculpted effect while remaining
inexpensive to produce. *(Photo courtesy of Robert W. Skinner,
Boston)*

Vase: ovoid body ending in a closed and flared rim, with
four long, angular buttresses, light green matte, 5″ × 2″,
$350–$450.

Vase: double-gourd form, four buttressed handles, porous
green and gunmetal matte, 7″ × 5″, *$350–$450.*

Vase: four-sided, straight-walled, four handles forming a
flat, circular opening, dark green matte, 9″ × 4″, *$400–
$450.*

Vase: small mouth centered by four buttress handles running full length to base, 7″, *$300–$350.*

Vase: two strap handles, porous green matte finish, 9″ ×
5″, *$350–$400.*

Vase: embossed flowers and leaves running up the side,

ending with geometric band at the opening, green glaze with gunmetal tailings, 10″ × 7″, *$800–$900*.

Vase: cylinder, with pinched and flared neck, two buttresses running from top to bottom, daffodil yellow matte finish, 6″ × 2″, *$350–$450*.

Vase: bulbous, with closed, collar rim, green matte glaze, 8″ × 5″, *$325–$375*.

Vase: bulbous, with four vertical buttresses forming pierced handles at the top and ending as flanges at the bottom, matte green cover, 7″ × 4″, *$500–$600*.

Vase: cylindrical, flared at either end, with four buttressed handles ending in 90-degree angles, matte blue glaze, 7″ × 4″, *$800–$900*.

Vase: buttress, green matte glaze with touches of shiny gray, 6″, *$350–$400*.

Vase: wide rim and elongated neck on flaring form centered by four long, angled handles to base, brown matte glaze, 7″, *$500–$600*.

Vase: four handles, green matte glaze, 7″, *$750–$850*.

Vase: bulbous form, rolled rim, six ruffled feet at the bottom, feathered green matte glaze, 10″ × 5″, *$650–$750*.

Vase: four-handles, flaring cylindrical form with four oblong openings between each handle, pea green matte, 13″ × 4″, *$1250–$1500*.

Vase: double gourd, all-over green and gunmetal matte, 7″ × 4″, *$125–$150*.

Vase: embossed flowers encircling top portion of the pot, with green matte finish, 9″ × 4″, *$225–$250*.

Vase: bulbous bottom, tapering to thin pinched neck and small flared rim, green matte finish, 5″ × 5″, *$225–$275*.

Vase: two buttressed handles, collar neck, rolled rim, with

blue-gray glaze dripping onto rust glaze, 7″ × 4″, *$200–$225*.

Vase: green and yellow lava glaze, 9″ × 4″, *$500–$600*.

Vase: green matte, ball shape with small top opening, touches of gray around top, 4″, *$125–$150*.

Vase: green matte glaze, four arms at neck, 11″, *$1100–$1400*.

Vase: two loop handles, dark green matte glaze, 6″ × 8″, *$400–$500*.

Vase: flared top edge, four arms from under lip to ball-shaped bottom section, 7″, *$550–$650*.

Vase: two square handles top to bottom, green matte with touches of gray, 5″, *$350–$400*.

Vase: two handles, green mate glaze, 4″, *$275–$325*.

Vase: green matte, molded lily design with leaves and fern, 12″, *$325–$375*.

Wall pocket: circular bottom and rectangular top, embossed with pinwheel motif, 7″ × 5″, *$100–$125*.

Wall pocket: spiked leaves under green matte finish, 14″ × 7″, *$450–$500*.

TIFFANY POTTERY

Shopmarks:
Incised letters *L.C.T.*

Etched in glaze, L.C. TIFFANY or FAVRILE POTTERY or
BRONZE POTTERY

Principal Contribution:
Decorative vases with floral themes

Founder:
Louis Comfort Tiffany

Born: 1848   Died: 1933
Founded: 1898–1905   Closed: 1919

Studios and Salesrooms:
Tiffany Pottery
Corona, New York
ca. 1898–1919

Tiffany & Company (showrooms)
New York
1905–current

"Mr. Louis Tiffany is busy experimenting in pottery, which no
doubt means that he will finally produce something as artistic as
his Favrile glass. In an interview with the manager, our representative was told that as of yet, Mr. Tiffany is in the experimental stage, but that he has been so charmed with the work of
artist potters at the Paris exposition, that he came home with
the determination to try it, and that he would probably produce
something in the lustre bodies."

—*Keramic Studio magazine*
December 1900[1]

Success breeds success, and in the case of Louis Comfort Tiffany, his success in the fields of metalware, lighting, jewelry,
and glassware paved the way for his entry into the art pottery
field. For many years some collectors have presumed that Tiffany's secret pottery experiments at his plant in Corona, New
York, were intended to supplant his purchase of lamp bases
from the Grueby Pottery Company, but research has indicated

1. *Keramic Studio,* II (December 1900).

that Tiffany's interest lay not simply in duplicating Grueby's line (as many potteries did attempt) but in creating his own retail line of art pottery.[2]

Development of Tiffany's art pottery proceeded at a moderate pace between its initial conception around 1898 and its first public showing at the Louisiana Purchase Exposition in St. Louis in 1904. Even then there were only three examples in the pottery exhibit, each "ivory-glazed white semi-porcelain [made from] clay from Ohio and Massachusetts."[3] It was not until late the following year, however, that examples of Tiffany's *favrile* pottery were offered for sale in his newly opened Fifth Avenue salesroom. The delay has been credited not to any lack of interest on the part of Louis Tiffany, but is reflective of the financial cushion other branches of his business provided his pottery experiments.

While Tiffany often referred to his pottery as *favrile* pottery, meaning "handmade," it appears that a large portion of the wares were cast in molds rather than thrown on a potter's wheel. Tiffany himself played an influential role in the designs of the vases and bowls, reflecting his personal interest in Oriental ceramics, his contact with European Art Nouveau designers of the era, and his decided preference for forms incorporating floral motifs. In some instances Tiffany designers would spray an actual plant or flower with shellac or a similar hardening finish, then coat it with plaster-of-Paris to form a naturalistic mold. On other examples details such as insects, birds, or flowers would be cast onto the base and then accented with additional handwork before firing. Among the most favored of the Tiffany wares today are those that were "treated sculpturally so that the decoration creates the form of the vase."[4]

Just as there was a wide range of shapes and floral decorations coming from the Tiffany pottery kilns, so were there a number of different glazes. "Originally the color of Favrile

2. Martin P. Eidelberg, "Tiffany Favrile Pottery," *Connoisseur* (September 1968), pp. 57–61.
3. Ralph and Terry Kovel, *The Kovels' Collectors Guide to American Art Pottery* (New York: Crown Publishers, 1974), p. 268.
4. Martin P. Eidelberg, "Tiffany Favrile Pottery," *Connoisseur* (September 1968), p. 59.

pottery was almost exclusively a light yellow-green shading into darker tones and hence resembling 'old ivory,' the name sometimes applied to it," Paul Evans has noted.[5] After the early light yellow glaze came a mottled green by 1906, along with crystalline, textured, and matte surfaces in a number of different colors. In a few instances a bronze plating was applied over the form, not unlike that being popularized by Charles Clewell.

The line of Tiffany pottery, however, did not prove to be as successful as its founder had hoped. As a late entry into the art pottery field, Tiffany's tenure in the marketplace was shortened not by the quality of the work but by the changing climate of the Arts and Crafts movement, the dwindling art pottery market, and the intense competition among the various mass producers of artwares. Fine examples are today considered a rarity, due in part perhaps to the possibility that the company may have employed a stockroom practice similar to that applied to their glassware: "if it was not sold after being displayed at three retail showrooms, it was either offered to employees at a discount, given as a gift or destroyed."[6]

Selected Prices

Vase: wide mouth on double-gourd form molded with lilies, mottled green glaze, 14″, *$800–$900.*

Vase: ringed neck on swollen cylindrical form tapering toward base, pale green glaze, 20″, *$500–$600.*

Vase: oviform, with collar rim, embossed flowers and leaves, spinach green high glaze, 7″ × 4″, *$800–$900.*

Vase: cylinder with bulging top, embossed maple leaves and pods, buttermilk matte glaze highlighted with brown, 7″ × 4″, *$1100–$1500.*

Vase: bulbous form with footed base and flared collar rim, gold high-glaze, 7″ × 8″, *$400–$450.*

5. Paul Evans, *Art Pottery of the United States* (New York: Charles Scribner's Sons, 1974), p. 283.
6. Ibid.

Vase: cylinder with crisply embossed leaf and floral design in white bisque, 12″ × 4″, $400–$500.

Vase: green drip over light green stylized vase, 9″ × 8″, $450–$550.

Vase: drip glaze over yellow-tan high gloss, 8″ × 10″, $900–$1100.

Vase: copper-clad form with silver finish that has a greenish patina, 7″, $700–$800.

VAN BRIGGLE POTTERY

Shopmark:[1]
Incised conjoined double-A, with one or more of the following:
1901–1920: Year and often form number (1-904)
1901–1905: Roman numeral denoting type of clay used[2]

1. For more information see Scott H. Nelson et al., *A Collector's Guide to Van Briggle Pottery* (Indiana, PA: Halldin Publishing, 1986).

2. A previous and widely held theory attributed each of the Roman numerals to Artus Van Briggle, Anne Gregory (Van Briggle), and Harry Bangs. Painstaking research by authors Robert W. Newton, Lois K. Crouch, Euphemia B. Demmin, and Scott Nelson (*A Collector's Guide to Van Briggle Pottery*, published in 1986) shed additional light on the markings, revealing a document written by Artus Van Briggle in 1902 explaining that the Roman numerals referred to the type of clay used in the ware. Their evidence and conclusions have been accepted and promoted by respected scholar Paul Evans in the 1987 edition of his book *Art Pottery of the United States* (see Note 6).

1904–1920: Occasionally name or initials of potter
1906–1912: Date and occasionally COLORADO SPRINGS
or abbreviation
1922–1926: Addition of VAN BRIGGLE/USA
Post-1920: Addition of VAN BRIGGLE/COLO. SPRGS. and occasionally ORIGINAL (hand-thrown piece), HAND-CARVED
(incised decoration), HAND DECORATED (slip decoration)[3]
1955–1968: High-gloss glaze with ANNA [sic] VAN BRIGGLE

Principal Contributions:
Hand-thrown and molded vases and bowls in matte glazes

Founder:
Artus Van Briggle
Born: 1869   Died: 1904
Founded: 1901   Closed: current

Studios and Salesrooms:
Van Briggle Pottery Company
Colorado Springs, Colorado
1901–current

"The history of the founding of the Van Briggle Pottery against
the odds of poor health, insufficient money, and untrained helpers
is well-known, but only a few intimate friends know how almost
overwhelming the struggle. The Van Briggles were working day
and often half the night and the kilns were turning out beautiful
pottery. To make it in quantity to pay expenses, that was the
problem."

—*Alice Shinn*, describing
the pottery of 1902[4]

"He does not work for the sake of working, but rather with the
purpose of producing a beautiful and perfect ware; of understanding every detail of vase building, so that he may create and teach;

3. Elisabeth Cameron, *Encyclopedia of Pottery & Porcelain: 1800–1960*
(New York: Facts on File Publications, 1986), p. 337.
4. Scott H. Nelson et al., *A Collector's Guide to Van Briggle Pottery*
(Indiana, PA: Halldin Publishing, 1986), p. 17.

in a word, that he may be the competent head and master of his enterprise."

—*The Craftsman*
1903[5]

Artus Van Briggle died in 1904 at the age of thirty-five. A gifted painter, an eloquent designer, and a determined creator of lost glazes, his potential for greatness could only have been destroyed by the disease that haunted him the final five years of his life. Stricken by tuberculosis while living in Ohio, Van Briggle left his friends and the studios where he had trained at Rookwood Pottery for over twelve years and in 1899 moved to Colorado Springs, where he hoped to continue his pottery experiments in the dry mountain air.

Van Briggle's last three years in Ohio had been divided among his painting, his decorating work at Rookwood, and his attempts to discover the lost secret of the famed Chinese "dead glaze." By 1898 his attempts were successful, and his first Lorelei vase traveled with him the following year to Colorado. His first year was discouraging, but in 1900 his fiancée, Anne Gregory, arrived, and his arduous glaze experiments in a borrowed kiln began to show promising results. With the financial help of friend and patron Maria Nichols Storer (the founder and former owner of Rookwood), the young couple built a small pottery in the yard behind Van Briggle's house. By the end of 1901 the pottery had produced nearly three hundred new pieces, all of which sold immediately; thus encouraged, the Van Briggle Pottery Company was formally organized in 1902, and the resulting infusion of capital from the sale of stock enabled Van Briggle both to improve his facilities and to enlarge his staff.

Anne left her teaching job, and the two were married in June 1902, but despite continued artistic recognition the expenses and energies demanded by the hand-thrown pottery and delicate matte glazes took their toll on Van Briggle. The winters of 1902 and 1903 were spent convalescing in Arizona while the

5. Irene Sargent, "Chinese Pots and Modern Faience," *The Craftsman* (September 1903), p. 423.

Three early and important Van Briggle pieces: the nine-and-one-half-inch "Lorelei" vase on the left dates from 1900; the seven-inch handled jug with stopper is from the same year; the twelve-inch tulip vase is dated 1902. All were designed by Artus Van Briggle. *(Photo courtesy of David Rago, Trenton)*

staff, under the direction of nineteen-year-old Frank Riddle and experienced potter Ambrose Schlegel, continued to turn out vases and bowls based on Van Briggle's sketches. Although Van Briggle was resigned to the use of molds, required for the firm to achieve financial success, it was not his intent "that molds were to be used for mass manufacture, which they were in the late period—to the extent that aging of the molds resulted in considerable loss of detail."[6] In early 1904 the pair returned to the pottery in Colorado Springs, but Van Briggle's health had deteriorated to the point that he was confined to bed. Anne Van Briggle assumed her husband's role as manager while he continued to sketch new designs until his death on July 4.

6. Paul Evans, *Art Pottery of the United States* (New York: Feingold & Lewis, 1987), p. 300.

As these examples illustrate, the decoration on Van Briggle pottery consisted primarily of molded plant or abstract forms. Early dated pieces are sought by collectors not just because of their rarity but for the clear definition of the decoration, which gradually deteriorated the longer the molds were used. *(Photo courtesy of Don Treadway, Cincinnati)*

Anne Louise Gregory (1868–1929), an artist in her own right, proved a capable manager. Numerous awards and a new building with two enormous kilns soon followed. By 1908 production had increased in variety as well as in number (peaking at six thousand items per year from 1909 to 1911),[7] as vases and bowls were complemented with lamps, tiles, candlesticks, bookends, flower frogs, and novelty items. Anne remarried that same year. By 1910, however, the pottery was struggling to remain solvent. With her new husband's encouragement, Anne left the pottery in 1912 to resume painting, at which time the pottery was leased and in 1913 sold. Anne Gregory Ritter died of cancer in 1929.

The pottery struggled from 1912 until 1920 but survived two changes in ownership and a serious fire in 1919. The new owners

7. Scott H. Nelson et al., *A Collector's Guide to Van Briggle Pottery* (Indiana, PA: Halldin Publishing, 1986), p. 131.

in 1920, I. F. and J. H. Lewis, maintained control of the firm until 1969, during which time the pottery continued to expand with an extensive line of commercial artwares and novelty items that were distributed across the country and abroad. The vast majority of post-1920 production was both molded and mass-produced. At times the forms that Artus Van Briggle had designed were reissued. According to Paul Evans, "since 1920 there has been a steady deterioration in the quality of the design, execution and glazes, the only reminder of the art pottery output being the addition of "Art Pottery" to the firm's name as the production of art pottery ended."[8] The few pieces hand-thrown after 1920 are generally incised with the word *Original*. A flood in 1935 destroyed much of the pottery and nearly all of its inventory of molds. The pottery was again sold in 1969 and has remained in operation ever since.

By far the most desirable of the hundreds of thousands of examples of vases and bowls bearing the Van Briggle trademark are those designed and executed while Artus Van Briggle was still alive. His early work often incorporated sculpted human or plant forms as low relief that "emphasizes the lines and contours of the vase which it beautifies."[9] A number of different colors were employed, often two or three incorporated into one piece; they were most often fired with Van Briggle's special "dead matte glaze" or a semimatte glaze. After his death the staff continued to produce limited numbers of his designs using molds; those dated prior to the sale of the pottery in 1913 are also among the most highly respected of the body of Van Briggle pottery work, as many of the early glaze formulas were perfected under Anne's leadership. As new designers were brought in, additional forms were produced, along with new glazes. Those dated between 1913 and 1920—when the pottery went through no less than three changes in ownership—are understandably more erratic and must be carefully evaluated on the basis of form, glaze, and quality of workmanship.

8. Paul Evans, *Art Pottery of the United States* (New York: Feingold & Lewis, 1987), p. 300.

9. Irene Sargent, "Chinese Pots and Modern Faience," *The Craftsman* (September 1903), p. 424.

Along with the misconception regarding the use of Roman numerals on early Van Briggle pottery (see Note 2) confusion has emerged surrounding the discovery of several pieces marked "Anna Van Briggle." Despite what many collectors and dealers would like to believe, these were not the work of either Artus or Anne Van Briggle (note the variance in the spelling). Instead, these were produced in mass quantity between 1955 and 1968 as a commercially motivated commemorative that is regarded today as no more than a novelty. Of slightly more interest are the pieces made in 1956 marked with the letter *G* enclosed in a circle. For approximately three months, these pieces were coated with a special high-gloss glaze containing specks of gold powder.

Selected Prices

Bowl: short neck on squat, bulbous form in mottled green glaze, undated, 4″ × 7″, *$85–$95.*

Bowl: closed form with embossed dragonflies, red with exposed clay, dated 1906, powder blue matte, 3″ × 5″, *$375–$425.*

Vase: tall, swollen, cylindrical form tapering toward base, molded with petaled flowers on long stem, matte pale blue with dark blue highlights, undated, 12″, *$125–$150.*

Vase: #167, elongated form with iris swelling toward base with two loop handles, darker blue on pale blue, undated, 13″, *$150–$175.*

Vase: embossed, stylized leaves and trefoils, under grayblue and green matte crystalline glaze, dated 1903, 7″ × 3″, *$375–$425.*

Vase: stylized poppy buds and jagged leaves in heavy relief, olive green matte finish, dated 1904, 10″ × 5″, *$650–$750.*

Vase: bulbous bottom tapering to small collared rim, with

double rows of embossed, stylized leaves, under rose matte glaze, dated 1903, 10″ × 5″, $1200–$1400.

Vase: diagonally incised collar rim, embossed with designs of geometric disk patterns, matte green, dated 1902, 5″ × 5″, $800–$900.

Vase: cylindrical form with stepped-in rim, embossed bell-flowers under lime green matte finish, dated 1903, 6″ × 3″, $600–$700.

Vase: with two handles, bulbous form with heavily embossed band of green leaves encircling the base, purple matte finish, dated 1903, 9″ × 6″, $1250–$1500.

Vase: flat and bulbous bottom, bulging form, cylindrical neck, light green-orange matte, dated 1902, 6″ × 4″, $350–$400.

Vase: flaring bottom, cylindrical neck, spade-shaped leaves under flowing blue matte, dated 1902, 4″ × 3″, $400–$450.

Vase: cylindrical form, vertical, arched leaves, dark green matte, dated 1906, 5″ × 4″, $200–$225.

Vase: bulbous, with closed rim, red and speckled green matte glaze, dated 1905, 5″ × 5″, $225–$250.

Vase: squat, bulbous form with embossed heart-shaped leaves, green-blue matte finish, dated 1903, 2″ × 5″, $450–$500.

Vase: flaring, cylindrical form with bulbous rim, embossed, stylized poppy buds and stems, blue-green matte glaze, dated 1902, 4″ × 4″, $400–$450.

Vase: bulbous form with rounded rim, embossed bumps around opening, and vertical lines from midsection to base, pea green matte, dated 1903, 4″ × 4″, $275–$325.

Vase: flaring cylindrical form, closed and flared rim, decorated with embossed tulips and leaves under light green matte finish, dated 1904, 6″ × 3″, $900–$1000.

Vase: seafoam green with collar rim, embossed stylized floral motif encircling body, dated 1912, 8″ × 3″, *$175–$200.*

Vase: squat form with tapering neck, six embossed tulips encircling ochre matte glaze, dated 1903, 4″ × 5″, *$400–$450.*

Vase: closed form, maroon matte glaze, dated 1904, 5″ × 7″, *$175–$200.*

Vase: with two handles, dark pink on rose matte glaze, dated 1906, 11″ × 4″, *$400–$450.*

Vase: light turquoise blue matte glaze, dated 1914, 4″ × 5″, *$125–$150.*

Vase: #104, pale blue-green matte over medium grayish brown, dated 1904, 4″, *$350–$400.*

Vase: #370, yellow matte glaze with red around top, dated 1907, 4″, *$225–$250.*

Vase: #692, floral design on red clay body, green matte with touch of yellow on buds, ca. 1908–1911, 7″, *$250–$300.*

Vase: #196, bluish green matte glaze, on finely molded floral design, dated 1903, 5″, *$450–$500.*

Vase: #694, light to deep pink matte glaze, touch of pale green around top, dated 1914, 7″, *$300–$350.*

Vase: dark brown clay body, light blue matte glaze, molded butterfly decoration, dated 1917, 2″, *$85–$95.*

Vase: #636, deep rusty brown clay body, green matte glaze with dark green flecks, ca. 1908–1911, 6″, *$175–$200.*

Vase: #451, light green matte glaze, dated 1906, *$300–$350.*

Vase: #205, two handles, green matte glaze, dated 1906, 5″, *$175–$200.*

VOLKMAR POTTERY

 VOLKMAR KILNS
METUCHEN, N.J.

Shopmarks:
(Pre-1888) Letters *C* and *V* overlaid
(1895–1896) Impressed VOLKMAR & CORY
(1896–1903) Impressed CHAS. VOLKMAR or CROWN POINT
WARE or stylized letter *V* (but without a year)
(After 1903) Stamped VOLKMAR KILNS/METUCHEN, N.J.

Principal Contributions:
Art pottery and tiles with underglaze decorations

Founder:
Charles Volkmar
Born: 1841   Died: 1914
Founded: 1882   Closed: ca. 1911

Studios and Salesrooms:
Charles Volkmar Pottery
Tremont (Bronx), New York
1882–1888

Menlo Park Ceramic Company
Menlo Park, New Jersey
1888–1893

Volkmar & Cory
Corona (Queens), New York
1895–1896

Crown Point
Corona (Queens), New York
1897–1902

Volkmar Kilns or
Charles Volkmar and Son
Metuchen, New Jersey
1903–ca. 1911

"Volkmar's importance in the New York area is due to the fact
that, besides exhibiting widely, he also taught classes at his pottery, first in Corona, Long Island, and, from 1903, in Metuchen,
New Jersey."

—*Robert Judson Clark*[1]

Charles Volkmar was born into an artistic family, his grandfather having been an engraver and his father a painter; thus,
it was not surprising when Charles chose to follow in their footsteps. At age eighteen he was an accomplished etcher and at
twenty-two was studying in Europe, where he was to spend
nearly sixteen of his next seventeen years working in the studios of numerous important potters, including the Haviland family's porcelain factory in Limoges, France.

Volkmar moved back to the United States in 1879, began
teaching, and built a kiln in Greenpoint, New York, where he
experimented with making Limoges-style tiles. One of his earliest commissions was a fireplace for the Salmagundi Club, for
which he worked as both a potter and a pottery tutor for several
years thereafter. The small Greenpoint (Long Island) kiln led
to the establishment of his first complete pottery operation at
his home in the Bronx around 1882. Volkmar concentrated his
efforts primarily on decorative tiles, along with plaques and
vases (molded and hand-thrown), in both the applied technique
and underglaze. According to Paul Evans, "the decorative motif
apparently most preferred by the artist was a landscape with
water and some living creatures, often a duck, goose or cow. In

1. Robert Judson Clark, ed., *The Arts and Crafts Movement in America:
1876–1916* (Princeton, NJ: Princeton University, 1972), p. 180.

all, about twelve colors were used: yellow, orange, light and dark blue, red, pink, light and dark brown, a 'cold' and a 'warm' green and black."[2]

The popularity of Volkmar's decorated tiles led to his decision to expand in that direction by forming a partnership with J. T. Smith in Menlo Park, New Jersey, where they organized the Menlo Park Ceramic Company in 1888. The tiles of the firm were widely acclaimed, leading to commissions in the Boston Public Library, the Rockefeller home in Tarrytown, New York, and the Fulton National Bank in Manhattan. The partners were unable to work together, however, perhaps due in part to Volkmar's independent spirit, and the firm was dissolved by 1893. Whatever the reason, Volkmar returned to New York and by winter of 1895 had taken on another partner, Miss Kate Cory, an artist; together they designed and decorated award-winning art tiles, mugs, and plaques, often selecting popular historical subjects as their motifs.

Once again, however, success could not sustain the partnership. Volkmar may have insisted on major changes in their production, for after Miss Cory left in 1896, he phased out the traditional historical scenes and set out to achieve "rich but delicate color qualities, subdued in tone . . . as are only possible to secure in the underglaze treatment of pottery."[3] An exhibition in New York City elicited praise from a number of publications for his "simple shapes and single colour glazes [done] with admirable restraint. His greens, blues, and yellows are pure, colorful, and even to a high degree."[4]

As Martin Eidelberg noted in the Princeton Exhibition catalog in 1972, "by the turn of the century Volkmar was following the general tendency towards mat or dull glazes although he seems, curiously, not to have been entirely happy with this development."[5] Eidelberg also observed that prior to 1900, "Volkmar was making landscape tiles . . . , thus paralleling, if not

2. Paul Evans, *Art Pottery of the United States* (New York: Charles Scribner's Sons, 1974), p. 310.

3. Margaret Whiting, *House Beautiful* (October 1900).

4. *International Studio* (November 1900).

5. Robert Judson Clark, ed., *The Arts and Crafts Movement in America: 1876–1916* (Princeton, NJ: Princeton University, 1972), p. 180.

preceding Rookwood, whose work in this genre is better known. The soft, mat glazes, well suited to the poetic mood of the scene, reveal his development away from his earlier, underglaze work."[6]

Selected Prices

Due to the infrequency with which examples of this pottery appear on the market, establishing an in-depth price guide has not yet been possible. Until additional information is compiled, readers are advised to seek counsel from experienced collectors before either buying or selling important pieces.

WALLEY POTTERY

WƆW

Shopmark:
Impressed letters *W J W*

Principal Contributions:
Hand-thrown vases, bowls, and mugs in a variety of quality glazes

Founder:
William J. Walley
Born: 1852   Died: 1919
Founded: 1898   Closed: 1919

Studios and Salesrooms:
Walley Pottery
West Sterling, Massachusetts
1898–1919

6. Robert Judson Clark, ed., *The Arts and Crafts Movement in America: 1876–1916* (Princeton, NJ: Princeton University, 1972), p. 181.

"To me there is more true art in a brick made and burnt by one man than there is in the best piece of molded pottery ever made."

—*William J. Walley*
1906[1]

After a series of discouraging setbacks, art potter William J. Walley purchased a deserted pottery in West Sterling, Massachusetts, in 1898 and founded a one-man operation demonstrating his concern for quality art pottery over quantity. Utilizing clay dug near his pottery, Walley turned, decorated, glazed, and fired his work by himself, declaring "I am just a potter trying to make art pottery as it should be made."[2] He experimented with both matte and glossy glazes, most often in green, red, and brown, producing a small number of vases, bowls, and mugs that are highly sought after today for both their rarity and their quality glazes.[3] The pottery closed at his death in 1919.

Selected Prices

Due to the infrequency with which examples of this pottery appear on the market, establishing an in-depth price guide has not yet been possible. The examples listed below are indicative only of the value of pieces of similar form and decoration. Until additional information is compiled, readers are advised to seek counsel from experienced collectors before either buying or selling important pieces.

Bowl: squat and bulbous, with four rounded edges and feet, burgundy, gray and lime green flambé matte glaze, 4″ × 6″, $225–$250.

---

1. Paul Evans, *Art Pottery of the United States* (New York: Charles Scribner's Sons, 1974), p. 316.
2. Ibid.
3. See Martin Eidelberg, ed., *From Our Native Clay* (New York: Turn of the Century Editions, 1987), p. 103.

Vase: relief leaves decoration in green and brown, luster glaze, 7″, *$625–$700.*

Vase: undecorated, green and brown matte glaze, 4″, *$125–$150.*

Vase: flared, elongated neck on bulbous form tapering toward base, mottled green glaze, 9″, *$175–$200.*

WALRATH POTTERY

Shopmark:
Incised WALRATH POTTERY around letters *MI*
(Mechanics Institute)

Principal Contribution:
Limited line of matte-glazed art pottery featuring
conventionalized decoration

Founder:
Frederick E. Walrath
Born: 1871   Died: 1920
Founder: ca. 1903   Closed: ca. 1918

Studios and Salesrooms:
Walrath Pottery
Rochester, New York
ca. 1903–ca. 1918

"Frederick Walrath . . . has successfully solved the difficult problem of incorporating flowers and leafage into the decoration of pottery without any suggestion of realism, without detracting in any way from the artistic ensemble."

—*International Studio*
1911[1]

While Frederick Walrath is considered by scholars to be a studio potter rather than the owner of an art pottery, that distinction has certainly had no effect on the demand for his rare and characteristic Arts and Crafts–style pottery. Although he worked in 1907 and 1908 for the Grueby Pottery, most of Walrath's career thereafter was dedicated to teaching young potters at the Mechanics Institute in Rochester, New York (1908–1918). There he was able to produce his noted "two-color wares . . . [in which] decorative motifs were generally conventionalized versions of plants, trees and flowers."[2]

Walrath's flowing matte glazes were recognized in 1912 in *The Craftsman* magazine and, like the pottery produced at Marblehead, have been prized by Arts and Crafts collectors ever since. "The similarity between the works of Arthur Baggs [at Marblehead Pottery] and Frederick Walrath can be traced to the fact that both had been students of Charles F. Binns at Alfred University. The simple, well-proportioned shapes of the vessels and the multi-toned, sober mat glazes give them a strength that accords well with the spirit of the Arts and Crafts Movement after 1900. The conventionalization of natural motifs and the arrangement of horizontal bands and vertical accents contribute to the architectural sensibility of these works."[3]

1. Paul Evans, *Art Pottery of the United States* (New York: Feingold & Lewis, 1987), p. 400.

2. Ibid.

3. Martin Eidelberg, ed., *From Our Native Clay* (New York: Turn of the Century Editions, 1987), p. 38.

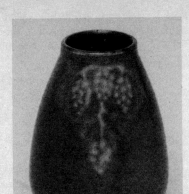

This seven-inch Walrath vase is decorated with stylized orange-yellow pine cones and needles on a matte green ground, making it a natural complement to an Arts and Crafts interior. *(Photo courtesy of Don Treadway, Cincinnati)*

Walrath concluded his career, which ended prematurely at the age of forty-nine, as chief ceramist at Newcomb College Pottery from 1918–1920.

Selected Prices

Due to the infrequency with which examples of this pottery appear on the market, establishing an in-depth price guide has not yet been possible. The examples listed below are indicative only of the value of pieces of similar form and decoration. Until additional information is compiled, readers are advised to seek counsel from experienced collectors before either buying or selling important pieces.

Bowl: crouched nude woman in center, glazed in pea green matte, 6″ × 7″, $300–$350.

Bowl: closed, stylized landscape showing green pine trees, medium blue matte ground, 2″ × 4″, $300–$350.

Bowl: pea green with brown-pink water lilies and light

green pads, attached wavelike flower holders supporting a full figure of a nude woman glazed in light brown-pink, 10″ × 8″, *$900–$1000*.

Bowl: stylized landscape with green pine trees against a medium blue matte ground, 2″ × 4″, *$275–$325*.

Mug: brown-green and yellow-orange matte glaze with stylized decoration, 5″ × 3″, *$250–$275*.

Vase: green-brown matte glaze with floral design, 5″ × 4″, *$650–$750*.

Vase: dark blue tree decoration on light gray-blue matte glaze background, 2″ × 4″, *$200–$225*.

Vase: decorated with yellow and orange pine cones and needles on a green matte background, 7″, *$800–$900*.

Vase: short neck and angled shoulder on squat cylindrical form slightly tapering toward base, decorated with stylized petaled clover on angular stems, slight orange and pale green on olive green ground, 5″, *$1000–$1250*.

WELLER POTTERY

LONHUDA

LOUWELSA WELLER

Shopmarks:
Numerous forms and variations, including the following:
(1895–1896) Impressed *LONHUDA* above letters *LF* enclosed in a shield
Incised or impressed name of the form above the word *WELLER*

Incised or impressed name of the form above the word
WELLER, all around and/or encased in a circle
Rubber stamp, WELLER WARE
(After 1915) The printed word *WELLER* incised or in relief
(After 1930) Script signature, *WELLER*
(After 1930) Paper label

Principal Contributions:
Underglaze-decorated art pottery, a quality iridescent line, and
molded commercial artware

Founder:
Samuel A. Weller
Born: 1851   Died: 1925
Founded: 1872   Closed: 1949

Studios and Salesrooms:
S. A. Weller Pottery
Fultonham, Ohio
1872–1888

Zanesville, Ohio
1888–1949

"The modeling and moulding rooms are on the second floor and
are quite picturesque with the many workers in their white
blouses and caps. Some are busy at the wheels, while others
bearing long boards filled with moulds gracefully balanced on
their heads, walk rapidly to the drying rooms where the moulds
are placed on shelves to dry."

—*The Sketch Book*
1906[1]

In the late nineteenth and early twentieth centuries the art pottery industry flourished around Zanesville, Ohio, where abundant supplies of inexpensive natural gas and high-quality clays,

1. May Elizabeth Cook, *Sketch Book* (May 1906); also appears in Ralph
and Terry Kovel, *The Kovels' Collectors Guide to American Art Pottery*
(New York: Crown Publishers, 1974), p. 291.

plus an extensive work force, attracted both artists and entrepreneurs. In 1872 a twenty-one-year-old potter by the name of Samuel A. Weller drew from a crude kiln his first batch of simple flowerpots, which he proceeded to sell door-to-door to the residents of nearby Zanesville. Forever alert and always looking for an edge over his competition, young Weller began decorating his plain flowerpots with common housepaint, and sales quickly increased. Soon he had expanded his line to include vases that he had thrown on the kick wheel he had built, and by 1888 the Weller Pottery had evolved from a primitive log cabin to a highly visible plant in Zanesville.

Samuel Weller never seemed content with the status of either his pottery or his plant. By 1890 he had moved out of his rented quarters and into a new factory that he had constructed; over the course of the next few years he continued to expand his operation, buying another plant and immediately building an addition to it. While one plant continued to produce popular wares, such as umbrella stands, jardinieres, and decorated flowerpots, Weller and his assistants were experimenting in the other with "the first fancy glazed ware in Zanesville."[2]

Of all the potteries operating in Zanesville, it soon became apparent that Weller and Roseville were to be the two most successful of the many commercial potteries attempting to duplicate the artistic achievements of the Rookwood Pottery in Cincinnati. Laura Fry, a decorator at Rookwood from 1881 until 1887, had developed and eventually patented "a technique of slip decoration using an atomizer, which allowed more delicate, even blending of colours than the previous method of application with a brush."[3] Her technique led to the highly successful Standard ware at Rookwood, which Weller and Roseville both attempted to duplicate. Fry left the Rookwood Pottery in 1887 and unsuccessfully attempted to prevent the firm from using her technique; the courts took several years to resolve the dispute, eventually ruling in favor of Rookwood, but not until 1898.

2. Paul Evans, *Art Pottery of the United States* (New York: Charles Scribner's Sons, 1974), p. 323.

3. Elisabeth Cameron, *Encyclopedia of Pottery & Porcelain: 1800–1960* (New York: Facts on File Publications, 1986), p. 133.

What the Weller Pottery lacked in originality they attempted to compensate for by duplicating many of the styles made popular by Rookwood. Both the Indian motif and the silver overlay appeared first in Rookwood's line but soon were also offered at a slightly lower cost by Weller. Nevertheless, modern collectors have not shunned high-quality examples such as this large mug. *(Photo courtesy of David Rago, Trenton)*

Meanwhile, Miss Fry went to work for William Long at Lonhuda Pottery from 1892 to 1894, where she taught him her technique for blending colors. Rather than wait for the outcome of the court case, Weller persuaded William Long in 1895 to move production of his Laura Fry–inspired Lonhuda line to one of Weller's buildings, and by 1896 Weller had both procured Laura Fry's technique and discouraged Long from remaining with the firm.

Unabashed, Weller's "high-glazed ware, generally in red to brown colors and hand-decorated with fruits, flowers, or portraits (frequently of Indians), was named Louwelsa,"[4] taking a portion of his young daughter's name, Louise, and adding to it the first three letters of his last name plus the initials of his first and middle names. Weller replaced Long with Charles Babcock

4. Paul Evans, *Art Pottery of the United States* (New York: Charles Scribner's Sons, 1974), p. 323.

Upjohn (1866–1953), who served as a designer and the firm's art director from 1897 until he left in 1904. In addition to the popular Louwelsa line, Weller and Upjohn quickly produced additional forms, including the well-known Dickens Ware (which later became known as I Dickens, to avoid confusion with II Dickens and later III Dickens—each line becoming less reliant on costly hand-decorating techniques). Frederick H. Rhead (1880–1942), who was to become art director at Weller's archrival, Roseville, worked with Weller for only a few months in 1903 and 1904 but created two new lines: the simpler III Dickens, in which "the design was covered with a clear glaze, often bearing an applied black cameo-type disc with the head of Dickens in white and a Dickens inscription in white on a similar disc";[5] and Jap Birdimal, "produced by outlining the decoration—geometric, scenic or with a Japanese motif—with a white slip squeezed from a bag through a fine nozzle, usually on a gray or blue background."[6]

While Rookwood maintained its superiority over its Zanesville imitators—Roseville, Owens, and Weller—competition in Zanesville remained heated. In 1901 Samuel Weller went after the French artist Jacques Sicard (1865–1923), who had developed a unique metallic iridescent luster; but Sicard agreed to come to work for Weller only under his terms, which included strict privacy. Sicard, no doubt, had heard about Weller's relationship with William Long six years earlier. Sicard remained with Weller from 1902 until 1907; during that time he and his assistant, Henri Gellie, designed and decorated a line called Sicardo, of "rather simple shapes with floral and other motifs in metallic lusters on an iridescent ground of different tints ranging from rose and blue to crimson and purple."[7] Sicard moved back to his homeland in 1907, taking his secret formula with him, but Samuel Weller persisted in advertising his line of

5. Paul Evans, *Art Pottery of the United States* (New York: Charles Scribner's Sons, 1974), p. 324.

6. Ibid.

7. Ibid., p. 325.

Three popular Weller styles: a Jap Birdimal vase on the left, a Hunter squat pitcher in the center, and a Louwelsa high-glaze mug with rare silver overlay at right. *(Photo courtesy of David Rago, Trenton)*

Sicardo Weller for five years until all remaining examples had been sold.

The Sicardo line has since emerged as the most highly regarded of the numerous forms of Weller art pottery. "The glowing tones, of red, purple, blue, and green," have been described by Martin Eidelberg as, "the ceramic industry's equal to Louis C. Tiffany's glass."[8] The glaze, he also notes, "is like the lustrous surface sheen of oil on water."[9]

Weller and Roseville battled for the commercial artware market for nearly twenty years, until the decline in public demand after World War I led first Roseville and then, in 1925, Weller to cease production of hand-decorated art pottery. Before then dozens of new lines and hundreds of forms (most of them molded) had been introduced and touted in their advertising. "After 1910 most of the new lines required a minimum of individual artistic

8. Martin Eidelberg, ed., *From Our Native Clay* (New York: Turn of the Century Editions, 1987), p. 36.
9. Ibid., p. 15.

work, and by the beginning of World War I production of prestige ware was abandoned; among the last to go [was] Louwelsa (which had been produced in over 500 shapes and sizes)."[10]

Samuel Weller died in 1925, and although his descendants retained control of the firm, without someone with Weller's degree of unbridled determination it was destined to close. The Depression saw a drastic drop in production, which enabled it to survive longer than most of its earlier competitors, but it bowed to pressure from less expensive foreign imports in 1948.

Selected Prices

Jardiniere: with pedestal, embossed forest scene in green and brown matte glazes, 8″ × 10″, $250–$300.

Pitcher: Sicardo four-sided, straight-walled pitcher, with two of the sides embossed, one showing an Art Nouveau woman with flowing gown and hair, another side showing whiplash-curved vines and fruit, the other two sides have a lightly raised intertwining vine design, spout created by a larger flower, handle formed by an iridescent stem, 22″ × 7″, $1500–$1750.

Umbrella stand: cylindrical form with Roman key motif at top and base, 20″, $150–$175.

Umbrella stand: cylindrical form with molded band of petaled flowers, matte green glaze, 20″, $150–$175.

Vase: fluted rim on squat bulbous form molded into six lobed sections, overall iridescent floral and scroll design, 5″ × 8″, $250–$300.

Vase: Indian portrait, rolled rim on swollen cylindrical form tapering toward base, painted with Indian brave, 11″, $400–$450.

10. Paul Evans, *Art Pottery of the United States* (New York: Charles Scribner's Sons, 1974), pp. 326–327.

Vase: detailed tree decoration on bands of layered yellow, blue, red and yellow iridescent glaze, 6″, $100–$125.

Vase: Sicardo, trefoil form with geometric floral pattern, iridescent glaze, 7″, $250–$275.

Vase: tall cylindrical form with a slight twist swelling toward base, iridescent purples and blue poppy design, 12″, $400–$500.

Vase: cylindrical, with overall amber leaf and dot design, on maroon vase, 11″, $350–$400.

Vase: bulbous, two-handled, with swirling Art Nouveau-style flowers in glowing, iridescent blues, green, and crimson, 9″ × 10″, $1000–$1250.

Vase: Hudson, painted with large blue and yellow iris blossoms and green spiked leaves, 15″ × 8″, $350–$400.

Vase: Sicardo, with blown-out grapes and vines, painted grape leaves, iridescent purple, blue, green, and crimson glaze, 22″ × 9″, $4000–$5000.

Vase: bulbous bottom, tapering to small rim with embossed beetles and leaves under a purple-to-light-blue glaze, 5″ × 4″, $325–$375.

Vase: cylindrical form with four oval indentations around the opening, decorated with silver and crimson leaves and berries, 11″ × 4″, $475–$575.

Vase: Dickensware, with two handles, polychrome portrait of an Indian in plumed headdress, against amber shaded to pale green, 7″ × 5″, $225–$275.

Vase: slip-painted with blue and white irises and light green leaves against pale green shaded to pink matte ground, 15″ × 7″, $400–$450.

Vase: two-handled form with ruffled rim and embossed swirling Art Nouveau design in celery green matte glaze, 9″ × 7″, $150–$175.

Vase: corset-shaped Sicardo in burgundy with highly stylized vine design in iridescent silver glaze, 8″, *$200–$225*.

Vase: high-glaze, cylinder, with pink, gold, and black bird perched on a black branch with green leaves against an ivory background, 8″ × 4″, *$250–$300*.

Vase: Sicardo, three-sided, trailing vines with leaves and berries in metallic gold against iridescent green and violet ground, 5″ × 3″, *$225–$250*.

Vase: cylinder, with lavender and blue lilacs on pale pink shaded to grayish green ground, 13″ × 4″, *$200–$225*.

Vase: two-handled, with white flower, stem, and leaves against brown to olive green high-gloss background, 8″ × 3″, *$175–$200*.

Vase: Eocean cylinder vase slip-decorated with a pink rose and green leaves against a black to pale blue ground, 9″ × 3″, *$100–$125*.

Vase: Hudson two-handled bulbous vase with a collar neck by Sarah McLaughlin, slip-decorated with pink and white lilies of the valley with light green leaves against a pale violet to pink ground, 7″ × 6″, *$100–$125*.

Vase: embossed scene of a brown bird watching over its nest eggs in the forest, 8″ × 3″, *$75–$85*.

Vase: Art Nouveau, bisque finish in pale peach and greens, molded Art Nouveau–style leaves and vines, flowers around top in deep peach color forming top edge, 13″, *$175–$200*.

Vase: Fudzi, bisque finish, blue to dark orange, incised decoration of large flowers in orange high-glaze, high-glaze inside, 8″, *$175–$200*.

Vase: Hudson, light to deeper green matte glaze, large white water lilies and buds with yellow and brown centers, lily pads touched with reddish/orange, 12″, *$350–$400*.

Vase: Hudson, pink to deep green, floral decoration of white and green flowers centered with yellow and orange, 7″, *$125–$150*.

Vase: Hudson, dark blue, red and green band around top, deep rose and pink flowers, green leaves, 10″, *$125–$150*.

Vase: Sicardo, multiple handles surrounding base, floral decoration with iridescence, 10″, *$500–$600*.

Vase: Sicardo, vine design, reds and greens with gold and purple, 4″, *$200–$225*.

WHEATLEY POTTERY COMPANY

Shopmarks:
(1880–1882) Incised *T.J.W. & CO* or signature
T.J. WHEATLEY, often with the year
(1903–1927) Paper label with letters *WP* enclosed in a circle beside the words *WHEATLEY/CINCINNATI, O.*

Principal Contribution:
Early high-relief and underglaze art pottery

Founder:
Thomas J. Wheatley
Born: 1853   Died: 1917
Founded: 1903   Closed: 1927

Studios and Salesrooms:
T. J. Wheatley & Company
Cincinnati, Ohio
1880–1882

Wheatley Pottery Company
Cincinnati, Ohio
1903–1927

Thomas J. Wheatley will be remembered more as an early pioneer in underglaze decoration than a manufacturer of art pottery. In 1880, the year in which he started his first individual pottery, Wheatley was granted a controversial patent for a method of applying underglaze colors and slips to a damp form; regardless of the actual source for this technique, the patent proved ineffective in restricting the use of the technique. In 1882 Wheatley ended his association with the Cincinnati Art Pottery, which he had helped form in 1880. His two-year-old firm failed that same year, as the Cincinnati market was unable to absorb the growing number of underglaze wares being produced.[1]

Wheatley formally reentered the Cincinnati pottery scene in 1903 with the formation of the Wheatley Pottery Company. Although the firm remained in business under that name until 1927, the production of art pottery was practically eliminated by 1910, when a fire destroyed much of the plant. Loss of the fragile Wheatley paper label has complicated the process of identifying the art pottery of the firm which was "characterized by a colored matt glaze over relief work, chiefly in dark shades of green, yellow and blue."[2]

Selected Prices

Due to the infrequency with which examples of this pottery appear on the market, establishing an in-depth price guide has not yet been possible. The examples listed below are only indicative of the value of pieces of similar form and decoration. Until additional information is compiled, readers are advised to seek

1. Martin Eidelberg, ed., *From Our Native Clay* (New York: Turn of the Century Editions, 1987), pp. 10–11.
2. Paul Evans, *Art Pottery of the United States* (New York: Charles Scribner's Sons, 1974), p. 335.

This twelve-inch Wheatley gourd vase reveals more than just a coincidental similarity to the popular Grueby gourd vase. Although the styles and matte green glazes are nearly identical, values are not, as the Wheatley is generally worth only 25 to 33 percent of a comparable Grueby. *(Photo courtesy of David Rago, Trenton)*

counsel from experienced collectors before either buying or selling important pieces.

Bowl: matte green glaze, relief decorated leaves, 3″ × 11″, $250–$300.

Vase: square, with stepped-in rim and base, pink dogwood blossoms in slip-relief against a light to olive green ground, 9″ × 7″ × 3″, $250–$300.

Vase: bulbous, with cylindrical neck, eight embossed buds and alternating leaves, medium green matte finish, 11″ × 11″, $650–$750.

Vase: matte green glaze, decorated with berries and leaves in relief, 12″, $500–$600.

Vase: bulbous, with cutaway stylized leaf decoration encircling the base and green mottled matte glaze, 7″ × 8″, $200–$225.

Vase: bulbous, high glaze, with flared neck and rolled rim, spray of orange wild roses and green leaves against vivid blue ground, 8″ × 7″, *$300–$400.*

WHITE POTTERY

White

Denver

Denver

Shopmarks:
(Early) Incised *DENVER*, occasionally with the small letter *w* inside the *D*
(Pre-1920) The year incised along with the word *DENVER*

Principal Contribution:
Undecorated, hand-thrown art pottery

Founders:
Frederick J. White
Born: 1838   Died: 1919

Francis G. White
Born: 1869   Died: 1960
Founded: 1894   Closed: ca. 1955

Studios and Salesrooms:
F. J. White and Son
Denver, Colorado
1894–ca. 1909

Denver Art Pottery
Denver, Colorado
ca. 1909–ca. 1955

The father-and-son team of Frederick and Francis White traced their pottery heritage back to England, where the elder

White's father had trained his son in the potter's art. Beginning around 1909 a line of hand-thrown art pottery was added to the firm's successful production of household dinnerware, mugs, bowls, and flowerpots. Featuring a "distinctive gray semi-matt, grainy-appearing glaze,"[1] the Denver Gray Ware line of simple vases, jardinieres, and lamps was one of the firm's first entries into the art pottery market. It was followed by a swirled clay form similar to that being produced at the same time by Niloak. The art pottery line eventually gave way to the dinnerware production, which sustained the firm through the Depression to the mid-1950s.

Selected Prices

Due to the infrequency with which examples of this pottery appear on the market, establishing an in-depth price guide has not yet been possible. Until additional information is compiled, readers are advised to seek counsel from experienced collectors before either buying or selling important pieces.

ZANESVILLE ART POTTERY

LA MORO

Shopmark:
Impressed word *LA MORO*

Principal Contributions:
Art pottery vases, plus line of household wares

Founder:
David Schmidt

Born: 1847   Died: undetermined

Founded: 1896   Closed: 1920

---

1. Paul Evans, *Art Pottery of the United States* (New York: Charles Scribner's Sons, 1974), p. 338.

Studios and Salesrooms:
Zanesville Roofing Tile Company
Zanesville, Ohio
1896–1900

Zanesville Art Pottery Company
Zanesville, Ohio
1900–1920

As a young man just recently having arrived in America from his homeland of Germany, David Schmidt learned the trade of a roof tiler in Pittsburgh, Pennsylvania, but eventually established a business of his own as an importer of slate and clay roof tiles.[1] In 1896 he persuaded a group of friends to finance the Zanesville Roofing Tile Company, which he organized and directed. Four years later, however, the firm made a drastic shift from producing clay roof tiles to both art pottery forms and commercial pottery, which were becoming the staple products of a number of Zanesville potteries.

The plant employed approximately one hundred workers, most of whom were temporarily laid off when the first of two disastrous fires swept through the plant in 1901. The founders immediately constructed a new plant, and the Zanesville Art Pottery increased its exposure and enhanced both its reputation and its sales through an exhibition at the 1904 Louisiana Purchase Exposition in St. Louis. Included in the designs of the young firm was a hand-painted art pottery form called La Moro, which shared many similarities with Samuel Weller's high-glaze Louwelsa line. In addition the firm also "produced . . . a matt-ground ware with light-colored slip decorations, similar to Owens' matt Utopian and Clifton's Tirrube."[2]

1. Elisabeth Cameron, *Encyclopedia of Pottery & Porcelain: 1800–1960* (New York: Facts on File Publications, 1986), p. 297.
2. Paul Evans, *Art Pottery of the United States* (New York: Charles Scribner's Sons, 1974), p. 341.

By 1910, as reported by *The Clay Worker*,[3] the work force at the Zanesville Art Pottery had increased to approximately two hundred persons, but another major fire forced the firm to rebuild once again. In 1920, however, Samuel Weller purchased the company and its plant and switched its line of production to that of Weller ware.[4]

Selected Prices

Jug: brown and white glaze, 10″, *$25–$35*.

Vase: Landsun, 11″, *$90–$100*.

Vase: Sheenware, with flared lip, 9″, *$30–$40*.

3. Paul Evans, *Art Pottery of the United States* (New York: Charles Scribner's Sons, 1974), p. 341.

4. Ralph and Terry Kovel, *The Kovels' Collectors Guide to American Art Pottery* (New York: Crown Publishers, 1974), p. 326.

PART 3

Metalware, Lighting, and Accessories

Evaluating Arts and Crafts Metalware

□

Robert C. Rust and Edythe "Kitty" Turgeon

with

Bruce Johnson

Robert C. Rust and Edythe "Kitty" Turgeon are partners in the Roycroft Associates Design Studios & Gallery and the Roycroft Gift Shop, located in the original Copper Shop on the National Historic Landmark Roycroft campus in East Aurora, New York. Kitty was one of the founders of the Roycrofters At Large Association, and both she and Robert Rust have served as presidents of that organization. Former owners of the Roycroft Inn, both have lectured and written extensively on the Arts and Crafts movement. They presently live in the National Historic Landmark Alexis J. Fournier House, an Arts and Crafts-style bungalow located in the landmark district of East Aurora.

"THE BOYS IN THE Copper Shop were a rough and ready group," according to Rix Jennings, artist and Roycrofter, whose career has spanned both eras of production at the East Aurora, New York, shops. "Guess they just had to laugh and kid with one another in a display of energy that seems to be incorporated in the pieces themselves."

The Roycroft Copper Shop was perhaps the largest and certainly the best known of the many Arts and Crafts–era metalsmithing shops that emerged in the first part of the twentieth century. Distinguishing between quality craftsmanship and shoddy work, however, involves more than just turning an item upside down to locate the maker's mark. All of the Arts and Crafts–era shops, from Roycroft and Tookay to Craftsman, Benedict, Van Erp, and the regional mechanical training high schools, produced superb examples of metalwork; and just as a painting by Picasso or Van Gogh can range from $50,000 to $5 million, pieces of Arts and Crafts metalware can range from $5 to $50,000 in value.

Nearly all Arts and Crafts metalware can be evaluated by using a few guidelines. The artist or craftsman who made each piece is probably, though not always, the major reference point. During this era there were many craftsmen and craftswomen working at home in their attics or cellars producing work equal to that of some of the best formal studios. Many of their pieces were marked, though some may not yet have been identified. Knowing what each of the important shopmarks looks like is a valuable tool to have when deciding to invest any sum of money on a vase or pair of bookends. But even the best, including Roycroft, Kipp, and Craftsman, occasionally produced lesser-quality work. We must take into account the fact that many of the larger shops and studios could afford to hire apprentices or journeyman metalsmiths to help in both the production and the finishing processes. In a shop as large as the Roycroft Copper Shop, a core group of approximately ten metalsmiths would have been assisted by a large number of apprentices over three decades of production. In some instances the work of the apprentices might not be judged worthy of the shop's particular mark but might still be taken home and used, only to be recirculated years later through an estate sale. More often, apprentices would be assigned to simple items, such as letter openers and bookends, where they could learn the trade without hindering production.

An assortment of Arts and Crafts hand-hammered copper-wares: Art Deco–style Roycroft five-inch bookends; Dirk Van Erp warty seven-inch vase; an unsigned nineteen-inch tray; a pair of Gustav Stickley thirteen-inch wall sconces; a seven-inch Roycroft American Beauty vase; a six-inch Roycroft cylinder vase with nickel-silver overlay; a five-piece Roycroft desk set; and a pair of twelve-inch Roycroft candlesticks. *(Photo courtesy of David Rago, Trenton)*

If a low-quality piece with a reputable shopmark surfaces, it may well have been the work of one of the apprentices.

A second consideration is the material that was used. Many shops, concerned only with producing the Arts and Crafts "look," used lighter-weight copper for all of their work. As the interest in the Arts and Crafts movement dwindled after 1915, even the more respected shops began to use lighter and less expensive materials. Experienced collectors have learned that the weight, or "feel," of an early piece will be more substantial than most later pieces. Regardless of when it was made, a quality piece of metalwork will, by its weight alone, stand out from the rest. In time you will develop an intuitive sense for evaluating quality pieces. You will know when you hold a fine piece in your hands, for it will virtually sing to you.

A third consideration in evaluating Arts and Crafts metalware is the finish. Often referred to as the patina of the piece, the finish can have a dramatic effect on the value of any piece of metalware. The patina may have developed over the years since it was made, may have been applied in the finishing room before it was sold, or both. The reddish brown glow of a piece left untouched since 1910 is both the most commonly found and the most popular. Roycroft, Stickley, and Van Erp each had their secret and not so secret formulas for their finishes. One particular form of metalware might not have the same finish applied to it each time; clients could even specify which they preferred, much as car styles and extras are available options today. These studios and shops offered a variety of finishes in an attempt to satisfy, within a certain framework, the tastes and styles of the day.

In some instances the copper was left in its natural state and permitted to darken slowly over the years. More often a deep brown patina was applied to the copper by dipping it in chemical solutions in the finishing rooms. The most popular of the Roycroft patinas was Aurora Brown, described as a "golden red brown finish." The Roycroft finishing rooms also developed several other finishes, including a rarely found blue-bronze patina, a limited line of Italian polychrome pieces featuring a greenish patina in the hammered areas, the more common Sheffield silver-plated wares, and the popular brass-plated copper items. At one time collectors were known to purposely remove the original patina and replace it with one considered more desirable, but today each type of finish has attracted its own group of collectors who value the merits of their particular type of finish.

As interest in Arts and Crafts metalware has grown, it has spurred an interest in duplicating the original patina that has often been destroyed by an enthusiastic, yet uninformed owner. In a few instances the repatination technique has been developed by craftsmen-chemists to such a fine art that even the most experienced collector cannot distinguish between it and an original. In all too many cases the repatination attempt leaves the piece with a mottled, unnatural-appearing patina rather than a uniform one. Distinguishing between the two is important, for even a fine example of repatination work will not be as valuable as an original, untouched example. To illustrate, a vase valued at $300 in its original patina would be worth no more than $225 if it has been repatinated. Nevertheless, had that same piece been polished to a blinding brightness, it might be worth only $75 on the basis of its design alone. For that reason, repatination, like refinishing, can serve a useful purpose, so long as a repatinated piece is both identified as such and priced accordingly.

Many repatinated pieces can be identified on close examination. Experienced collectors have learned to look on the bottoms of pieces they suspect may have been repatinated, for if the bottom has a perfect, unscarred appearance, either the piece was never used or has been recently treated to a chemical bath. In a similar manner, high spots on the outside of the piece should show some evidence of wear. If the piece has a perfect patina, beware; even a seldom-used piece of metalware should show some evidence of having survived for as many as eighty-eight years.

Another consideration in evaluating a piece of Arts and Crafts metalware is the hammering technique. Three different techniques dominated Arts and Crafts production: hand hammering, machine hammering, and no hammering (referred to as "spun copper"). Collectors show a decided preference for the hand-hammered examples that typified early, quality work. Hammering was associated with handcraftsmanship, and the finest pieces of the era are an honest reflection of that association. Cost-conscious companies soon developed a means of achieving the hammered effect without additional hand labor; machines were invented that would produce a uniform hand-hammered effect on a sheet of copper or brass before it was ever turned over to the craftsman. Collectors can determine whether a piece was hand-hammered or machine-hammered by inspecting the planishing marks closely. The machine-hammered marks will be nearly identical in pattern, depth, and dimensions; each hand-hammered mark will be slightly different from the one next to it. To a serious collector the fine difference is crucial.

The spun-copper pieces began appearing as the Arts and Crafts movement started to lose momentum and people began to turn toward yet another style of interior design. Just as

Although unsigned, this twenty-seven-inch Arts and Crafts table lamp demonstrates uniform hammering, a pleasing patina, and a mica shade with riveted struts and rolled rim influenced by Dirk Van Erp. *(Photo courtesy of David Rago, Trenton)*

quickly as pegged joints became associated with outdated furniture, hand-hammered marks were deemed old-fashioned. In an effort to remain current, many shops began offering copper wares in a smooth, unhammered style. Unfortunately, by this time the weight of the copper being used had also been reduced, and the net result was that the spun-copper pieces rarely equaled the quality of workmanship, design, or materials of the earlier examples.

Like furniture from this era, the condition of the metalware is also an important consideration when determining the value of a piece. Normal wear is both expected and appreciated as a sign that a piece has proved beneficial in many people's lives. It is not an indication that a piece should be repatinated, for that process should be reserved only for those pieces that have been polished. Minor dents, like normal wear, will not detract from the value of a piece so long as they do not detract from the beauty as well. Rare and important pieces can actually be seriously damaged in the attempt to remove a minor dent, for the stress applied to the metal can adversely affect the finish, especially if it is an early form of lacquer applied to the patina to retard additional darkening.

One of the areas most difficult to define is that of design. Distinguishing between a piece of pleasing proportion and one that appears somewhat awkward or unnatural is often subjective and always open to debate. To an untrained eye two pieces of furniture, pottery, or metalware may seem nearly identical; however, minor differences in dimension, subtle embellishment, or proportion can push the price of one to astronomical heights while the other may languish on the shelf. Defining what is considered a desirable design comes from experience, most notably from studying pieces illustrated in catalogs and sold at auctions, where prices and designs can be compared. If certain forms emerge as more valuable than others with a similar patina, wear, material, and workmanship, the reason may be the design.

Rarity always plays a role in the determination of the value of any piece. Roycroft letter openers were mass-produced, even if by hand, and remain one of the least expensive of all of their wares. The small number of lamps that featured a collaboration between Dard Hunter and Karl Kipp in 1909 and 1910 are considered extremely rare and for that reason, along with their excellent design, are considered the most valuable of their kind. Determining which pieces are rare, however, is difficult, for production figures have never been discovered that would indicate exactly how many examples of each particular design were produced. Instead, to judge the relative rarity of a piece, collectors have to rely on the number of times that particular form becomes available. When an item appears for the first time at a major auction, it is bound to stir excitement in a crowd of bidders; but if the resulting publicity draws out a dozen more examples the following year, then the first price may never be equaled, let alone surpassed. The rarity factor is often overlooked in the rush by collectors toward a piece with a popular shopmark. This was illustrated recently at a New York auction, when two very similar but not identical designs were offered in two copper vases. The first was made by Karl Kipp in the early days of his Tookay Shop after he left the Roycroft in 1912 to become an entrepreneur craftsman for four years. The second was a similar design but was produced in the Roycroft Copper Shop sometime after 1915. This later Roycroft piece brought three times what was paid for the Kipp piece, for no other

More Arts and Crafts metalwares: a five-inch Dirk Van Erp copper bowl; a seven-inch Roycroft American Beauty vase; a thirteen-and-one-half-inch Dirk Van Erp inkwell; a four-inch letter holder from Albert Berry's Crafts Shop in Seattle; a Roycroft calender/note pad; a three-inch Dirk Van Erp matchbox holder; and a pair of Roycroft six-inch leather bookends. *(Photo courtesy of D. J. Puffert, Sausalito)*

reason than the lack of knowledge on the part of the bidders. The Kipp piece may well have been the master's own effort, rather than a production piece from a large and recognizable shop. In the future, as more information becomes available to more collectors, the Kipp piece may well turn out to have been the bargain of that day.

Collecting metalware of the Arts and Crafts era may perhaps be the most enjoyable of all the areas discussed in this study, for it has been widely distributed, both in its day and ours; much of it remains both inexpensive and practical; and it complements the other areas. Even if your interest is only in books from this period, hand-hammered bookends display them as they were meant to be seen. The metalware blends well with the art pottery of this time, especially that from shops such as Marblehead, Walrath, Grueby, and Hampshire, which adopted Arts and Crafts designs. And the heavy, often dark furniture of Roycroft, Stickley, and Limbert appreciates the glow of copper, brass, or silver to enliven its otherwise staid appearance. The complete Arts and Crafts collector is the well-balanced collector: furniture, pottery, metalware—and information.

Gorham Manufacturing Company

TRADE-MARK.

STERLING

Shopmarks:
Outline of a lion, an anchor, and the letter *G*, all beneath outstretched eagle and word *MARTELÉ*

Principal Contribution:
Hand-hammered silver line with Art Nouveau embellishments

Founder:
Jabez Gorham
Born: 1792   Died: 1869
John Gorham
Born: 1840   Died: 1898
Founded: 1831   Closed: current

Studios and Salesrooms:
Gorham Manufacturing Company
Providence, Rhode Island
1831–current

"A very fine ground effect is produced by finishing the article
first, then peaning it in regular courses and then chasing devices
in the rough surface, smoothing the chased parts. The effect has
a remarkably fine appearance."

—*Diary of a Silversmith*
1876[1]

When twenty-one-year-old John Gorham joined his father, Jabez
Gorham, in 1841 in what was then to be known for a brief period

1. Charles H. Carpenter, Jr., *Gorham Silver: 1831–1981*, (New York:
Dodd, Mead & Co., 1982), p. 108.

of time as Gorham & Son, he brought a desire for innovative expansion to the stable, conservative business foundation that his father had established. Against the advice of his father, who retired in 1847 rather than risk his savings in the firm's expansion, John Gorham borrowed the money to build a new factory, increased both his work and sales force, and expanded their line from silver spoons to hollowware, such as tea sets, bowls, and presentation pieces. Over the course of the next five decades Gorham was to encounter numerous setbacks, but each proved to be but a temporary hindrance to his goal—to make Gorham silver the most respected in the country.

One of his first important designers was George Wilkinson (1819–1894), who created some of Gorham's most impressive high Victorian styles before his death. His place was then taken by William C. Codman (1839–1921), who was responsible for Gorham's entry into the Art Nouveau and Arts and Crafts styles of silver production. George Wilkinson had helped raise Gorham to where its chief competitor was Tiffany and Company, but it was Tiffany who captured world attention in 1876 with the introduction of hand-hammered silver. As author Charles H. Carpenter, Jr., observed, "The idea of leaving a hammered surface on a piece of silverware is a complete reversal of the traditional idea of smoothing out hammer marks in a finished object. Hammer marks of various kinds have been left on silverware since the beginnings of the craft, but it was usually thought that such marks were an indication that the piece had not been quite finished."[2] Although Tiffany acknowledged his indebtedness to the Japanese for the idea of hand-hammering, the fame was still Tiffany's. Gorham quickly introduced its own style of hammering, which differed from that of Tiffany; whereas Tiffany hammering appears more uniform and controlled, Gorham silver reveals the freedom given each silversmith to select the size and pattern of hammering deemed appropriate to his particular piece.

By 1877, when the Arts and Crafts movement was still more than twenty years away, silversmiths across the country had

2. Charles H. Carpenter, Jr., *Gorham Silver: 1831–1981* (New York: Dodd, Mead & Co., 1982), p. 108.

adopted the hammering technique introduced by Tiffany. The emergence of the Arts and Crafts movement found an audience philosophically receptive to hand-hammered metalware, and as Carpenter points out, "the hammered surfaces were not only beautiful in the way they broke up light into glittering reflections, they were also practical. Hammered silver didn't show finger marks as easily as plain, highly polished silver."[3]

Although the hand-hammered effect is most often associated with the Arts and Crafts movement, Gorham's first ventures into this technique were inspired by the Art Nouveau style. In 1890 the new Gorham Manufacturing plant was opened, and the company entered into a period of continued artistic and financial achievement. Although not considered at the time as important as their other projects, in 1893 Gorham experimented with applying silver overlay on Rookwood vases and ewers. The silver was not signed and the project was not continued, making those surviving examples extremely valuable today.

In 1896 William Codman introduced what was to later be named Martelé (French for "hand-hammered") silver. The line was put into full production by 1900, reflecting Gorham's decision to "take a direction toward expensive, prestigious, hand-made silverwares . . . a direct outgrowth of the English Arts and Crafts movement."[4] But while most other silversmithing firms were executing Colonial Revival forms in the hand-hammered Arts and Crafts technique, William Codman's craftsmen at Gorham applied the same technique to the Art Nouveau style. Although the Gorham factory was the most advanced of its kind, the Martelé line was made entirely by hand. Hammering was subtle, and a mild oxidation chemical was applied to highlight the carvings.

The Gorham Martelé line garnered numerous awards at the 1904 St. Louis Exposition, but as the Arts and Crafts movement progressed, desire for their "floral and naturalistic imagery . . .

3. Charles H. Carpenter, Jr., *Gorham Silver: 1831–1981* (New York: Dodd, Mead & Co., 1982), p. 108.
4. Ibid., p. 223.

The nine-inch silver Gorham pitcher is decorated with a chased poppy and wild flower design and marked Martelé; the silver plate (11″ × 9″) is also signed Martelé and features an Art Nouveau motif. *(Photo courtesy of Robert W. Skinner, Boston)*

in the French Art Nouveau design"[5]—even in a hand-hammered technique—began to falter. By 1912 the line had been discontinued except for a few special commissions. William Codman, who personally designed the vast majority of the Martelé pieces, retired in 1914 at the age of seventy-five. The Gorham company responded with a number of new designs, including an Art Deco line, and has enjoyed continued success.

Selected Prices

Centerpiece: Martelé sterling silver, oval form with raised, shaped edge with chased anemones and bud border with swag stems on scrolled raised foot, mongrammed interior, 4″ × 13″ × 11″, $2000–$2250.

Cigarette holders: beaded rim over band of chased hands

5. Wendy Kaplan, ed., *The Art That Is Life: The Arts and Crafts Movement in America, 1875–1920* (Boston: Museum of Fine Arts, 1987) p. 156.

holding cigars in repeating design, angled bowl on pedestal fitting into scored marble base, silver hallmarked, 4″, *$210–$235.*

Inkwell: #2342 Martelé sterling silver, square lid with leaves and poppies on oval form, with pen tray with vines on raised S-curve feet, 6″ × 11″, *$2000–$2250.*

Pot: #9988 Martelé sterling silver, bud finial on fluted hinged lid, elongated lobed neck, spout and curved handle on sectioned melon-shape base, chased with violets and buds, raised scroll foot, 11″, *$2000–$2250.*

THE JARVIE SHOP

Jarvie

Shopmark:
Script signature JARVIE or MADE BY THE JARVIE SHOP

Principal Contributions:
Candlesticks and lanterns, hand-hammered bowls, trays, desk sets, and accessories

Founder:
Robert R. Jarvie

Born: 1865   Died: 1941
Founded: 1904   Closed: ca. 1920

Studios and Salesrooms:
The Jarvie Shop
Chicago
1904–ca. 1920

"Determined to succeed—being a Scotchman—Mr. Jarvie purchased sheet iron and rivets, and at a temporary work bench set up in one corner of the dining-room of his apartment, began his serious work as a craftsman. Only the angels who hover above the earnest arts and crafts workers can tell why he was not driven forth from that building by the irate tenants below, when nightly the sound of his hammer was persistently heard."

—*The Craftsman*
1903[1]

When Robert Jarvie passed away in 1941 at the Scottish Old People's Home outside Chicago, he may well have considered his venture into metalsmithing a failure. Like so many of the craftsmen whose shops—furniture, pottery, and metalware—flourished during the reign of the Arts and Crafts movement, he was unable to survive the swing in public tastes that coincided with World War I.

Jarvie was a thirty-five-year-old Department of Transportation official for the city of Chicago when he entered two simple iron lanterns in a 1900 Arts and Crafts Society exhibition. They and several subsequent candlesticks displayed at the Art Institute show in 1903 attracted the attention of both the press and the public, prompting *The Craftsman* to comment that "one has but to visit the department and the so-called art stores crowded with impossible creations of metal, gauze, silk, beads and paper, in order to appreciate the quiet but satisfying beauty of Mr. Jarvie's lampshades. The motive in all Mr. Jarvie's work is utility and simple beauty rather than a striving for striking effects."[2]

By 1904 Jarvie had received enough encouragement and commissions to leave a secure future with the city and open the Jarvie Shop in the Fine Arts Building in downtown Chicago. Much of his early work consisted of iron lanterns with horn shades (procured from the nearby stockyards) and candlesticks cast from brass or copper and "brush polished, a

1. "An Appreciation of the Work of Robert Jarvie," *The Craftsman* (December 1903), p. 272.
2. Ibid., pp. 274–275.

A pair of twelve-and-one-half-inch copper candlesticks made by Robert Jarvie ranks among his most respected work for their delicate balance of proportion and form. *(Photo courtesy of Christie's, New York)*

process which leaves the metal with a dull glow."[3] As the observer from *The Craftsman* went on to describe, "Some pieces are cast in bronze and their unpolished surfaces are treated with acids which produce an exquisite antique green finish."[4]

The "Candlestick Maker," as he was soon called, designed a number of "slender candlesticks which so fluidly glided between a finely proportioned base and socket,"[5] but he was unable to meet the growing demand for his work. In addition to his famous candlesticks and lanterns, he and a pair of young apprentices were kept busy producing a number of related copper and brass accessories, including inkwells, bowls, smoking sets, trays, bookends, and wall sconces. By 1910 Jarvie had widened his

3. "An Appreciation of the Work of Robert Jarvie," *The Craftsman* (December 1903), p. 273.

4. Ibid.

5. Sharon Darling, *Chicago Metalsmiths* (Chicago: Chicago Historical Society, 1977), p. 55.

scope to include silver and gold, which led to a number of commissions for hand-hammered silver trophies, engraved silver pitchers and punch bowls, and a line of silver tea sets in the Colonial style of Paul Revere.

Despite glowing reviews, such as one in *The Craftsman* declaring that "the graceful outlines and soft lustre of the unembellished metal combine to produce dignity as well as beauty,"[6] by 1920 Jarvie was forced to close his shop and take a job as a salesman for one of Chicago's popular silver firms. Nearly seventy years later all of the work of Robert Jarvie is actively sought by Arts and Crafts collectors. Especially prized are matched pairs of copper, brass, or silver-plated candlesticks, although even individual candlesticks attract a great deal of attention from Arts and Crafts collectors, for, as one reviewer noted in 1903, "the possessor of one of the Jarvie candlesticks must feel that nothing tawdry or frivolous can be placed by its side."[7]

Selected Prices

Production at Jarvie's shop remained limited, thus examples of his work are considered both rare and, in many cases, extremely valuable. While candlesticks are the most often discovered examples of his work, the difference between a $300 pair of brass candlesticks and a $3,000 pair of similar-appearing candlesticks is too subtle to be described in this study. As in all metalwork, style, patina, and rarity are the determining factors in evaluating Jarvie's work. Advanced collectors should be consulted before buying or selling important Jarvie pieces.

6. "An Appreciation of the Work of Robert Jarvie," *The Craftsman* (December 1903), p. 273.
7. Ibid., pp. 273–274.

THE KALO SHOP

Shopmarks:
(Early) Word KALO
(Later) Words HAND BEATEN or HAND WROUGHT AT
THE KALO SHOP(S)/STERLING/CHICAGO and/or NEW
YORK and/or PARK RIDGE[1]

Shopmark Dating Key:
PARK RIDGE (1905–1914), NEW YORK (1914–1918), HAND
BEATEN (1905–1914), HAND WROUGHT (after 1914)[2]

Principal Contributions:
Copper and silver bowls, trays, desk sets, jewelry, and silver
dining ware

Founder:
Clara P. Barck
Born: 1868   Died: 1965 (retired 1940)
Founded: 1900   Closed: 1970

Studios and Salesrooms:
Kalo Shop
Chicago
1900–1970

New York (salesrooms only)
1914–1918

1. For more information on dating Kalo works, see Sharon Darling, *Chicago Metalsmiths* (Chicago: Chicago Historical Society, 1977), p. 48.
2. Wendy Kaplan, ed., *The Art That Is Life: The Arts and Crafts Movement In America, 1875–1920* (Boston: Museum of Fine Arts, 1987), p. 279.

This Kalo tea set relies on the ribbing in the body of the teapot, cream pitcher, and sugar bowl for its decoration. Insulators on the handles and finial are of ivory. The scalloped tray measures nineteen and one-half inches by twelve inches. *(Photo courtesy of Robert W. Skinner, Boston)*

"Beautiful, Useful, and Enduring"

—The Kalo Shop motto

What eventually grew to become Chicago's most prolific source of handmade silver tableware began in 1900 as thirty-two-year-old Clara Barck's small leather shop on Dearborn Street. From the beginning one of her intentions was to establish a business that would both teach and train young women interested in arts and crafts, and when she married metalsmith George S. Welles in 1905, the "Kalo girls" soon had the opportunity to add metalwork and jewelry to their skills.

While their early work concentrated on copper bowls, trays, and desk sets, in addition to jewelry, Clara Welles soon expanded their small but growing operation into handmade silverwork. Simple bowls, candlesticks, tea and sugar sets, pitchers, and flatware in the current Arts and Crafts style featuring a hammered surface found a number of ready buyers, even long after the fervor had cooled. As Sharon Darling observed in her detailed study, "A few pieces of Kalo hollowware made before 1914 displayed flaring side handles and were set with stones in the manner favored by Charles R. Ashbee and other silversmiths of the British Arts and Crafts movement. Such designs were soon abandoned, however, in favor of soft curves which gave objects a gently rounded look."[3]

As the firm's reputation for quality grew, the staff was besieged with applications from aspiring silversmiths, both male and female. At any given time workers in the shop would consist of students, apprentices, and trained employees, many of whom later established their own silver shops in Chicago. Awards and recognition soon followed, and their fame, both artistic and popular, spread across the country. While many of their popular styles were continued for several years, the "substantial handwrought hammer-textured silverware designed by Mrs. Welles in plain, paneled, and fluted shapes, infrequently ornamented with chasing, was consistently expressive of the metal and revealed subtle shifts in styles and tastes."[4]

Clara Barck Welles retired in 1940 and in 1959 gave the Kalo Shops to four of her loyal employees.

Selected Prices

Bowl: wide hammered-copper form with curled edge, silvered interior, 3″ × 9″, *$150–$175*.

Bowl: copper form with silver wash, 2″ × 5″, *$100–$125*.

Bowl: #20H, sterling silver, three indentations around top, 3″ × 4″, *$200–$225*.

Bowl: #P12M, hand-hammered silver, linear design around top, 2″ × 6″, *$200–$225*.

3. Sharon Darling, *Chicago Metalsmiths* (Chicago: Chicago Historical Society, 1977), p. 45.

4. Wendy Kaplan, ed., *The Art That Is Life: The Arts and Crafts Movement in America, 1875–1920* (Boston: Museum of Fine Arts, 1987), p. 279.

Bowl: sterling silver, showing a conventionalized repoussé design repeated five times, 3″ × 4″, *$300–$350.*

Box, stamp: sterling silver, ebonized fruitwood finial with beaded base on squat cylindrical form, with applied initials, 2″ × 2″, *$150–$175.*

Cup, child's: silver with two embossed ducks on one side, applied curved handle, 3″ × 4″, *$175–$200.*

Ice bucket: with liner, octagonal form tapering to footed base, corresponding liner with tab handles and pierced bowl, 5″, *$600–$700.*

Ice tongs: sterling silver, simple handle with cut-corner detail and a chased rib border, shaped pierced bowls, 8″, *$150–$175.*

Pitcher: sterling silver, short neck with rolled rim on decagonal body, squared hollow handle, bright finish, 9″, *$600–$700.*

Pitcher: sterling silver, paneled octagonal cylindrical form slightly indenting to a molded base, raised flat spout, rolled rim, square hollow handle, 9″, *$650–$750.*

Spoon, serving: sterling silver, painted bowl with long, flaring handle, embossed *Y* at the handle end, 14″ × 1″, *$100–$125.*

Spoon and bowl: sterling silver, #7, 10″ long, *$100–$125.*

Tea set: tall teapot with ribbed body, ribbed creamer and sugar bowl, platform bases, large oval scalloped tray, ivory handle and finial, 19″ × 12″, *$2000–$2250.*

Tray, serving: silver, circular, with attached center ring, 11″, *$250–$275.*

Tray: #3, sterling silver, hand-hammered, three indentations around top in clover leaf shape, 6″, *$100–$125.*

Tray: serving, sterling silver, with three lobes on each end, 5″ × 14″, *$325–$375.*

KARL KIPP
(The Tookay Shop)

This ad first appeared in *The Craftsman* magazine in 1912, displaying the Tookay shopmark in the upper corners. The lower ad is indicative of the bond formed between the two former Roycrofters.

Shopmark:
The initials *KK* (first one reversed) enclosed in a circle

Principal Contributions:
Hand-hammered copper bowls, vases, and accessories

Founder:
Karl Kipp

Born: ca. 1881   Died: undetermined
Founded: 1911   Closed: 1915

Studios and Salesrooms:
Roycroft Copper Shop
East Aurora, New York
1908–1911
1915–1931

Tookay Shop
East Aurora, New York
1911–1915

"The rare coloring of these pieces adds to their individuality and charm."

—Tookay advertisement,
The Craftsman, 1912[1]

Predicting both the artistic and commercial success of Karl Kipp's metal designs would have been difficult in 1908. The twenty-seven-year-old banker had left his job and moved his family to East Aurora, New York, where he asked to work in one of the craft shops in Elbert Hubbard's Roycroft colony of artisans.[2] Hubbard first assigned Kipp to the bookbindery, which had been in operation since before the turn of the century, as Hubbard's primary interest always had been and continued to be publishing. While Hubbard's own skills lay in his flowery style of persuasive writing and speaking, he was quick to recognize and promote talented individuals. By 1908 many metalshops—from Gustav Stickley's Craftsman Shops outside nearby Syracuse to Arthur J. Stone's silversmiths in Gardner, Massachusetts—were producing hand-hammered silver, copper, and brass wares, but Hubbard's small metalshop had grown only to where it was producing copper pulls for their limited line of furniture and trim for their doors and interiors. Hubbard soon realized that Kipp had a natural sense for design and appointed him head of the Roycroft Copper Shop. From the bookbindery Kipp brought Walter Jennings, and the two men set about reorganizing and expanding the metalsmith operation at Roycroft.

1. "Craftsman Advertising Department," *The Craftsman* (September 1912).
2. For more information see Roycroft entries under Metalware and Furniture, pp. 482 and 103, respectively.

With no prior experience and no one in East Aurora to train him, Kipp demonstrated a remarkable natural talent for design. From the very beginning his work reveals a familiarity with the designs of the Vienna Secessionists, led by Josef Hoffmann, whose work was illustrated in current magazines and art books that Elbert Hubbard subscribed to and encouraged his craftsmen to read. Within a year the Roycroft Copper Shop was able to release a catalog of the wares they had made available; what is striking about some of these early designs is their advanced degree of sophistication: Kipp had incorporated cut-out squares into geometric motifs reflective of Josef Hoffmann's designs as fluently as a craftsman who had worked with metalwares for several years rather than for only a matter of months.

In 1909 Dard Hunter returned from a sabbatical in Vienna and met Kipp for the first time. Hunter had become a Roycrofter in 1903 but was away from his duties in the book-design and stained-glass departments studying in Europe when Kipp arrived in East Aurora. The two became good friends and together designed and created a number of unique lamps and lighting fixtures. Their collaboration in the Roycroft shops was brief, however, for Hunter left in early 1910, but not before he had added to Kipp's education in modern design. Subsequent issues of *The Fra* magazine introduced metalwares with square silver overlay and candlesticks on chamfered squares or rectangular bases that became standard in Roycroft production for several years.

The Roycroft Copper Shop grew rapidly under Kipp's leadership, but in 1911 he and his first assistant, Walter Jennings, left the Roycroft campus to form the Tookay Shop a short distance away. The reasons for their sudden departure have never been made clear; the two men may have differed with Elbert Hubbard over the Copper Shop operation or may simply have been convinced that they could duplicate the success of the Roycroft Copper Shop on their own without watching the majority of the profits go to Hubbard.

Whatever the reason, the Tookay Shop was in operation by 1912, when the first advertisements began appearing in *The Craftsman* magazine—a double annoyance, no doubt, to Elbert Hubbard. Kipp's new shopmark, two *K*'s, began appearing on

The buttressed vase (7¾″) found with and without the square silver-nickel overlays has been attributed to Kipp, as has the cylinder vase with the silver-nickel band. However, each of these particular pieces is marked with the Roycroft orb-and-cross, although a buttress vase without the overlay squares was produced and signed with the double-K mark at the Tookay Shop. *(Photo courtesy of David Rago, Trenton)*

his designs, many of which were executed in pewter and silver, perhaps in an attempt to distinguish his new work from that being manufactured in the Roycroft Copper Shop. There the workers he had trained continued to produce copper wares based on his previous designs and stamped with the familiar orb-and-cross. Kipp and Jennings were on their way to establishing a successful business with a sales outlet in New York City when World War I erupted. On May 7, 1915, a German submarine torpedoed the *Lusitania*, sending Elbert and Alice

Hubbard, along with more than one thousand others, to a watery grave. The shock swept through the country and the Roycroft campus. Thirty-two-year-old "Bert" Hubbard assumed control of his father's operation and almost immediately went to Kipp and Jennings to ask that they return to the Roycroft Copper Shop. It is uncertain whether Kipp and Jennings had grown somewhat disillusioned with self-employment or were beginning to feel the effect of the shortage of copper and brass caused by the war effort, but the pair returned that same year.

While Bert Hubbard never pretended to be the charismatic leader his father was, his business sense was just as keen. With Kipp and Jennings back in the Copper Shop, he instituted a national sales campaign for Roycroft metalwares. Rather than limiting sales to visitors to the campus and readers of their publications, Hubbard offered established retail stores across the country the opportunity to sell a wide range of Roycroft products in their showrooms, including books, leather items, and metalwares.[3] As a result, production in the Copper Shop increased dramatically. Kipp continued to create new designs for the staff of nearly thirty-five apprentices and experienced metalsmiths, who churned out thousands of bookends, desk sets, bowls, vases, candlesticks, and ashtrays. Although designers such as Dirk Van Erp criticized the restraint placed on the artistic freedom of the Roycroft metalsmiths, the emphasis remained on the production of uniform, quality metalwares rather than time-consuming experimental designs.

When the Arts and Crafts movement began to give way to new styles in the early 1920s, Kipp responded with a number of new designs. Unfortunately, a reduction in the weight of the copper being used detracted from some of his designs, yet they still reveal a man in tune with the times. Some of Kipp's Art Deco bookends, for instance, preceded those of several of the best known metalware designers of that era. Once the Depression set in, however, it became evident that bankruptcy was inevitable. Sales dropped, and gradually most of the Copper Shop employees were released. Karl Kipp retired from the

3. For a list of the outlets see Charles F. Hamilton, *Roycroft Collectibles* (New York: A. S. Barnes & Co., 1980), pp. 63–67.

Roycroft Copper Shop in the early 1930s and chose not to re-open the Tookay Shop.

Selected Prices

While Roycroft collectors have long known of Karl Kipp, unfortunately the general public, including a large number of Arts and Crafts collectors, has not. As yet, no one has come forth with any biographical information or critical analysis regarding Kipp that would further document his role in Arts and Crafts metalwork design. Although Tookay Shop collectors have their own personal price guides for determining how much they will pay for a particular design, the information and examples necessary to establish a reliable price guide have not yet reached the marketplace. Until they do, collectors will need to evaluate carefully each piece they encounter. At present those pieces with the double-K mark tend to run parallel to the identical Kipp designs bearing the Roycroft orb-and-cross, but the simple fact that the Tookay Shop output remained small, spanning only four years, should ensure that those designs with the double-K mark will soon begin to increase in value at a faster rate.

THE ROYCROFTERS

The straight tail on the *R* and the addition of the word *Roycroft* indicate that this piece was produced after 1915.

Shopmarks:
The letter *R* within a circle topped by a cross[1]
(Pre-ca. 1910) The tail of the letter *R* ends in a tight curl
(Post-ca. 1910) The tail of the letter *R* remains relatively straight
(Post-ca. 1915) Addition of the word *ROYCROFT*

Principal Contributions:
Copper vases, bowls, bookends, desk sets, candlesticks, and lamps

Founder:
Elbert Hubbard
Born: 1856   Died: 1915
Founded: 1895   Closed: 1938

Studios and Salesrooms:
The Roycroft Shops
East Aurora, New York
1895–1938

"Beautiful objects should be owned by the people. They should be available as home embellishments and placed within the reach of all. The Roycroft artists in metal believed this so they designed and created hand-hammered copper vases, trays, bowls, candlesticks, lighting fixtures and a hundred and one other objets d'art—individual pieces of craftsmanship that were lasting, beautiful and worthwhile."

—*Roycroft catalog*
1919[2]

By the year 1909 the Arts and Crafts movement and its principal players were well established in their respective studios and workshops. Names such as Grueby, Stickley, Teco,

---

1. Unsigned pieces, which can be positively identified by using a Roycroft catalog, are the result of a Roycroft tradition in which the staff members were permitted to work on pieces during their free time, so long as those pieces were for use in their own homes. Such pieces, along with apprentice work failing to meet Roycroft standards, would normally not be stamped.

2. Nancy Hubbard Brady, ed., *The Book of the Roycrofters* (East Aurora, NY: House of Hubbard, 1977), p. 10.

Rookwood, Limbert, and Roycroft had grown familiar to the thousands of readers of magazines such as *House Beautiful, Ladies' Home Journal, Studio, Beautiful Homes,* and *The Craftsman.* All were continuing to expand their popular lines, and in East Aurora, Elbert Hubbard was preparing to add yet another dimension to the growing Roycroft production.

For nearly ten years his artisans had produced books, leathercrafts, and oak furniture, much of it embellished with hammered copper pulls and strap hinges created in the small metal shop near the main inn, but metalware production had been hampered by a lack of internal leadership and direction in design. As described in the landmark 1972 exhibition headed by Robert Judson Clark, "Local residents were employed [in the Roycroft shops], but significantly large numbers of people came to East Aurora from across the country to find work. An apprentice system was set up, and workers learned various crafts, migrating from shop to shop. The cultural life included lectures, frequently by Hubbard, concerts and organized sports. While Hubbard wrote, edited his magazines, and made lecture tours, his admirable wife Alice kept the books and supervised the business."[3] Hubbard, although a man of many ideas, was not trained or experienced in the design aspect of either furniture or metalware. Aware, no doubt, of the Craftsman Shops' line of hammered bowls, trays, and lighting fixtures illustrated in Gustav Stickley's catalogs and monthly magazine, Hubbard could not begin large-scale production until he found the man who could provide the designs and organization necessary to compete with Stickley and the growing number of metalsmiths working in the popular Arts and Crafts style.

For Hubbard and the Roycroft shops that man was Karl Kipp, a balding banker who, like many Roycroft converts, had journeyed to East Aurora willing to work in whatever capacity his skills could best be utilized. Kipp arrived in September 1908 and was assigned to the bookbindery but was soon singled out by Hubbard to organize and direct the Roycroft copper shop. From the bookbindery Kipp selected Walter U. Jennings to assist him,

3. Robert Judson Clark, ed., *The Arts and Crafts Movement in America: 1876–1916* (Princeton, NJ: Princeton University, 1972), p. 45.

and by the time the 1910 catalog went to press, the copper shop had begun production on a number of hammered-copper desk sets, a smoker's set, a nut bowl set, candlesticks, and vases. According to Mary Laura Gibbs, "Kipp conceived each design and then turned the prototype over to an assistant, who made the special tools to execute the details more rapidly."[4] Characteristic of these early Kipp designs were small square cutouts, appearing in the handle of the nut spoon, in the letter opener, and in the sides of the smoking set's tray, or a silver square applied to the copper forms.[5]

The year 1909 also marked the return of Dard Hunter (1883–1966) to the Roycroft campus. Hunter, who later emerged as a world authority on papermaking, had been introduced to the book designs of William Morris, not by Elbert Hubbard but by Hunter's father, a small-town Ohio newspaper publisher. Like Kipp, Hunter journeyed to East Aurora to meet and work with Elbert Hubbard but at an earlier age. When the twenty-year-old Hunter arrived in East Aurora in 1903, book design and production at Roycroft was well organized but lacked sophistication. Hubbard's extensive library included a number of current German publications, which influenced Hunter's subsequent Roycroft designs and his decision to journey to Vienna in 1908.

Hunter's early years at Roycroft were also involved with stained-glass design, and "by 1906 he was making windows, lampshades and lighting fixtures of leaded glass for the Roycroft Inn and Shops."[6] Hubbard appointed Hunter head of the stained-glass department at Roycroft and in 1908 encouraged and possibly financed Hunter's sabbatical in Europe. The designer returned in 1909 and immediately set about incorporating much of what he had seen of the work of the Vienna Secessionists into his stained-glass designs. By that time the Roycroft copper shop had been organized by Karl Kipp, undoubtedly much to Hunter's delight, and the pair quickly

4. Robert Judson Clark, ed., *The Arts and Crafts Movement in America: 1876–1916* (Princeton, NJ: Princeton University, 1972), p. 47.

5. Mary Roelofs Stott, *Rebel with Reverence* (Watkins Glen, NY: American Life Foundations, 1984), pp. 66–69.

6. Wendy Kaplan, *The Art That Is Life: The Arts and Crafts Movement in America, 1875–1920* (Boston: Museum of Fine Arts, 1987), p. 168.

collaborated on several lighting fixtures—Hunter designing the stained-glass shades, Kipp taking charge of the bases—which appeared in the 1910 catalog. These rare ceiling and wall fixtures with Kipp's silver squares or cutouts and Hunter's simple geometric glass patterns are among the most valued of all Roycroft production.

Dard Hunter returned to Vienna in 1910 and never worked for Elbert Hubbard again. Karl Kipp continued to manage the copper shop for only one additional year, leaving in 1911 and taking his top assistant, William U. Jennings, with him across the small town of East Aurora to establish, in direct competition with Elbert Hubbard, The Tookay Shop. Kipp's and Jennings's reasons for leaving were not made public, but since Hubbard was never known for being generous with his payroll, financial and family responsibilities and the lure of self-employment may well have been critical factors in their decisions.

As evidence of his organizational abilities, the Roycroft copper shop survived the departure of Karl Kipp and continued to expand production. In 1912 and 1913 the shop executed several hundred ceiling fixtures, table lamps, dresser and desk pulls, and related accessories for the renowned Grove Park Inn outside Asheville, North Carolina. In 1915, however, the world and the Roycroft family of artisans were sticken with the news of the sinking of the *Lusitania*. Elbert and Alice Hubbard were among the more than one thousand travelers who drowned in the North Sea after the precipitous German submarine attack. Their son, Elbert Hubbard II (1883–1970), affectionately called Bert, took overt the Roycroft operation at age thirty-two and immediately persuaded Karl Kipp and Walter Jennings to return to the Roycroft copper shop.

Kipp remained at the Roycroft copper shop until the Depression cut sharply into sales and production. Walter Jennings, who had resigned a secure management position with a knitting mill in 1908 to move his wife and three small children to East Aurora to become a Roycrofter, stayed with Bert and the Roycroft copper shop until 1933. He then worked for approximately seven years with another former Roycroft coppersmith, Arthur Cole, who had left several years earlier to establish his own shop, the Avon Coppersmith, in Avon, New York. In the early 1940s, however, Jennings returned to East Aurora finally to establish his own copper shop.

The Roycroft Shops fell victim to the Great Depression, though formal bankruptcy did not take place until 1938. Over the course of the next forty years a number of unsuccessful owners were able to preserve the key structures on the campus but not without the loss of many of the original Roycroft furnishings. Efforts are continuing today to save the Roycroft Inn and the other buildings of the East Aurora campus; they were furthered by the organization of a group of artisans and Roycroft collectors, historians, and preservationists in 1976 under the name "Roycroft Renaissance." Their Roycroft reproductions and other items designed and produced in the Roycroft spirit are marked with an orb-and-cross similar to the original mark but encompassing a pair of *R*'s to distinguish it clearly from the early mark.

National distribution of Roycroft metalwares was assured in 1915 when Elbert Hubbard II decided to supplement the gift shop and mail order sales with Roycroft displays in established retail stores across the country. The opportunity was immediately grasped by a number of prestigious stores, including Marshall Field in Chicago, Lord & Taylor in New York, and Stix, Baer & Fuller in St. Louis. By 1924 the list of retail outlets had grown to more than 320, with distribution spread to every state in the country.[7] In a move that his father would have appreciated, Elbert Hubbard II did not offer to place the items, which included Roycroft books, leathercrafts, and copper wares, on consignment but instead sold them to the participating store at a 33 percent discount. Any items that failed to sell in the store were eventually reduced in price or given to local employees rather than being returned to East Aurora, thus enabling collectors fifty years later to find examples from the Roycroft Shops in every part of the country.

As Charles Hamilton summarized in his book *Roycroft Collectibles*, "It wasn't until about 1909 that a truly well organized and talented Copper Shop group began turning out the fine

7. Charles Hamilton, *Roycroft Collectibles* (New York: A. S. Barnes & Co., 1980), pp. 63–67.

The Roycroft bookends on the left were designed to display the tooled cover of the standard-size edition of Hubbard's books, while the smaller hammered-copper bookends were intended for the miniature soft-bound editions. The low bowl, the calendar holder, and the curved bookends with decorative riveted trim are characteristic of their production work. The ten-inch-by-twenty-four-inch tray in the background is by Dirk Van Erp. *(Photo courtesy of D. J. Puffert, Sausalito)*

specimens of the craft. But from then on, until the Roycroft folded in 1938, their output was amazingly large for a hand-crafted line. The variety of products grew and grew and the quality was superb. They worked in copper, brass, silver, silver plate, and etched silver and brass."[8] Among the more commonly found Roycroft items are the standard hammered-copper ash-trays and smoking sets (even though Elbert Hubbard campaigned on the Chautauqua circuit against smoking), vases, bowls, and desk accessories. What has failed to ignite any interest in Arts and Crafts collectors are the smooth copper pieces produced after 1920; the silver-plated pieces, some of which are marked "Silverplate" and/or "Sheffield," also have only a small following unless the design of the piece is particularly unique and exciting. Many of the standard copper items were brass-plated, and as a result years of hard use may have worn the plating off the high spots, exposing the bright copper beneath it and reducing its value in the eyes of many collectors.

Among the more desirable of the Roycroft metalwares are bud vases with Steuben glass inserts from the Corning Glass

8. Charles Hamilton, *Roycroft Collectibles* (New York: A. S. Barnes & Co., 1980), p. 58.

Company, as well as Roycroft lamps with Corning's Steuben lampshades. As more and more collectors have attempted to assemble Arts and Crafts room settings, the value of nearly all Roycroft lamps has increased, the only exception, as with all examples, being those pieces that have been polished. Like Stickley's Craftsman Shops, the Roycrofters treated their metalwares either chemically or with heat to produce a patina resembling that found on pieces that have been exposed to the air for several decades. Polishing removes not only the original patina but also the additional patina the piece has acquired since it was first sold. As every experienced Roycroft collector will attest, restoring both patinas—and the value of the piece—is virtually impossible.

Roycroft metalwares remain the most popular of all of the Arts and Crafts shops, for they are attractive, useful, available, and, for the most part, reasonably priced.

Selected Prices

Ashtray: hammered copper, stacking set of three with stylized flower form, 4″, *$40–$50.*

Ashtray: hammered copper with cigarette rest, 1″ × 4″, *$20–$30.*

Ashtray: hammered copper on oak pedestal, copper strap handle on matchbox holder over shallow round bowl, round oak base, 29″, *$150–$175.*

Bookends: hammered copper, tall rectangular form with stylized repoussé flower and tooled border, one open frame, one with full panel, 8″ × 6″, *$75–$95.*

Bookends: hammered copper, semicircular arch on rectangular plate, 3″ × 6″, *$85–$95.*

Bookends: overlapping graduated triangles in copper on brass ground, Art Deco style, 5″ × 4″ × 3″, *$125–$150.*

Bookends: hammered copper with large, heavily embossed poppy on each, 6″ × 5″, *$175–$200.*

Bookends: hammered copper with heavily embossed poppies, brass wash, 5″ × 5″, *$150–$175.*

Bookends: hammered copper with dark patina, floral decoration, 3″ × 3″, *$55–$65.*

Box, cigar: hammered copper, applied medallion with initials on rectangular hinged lid with tooled border, cedar-lined, 2″ × 9″ × 6″, *$200–$225.*

Bowl: hammered copper, wide, deep form in dark brown patina, 5″ × 10″, *$100–$125.*

Bowl with ladle: hammered copper, three-footed form with broad planishing marks, bowl 3″ × 7″, *$200–$225.*

Bowl: hammered copper with brass outer wash, 1″ × 7″, *$55–$65.*

Bowl: hand-hammered copper with brass highlights, 3″ × 6″, *$75–$85.*

Bowl: hammered copper with crimped design top, 3″ × 4″, *$70–$80.*

Bowl: hammered copper, 1″ × 5″, *$30–$40.*

Candlesticks: hammered copper, flattened rim and socket on cylindrical stems and wide floriform bases, pair, 8″, *$90–$115.*

Candlesticks: hammered copper, angled flattened rim and deep socket on cylindrical standard and flattened disk base, pair, 10″, *$100–$125.*

Candlesticks: hammered-copper design with two square rods riveted to a square base, pair, 7″, *$200–$225.*

Candlesticks: hammered copper, each with four feet that continue into long strips to form the body, riveted at top and bottom with circular bobeche, 12″ × 4″, *$500–$600.*

Candlesticks: silver on copper, with bobeches resting on two squared shafts supported by a pyramidal, four-sided base, pair, 8″ × 3″, *$250–$300.*

Crumber: hammered copper with silver wash, two-piece set with stylized decoration, *$20–$30.*

Desk set: five pieces of hammered copper with radially hammered pattern, consisting of a letter holder, calendar holder, letter opener, inkwell, and blotter, 3″ × 5″ × 1″, *$225–$250.*

Desk set: four pieces, hammered bronze and copper with textured honeycomb finish, consisting of inkwell with hinged lid, calendar stand, tray, letter opener, *$175–$200.*

Lamp, desk: #903, hammered copper, round dome with mica panels on square standard and base, 14″, *$250–$300.*

Lamp, desk: ten-sided shape with purple and light green leaded glass, brass base, cylindrical shaft, 19″ × 15″, *$650–$750.*

Lamp, table: hammered copper and leaded glass, conical shade of long, thin triangular channels of green-yellow glass ending in small rectangles of pink and green, broad, circular foot, 20″ × 16″, *$2500–$2750.*

Lamp, desk: hammered-copper helmet shade supported by cylindrical copper shaft, ending in flared circular base, 16″ × 7″, *$300–$400.*

Lamp, table: four-piece hammered-copper base, center shaft, and three legs ending in Greek key feet on triangular platform, three-socket ball connector, with tapering, six-sided mica shade, 17″ × 10″, *$275–325.*

Lamp, desk: hammered copper, wide, domed shade with four straps and band of mica, resting on a flaring cylindrical shaft and broad, circular base, fully riveted, 15″ × 10″, *$1500–$1750.*

Lamp, table: hammered brass and copper, cylindrical shaft and tapering, domed shade in brass and copper, 16″ × 7″, *$350–$400.*

The classic American Beauty vase was produced by the Roycroft-ers for several years and ranged in size from the seven-inch bud vase to a twenty-two-inch model engraved for the Grove Park Inn in Asheville, North Carolina, for which the Roycroft Copper Shop furnished over six hundred pieces of hammered copper in 1913. *(Photo courtesy of David Rago, Trenton)*

Letter opener: hammered copper with curled handle, 7″ $25–$35.

Sconces, wall: hammered copper, arrowhead backs, incorporating candle sockets, pair, 8″, $100–$125.

Smoking set: hammered-copper oval tray, attached match holder, three loose canisters with riveted sides, 14″ × 6″, $300–$350.

Vase: hammered copper with brass wash, heavy-gauge cylindrical, tooled stylized flowers and green stems, 10″ × 3″, $300–$350.

Vase: American Beauty #211, hammered copper, cylindrical neck extending from bulbous base and ending in flared rim, covered with brass-wash patina, 7″, $150–$175.

Vase: American Beauty #210, same as above, 12″, $200–$225.

Vase: American Beauty #201, same as above, 19″, $300–$350.

Vase: hammered copper, cylinder, with four angled, tooled buttresses riveted to the body, nickel-silver square alternating between the top of each buttress, 8″ × 4″, $850–$950.

Vase: hammered copper, with gently closing top, decorated with pierced and applied nickel-silver banded design, 6″ × 3″, $250–$275.

Tray, serving: hammered copper with double handles, 11″ diameter, $85–$95.

Tray: hammered copper, 8″ diameter, $45–$55.

SHREVE & COMPANY

Shopmarks:
(1883–1909) Bee within a shield
(1909–1922) Bell within a box, SHREVE & CO.

Principal Contribution:
Quality hand-hammered silver with applied strapwork

Founder:
George C. Shreve
Born: ca. 1825   Died: 1893
Founded: 1852   Closed: current

Studios and Salesrooms:
Shreve & Company
San Francisco, California
1852–current

"When President Theodore Roosevelt visited San Francisco, the citizens presented him with a 10-inch high golden bear, cast from solid gold from Shreve's."

—Shreve employee[1]

The California Gold Rush of 1848 and statehood two years later attracted thousands of fortune-seekers from across the United States. While most never found the mother lode, they remained to open new business, such as the Shreve jewelry store founded in 1852 by George C. Shreve and his half-brother Samuel in San Francisco. Beginning as a jewelry store rather than a manufacturing operation, Shreve & Company grew to become one of the most successful silversmith operations in the state after 1883. Their output was both substantial and varied, ranging from custom-made flatware, souvenir spoons, and hollowware to platters and tea sets.

When the earthquake of 1906 destroyed most of their plant, it forced Shreve & Company to retool and enabled them to introduce new lines in the popular Arts and Crafts style. Their first catalog after the earthquake revealed a wide variety of silver wares, including a number of flatware patterns. While not generally known for their innovative designs, the Shreve & Company Arts and Crafts silver retained the high standards of quality for which the firm had been known for several decades. Many of their new designs were actually standard silver forms adapted to the Arts and Crafts style by adding strapwork and rivets to the exterior. As one observer noted, "the decorative rivets have their counterpart, occasionally seen on Mission-style

1. Edgar W. Morse, *Silver in the Golden State* (Oakland, CA: Oakland Museum, 1986), p. 17.

This outstanding Shreve silver lamp (19¾″ × 15½″) features six mica panels beneath a scrollwork shade design. The shade and base are both lightly hammered; the monogram *GMC* in relief on the base would seem to indicate it was a commissioned piece. *(Photo courtesy of Christie's, New York)*

furniture, in pegs that serve no structural purpose."[2] The strapwork evokes medieval images that were also mirrored in the strap hinges that Gustav Stickley designed at the Craftsman Shop and that the Roycrofters utilized in East Aurora.

Although Shreve & Company's attempt to fulfill the demand for Arts and Crafts–style silver on the West Coast was not always an artistic success, their high standards of craftsmanship and materials never suffered. By 1968 the firm eventually returned to what it had been over a hundred years earlier—a very successful retail jewelry business.

Selected Prices

Basket: sterling silver, with decorative scalloped handle, and with two engraved and reticulated coats of arms on

2. Wendy Kaplan, ed., *The Art That Is Life: The Arts and Crafts Movement in America, 1875–1920* (Boston: Museum of Fine Arts, 1987), p. 283.

either side of its undulating rim, stemming from an oval base, 8″ × 14″ × 10″, *$500–$550.*

Bowl: sterling silver, wide mouth with beaded rim on round form with applied silver balls, footed base, 5″ × 9″, *$900–$1000.*

Breakfast set: sterling silver, one-pint coffee, creamer, open sugar, and shaped-edge oval tray, cylindrical form flaring at base, straight spout, strapwork borders, *$1000–$1250.*

Creamer and sugar: strap detail around rim, double C-scroll handle on squat bulbous form, 2″ × 4″, *$175–$200.*

Pitcher: sterling silver, with stylized leaf and rivet design, 11″ × 9″, *$450–$550.*

Plate, cake: sterling silver, shaped shallow plate with strapwork edge on cylindrical stem flaring toward domed base, 5″ × 10″, *$250–$300.*

Tray, bread: sterling silver, oval with shaped edge and flat strap border, hammered texture, 14″, *$400–$450.*

STICKLEY BROTHERS

Shopmark:
Model number impressed in metal, generally with STICKLEY BROTHERS paper label

Principal Contribution:
Limited line of hand-hammered copper metalware

Founders:
Albert Stickley
Born: 1862   Died: 1928

John George Stickley
Born: 1871   Died: 1921
Founded: 1891   Closed: ca. 1940

Studios and Salesrooms:
Stickley Brothers, Inc.
Grand Rapids, Michigan
1891–ca. 1940

According to their 1908 catalog, the Stickley Brothers Company, under the leadership of Albert Stickley,[1] offered a line of "Russian hand-beaten copper."[2] Grand Rapids author Don Marek estimates that their metalwork was first introduced in 1904, citing a tray, "probably inspired by English work, as was Gustav Stickley's similar design,"[3] as an example of the commendable work of their metalsmiths. While examples of every item illustrated have not yet surfaced, their catalog depicts a variety of lighting devices, including chandeliers (referred to as "electroliers"), table lamps, candlesticks, and electric sconces. In addition, they offered a number of different umbrella stands, jardinieres, plaques, boxes, pitchers, and desk accessories in copper or brass.

Like their furniture, surviving examples reveal a variety of designs, reflecting influences of both the European Art Nouveau and the English Arts and Crafts styles, and differences in quality of material and workmanship. One theory proposes that the earlier, heavier Stickley Brothers copper pieces were imported from Russia, and the later, lighter, and less commendable examples were made in Grand Rapids, Michigan, in the Stickley Brothers metalshop. Signed examples are not as common as those from the Roycroft and the Craftsman shops; thus,

1. For more information on Albert Stickley and the formation of the company, see the Stickley Brothers entry in the Furniture section, p. 121.
2. *Quaint Furniture: Arts and Crafts* (1908: reprint, New York: Turn of the Century Editions, 1981), p. 5.
3. Don Marek, *Arts and Crafts Furniture Design: The Grand Rapids Contribution, 1895–1915* (Grand Rapids, MI: Grand Rapids Art Museum, 1987), p. 52.

While the cane isn't copper, the twenty-six-inch Stickley Brothers umbrella stand is. The riveted rim and flared base, plus the embossed sphere on each of the six panels, makes an attractive, though not inspiring, design. *(Photo courtesy of David Rago, Trenton)*

determining a value is totally dependent on the design, condition, and quality of each individual piece.

Selected Prices

While metalwork bearing the Stickley Brothers paper label is relatively scarce, neither its quality of materials nor its attractiveness of design has stirred much interest on the part of collectors. The earlier, possibly imported copper wares are considered more valuable than their later, domestic wares, but neither has garnered as much attention as any of the other shops discussed in this section. As a general rule, Stickley Brothers metalware of quality and design similar to that of the Roycroft Copper Shop will bear similar values.

GUSTAV STICKLEY
and the
CRAFTSMAN SHOPS

Shopmarks:
Impressed joiner's compass around motto, *Als ik kan*

Principal Contributions:
Copper trays, bowls, desk sets, and lamps

Founder:
Gustav Stickley
Born: 1858   Died: 1942
Founded: 1898   Closed: 1916

Workshops and Salesrooms:
The United Crafts
Eastwood, New York
1898–1904

Craftsman Workshops
Eastwood, New York
New York City
1905–1916

"Having begun with the necessary drawer and door pulls, hinges and escutcheons, done from simple designs which were in harmony with the furniture, it was natural that we should go on with the making of other things along the same lines, as in the

Craftsman scheme of interior decoration and furnishing there is a well-defined place for the right kind of metal work."

—*Gustav Stickley*
1910[1]

Though having professed at one point to personally preferring wood knobs over hand-hammered hardware, Gustav Stickley did not sacrifice any cost when it came to either the hardware on his Craftsman furniture or the copper, brass, and iron accessories his metalsmiths also produced. Without exception, the hardware accompanying Stickley's Arts and Crafts furniture is the best of its genre; of all of the other furniture manufacturers, only the Roycrofters approached the quality of the Craftsman hardware. While L. & J. G. Stickley were content with smaller copper pulls, Charles Limbert and Albert Stickley more often than not purchased mass-produced hardware from the Grand Rapids Brass Company.[2] Although production figures have never come to light, it would appear that the Craftsman Shops output was substantial in comparison with similar operations, though judging by what has surfaced in recent years, they were not as prolific as the Roycrofters, who garnered a steady income from the sale of their metalwork to visitors on the Roycroft campus and in outlets around the country. The Craftsman trays, bowls, lamps, and sconces that have survived, however, reflect the high degree of both materials and craftsmanship invested in each piece.

The Craftsman catalogs of both 1904 and 1910 illustrate the emphasis Stickley placed on lighting fixtures.[3] As America was blowing out candles and flipping on light switches in the first decade of the new century, furniture, metalware, and even

1. *Stickley Craftsman Furniture Catalogs* (New York: Dover Publications, 1979), p. 82.

2. Don Marek, *Arts and Crafts Furniture Design: The Grand Rapids Contribution, 1895–1915* (Grand Rapids, MI: Grand Rapids Art Museum, 1987), p. 63.

3. Stephen Gray, ed., *Collected Works of Gustav Stickley* (New York: Turn of the Century Editions, 1981); also *Stickley Furniture Catalogs* (New York: Dover Publications, 1979).

This impressive copper serving tray is stamped with the Craftsman logo on the reverse and features four pierced handles alternating with four repoussé abstract flower motifs. *(Photo courtesy
of Christie's, New York)*

pottery companies were scrambling to fill the need for electric
lamps and ceiling fixtures. While Stickley's 1904 catalog offered
four styles of copper serving trays, two copper wall plaque designs, and no vases, customers had their choice of no less than
thirty-three different types of lighting fixtures: six using candles, nine dependent on oil, and eighteen electric.

Although Craftsman metalwork might utilize either copper,
brass, or iron, depending on the design, all shared two characteristics that continue to cause confusion years later. First, the
planishing marks made by the metalsmith's hammer were purposely left in the surface. Collectors accustomed to smooth silver and polished brass may have assumed such marks were
evidence of crude, untrained work, but those familiar with the
Arts and Crafts era's attempt to recapture the spirit of medieval craftsmanship realize that the marks were no reflection on
the skill of the coppersmith. Second, metalwork of the period
was treated in the shop to give it a dark patina that normally
would require years of exposure to the air. As Stickley described in *The Craftsman* magazine, "If a very dark finish is
desired, the copper may be heated long enough to turn it black

and then rubbed with the powdered pumice stone, which will brighten the raised places on the metal, leaving the sunken places dark. The tray should not be lacquered as age gives the best possible finish, and this is prevented by lacquering."[4] Owners who have discovered metalwork made during the Arts and Crafts era and who have also incorrectly assumed that the tarnishing was unintentional have caused permanent damage by polishing it. With but rare exception, attempts to repatinate polished metalwork have been less than satisfactory.

The Craftsman Shop's nine-piece copper desk sets that were being offered by 1910 have provided current Arts and Crafts collectors with additional opportunities to purchase a hand-hammered example impressed with the famous joiner's compass mark. While most Craftsman trays, plaques, and rare lighting fixtures are highly coveted collector's items, individual pieces from the desk sets—inkwells, letter openers, letter holders, calendars and pen trays—continue to surface at auctions, flea markets, and antiques shops, where they generally sell for reasonable prices.

Just as he provided furniture plans for the home craftsman, Stickley also published numerous articles in *The Craftsman* magazine illustrating for his readers the basics of metalsmithing. In addition, he also offered to provide sheets of copper or brass, mica for lampshades, and for those who were also building their own Mission oak furniture "the same metal trim which we use ourselves, so that when they make Craftsman furniture in their own workshops from designs which we furnish them, they need not be at a loss for the right metal trim."[5]

In keeping with the Arts and Crafts philosophy of the importance of harmony in the total home environment, Gustav Stickley also introduced a line of Craftsman fabrics: table scarves, window curtains, pillow covers, and centerpieces. Designs included trees, seed pods, lotus plants, zinnias, and geometric patterns. Articles on linens began appearing in *The Craftsman* as

4. "Lessons in Metalwork," *The Craftsman* (October 1907), pp. 101–102.
5. *Stickley Craftsman Furniture Catalogs* (New York: Dover Publications, 1979), p. 82.

The two Arts and Crafts linens in the rear have not been identified, but the forty-seven-inch circular tablecloth at the lower left is a Craftsman pattern. The orange and yellow magnolia petals are applied to an ivory background. The six luncheon napkins are also a Craftsman pattern, with the familiar "china tree" motif in each corner. *(Photo courtesy of David Rago, Trenton)*

early as May 1903 and continued for several years; in addition to offering Craftsman fabrics for sale, Stickley also encouraged his readers to embroider their own appliqué in designs that he illustrated.

Unlike their furniture and metalware, Craftsman linens were not destined to survive several decades of daily use. Examples that can be identified through comparisons with those pictured in his catalogs are extremely rare and have become treasured by modern Arts and Crafts collectors. In their place, collectors display table scarves and centerpieces from unknown sources, many of which may well have been made in private homes by young women, not unlike the practice of china painting a few years earlier. Unidentified Arts and Crafts–style linens are one of the true bargains remaining from this era, for they often remain tucked away in a stack of Victorian linens and lace in cedar chests, antiques shops, and flea market booths. Most can be purchased for between $10 and $50 and add yet another dimension to the furniture, pottery, and metalware of the period.

Selected Prices

Ashtray: #271, hammered-copper form with four repoussé balls, 7″, *$200–$225*.

Candlestick: hammered-copper cylinder set in bowl base, finger grip on cylinder, removable bobeche, 9″, *$750–$850*.

Jardiniere: hammered copper with flared cylindrical body, riveted seams, two handles, repoussé spade motifs, 19″ high, *$1000–$1250*.

Lamp, floor: hammered-copper harp atop oak pedestal with four flared supports at bottom, 57″, *$1250–$1500*.

Lamp, table: hammered-copper base with deep hammering, wicker shade, 25″, *$900–$1000*

Lamp, table: #504, oak and copper base with cloth-lined wicker shade, pyramid base, 23″, *$850–$950*.

Letter opener: hammered copper, scooped top for hand, 11″, *$125–$150*.

Linen: circular tablecloth with magnolia motif in yellow and orange on cream ground, 48″, *$250–$300*.

Plaque, wall: hammered copper with four repoussé spade motifs along border, recessed center, 15″ diameter, *$900–$1000*.

Sconce, wall: #400, hammered-copper bracket with three-link chain, suspended Steuben glass shade, 10″, *$550–$650*.

Tray: circular, hammered copper, no handles, 9″, *$100–$125*.

Tray: circular, hammered copper, no handles, 13″, *$175–$200*.

Tray, serving: circular, hammered copper, with repoussé flower motifs and four pierced handles, 20″, *$650–$750.*

Umbrella stand: #383, hammered-copper cylindrical form with flared rim, double handles, repoussé spade motif, 25″, *$1000–$1250.*

Vase: #26, flared form top and bottom, 11″, *$400–$450.*

ARTHUR J. STONE

Shopmarks:
(Pre-1906) Metalsmith's hammer conjoined with the letter *S*
(1906–1937) Metalsmith's hammer conjoined with the word
STONE
(After 1937) Addition of the letter *H* within a shield

Principal Contribution:
Wide range of domestic silver items in the Arts and Crafts style

Founder:
Arthur J. Stone
Born: 1847　　　Died: 1938
Founded: 1901　　Sold: 1937

Studios and Salesrooms:
Arthur J. Stone, Silversmith
Gardner, Massachusetts
1901–1937

"Pieces . . . are all raised from the flat by hammering except when the parts are too small to make this process practical. The work is designed, directed, and ornamented by Mr. Stone. It is stamped with his mark and also the initial of the hammerer."

—Advertising leaflet
1914[1]

Trained in England as a silversmith and influenced by the writings of John Ruskin and William Morris, twenty-seven-year-old Arthur J. Stone came to America in 1884 and went to work for a number of silver manufacturing firms. In 1901, at the age of fifty-four, Stone's lifelong dream was realized when he opened his own silversmith shop in Gardner, Massachusetts. His work immediately attracted the attention of members of the Boston Arts and Crafts Society, who bestowed numerous awards on Stone, leading to a silver award at the Louisiana Purchase Exposition in St. Louis in 1904. One of his entries, a copper and silver jardiniere, characterized his emerging style with its "curving outline, the faint hammer marks on the surface, and the encircling repoussé wreath of oak leaves and inlaid silver acorns."[2]

While much of his earliest work was in the form of presentation and ecclesiastical silver, as word of his skill spread, Stone had to hire apprentice and journeymen silversmiths to assist him in producing a wide range of domestic silver wares: tea sets, bowls, boxes, trays, and vases. Stone was respected as much as a teacher of young silversmiths as a designer and craftsman; he instituted a profit-sharing plan with his employees and permitted key assistants to add their initials below that of the firm's shopmark on their work.

Stone preferred working with his own designs, opting to incorporate the best elements of earlier styles and techniques into a unique rendition that captured both his philosophy and the spirit of the Arts and Crafts movement. His decoration remained subtle; he preferred not to detract from the form itself.

1. Elenita C. Chickering, "Arthur J. Stone, Silversmith," *Antiques* (January 1986), p. 279.
2. Ibid., p. 278.

This fine assortment of silver demonstrates the high-quality design and workmanship of Arthur J. Stone and two of his contemporaries. The ten-inch and seven-inch pitchers both bear the Stone mark, while the silver, footed fruit bowl is by Georg Jensen; the flared vase is French. *(Photo courtesy of Robert W. Skinner, Boston)*

Some of his most coveted work features gold inlay. Stone's interest in botany is legendary, as he was known to traverse nearby fields and streams in search of new forms with which to embellish his work. His personal involvement with both his clients and their commissions brought them back time and time again.

Arthur Stone suffered a stroke in 1926 but remained active as the firm's chief designer. As a credit to his talent, "the spare, ascetic quality of Stone silver insured his shop's success when Arts and Crafts metalwork styles and textures became unfashionable."[3] The reputation established by Arthur Stone enabled the firm to continue past his death in 1938.

Selected Prices

Bowl: sterling silver, wide-mouthed form with chased band incorporating triangle and scroll medallion on flared foot, 5″ × 8″, $1000–$1250.

3. Wendy Kaplan, ed., *The Art That Is Life: The Arts and Crafts Movement in America, 1875–1920* (Boston: Museum of Fine Arts, 1987), pp. 282–283.

Bowl: sterling silver, fine-lobed round form with triple rib border, 1″ × 8″, $200–$250.

Bowl: copper, wide mouth on squat bulbous form, designed with tooled scroll feather and loop design, 3″ × 5″, $650–$750.

Box, pill: sterling silver, straight-sided oval form, 1″ × 2″, $150–$175.

Dish: ivory finial on rounded square cover fitting into corresponding lower half, 4″ × 7″, $425–$475.

Napkin ring: sterling silver, chased and openwork decoration with berries and leaves, 2″, $100–$125.

Pepper shaker: baluster form with urn finial on diamond-patterned cover, rib detail at shoulder, 4″, $150–$175.

Pitcher: sterling silver, flat molded rim with curved lip on wide mouth, scroll handle, squat body swelling toward bulbous base, ring foot, 7″, $700–$800.

Pitcher: sterling silver, molded curved rim in ribbed pear-shaped body and flared molded base, hollow curved handle, 10″, $1000–$1250.

Platter: sterling silver, molded rim, oval form with shaped ribbed inner edge, 18″, $750–$850.

Platter: sterling silver, molded rim, oval form with shaped ribbed inner edge, 16″, $400–$500.

Spoon: serving, antique pattern, 9″, $100–$125.

Spoon: martini, antique pattern, 12″, $85–$100.

Tray: sterling silver, molded wavy edge on oval form with stylized pad feet, 5″, $300–$350.

TIFFANY STUDIOS

**TIFFANY STUDIOS
NEW YORK**

Shopmark:
Impressed TIFFANY STUDIOS / NEW YORK

Principal Contributions:
Stained-glass windows, glassware, lamps, and metal accessories

Founder:
Louis Comfort Tiffany

Born: 1848	Died: 1943
Founded: 1902	Closed: 1938

Studios and Salesrooms:
Louis C. Tiffany & the Associated Artists
New York
1879–1885

Tiffany Glass Company
New York
1886–1902

Tiffany Studios
New York
1902–1938

"Louis Comfort [Tiffany's] relative avoidance of silver as an art
material may have had a psychological implication—perhaps one
that is almost too obvious. His father and his father's firm were
world famous for their silverware, and it would have only been

natural for him to want to make it on his own as an artist—in another field."

—*Charles H. Carpenter, Jr.*[1]

Louis C. Tiffany was raised in a world of riches—most notably of silver. His father, Charles Lewis Tiffany (1812–1902), was well on his way to having created an empire made of silver and jewels when Louis was born. As a young man he traveled extensively and studied art in Europe, returning in 1879 to establish a popular interior decorating firm that was hired in 1883 to furnish a portion of the White House for President Chester A. Arthur. Tiffany continued to travel and to explore new avenues of artistic expression. In Paris he was enthralled by the work of Emile Gallé and became close friends with Samuel Bing; on his return to New York he redirected his focus and by 1896 had introduced both his famous stained-glass lamps and his line of *favrile* (handmade) glass.

Many of the bases for his decorative stained-glass shades were purchased from art pottery firms, most notably Grueby but also Wheatley and Hampshire. The majority, however, were of bronze, cast in an Art Nouveau style. In 1902, on the death of his father, Louis C. Tiffany was named vice-president and artistic director of Tiffany & Company, which had continued to excell in Victorian silver. That same year the name of the Tiffany Glass Company was changed to Tiffany Studios to reflect their wide range of production. The Tiffany fortune had been built on the carriage trade, but the intent of Tiffany Studios was the "mass production of beautiful household objects that brought affordable art into the middle class house."[2]

While Tiffany experimented with art pottery[3] and continued to produce stained-glass lamps, his line of *favrile* glass

1. Charles H. Carpenter, Jr., *Tiffany Silver* (New York: Dodd, Mead & Co., 1978), p. 50.
2. Wendy Kaplan, ed., *The Art That Is Life: The Arts and Crafts Movement in America, 1875–1920* (Boston: Museum of Fine Arts, 1987), p. 152.
3. For more information see Tiffany Pottery, p. 418.

The twelve-inch circular tray, the bronze inkwell, and the brass planter were produced by Tiffany Studios and feature their characteristic stylized decorations. The Roycroft desk set provides a contrast in the styles of the two firms. The small desk lamp is unmarked. *(Photo courtesy of D. J. Puffert, Sausalito)*

overshadowed all phases of his expanding operation during the first decade of the twentieth century. Tiffany's interest in metalware was a complete contrast—in both style and materials—to that of Tiffany & Company. Silver production at Tiffany Studios was restricted to special commissions, and even then the intent of the decoration and subtle hammering was to reduce the traditional mirrorlike surface of the silver. Metalware production at Tiffany Studios centered on bronze, often in combination with glass. Small desk lamps, desk accessories, boxes, and bowls in a wide range of reasonably priced styles comprised the majority of their metalware production. Motifs ranged from abstract Art Nouveau to Egyptian and American Indian designs to natural forms, including dragonflies, flowers, and plants.

Louis C. Tiffany's involvement in Tiffany Studios declined after 1919, but he continued to experiment with his favorite medium—stained glass—until the studios closed in 1938.

Selected prices

Bowl: bronze, shallow form with band of repeating pierced flowers, 9″, $85–$95.

Candlestick: #11489, bronze, removable bobeche, lobed socket with green glass on slender stem and disk foot, 17″, $400–$500.

The Egyptian scarab, or beetle, was a popular motif in the Arts and Crafts era. Here it forms the *favrile* glass shade of a Tiffany Studios desk lamp (8½″ × 6½″) with a bronze base. *(Photo courtesy of Robert W. Skinner, Boston)*

Candlesticks: bronze, removable bobeche on bulbous socket resting on three fingers, tall slender stem on disk base, pair, 19″, $300–$350.

Humidor: etched metal over glass panel, 6″ × 4″, $225–$250.

Inkwell: nautical design with dolphin corners, clamshell lid, $250–$300.

Inkwell: zodiac pattern in dark bronze patina, $125–$150.

Inkwell: etched metal in pine needle design over green slag glass, $250–$300.

Lamp: #319, three-light, three lily shades supported by three arms extending upward from a circular base, base has original green/brown patina, 13″, $2250–$2500.

Lamp: leaded glass, shade consists of multiple shades of green and white, glass with swirling leaf design in yellow, 23″ × 18″, $5000–$6000.

Lamp: #269, green-blue *favrile* glass molded as a scarab on two branches and domed ribbed base, 8″ × 6″, *$250–$300*.

DIRK VAN ERP

Shopmarks:
Hammered mark of windmill over words *DIRK VAN ERP* in box
(1910–1911) Addition of name D'ARCY GAW in the box above that of DIRK VAN ERP
(After 1911) Gap in right side wall of box
(After 1915) Right side wall of box missing
(After 1915) Addition of words *SAN FRANCISCO*
(After 1940) Addition of words *HAND WROUGHT*

Principal Contributions:
Mica-shade copper lamps, bowls, vases, and accessories

Founder:
Dirk Van Erp
Born: 1860   Died: 1933
Founded: 1908   Closed: ca. 1950

Studios and Salesrooms:
Dirk Van Erp Studio or The Copper Shop
Oakland, California
1908–1910

San Francisco, California
1910–ca. 1950

"He had it in his head and his hands. There was no lost motion whatsoever when he started to make a piece. [Either] it came out a very nice piece [or] it never got finished."

—*William Van Erp*,
speaking of his father[1]

Born in the Netherlands in 1860, Dirk Van Erp received his first training in metalsmithing in the family business, where he helped produce kitchen utensils and milk containers. The lure of unbridled opportunities in America attracted the young Van Erp, the eldest of seven children, and he traveled to California in 1885, where at the age of twenty-six he found employment in the San Francisco shipyards.

While his experience as a metalworker provided him with a steady income in the shipyards, Van Erp eventually began producing metalwares in his home, utilizing brass shell casings, and by 1906 was consigning the finished products to area art dealers. Encouraged by the response, Van Erp opened a studio in Oakland in 1908 at the age of forty-eight. By 1910 he had moved his shop to San Francisco and taken on a partner—D'Arcy Gaw, a young designer from Canada who had been experimenting with electric lamps since 1902.[2] Although the partnership lasted only one year before Miss Gaw returned to Chicago to resume a career in interior design work, the collaboration proved to be instrumental in Van Erp's development. Miss Gaw's lamp designs provided Van Erp with the ideal format to display his skills as

1. Bonnie Mattison, *California Design 1910* (Pasadena, CA: California Design Publications, 1974), p. 78.
2. Wendy Kaplan, ed., *The Art That Is Life: The Arts and Crafts Movement in America, 1875–1920* (Boston: Museum of Fine Arts, 1987), p. 275.

a coppersmith. "Substantial and functional, [the] lamp exemplifies inspired coppersmithing skills, particularly in the use of copper for both the base and the shade to create a unified composition."[3] Using mica panels in the shade, Van Erp created lamps that "give warm tones harmonizing with the softly reflective patinated copper base."[4]

Van Erp was assisted in his San Francisco studio first by his daughter Agatha Van Erp and Harry Dixon (who went on to open his own shop in 1921) and later by his son William. After Miss Gaw left San Francisco in 1911 to establish a design studio in Chicago, Van Erp continued to produce electric lamps, often using designs commissioned from other artists. In addition, the studio produced a number of smaller copper accessories, including bowls, vases, and desk sets. Dirk Van Erp retired in 1929, turning operation of the shop and studio over to William.

While nearly all of the work of Dirk Van Erp is sought by Arts and Crafts collectors today, his lamps rank highest. By 1915, when output at the shop reached its peak, Van Erp had hired enough assistants so that lamp production was divided, with the apprentices assembling shades while the more experienced craftsmen hammered out the bases. As Bonnie Mattison has pointed out, "Patterns were used for both the bases and the shades. Even so, subtle variations of proportion and planishing distinguish each example of a given design."[5] Distinguishing between a multithousand-dollar lamp—such as the rare twenty-five-inch-high model that drew a final bid of $65,000 at Christie's on June 20, 1987—and one of the more common $3,000 to $4,000 lamps requires careful attention to design, condition, technical details, and degree of rarity. Serious Van Erp collectors show a decided preference for his earlier work, which is identified through the shopmark box and the style of the lip of the shade. In Van Erp's pre-1911 lamps, the lip of the shade

3. Wendy Kaplan, ed., *The Art That Is Life: The Arts and Crafts Movement in America, 1875–1920* (Boston Museum of Fine Arts, 1987), p. 275.

4. Ibid., p. 276.

5. Bonnie Mattison, *California Design 1910* (Pasadena, CA: California Design Publications, 1974), p. 78.

The closed-box shopmark, rolled shade rim, and riveted strut arrangement indicate that this is an early Dirk Van Erp lamp (21″ × 20½″). The tall, tapering bulbous base is also a form that Van Erp collectors appreciate. *(Photo courtesy of David Rago, Trenton)*

formed a very small, tight rim. After 1915 a definite horizontal band evolves, often as wide as one inch. The earlier lampshades also feature struts riveted to the outside of the cap at the top, whereas later the struts ended under the cap. Among the rarest of all of his lamps are his floor models and a unique hanging desk lamp.

In a similar vein, the large bowls and vases with a "warty" texture and "usually accompanied by 'fire-color', a brilliant red achieved by heating the copper during the annealing process,"[6] also are considered rare and thus more valuable than the standard hand-hammered wares. These examples were not smoothed with the small planishing marks of the finish hammer but instead reveal the rough texture created by the ball-peen hammer used to form the shape. For those collectors desiring an example of Van Erp's work, smaller items, such as vases, trays, or letter

6. Bonnie Mattison, *California Design 1910* (Pasadena, CA: California Design Publications, 1974), p. 79.

This Gustav Stickley desk provides an appropriate place for a Dirk Van Erp mica-shade lamp (17″ × 18″). The narrow border around the rim of the shade and this particular strut design would indicate a middle-period origin. *(Photo courtesy of D. J. Puffert, Sausalito)*

openers, can still be purchased for reasonable amounts, especially if they are beginning to show wear or slight damage.

Speaking of the lamps in particular, scholar Robert Judson Clark touched on one important reason why the work of Dirk Van Erp was successful both during his lifetime and after: "Its shape and color, as well as the glow from the mica shade, were perfect complements for the oak furniture and paneled interiors of the American bungalow during the mature phase of the Arts and Crafts movement in this country."[7] Modern collectors have shown that they too recognize what a Dirk Van Erp lamp can mean to an Arts and Crafts interior.

7. Robert Judson Clark, ed., *The Arts and Crafts Movement in America, 1876–1916* (Princeton, NJ: Princeton University, 1972), p. 90.

Selected Prices

Since the distinctions between a $1,000 and a $10,000 Dirk Van Erp lamp may not be evident in a price guide description, his mica-shade lamps have purposely been omitted from this listing. Providing the mica is intact and the base unpolished, any Dirk Van Erp lamp has the potential of being worth a minimum of $1,000. The best advice for any collector preparing either to buy or to sell a Dirk Van Erp lamp is to have it first inspected and appraised by a qualified expert familiar with the implications of a rolled rim, riveted strut, and unbroken shopmark.

Basket: pierced, banded handle riveted to a boat-shaped base, 10″ × 8″, *$400–$450.*

Bookends: hammered copper, with ribbon border, 3″ × 4″, *$100–$125.*

Bowl: hammered copper, seven-sided, 2″ × 10″, *$175–$200.*

Bowl: hammered copper with detailed round copper base, 3″ × 6″, *$250–$300.*

Bowl: hammered copper with deep patination, ruffled edge, 2″ × 5″, *$150–$175.*

Candlestick: four-sided form riveted to hexagonal base, ending with hexagonal bobeche and riveted candle cup, 9″ × 5″, *$200–$225.*

Desk set: copper pen tray, inkwell, and stamp holder, *$300–$350.*

Inkwell: hammered copper with mid-dark patina, geometric design on the four corners of the lid, 3″ × 3″, *$175–$200.*

Jardinere: hammered copper, large and bulbous form with rolled rim and tapered base, 10″ × 12″, *$1000–$1250.*

Letter opener: hammered copper, with cut-out design on handle, 8″, *$85–$95.*

This five-inch copper vase and three-inch inkstand reflect the hammered surface and deep patina characteristic of Van Erp's work. The cut-out design on the lid was reportedly executed by Van Erp's daughter Agatha. *(Photo courtesy of Christie's, New York)*

Matchbox holder: hammered copper, 3″ × 3″, *$85–$95.*

Tray, smoking: hammered copper with cigarette rest and matchbox holder, 3″ × 7″, *$95–$120.*

Tray, serving: hammered copper with handles, stylized rounded corners, 22″ × 12″, *$500–$600.*

Tray, serving: hammered copper, riveted handles on rectangular form, 10″ × 24″, *$550–$650.*

Tray: hammered copper, round form with tooled inner circle and loop handles, 12″, *$250–$300.*

Vase: hammered copper in early style, 8″ × 7″, *$500–$600.*

Vase: hammered copper with light brown patina, 10″ × 11″, *$650–$750.*

Vase: hammered copper with red "warty" texture, flared

base, bulbous top, rolled rim, covered with red-brown finish, 7″ × 6″, *$1000–$1250*.

Vase: hammered copper with red "warty" texture, bulbous, squat form with rolled rim, 4″ × 6″, *$600–$700*.

Vase: hammered copper in flaring cylindrical form, with stepped-in, rolled rim, 8″, *$850–$950*.

OTHER METALWARE SHOPS AND STUDIOS

"The word 'hand-wrought' means much or little of itself. It may stand only for sturdy usefulness, or for exquisite perfection of symmetry and design. It may accompany ignorant, careless workmanship or the skilled intelligence of long experience."

—*Arthur J. Stone*
1934[1]

The proponents of the Arts and Crafts movement, from William Morris and John Ruskin in England to Gustav Stickley and Jane Addams in America, attempted to improve the life of the common worker through renewed recognition of the value of handcraftsmanship. From a purely business standpoint, Stickley's offer to provide plans and hardware for furniture, copper and mica for lamps, and encouragement for anyone interested in constructing his or her own Arts and Crafts furnishings may

1. Wendy Kaplan, *The Art That Is Life: The Arts and Crafts Movement in America, 1875–1920* (Boston: Museum of Fine Arts, 1987), p. 283.

have seemed self-defeating, but his attitude was typical of the truly zealous reformers. As a result, inspired craftsmen and craftswomen all across the country began experimenting with the design and fabrication of their own furniture, pottery, and metalware. While most never rose to nor maintained the level of the well-known firms, examples of their work continue to surface. Many were attracted to metalware for obvious reasons. Unlike furniture it did not require a large workshop; unlike pottery it did not require a kiln. Tools, for the most part, were simple, often improvised. Those craftsmen who found the work rewarding and, in at least some part, financially promising opened their own studios or joined existing firms as apprentices or journeyman metalsmiths.

The sheer number of craftsmen and craftswomen whose work and whose lives were never well documented has dictated that a complete listing—let alone a detailed analysis—of their names, their locations, their shopmarks, and their work can never be amassed. As was emphasized in the introduction of this section, the evaluation of Arts and Crafts metalware is more dependent on the individual piece than on the name of the craftsman who produced it. Nevertheless, the compilation of information on the craftsmen of this era must continue. One of the finest studies was conducted by Sharon Darling, entitled *Chicago Metalsmiths* (Chicago: Chicago Historical Society, 1977). The large number of Chicago craftsmen included below is indicative as much of Miss Darling's research as it is of Chicago's support of the Arts and Crafts movement at the turn of the century. It can only be hoped that writers and researchers in every major city will undertake similar studies in order that they might share what information is available on Arts and Crafts craftsmen with today's growing number of collectors.

ALBERT BERRY'S CRAFTS SHOP
Seattle, Washington
> Active: ca. 1904–ca. 1930

> Quality hand-hammered copper wares, desk sets, often incorporating fossilized walrus tusk

> Shopmarks: ALBERT BERRY in script under initials *A.A.* flanking a metalsmithing hammer

BERRY'S CRAFT SHOP/ SEATTLE encircling large initial *B*

APOLLO STUDIOS
New York, New York
   Active: ca. 1909–1922
   Brass and copper kits for amateur metalworkers, jewelry
   Shopmark: APOLLO STUDIOS/ NEW YORK

ARTS CRAFTS SHOP
Buffalo, New York
   Active: ca. 1905–1906 (became Heintz Art Metal Shop)
   Otto L. Heintz (dates unknown)
   Copper bowls, candlesticks, and accessories with enamel decoration
   Shopmark: ARTS CRAFTS SHOP/ BUFFALO

AVON COPPERSMITH
Avon, New York
   Arthur Cole (dates unknown)
   Active: ca. 1910–ca. 1940
   Former Roycrofter who worked in hand-hammered copper accessories
   Shopmark: AVON COPPERSMITH

BENEDICT ART STUDIO
East Syracuse, New York
   (Formerly Onondaga Metal Shop)
   Harry L. Benedict (dates unknown)
   George N. Couse (dates unknown)
   Active: ca. 1904–undetermined
   Hand-hammered trays, lamps, desk sets, bowls, and accessories in copper, iron, and brass
   Shopmark: letters *BB* and bee enclosed by diamond

BENNETT, BESSIE
Chicago, Illinois
   Dates unknown
   Active: 1902–1921
   Arts and Crafts–style copper wares
   Shopmark: undetermined

BLANCHARD, PORTER
Boston, Massachusetts; Los Angeles, California
   1886–1973
   Active: 1909–1973

High-quality silver and pewter, specializing in flatware
(founded Arts & Crafts Society of Southern California)
Shopmark: (pre-1933) initials *P.B.* in an oval

BOWLES, JANET PAYNE*
New York, New York; Indianapolis, Indiana
1876–1948
Active 1907–ca. 1935
Silversmith, often working in abstract forms
Shopmark: undetermined

BOYDEN COMPANY, FRANK S.
Chicago, Illinois
Frank S. Boyden (1861–1943)
Fred C. Minuth (1884–1966)
Active: 1903—currently Boyden-Minuth Company
Jewelry, trophies, and ecclesiastical wares
Shopmarks: F.S. BOYDEN/ CHICAGO; letter *F* within a large letter *B*

BRADLEY & HUBBARD
Boston, Massachusetts
Active: early 20th century
Bronze and slag glass lamps, desk sets, and accessories
Shopmark: BRADLEY & HUBBARD MFG. CO. around triangle enclosing
outline of lamp

BRANDT METAL CRAFTERS
Chicago, Illinois
Active: ca. 1914–ca. 1923
Jewelry and housewares
Shopmark: BRANDT METAL CRAFTERS

BREESE, EDWARD H.
Chicago, Illinois
Dates unknown
Active: ca. 1921–1940
Jewelry and silverware in the Kalo Shop style
Shopmark: STERLING/ HANDWROUGHT/ E.H.B.

BROSI, FRED
San Francisco, California
Active: early 20th century

High-quality hammered-copper wares in style of Van Erp
Shopmark: YE OLDE COPPER SHOPPE

BURTON, ELIZABETH EATON
Santa Barbara, California
Dates unknown
Active: ca. 1910
Bronze, brass, and copper table lamps
Shopmark: undetermined

CARENCE CRAFTERS
Chicago, Illinois
Dates unknown
Silver, copper, and brass desk accessories
Shopmark: CARENCE CRAFTERS / CHICAGO

CELLINI SHOP, THE
Evanston, Illinois
Ernest Gerlach (1890–date unknown)
Active: 1914–current
(Early) Copper bowls and silver dinnerware in Kalo Shop style
Shopmark: (early) CELLINI SHOP/ EVANSTON/ HANDWROUGHT

CHICAGO ART SILVER SHOP
Chicago, Illinois
Edmund Boker (1886–date unknown)
Ernest Gould (1884–1954)
Active: 1912—currently Art Metal Studios
Art Nouveau copper, bronze, and silver housewares
Shopmark: STERLING/ HAND-MADE/ CHICAGO/ ART SILVER SHOP; initials *S.A.S.*

CHICAGO SILVER COMPANY
Chicago, Illinois
Knut L. Gustafson (1885–1976)
Active: 1923–1945
(Early) Hand-hammered flatware and dinnerware
Shopmarks: large letter *C*; initials *S.C.CO* encompassed by circle

COPELAND, ELIZABETH*
Boston, Massachusetts
1867–1957

Active: 1902–1937

Jeweler and silversmith, occasionally incorporating semiprecious stones into her silverwork

Shopmark: initials *E.C.*

COULTAS, WILHELMINA
Chicago, Illinois

Dates unknown

Active: 1910–1923

Jewelry designer

Shopmark: undetermined

CRAFTSMAN STUDIOS
Laguna Beach, California

Active: dates unknown

Lightweight copper bowls and accessories

Shopmark: anvil and hammer/ HANDMADE/ CRAFTSMAN, often with form number

DIXON, HARRY*
San Francisco, California

1890–1967

Active: 1908–1967

Apprentice under Dirk Van Erp from 1908 to ca. 1915; opened his own shop ca. 1922; copper and brass accessories

Shopmark: HDIXON/ SAN FRANCISCO

DODGE, WILLIAM WALDO
Asheville, North Carolina

Active: 1923–1943

Silversmith: trophies, flatware, dinnerware, lighting fixtures

Shopmark: ASHEVILLE SILVERCRAFT

ENOS COMPANY
New York, New York

Active: ca. 1913

Copper and brass lighting fixtures (advertised in *The Craftsman*)

Shopmark: undetermined

FOGLIATA, A.*
Chicago, Illinois

Dates unknown

Active: ca. 1903–1907

Jeweler and silversmith
Shopmark: undetermined

FRIEDELL, CLEMENS
Pasadena and Los Angeles, California
Active: 1892–1953
Silversmith: high quality hand-hammered dinnerware
Shopmark: STERLING FRIEDELL PASADENA

FROST ARTS AND CRAFTS WORKSHOP
Dayton, Ohio
George W. Frost (dates unknown)
Active: ca. 1915
Hand-hammered copper accessories (advertised in *The Craftsman*)
Shopmark: triangle encompassing company's initials

GERMER, GEORGE E.*
Boston, Massachusetts
1868–1936
Active: ca. 1893–ca. 1920
Ecclesiastical silverwork
Shopmark: inscribed GEORGE E. GERMER/BOSTON, MASS./ date

GLESSNER, FRANCES MacBETH*
Chicago, Illinois
1848–1922
Active: 1904–1915
Hand-hammered silver items
Shopmark: the letter *G* encompassing a bee

GYLLENBERG, FRANS J. R.*
Boston, Massachusetts
1883–unknown
Active: ca. 1905–ca. 1929
Hand-hammered copper wares
Shopmark: F.J.R.G.

HANDICRAFT GUILD
Minneapolis, Minnesota
Ernest A. Batchelder (1875–1957), founder
Founded: 1902
Metalwork and jewelry by independent craftsmen, teachers, and students
Shopmark: HANDICRAFT GUILD/ MINNEAPOLIS

HANDICRAFT SHOP*
Boston and Wellesley Hills, Massachusetts
Active: 1901–ca.1940

Jewelry, metalwork, and silversmithing by independent craftsmen and craftswomen

Shopmark: anvil and letters *H* and *S*, often with mark of craftsman

HANCK, MATTHIAS WM.
Park Ridge, Illinois
1883–1955

Active: 1911–1955

Jewelry and silver dinnerware

Shopmark: HANDMADE BY M.W. HANCK/ PARKRIDGE, ILL/ STERLING

HANDEL COMPANY
Meriden, Connecticut
Active: early 20th century

Bronze lamps

Shopmark: HANDEL and model number

HEINRICHS, JOSEPH
New York, New York
Active: ca. 1910

Quality hand-hammered copper bowls and accessories

Shopmark: JOS.HEINRICHS/ PARIS & NEW YORK/ PURE COPPER

HEINTZ ART METAL SHOP
Buffalo, New York
(Previously Arts Crafts Shop)

Otto L. Heintz and Edwin A. Heintz (dates unknown)

Active: ca. 1905–1935

Copper and bronze desk sets, bowls, and accessories with sterling silver overlay

Shopmark: initials H.A.M.S. in diamond over STERLING ON BRONZE and patent date

HULL HOUSE SHOPS
Chicago, Illinois
Jane Addams (1860–1935), founder
ca. 1898–ca. 1940

Copper, brass, and silver bowls, candlesticks, trays, and accessories

Shopmark: none

Two desk lamps produced by the Heintz Art Metal Shop in Buffalo, New York. The nickel-silver overlay is a familiar characteristic of their work. *(Photo courtesy of David Rago, Trenton)*

JULMAT, THE
Park Ridge, Illinois
  Julius O. Randahl (1880–1972)
  Matthias Wm. Hanck (1883–1955)
  Active: ca. 1910
  Hand-hammered housewares
  Shopmark: THE JULMAT/ HAND WROUGHT/ PARK RIDGE, ILL/ STERLING

KNIGHT, MARY KATHERINE*
Boston, Massachusetts
  1876–unknown
  Active: ca. 1905
  Silversmith
  Shopmark: shield enclosing letter *K* and knight on horseback/ STERLING

KOEHLER, FLORENCE*
Chicago, Illinois
  1861–1944
  Active: ca. 1900

Metalsmith, jewelry designer, often working in Art Nouveau designs

Shopmark: undetermined

LEBOLT & COMPANY

Chicago, Illinois
>J. Myer H. Lebolt (1868–1944)

>Active: 1899–current

>Jewelry and silver dinnerware

>Shopmark: letter *L* in diamond over LEBOLT/ HANDBEATEN

LEINONEN, KARL F.*

Boston, Massachusetts
>1866–1957

>Active: ca. 1903–ca. 1950

>Silversmith

>Shopmark: (early) Handicraft Shop mark and letter *L*

MARSHALL FIELD & CO.

Chicago, Illinois
>Craft Shop

>Active: ca. 1904–ca. 1950

>Silver jewelry, dinnerware, trays, tea sets, bowls, etc.

>Shopmarks: MADE BY MARSHALL FIELD & CO.; MADE IN OUR CRAFT
>SHOP/ MARSHALL FIELD & CO.; MF & CO/ ARTMETAL CRAFT

MULHOLLAND BROTHERS

Park Ridge and Evanston, Illinois
>Walter Mulholland (dates unknown)

>David E. Mulholland (dates unknown)

>Active: 1912–1934

>Silver dinnerware in Kalo Shop style

>Shopmark: letter *M* within outline of an anvil; MULHOLLAND, also
>CELLINI SHOP (retail outlet), and EVANSTON (1916–1919)

MUNSON, JULIA

New York, New York
>Dates unknown

>Active: ca. 1900

>Metalsmith with Tiffany Studios

>Shopmark: unknown

This hammered-copper table lamp (14″ × 15″) features three mica panels in a style inspired by Dirk Van Erp. While not as artistic as Van Erp's, Old Mission Kopperkraft is highly respected by Arts and Crafts collectors. *(Photo courtesy of Robert W. Skinner, Boston)*

NOVICK, FALICK
Chicago, Illinois
1878–1957

Active: 1909–1957

(Early) Plain copper bowls and pitchers in Kalo Shop style

Shopmark: STERLING/ HANDWROUGHT/ BY F. NOVICK/ CHICAGO

OLD MISSION KOPPERKRAFT
San Francisco, California
Active: ca. 1910

Copper bookends and accessories

Shopmark: OLD MISSION KOPPERKRAFT with outline of church

ONONDAGA METAL SHOPS
East Syracuse, New York
(Became Benedict Art Studio)

Active: ca. 1901–ca. 1904

Quality hand-hammered copper wares (possibly for Gustav Stickley)

Shopmark: conjoined initials *O M S*

PETTERSON STUDIO
Chicago, Illinois
> John Pontus Petterson (1884–1949)
>
> Active: 1912–1949
>
> (Early) Silver dinnerware influenced by Jarvie
>
> Shopmark: THE PETTERSON STUDIO/ CHICAGO; initials *TPS* enclosed in circle/ HANDMADE.

POND APPLIED ART STUDIOS*
Baltimore, Maryland
> Theodore H. Pond (1872–1933)
>
> Active studio: 1911–1914
>
> Silversmith
>
> Shopmark: dragonfly enclosed by KWO-NE-SHE and HAND/ WROUGHT/ STERLING/ POND

PRESTON, JESSIE M.
Chicago, Illinois
> Dates unknown
>
> Active: 1900–1918
>
> Jewelry designer; high quality candlesticks in style of Robert Jarvie
>
> Shopmark: PRESTON/ CHICAGO

RANDAHL SHOP, THE
Park Ridge, Illinois
> Julius O. Randahl (1880–1972)
>
> Active: 1911–current
>
> (Early) Hand-hammered bowls, tea seats, candleholders
>
> Shopmarks: RANDAHL/ HAND WROUGHT/ STERLING; initials *JOR* with silversmith's hammer

ROKESLEY SHOP*
Cleveland, Ohio
> Louis Rorimer (1872–1940)
>
> Active: ca. 1907–ca. 1916
>
> Jewelry, smaller metal items, silversmithing
>
> Shopmark: rectangle around ROKESLEY/ STERLING

SHAW, JOSEPHINE HARTWELL*
Boston and Duxbury, Massachusetts
> Dates unknown
>
> Active: ca. 1900–1935
>
> Acclaimed jewelry designer
>
> Shopmark: J.H. SHAW

SMITH METAL ARTS
Buffalo, New York
Active: ca. 1920
Hand-hammered copper, silver items
Shopmark: *S & Co* (letter *o* inside the *C*)

SORENSON, CARL
Philadelphia, Pennsylvania
Dates unknown
Active: ca. 1914
Hand-hammered copper desk accessories
Shopmark: large letter *C* encompassing smaller letter *S*

SWASTICA SHOP
Chicago, Illinois
Active: 1902–date unknown
Jewelry, hand-hammered metalware, leathers, and crafts
Shopmark: undetermined

SWEESTER COMPANY
New York, New York
Active: ca. 1900–1915
Silver and gold jewelry
Shopmark: *S & E* inside rectangle

T.C. SHOP
Chicago, Illinois
Emery W. Todd (dates unknown)
Clemencua C. Cosio (dates unknown)
Active: 1910–1923
Silver dinnerware, jewelry
Shopmark: THE TC SHOP/ CHICAGO/ HAND WROUGHT/ STERLING or letters *T C* conjoined

THATCHER SCHOOL OF METAL WORK
Woodstock, New York
Active: ca. 1911
Basic metalwork forms by students
Shopmark: undetermined

TRAUTMANN, GEORGE H.
Chicago, Illinois
Dates unknown
Active: 1910–1917

This twelve-inch-diameter pewter bowl was designed and signed by Harry Dixon, a former employee of Dirk Van Erp, after he had opened his own shop in San Francisco. The lamp base is by Fulper Pottery, and the shade was designed by Chicago metal-smith George Trautmann (17″ × 17″). *(Photo courtesy of D. J. Puffert, Sausalito)*

Lamps, sconces, chandeliers, lighting fixtures
Shopmark: G.H.TRAUTMANN/ RAVENSWOOD, CHICAGO

TRIO SHOP
Evanston, Illinois
Active: 1908–1915
Hand-hammered metalware by independent craftsmen
Shopmark: individual

TROY SCHOOL OF ARTS & CRAFTS
Troy, New York
Active: ca. 1907
Basic metalware forms, including desk accessories, by students
Shopmark: individual

VANDENHOFF, GEORGE A.
New York, New York
Dates unknown
Active: ca. 1913
Artistic brass and copper novelties (advertised in *The Craftsman*)
Shopmark: undetermined

VERMON COPPER COMPANY
(Location undetermined)
Dates unknown
Inexpensive copper accessories
Shopmark: conjoined letters *V.C.C./* VERMON/ HAND HAMMERED COPPER and form number

WATKINS, MILDRED G.*
Cleveland, Ohio
1883–1968
Active: ca. 1903–ca. 1960
Jeweler and noted silversmith
Shopmark: sailboat and MILDRED WATKINS/ STERLING

WINN, JAMES H.
Chicago, Illinois
1966–ca. 1940
Active: 1895–1927
Jewelry in both Arts & Crafts and Art Nouveau styles
Shopmark: WINN

WYNNE, MADELINE YALE*
Chicago, Illinois
1847–1918
Active: 1893–1909
Hand-hammered gold, silver, and copper bowls and jewelry
Shopmark: unknown

ZIMMERMANN, MARIE*
New York, New York
1878–1972
Active: 1903–ca. 1930
Hammered metal bowls in copper, silver, bronze, gold, with various chemical patinas; jewelry, accessories
Shopmark: MARIE ZIMMERMANN/ MAKER/ around *M Z* cipher

---

*Featured in Wendy Kaplan, ed., *The Art That Is Life: The Arts and Crafts Movement in America, 1875–1920* (Boston: Museum of Fine Arts, 1987).

Selected Bibliography

Anderson, Timothy, Moore, Eudorah, and Winter, Robert. *California Design 1910.* Pasadena, CA: California Design Publications, 1974; Santa Barbara, CA: Peregrine Smith, 1980.

Anscombe, Isabelle, and Gere, Charlotte. *Arts and Crafts in Britain and America.* New York: Rizzoli International Publications, 1978.

The Arts and Crafts Quarterly (periodical). David Rago, ed. and publ. Trenton: Arts and Crafts Quarterly, 1987–present.

The Artsman (periodical). Philadelphia: Rose Valley Press, 1903–1907.

Bavaro, Joseph, and Mossmann, Thomas. *The Furniture of Gustav Stickley: History, Techniques, Projects.* New York: Van Nostrand Reinhold, 1982.

The Book of the Roycrofters. Roycroft Shop catalog: 1919 and 1926 (catalog reprint). East Aurora, NY: House of Hubbard, 1977.

Brandt, Frederick. *Late 19th and Early 20th Century Decorative Arts.* Richmond: Virginia Museum of Fine Arts, 1985.

Brooks, H. Allen. *Frank Lloyd Wright and the Prairie School.* New York: George Braziller, 1984.

Callen, Anthea. *Women Artists of the Arts and Crafts Movement 1870–1914.* New York: Pantheon Books, 1979.

Cathers, David. *Furniture of the American Arts and Crafts Movement.* New York: New American Library, 1981.

———. *Genius in the Shadows: The Furniture Designs of Harvey Ellis.* New York: Jordan Volpe Gallery, 1981.

Champney, Freeman. *Art and Glory: The Story of Elbert Hubbard.* Kent, OH: Kent State University Press, 1983.

Clark, Garth, and Hughto, Margie. *A Century of Ceramics in the United States 1878–1978.* New York: E. P. Dutton, 1979.

Clark, Robert Judson, ed. *The Arts and Crafts Movement in America 1876–1916*. Princeton, NJ: Princeton University Press, 1972.

Cole, G. D. H., ed. *William Morris: Selected Writings*. Centenary edition. London: Nonesuch Press, 1948.

The Craftsman (periodical). Gustav Stickley, ed. Eastwood and New York: Craftsman Publishing, 1901–1916.

Cummins, Virginia. *Rookwood Pottery Potpourri*. Silver Spring, MD: Leonard and Coleman, 1980.

Danforth Museum of Art. *On the Threshold of Modern Design: The Arts and Crafts Movement in America*. Danforth, MA: Danforth Museum of Art, 1984.

Darling, Sharon. *Chicago Furniture: Art, Craft & Industry 1833–1933*. Chicago: Chicago Historical Society, 1984.

———. *Chicago Metalsmiths*. Chicago: Chicago Historical Society, 1977.

Davey, Peter. *Architecture of the Arts and Crafts Movement*. New York: Rizzoli International Publications, 1980.

Doros, Paul. *The Tiffany Collection of the Chrysler Museum at Norfolk*. Norfolk, VA: The Chrysler Museum, 1978.

Edwards, Robert, ed. *The Arts and Crafts Furniture of Charles Limbert* (catalog reprint). Watkins Glen, NY: American Life Foundation, 1982.

———. *The Byrdcliffe Arts and Crafts Colony*. Wilmington, DE: Delaware Art Museum, 1985.

Eidelberg, Martin, ed. *From Our Native Clay*. New York: American Ceramic Arts Society and Turn of the Century Editions, 1987.

Evans, Paul. *Art Pottery of the United States*, second edition. New York: Feingold & Lewis Publishing, 1987.

Freeman, John Crosby. *The Forgotten Rebel, Gustav Stickley and His Craftsman Mission Furniture*. Watkins Glen, NY: Century House, 1965.

Garner, Philippe. *Twentieth-century Furniture*. New York: Van Nostrand Reinhold, 1980.

Gray, Stephen, and Edwards, Robert, eds. *The Collected Works of Gustav Stickley* (catalog reprint). New York: Turn of the Century Editions, 1981.

Gray, Stephen, ed. *The Mission Furniture of L. and J. G. Stickley* (catalog reprint). New York: Turn of the Century Editions, 1983.

———. *The Early Work of Gustav Stickley* (catalog reprint). New York: Turn of the Century Editions, 1987.

———. *Lifetime Furniture* (catalog reprint). New York: Turn of the Century Editions, 1981.

———. *Limbert's Holland Dutch Arts and Crafts Furniture* (catalog reprint). New York: Turn of the Century Editions, 1981.

———. *Roycroft Furniture* (catalog reprint). New York: Turn of the Century Editions, 1981.

———. *Quaint Furniture: Arts and Crafts* (reprint of Stickley Brothers catalog). New York: Turn of the Century Editions, 1981.

———. *Arts and Crafts Furniture: Shop of the Crafters at Cincinnati* (catalog reprint). New York: Turn of the Century Editions, 1983.

Hamilton, Charles. *Roycroft Collectibles*. New York: A. S. Barnes and Co., 1980.

Hamilton, Charles, Turgeon, Kitty, and Rust, Robert. *History and Renaissance of the Roycroft Movement*. Buffalo, NY: Buffalo & Erie County Historical Society, 1984.

Hanks, David. *The Decorative Designs of Frank Lloyd Wright*. New York: E. P. Dutton, 1979.

Henderson, Philip. *William Morris: His Life, Works and Friends*. New York: McGraw-Hill, 1967.

Hunter, Dard. *My Life with Paper*. New York: Alfred Knopf, 1958.

Huxford, Sharon, and Huxford, Bob. *The Collectors' Encyclopedia of Weller Pottery*. Paducah, KY: Collector Books, 1979.

Kaplan, Wendy, ed. *The Art That Is Life: The Arts and Crafts Movement in America 1875–1920*. Boston: Museum of Fine Arts, 1987.

Keen, Kirsten Hoving. *American Art Pottery 1875–1930*. Philadelphia: Falcon Press, 1978.

Keramic Studio, a Monthly Magazine for the China Painter and Potter (periodical). Syracuse, NY: Keramic Studio Publishing, 1899–1930.

Koch, Robert. *Louis C. Tiffany's Glass, Bronzes, Lamps*. New York: Crown Publishers, 1971.

Kornwolf, James. M. H. *Baillie Scott and the Arts and Crafts Movement*. Baltimore: John Hopkins Press, 1972.

Kovel, Ralph, and Terry. *The Kovels' Collectors Guide to American Art Pottery*. New York: Crown Publishers, 1974.

Lambourne, Lionel. *Utopian Craftsmen: The Arts and Crafts Movement from the Cotswolds to Chicago*. Salt Lake City, UT: Peregrine Smith, 1980.

Ludwig, Coy. *The Arts and Crafts Movement in New York State 1890s–1920s*. Layton, UT: Peregrine Smith, 1983.

Makinson, Randell. *Greene and Greene: Architecture as a Fine Art*. Salt Lake City, UT: Peregrine Smith, 1977.

———. *Greene and Greene: Furniture and Related Designs*. Salt Lake City, UT: Peregrine Smith, 1979.

Manson, Grant Carpenter. *Frank Lloyd Wright to 1910: The First Golden Age*. New York: Van Nostrand Reinhold, 1958.

Marek, Don. *Arts and Crafts Furniture Design: The Grand Rapids Contribution 1895–1915*. Grand Rapids, MI: Grand Rapids Art Museum, 1987.

Nelson, Scott, Crouch, Lois, Demmin, Euphemia, and Newton, Robert. *A Collectors' Guide to Van Briggle Pottery*. Indiana, PA: Halldin Publishing, 1986.

The Newark Museum Collection of American Art Pottery. Newark, NJ: Newark Museum, 1984.

Page, Marion. *Furniture Designed by Architects*. London: The Architectural Press, 1983.

Poesch, Jessie. *Newcomb Pottery*. Exton, PA.: Schiffer Publishing, 1984.

Roycroft Handmade Furniture (1912 catalog reprint). East Aurora, NY: House of Hubbard, 1973.

Rubin, Jerome, and Cynthia. *Mission Furniture*. San Francisco: Chronicle Books, 1980.

Smith, Mary Ann. *Gustav Stickley: The Craftsman*. Syracuse, NY: Syracuse University Press, 1983.

Stickley Craftsman Furniture Catalogs (Gustav Stickley 1910 catalog and L. & J. G. Stickley 1912 catalog reprint). New York: Dover Publications, 1979.

Stickley, Gustav, ed. *Craftsman Homes*. New York: The Craftsman Publishing Co., 1909; Dover Publications, 1979.

———. *More Craftsman Homes*. New York: The Craftsman Publishing Co., 1912; Dover Publications, 1912.

Stott, Mary Roelofs. *Elbert Hubbard: Rebel with Reverence*. Watkins Glen, NY: American Life Foundation, 1984.

Tiller, a Bimonthly Devoted to the Arts and Crafts Movement (periodical). Bryn Mawr, PA: The Artsman, 1982–1983.

Twombly, Robert. *Louis Sullivan: His Life and Work.* Chicago: The University of Chicago Press, 1986.

William Morris and Kelmscott. London: The Design Council, 1981.

Wright, Frank Lloyd. *An Autobiography.* New York: Duell, Sloan and Pierce, 1943.

Index

About the Author

BRUCE JOHNSON has been collecting Arts and Crafts furniture, pottery, and metalware for more than twelve years. Since 1980 he has written the nationally syndicated antique restoration column "Knock On Wood" and recently completed his third book on that subject, entitled *The Weekend Refinisher* (Ballantine Books). Readers of *Country Living* magazine also know Mr. Johnson as the author of the regular "Antiques Across America" column. In addition to having written numerous articles for *Maine Antique Digest, Antiques Dealer Magazine, The Arts & Crafts Quarterly, Antique Week,* and *Country Living,* Johnson organized the first Arts and Crafts conference and antiques show held at the Grove Park Inn outside Asheville, North Carolina, in February 1988. He, his wife, Dr. Lydia Jeffries, and son, Eric, live in Durham, North Carolina, in an Arts and Crafts–style bungalow they have restored.

Readers who wish to be notified of the next price update for antiques of the Arts and Crafts movement or who have additional information on firms, shopmarks, or craftsmen and craftswomen of the movement are invited to write to Bruce Johnson, P.O. Box 6660, Durham, NC 27708.

The HOUSE OF COLLECTIBLES Series

☐ Please send me the following price guides—
☐ I would like the most current edition of the books listed below.

THE OFFICIAL PRICE GUIDES TO:

☐ 199-3	American Silver & Silver Plate 5th Ed.	$11.95
☐ 513-1	Antique Clocks 3rd Ed.	10.95
☐ 283-3	Antique & Modern Dolls 3rd Ed.	10.95
☐ 287-6	Antique & Modern Firearms 6th Ed.	11.95
☐ 738-X	Antiques & Collectibles 8th Ed.	10.95
☐ 289-2	Antique Jewelry 5th Ed.	11.95
☐ 539-5	Beer Cans & Collectibles 4th Ed.	7.95
☐ 521-2	Bottles Old & New 10th Ed.	10.95
☐ 532-8	Carnival Glass 2nd Ed.	10.95
☐ 295-7	Collectible Cameras 2nd Ed.	10.95
☐ 548-4	Collectibles of the '50s & '60s 1st Ed.	9.95
☐ 740-1	Collectible Toys 4th Ed.	10.95
☐ 531-X	Collector Cars 7th Ed.	12.95
☐ 538-7	Collector Handguns 4th Ed.	14.95
☐ 748-7	Collector Knives 9th Ed.	12.95
☐ 361-9	Collector Plates 5th Ed.	11.95
☐ 296-5	Collector Prints 7th Ed.	12.95
☐ 001-6	Depression Glass 2nd Ed.	9.95
☐ 589-1	Fine Art 1st Ed.	19.95
☐ 311-2	Glassware 3rd Ed.	10.95
☐ 243-4	Hummel Figurines & Plates 6th Ed.	10.95
☐ 523-9	Kitchen Collectibles 2nd Ed.	10.95
☐ 291-4	Military Collectibles 5th Ed.	11.95
☐ 525-5	Music Collectibles 6th Ed.	11.95
☐ 313-9	Old Books & Autographs 7th Ed.	11.95
☐ 298-1	Oriental Collectibles 3rd Ed.	11.95
☐ 746-0	Overstreet Comic Book 17th Ed.	11.95
☐ 522-0	Paperbacks & Magazines 1st Ed.	10.95
☐ 297-3	Paper Collectibles 5th Ed.	10.95
☐ 744-4	Political Memorabilia 1st Ed.	10.95
☐ 529-8	Pottery & Porcelain 6th Ed.	11.95
☐ 524-7	Radio, TV & Movie Memorabilia 3rd Ed.	11.95
☐ 288-4	Records 7th Ed.	10.95
☐ 247-7	Royal Doulton 5th Ed.	11.95
☐ 280-9	Science Fiction & Fantasy Collectibles 2nd Ed.	10.95
☐ 747-9	Sewing Collectibles 1st Ed.	8.95
☐ 358-9	Star Trek/Star Wars Collectibles 2nd Ed.	8.95
☐ 086-5	Watches 8th Ed.	12.95
☐ 248-5	Wicker 3rd Ed.	10.95

THE OFFICIAL:

☐ 445-3	Collector's Journal 1st Ed.	4.95
☐ 549-2	Directory to U.S. Flea Markets 1st Ed.	4.95
☐ 365-1	Encyclopedia of Antiques 1st Ed.	9.95
☐ 369-4	Guide to Buying and Selling Antiques 1st Ed.	9.95
☐ 414-3	Identification Guide to Early American Furniture 1st Ed.	9.95
☐ 413-5	Identification Guide to Glassware 1st Ed.	9.95
☐ 448-8	Identification Guide to Gunmarks 2nd Ed.	9.95
☐ 412-7	Identification Guide to Pottery & Porcelain 1st Ed.	$9.95
☐ 415-1	Identification Guide to Victorian Furniture 1st Ed.	9.95

THE OFFICIAL (SMALL SIZE) PRICE GUIDES TO:

☐ 309-0	Antiques & Flea Markets 4th Ed.	4.95
☐ 269-8	Antique Jewelry 3rd Ed.	4.95
☐ 085-7	Baseball Cards 8th Ed.	4.95
☐ 647-2	Bottles 3rd Ed.	4.95
☐ 544-1	Cars & Trucks 3rd Ed.	5.95
☐ 519-0	Collectible Americana 2nd Ed.	4.95
☐ 294-9	Collectible Records 3rd Ed.	4.95
☐ 306-6	Dolls 4th Ed.	4.95
☐ 359-7	Football Cards 7th Ed.	4.95
☐ 540-9	Glassware 3rd Ed.	4.95
☐ 526-3	Hummels 4th Ed.	4.95
☐ 279-5	Military Collectibles 3rd Ed.	4.95
☐ 745-2	Overstreet Comic Book Companion 1st Ed.	4.95
☐ 278-7	Pocket Knives 3rd Ed.	4.95
☐ 527-1	Scouting Collectibles 4th Ed.	4.95
☐ 494-1	Star Trek/Star Wars Collectibles 3rd Ed.	3.95
☐ 307-4	Toys 4th Ed.	4.95

THE OFFICIAL BLACKBOOK PRICE GUIDES OF:

☐ 743-6	U.S. Coins 26th Ed.	3.95
☐ 742-8	U.S. Paper Money 20th Ed.	3.95
☐ 741-X	U.S. Postage Stamps 10th Ed.	3.95

THE OFFICIAL INVESTORS GUIDE TO BUYING & SELLING:

☐ 534-4	Gold, Silver & Diamonds 2nd Ed.	12.95
☐ 535-2	Gold Coins 2nd Ed.	12.95
☐ 536-0	Silver Coins 2nd Ed.	12.95
☐ 537-9	Silver Dollars 2nd Ed.	12.95

THE OFFICIAL NUMISMATIC GUIDE SERIES:

☐ 254-X	The Official Guide to Detecting Counterfeit Money 2nd Ed.	7.95
☐ 257-2	The Official Guide to Mint Errors 4th Ed.	7.95

SPECIAL INTEREST SERIES:

☐ 506-9	From Hearth to Cookstove 3rd Ed.	17.95
☐ 530-1	Lucky Number Lottery Guide 1st Ed.	4.95
☐ 504-2	On Method Acting 8th Printing	6.95

TOTAL	

SEE REVERSE SIDE FOR ORDERING INSTRUCTIONS

FOR IMMEDIATE DELIVERY

VISA & MASTER CARD CUSTOMERS
ORDER TOLL FREE!
1-800-638-6460

This number is for orders only; it is not tied into the customer service or business office. Customers not using charge cards must use mail for ordering since payment is required with the order—sorry, no C.O.D.'s.

OR SEND ORDERS TO

THE HOUSE OF COLLECTIBLES
201 East 50th Street
New York, New York 10022

POSTAGE & HANDLING RATES

First Book $1.00
Each Additional Copy or Title $0.50

Total from columns on order form. Quantity_____ $_____
                                                                    (include postage
☐ Check or money order enclosed $_____ and handling)

☐ Please charge $_____to my: ☐ MASTERCARD ☐ VISA

Charge Card Customers Not Using Our Toll Free Number Please Fill Out The Information Below

Account No. _____Expiration Date_____
                        (All Digit·
Signature_____

NAME (please print)_____PHONE_____

ADDRESS_____APT. #_____

CITY_____STATE_____ ZIP_____